DATE DUE

#47-0108 Peel Off Pressure Sensitive

A DAY AT A TIME

A Day at a Time

The Diary Literature of American
Women from 1764 to the Present

EDITED BY MARGO CULLEY

The Feminist Press

AT THE CITY UNIVERSITY OF NEW YORK

NEW YORK

© 1985 by The Feminist Press at the City University of New York
All rights reserved. Published 1985
Printed in the United States of America
89 88 87 86 85 6 5 4 3 2 1

The lines from "Cartographies
of Silence" from *The
Dream of a Common Language,
Poems 1974-1977*, by Adrienne
Rich, are reprinted by permission
of the author and the publisher,
W. W. Norton & Company, Inc.
© 1978 by W. W. Norton &
Company, Inc.

Library of Congress Cataloging in Publication Data
Main entry under title:

A Day at a time.

    Bibliography: p.
    1. Women—United States—Diaries.   2. Diaries.
I. Culley, Margo.
CT3260.D395 1985   920.72'0973   85-13140
ISBN 0-935312-50-1
ISBN 0-935312-51-X (pbk.)

Cover and text design by Janet Halverson

Typeset by ComCom

Manufactured by Haddon Craftsmen, Inc.

TO THE MEMORY OF JOANNA BROWNE SEFTON [1877–1970],
AND TO
MARGARET SEFTON MULVEHILL,
URBAN SYLVESTER MULVEHILL,
AND
MAREA KATE SEFTON

Contents

Personal and Political

Preface

Diaries kept by American women contain a rich record of their lives through three centuries and are a powerful testament to their achievements, including their achievements as writers. The goal of this collection is to introduce a part of this vast body of literature with an emphasis on the large number of diaries that have been published but are now out-of-print. Calling this form of autobiographical writing "literature" identifies the many examples of fine writing contained in diaries and journals and also acknowledges that this periodic life-writing springs from the same source as the art created for a public audience: the urge to give shape and meaning to life with words, and to endow this meaning-making with a permanence that transcends time.

From well before the American Revolution to the present, large numbers of women have kept regular written records of their lives. With the major exception of black women's lives under slavery, virtually every aspect of women's experience finds expression in their diaries. Women we have never heard of, who were explorers, naturalists, miners, homesteaders, physicians, factory workers, political activists, preachers, farmers, and prisoners of war have all kept diaries. And the familiar aspects of women's domestic lives—pregnancy, mothering, nursing the sick, managing a household—all find full expression in their life-records. Taken together these texts document vividly the strength, resilience, and resourcefulness of American women. Their diaries and journals also mark with inescapable clarity the constraints under which women have lived in American culture and their pain.

Among the well-known American women who have kept journals that have been published in whole or part are Abigail Adams, Louisa May Alcott, Enid Bagnold, Ruth Benedict, Helen Bevington, Louise Bogan, Willa Cather, Kate Chopin, Janet Flanner, Charlotte Forten, Margaret Fuller, Lillian Hellman, Julia Ward Howe, Alice James,

Helen Keller, Fanny Kemble, Meridel LeSueur, Anne Morrow Lindberg, Maria Mitchell, Sylvia Plath, Eslanda Robeson, May Sarton,
Dorothy Thompson, and Laura Ingalls Wilder. This book, for the
most part, does not focus on these women of public achievement, but
on the life-writing of "ordinary" American women. Many, many
women have felt their lives "remarkable" enough to have kept a
written record, and thousands of their diaries have been edited and
published by the writers themselves, their families, or by scholars who
found the texts significant. And, of course, a number exponentially
greater than those that have been published remain in manuscript—
in attics, public libraries, historical societies, and university and college archives.

The materials chosen for this collection are arranged chronologi-
cally (according to the first diary entry) in order to create a mosaic
of American women's history and to suggest changes in the form,
content, and function of the diary as a verbal construct (issues discussed fully in the Introduction). In three groups from the eighteenth, nineteenth, and twentieth centuries, the texts in each section
echo certain themes in women's lives. Of the several diaries written
at the time of the American Revolution in "In the Fatherland," only
the record of Elizabeth Sandwith Drinker focuses on the war. Abigail
Bailey's and Nancy Shippen Livingston's narratives relate the power
and influence wielded by the men in their lives at a time in America
when women were without legal protections. Mary Vial Holyoke's
diary provides glimpses of the physical and emotional demands of
childbearing in the eighteenth century, while Elizabeth Fuller's diary
focuses on the work contributed by a single woman to the family
economic unit in colonial America.

A sense of movement and change dominates the second section,
"The Journey Out." In several diaries this movement is literal as in
the case of Sarah Peirce Nichols's "twelve mile walk." This section
reflects aspects of the massive migration of peoples in the nineteenth
century including Carolina Preus's travel from Norway to the
United States and the movement westward of Margaret Van Horne
Dwight, Amelia Stewart Knight, Helen Marnie Stewart, and Mary
Dodge Woodward. Ready for adventure, Annie Holmes Ricketson
joins her husband on board a whaling ship and Fannie Hardy joins
her father in white water canoeing on the Penobscot River in Maine.
In several instances in this section, the diarists' journeys are as much

spiritual as literal. Rebecca Jackson's religious conversion, Eliza Frances Andrews's passage through the Civil War, and Helen Ward Brandreth's journey from courtship to marriage leave each diarist profoundly changed.

Mary MacLane's intensely introspective journal appropriately introduces the twentieth-century texts in the "Personal and Political" section. The journey inward comes to dominate diary writing in the twentieth century, but the reader must remember that the idea of the diary as the arena of the secret, inner life is a relatively modern idea and describes only one kind of diary. As the excerpts in this section illustrate, twentieth-century diaries address a wide range of subjects and serve many purposes. In this century women have been witness to war and its consequences in their diaries as in the selections here from Elizabeth Ashe and Nell Giles. Several diaries in this section have explicitly political themes such as those of Barbara Deming, Joan Frances Bennett, and Barbara Smith. As an older and ailing woman in a nursing home, Joyce Horner uses her journal as a moving and powerful means of sustaining her inner resources. Love, work, travel, and adventure continue to be important themes in women's diaries of this century.

In making the selections for this volume, my goal was to include women writers in as wide a range of situations as possible. Young women and older women from a variety of cultures and class backgrounds, married women and women who never married, women loving men and women loving women, mothers and women alone —categories that in many cases overlap—are all represented. Texts were also chosen with concern that they discuss as wide a variety of topics as possible including love, friendship, work, war, nature, spirituality, birth, death, poetry, and politics. And they were selected and arranged with the intention that the excerpts would comment on one another in developing certain themes, such as race, in American life. With these goals in mind, I am conscious in the extreme of the limits of diary excerpts and every choice represents a compromise with other possible choices. My hope is that these brief examples of women's periodic life-writing will stimulate sufficient interest that the reader will use the bibliography to seek out these diaries and others in order to experience the integrity and power of entire texts.

Though some students of diary literature would insist on a distinction, I have used the words "diary" and "journal" interchangeably throughout the book. In the diary excerpts, spelling and punctuation remain as they appeared in the source, thus reflecting the editorial decisions of the original editor in the cases of the published diaries. In the very few instances where confusion of meaning might result from preserving original spelling, changes—indicated in brackets—have been made.

In preparing this book, I had the assistance of many people, first among whom are James and Kristen Cummings, who more than once offered me stimulating hospitality and access to their extraordinary private collection of near ten thousand published diaries. I am also in debt to the class-members of "Teaching Women's Literature from a Regional Perspective," who first demonstrated to me in their own work what riches lay in women's diary literature. Among them special thanks go to Carol Potter, who located and wrote about the diary of Helen Ward Brandreth, Jeannine Atkins, who introduced me to Mary MacLane, and Leslie Schwalm, who located and wrote about the diary of Rebekah Dickinson. I am most grateful to Betty Billings, who gave me a copy of this unpublished diary kept by "Aunt Marion." Thanks go also to Dorothy Johnson of the Common Reader Bookshop in New Salem, Massachusetts, who for years has been finding out-of-print diaries and other treasured books by and about women for me.

Majorie Karlson, Paula Mark, and the reference staff at the University of Massachusetts Library have been of crucial assistance with my research. Edla Holm and the interlibrary loan staff of the same institution, who have for years cheerfully filled my requests for obscure and peculiar items, also made it possible for me to complete the bibliographical aspect of this project. Reference librarians and archivists whom I have not met, including Hilary Cummings at the University of Oregon, Leo Dolenski at Bryn Mawr, Janet Ness at the University of Washington, and Virginia Adams at the New Bedford Historical Society, promptly and graciously replied to my requests for information.

I owe much to the members of the National Endowment for the Humanities Summer Institute on "Non-Traditional Women's Literature: Theory and Practice." It was for those Rose Towers colleagues, many of whom have remained a sustaining network of critics and friends, that this project was first begun. Florence Howe's enthusiasm for this book, and patience with it, along with the careful professionalism of Joanne O'Hare and Jo Baird at The Feminist Press have provided continuing support. As always I am grateful to my colleagues in English and Women's Studies at the University of Massachusetts, especially to Lee Edwards, Arlyn Diamond, Catherine Portuges, and Joseph T. Skerrett, Jr., who never made me feel bad that I was *still* working on my diary book. Kathleen Swaim, who dragged this Luddite into the computer age, made the book possible in this and all other ways.

A DAY AT A TIME

Introduction

As all the standard bibliographical sources show, American men kept journals in numbers far exceeding those kept by women until well past the middle of the nineteenth century.[1] One of the most fascinating questions about American diary literature is, therefore, how, in the twentieth century, the diary came to be a form of writing practiced predominantly by women writers. The reasons why women continued to choose periodic life-writing and men began to abandon the form are complex. The reason is not, as some writers about autobiography have suggested, that women's lives are fragmented and thus so are the forms of their writing. Nor is the reason that other avenues of literary expression were closed to women writers. The first argument embodies a type of life/art fallacy for which feminist critics must invent a pithy name in order to stop its easy use; the second, as abundant evidence now indicates, is also simply not true.

An important part of the answer to how and why diary literature became the province of women writers is the emergence of the self as the subject of the diary. If we come to the reading of diaries with only the modern idea of the diary as the arena of the "secret" inner life, we will distort or be disappointed in what we find in the journal pages written by American women throughout their history. It is only relatively recently (roughly in the last one hundred years) that the content of the diary has been a record of private thoughts and feelings to be kept hidden from others' eyes. Many eighteenth- and nineteenth-century diaries were semi-public documents intended to be read by an audience. Those kept by men, in particular, record a public life or are imbued with a sense of public purpose or audience. In the course of the nineteenth century, as a split between the public and private spheres came increasingly to shape the lives of women and men, those aspects of culture associated with the private became the domain of women. Simultaneously, changing ideas of the self, influenced by romanticism, the industrial revolution, and the "discov-

3

ery" of the unconscious contributed to changes in the content and function of the diary. As the modern idea of the secular diary as a "secret" record of an inner life evolved, that inner life—the life of personal reflection and emotion—became an important aspect of the "private sphere" and women continued to turn to the diary as one place where they were permitted, indeed encouraged, to indulge full "self-centeredness." American men, unused to probing and expressing this inner life in any but religious terms found, as the secular self emerged as the necessary subject of the diary, the form less and less amenable to them.

Also, toward the end of the nineteenth century, diary keeping in America became associated with gentility, and keeping a life-record among a "lady's" accomplishments. Etiquette books of the period containing prescriptive material about diary keeping suggest ways in which the genre became "feminized" ("Dear Diary"). Of course, the basic requirements of literacy and a modicum of leisure are the strongest determinants of who did and did not keep journals, and we can demonstrate how the ideology of "refinement" shaped the authorship in terms of class and race as well as gender.

The Changing Function and Content of the Diary

The American diary has its roots in the spiritual autobiography that charts the progress of the pilgrim's soul toward God, a function the diary still serves for some today. But throughout the eighteenth and nineteenth centuries in America, the secular journal served a number of semi-public purposes and the writers of many of these secular journals intended them to be read. Women diarists in particular wrote as family and community historians. They recorded in exquisite detail the births, deaths, illnesses, visits, travel, marriages, work, and unusual occurences that made up the fabric of their lives. Women for whom that fabric had been torn, who emigrated to this country, traveled as part of the westward migration, joined their husbands on whaling ships, or went to distant lands as missionaries, used journals to maintain kin and community networks. The diaries kept by these women functioned as extended letters often actually sent to those left behind.

If we look at two examples included in the collection here, we can chart the changes from diarist as family and social historian to the modern diarist whose principal subject is the self. Mary Vial Holyoke

(1737–1802) and Mary MacLane (1881–1929) kept their journals at opposite ends of the continent, but they are also separated from each other
by the romantic discovery of the secular self, the split between the
private and the public spheres emphasized by the industrial revolution, and the psychoanalytic celebration of individual consciousness.
Here is the record of Mary Vial Holyoke for the months of April and
May 1770 in Salem, Massachusetts:[2]

Apr. 7. Mr. Fisk Buried.
23. Went with Mr. Eppes to Mrs. Thomas. Took Down Beds.
26. Put Sals Coat in ye frame.
27. Made mead. At the assembly.
May 14. Mrs. Mascarene here & Mrs. Crowninshield. Taken very ill. The
Doctor bled me. Took an anodyne.
15. Kept my Bed all day.
17. Brought to Bed at 12 of a son.
19. The Baby taken with fits the same as ye others. Nurse came. Mrs. Vans
Died.
20. The Baby very ill. I first got up.
21. It Died at 11 °clock A.M. Was opened. The Disorder was found to Be in
the Bowels. Aunt Holyoke died.
22. Training. Mother Pickman here. Mrs. Sarjant yesterday.
23. My dear Baby buried.
28. Mrs. Pickman, Miss Dowse Drank tea here. Mrs. Jones, Lowell, Brown,
Cotnam, Miss Cotnam & Miss Gardner Called to see me.
29. Wrote to Boston and Cambridge. Mrs. Savage Brought to Bed. The
widow Ward lost 2 children with ye Throat Distemper from May 25th to
May 29th.
30. Cato went to Boston and returned.

Nearly 150 years later in Butte, Montana, Mary MacLane introduces herself in her journal with this Whitmanesque catalogue:[3]

And at this point I meet Me face to face.
I am Mary MacLane: of no importance to the wide bright world and dearly
and damnably important to Me.
Face to face I look at Me with some hatred, with despair and with great
intentness.
I put Me in a crucible of my own making and set it in the flaming trivial
Inferno of my mind. And I assay thus:
I am rare—I am in some ways exquisite.
I am pagan within and without.

I am vain and shallow and false.

I am a specialized being, deeply myself.

I am of woman-sex and most things that go with that, with some other *pointes*.

I am dynamic but devastated, laid waste in spirit.

I'm like a leopard and I'm like a poet and I'm like a religieuse and I'm like an outlaw.

I have a potent weird sense of humor—a saving and a demoralizing grace.

I have brain, cerebration—not powerful but fine and of a remarkable quality.

I am scornful-tempered and I am brave.

I am slender in body and someway fragile and firm-fleshed and sweet.

I am oddly a fool and a strange complex liar and a spiritual vagabond.

I am strong, individual in my falseness: wavering, faint, fanciful in my truth.

I am eternally self-conscious but sincere in it.

I am ultra-modern, very old-fashioned: savagely incongruous.

I am young, but not very young.

I am wistful—I am infamous.

In brief, I am a human being.

I am presciently and analytically egotistic, with some arresting dead-feeling genius.

And were I not so tensely tiredly sane I would say that I am mad.

The contrast between these two journal entries illustrates clearly the changes in the content, function, and form of the diary as created by American women writers in the last two hundred years. Eighteenth-century Mary Holyoke keeps her record as one might enter births and deaths in the family Bible. Her diary is typical of the period —a chronicle of who visited, who was ill, who was born, and who died, with events traditionally considered "historical," such as the military training she mentions, very much in the background. She begins this journal when she marries, as though to become the family and community historian is one of the duties of her new station in life. Her record with its factual fragments of sentences could not be more different from the later effusions of Mary MacLane. Mary Holyoke uses the first person pronoun only once in this two-month section. And one might say that the only evidence of a subjective reaction to the events she mentions is in the line where she uses the one adjective, "My *dear* Baby buried." In this single word is the germ of "self" that explodes in the pages of Mary MacLane's diary. What we do get in the Holyoke record that is utterly absent in the later text is a picture of family and community life, particularly the associations between the women of the community as they attend one another in the rituals of childbirth, illness, and death. This is not to say that the diary contains no record of an individual consciousness. Indeed in her very preoccupation with these details emerges her unique history. Mary Holyoke, though the wife of a prominent Salem physician, lost eight children in childbirth, a fact strongly influencing the selection of detail for her record.

The Mary MacLane diary, intended for publication when written, chronicles pure "Ego." Her favorite pronoun is the first person, as in the lines above, where "I am" is like a chant with "me" and "my" echoing choruses. But though she focuses intensely and exclusively on her own consciousness, we, ironically, know almost nothing about her. The diary contains no mention of routine daily activity, of family, of friends other than "the anemone lady." Utterly absent in this diary is the sense of self as part of a social fabric.

The self in Mary MacLane's record is no longer witness and chronicler but the *subject* of the record. In her exclusive focus on her own exquisitely analyzed individual sensibility, MacLane writes under the general influence of European romanticism, the specific tradition of the French *journal intime*, and in the context of the impact of Freud; but her most important predecessor, whom she mentions early in her journal, is Marie Bashkirtseff, a young Russian painter whose diary of utter self-absorption was first published in France in 1887. Marie Bashkirtseff always felt she would die young and she did succumb to tuberculosis in her mid-twenties. She undertook her diary with the hope that, if her painting did not bring her fame and immortality, the diary would. Again, she was correct. When edited by her mother from the eighty-four volumes Marie wrote, the published journal became phenomenally popular. With its translation into English in 1889 a kind of Marie Bashkirtseff cult developed in America. Women from Old Deerfield, Massachusetts[4] to Butte, Montana began keeping journals with the explicit expectation that their journals would make them famous, too. (One who took exception to the Bashkirtseff rage was Alice James, who refused to read the infamous journal and called Bashkirtseff "the perverse of the perverse.")[5] Marie Bashkirtseff readily admitted to "immense egotism" for which she was both adored and despised. But the wide popularity of her journal in America clearly gave American women "permission" to pay that kind of sustained attention to the self.

Reasons for "Keeping a Diary"

Marie Bashkirtseff's enthusiastic self-regard coupled with her acute consciousness of the passage of time identify two crucial, related, often unconscious motives for keeping a diary. In the year of her death, Bashkirtseff wrote a Preface to her diary in which she said: "The record of a woman's life, written down day by day, without any attempt at concealment, as if no one in the world were ever to read it, yet with the purpose of being read, is always interesting; for I am certain that I shall be found sympathetic, and I write down everything, everything, everything. Otherwise why should I write?"[6] Though few women diarists express such irrepressible self-admiration, keeping a diary, one could argue, always begins with a sense of self-worth, a conviction that one's individual experience is somehow *remark* able. Even the most self-deprecating of women's diaries are grounded in some sense of the importance of making a record of the life. As Bashkirtseff states, the writing act itself implies an audience and this audience will be the vehicle of preserving the life-record (in the act of reading) despite the passage of time and inevitable change. Even the phrase "keeping a diary" suggests this resistance to time, change, and ultimately, death. Though rarely expressed as directly as in Bashkirtseff's text, the essence of the impulse to keep a diary is captured in "I write, therefore I am." And will be.

Some American women diarists write explicitly for an imagined future audience who will survive them, as does Mollie Sanford on the Nebraska and Colorado frontiers, declaring, Bashkirtseff-like, "I do not want to be forgotten."[7] Most diarists do not write consciously or explicitly in defiance of death or what Bashkirtseff calls "oblivion"; but we can see how the smaller "deaths" or dislocations have often prompted journal keeping. Marriage, travel, and widowhood are all occasions creating a sense of a discontinuity of self—I was that, now I am this; I was there, now I am here. Keeping a life record can be an attempt to preserve continuity seemingly broken or lost. This can most clearly be seen in the numbers of women who left family and friends to travel West and used journals as a vehicle for maintaining severed networks. They were strongly informed by a sense of audience that shapes their accounts of wondrous and unfamiliar sights and their efforts to come to grips with a new life. Laura Downs Clark, who traveled with her new husband to the Firelands region of Ohio, kept a journal for her mother left behind. The diary reveals a tension between an objective record of daily events and her subjective response to her situation. Most of the entries are short: "June 24 [1818] Wednesday rained hard in the middle of the day— Salted down our pork & hung our fish up to dry." But every time her husband leaves her alone for any period of time, she records long entries that, in her words, "give full vent to my feelings."

July 10th . . . O! that parting moment when I was seated in the waggon to take (perhaps) a final farewell of all this world holds dear to me when I bid Grandmother farewell as she stood with weeping eyes to take her last look & I turned my back upon them (O! how my heart aches & the tears bedew my cheeks whilst writing this scene) it seems now as if that this moment was not realized enough at the time & it surely was not by me though no mortal tongue can express my feelings at that time how I catched the last glimmer of the Dear old habitation—the fields the trees & everything else seemed to wear a gloomy aspect at my departure was the ways of heaven ever more dark than in my leaving you—when I think of the little probability I have of seeing you again it seems as if I must fly! instantly fly to you. . . .[8]

The next entry returns to her earlier mode: "July 11th Saturday got out shingle enough to finish the roof and side up the end I had to cook for my men kept school & made a slipper for Mrs. Canfields baby— very hot weather indeed and very dry—." In this 1818 diary, we can almost feel the pressure of the internal, emotional life displacing social history as the necessary subject of the diary. Her usual entries are short and matter-of-fact. Those where she records her feelings are long, intense passages written while she is thinking of her mother, that is, in the *imagined* company of women.

Many diaries, of course, are not written for others' eyes, but for an audience who is the diarist herself. Charlotte Forten gives as complete an account of why she is keeping a diary as any woman in the mid-nineteenth century. In 1854, she writes:

A wish to record the passing events of my life, which, even if quite unimportant to others, naturally possess great interest to myself, and of which it will be pleasant to have some remembrance, has induced me to commence this journal. I feel that keeping a diary will be a pleasant and profitable employment of my leisure hours, and will afford me much pleasure in after years, by recalling to my mind the memories of other days, thoughts of much-loved friends from whom I may be separated . . . the interesting books that I read;

and the different people, places and things that I am permitted to see. Besides this, it will doubtless enable me to judge correctly the growth and improvement from year to year.[9]

Her phrase "even if quite unimportant to others" suggests the possibility in her mind that others *might* find her record of interest, but her stated purpose is to establish continuity between present and future selves.

Constructing the Self

As invaluable as women's life-records are as historical sources containing a kind of "truth" about women's lives not found in other places, we must remember that diaries and journals are texts, that is, verbal constructs. The process of selection and arrangement of detail in the text raises an array of concerns appropriately "literary," including questions of audience (real or implied), narrative, shape and structure, persona, voice, imagistic and thematic repetition, and what James Olney calls "metaphors of self."[10] The act of autobiographical writing, particularly that which occurs in a periodic structure, involves the writer in complex literary as well as psychological processes. It is a paradox that the process whose frequent goal is to establish self-continuity involves at its heart a dislocation from the self, or a turning of subject into object. Even in some of the earliest American women's diaries we can see this kind of "double consciousness," as the self stands apart to view the self. Rebekah Dickinson, a single woman living in Hatfield, Massachusetts in 1787, is very much conscious of herself as different from those around her and she fills the pages of her journal with this sense of "otherness": " . . . wondered how my lot fell by my Self alone how it Came about that others and all the world was in Possession of Children and friends and a hous and homes while i was so od as to Sit here alone . . . "[11] She writes of herself being "as lonely as tho i was Cast out from all the rest of the People and was a gasing stock for the old and young to gaze upon." In using her journal as a vehicle for religious self-examination, Dickinson knows herself as God would know her (completely, truly, and from within) and also views herself from the imagined position of those around her. The painful sense of "otherness" that fills the pages of this journal is borne of her awareness of being alone as she experiences it subjectively, compounded by her sense that others view her as an odd object.

An important vehicle in this process of objectifying the self is the audience of the journal. Some journals, as we have seen, are intended for real audiences but in many more the audience is implied. In some instances, the diary itself takes on this role as it is personified. "Dear diary" is a direct address to an ideal audience: always available, always listening, always sympathetic. Charlotte Forten addresses this audience on the last day of 1856: "Once more my beloved Journal, who art become a part of myself,—I say to thee, and to the Old Year,— Farewell!" Later she writes: "And now farewell, farewell to thee! my dear old friend, my *Only confidant!*—my journal!" In another passage where she seems to be speaking to a loved one, she is also speaking to the diary itself. "What name shall I give to thee, oh *ami inconnue?* It will be safer to give merely an initial—A. And so, dear A., I will tell you a little of my life for the past two years."[12]

Others who have given their journals names include Helen Ward Brandreth, a young upper-class girl in New York state, who in 1876 begins her diary: "I have determined to keep a journal. I shall call it Fannie Fern." She cautions Fannie, questions her, and apologizes to her ("I am afraid that you will think me dead or that something awful has happened to me").[13] Carol Potter, who has written about this diary kept by her great-grandmother, says in her own diary: "Most people would laugh to think that a personal diary was of such significance to a person, but this one is to me. When Nellie [Brandreth] writes—my dearest darling Fan—over and over, I know how she felt about that little book. It was a friend and so is this dumpy little blue notebook. How I wish I had started in a really nice bound notebook. But one never knows what will become of a first meeting or even a few."[14]

A contemporary diarist who knows what the relationship between writer and journal may become writes: "This notebook becomes my own little cheerleader, conscience, reckoner. You said it, now do it, it yells—OK, OK. WHAT?? It says—what's holding you up? What's the paralysis?" (March 1, 1977). Two days later she writes: "This journal has become my friend, my compulsion also . . . I need this writing. It is saving me . . . releasing me . . . But there is no one here to hold me, to tell me it's alright and yes—you can do it!—Right about now I feel the biggest, grandest need to be mothered."[15]

The importance of the audience, real or implied, conscious or unconscious, of what is usually thought of as a private genre cannot be overstated. The presence of a sense of audience, in this form of writing as in all others, has a crucial influence over what is said and how it is said. Friend, lover, mother, God, a future self—whatever role the audience assumes for the writer—that presence becomes a powerful "thou" to the "I" of the diarist. It shapes the selection and arrangement of detail within the journal and determines more than anything else the kind of self-construction the diarist presents. In naming her diary after the popular novelist Fanny Fern, Helen Ward Brandreth casts herself in its pages as the heroine of a piece of romantic fiction. She describes to "Fan" her "spooners," her flirtations, her engagement to the "wrong man," and her scheming to free herself for the "right man."

I danced with him about six times; then he asked me to go out on the stoop with him. Of course I went and when we got out there he took off his glove and wanted to hold my hand. I resisted the temptation for awhile, but, O Fan, I am *so* ashamed; at last I yielded. My hand trembled so that I was afraid he would notice it. O Fan, Fan!! I will die if he marries Birdie, For he does like her more than anybody else. At present.[16]

As we read Brandreth's journal we can see how its pages contain not *self* in any total sense, but a self which is to some degree a fiction, a construction. Even Mary MacLane, who attempts to write *everything,* is aware of this phenomenon and the crucial role of audience in the process. "I am trying my utmost to show everything—to reveal every petty vanity and weakness, every phase of feeling, every desire. It is a remarkably hard thing to do, I find, to probe my soul to its depths, to expose its shades and half-lights." She later concludes: "I am in no small degree, I find, a sham—a player to the gallery."[17] Whether "the gallery" is the personified diary, a real or implied audience, all diarists are involved in a process, even if largely unconscious, of selecting details to create a persona. The presence of the "gallery" is strongly felt in the journal of Alice James, brilliant and tortured invalid, who casts herself in her journal as an ironic social satirist. In what Robert Fothergill calls "the unique instance in the genre of a self-presentation which is almost unremittingly comic,"[18] we see clearly the distance possible between the character created in the diary and the far more complex life lived.

The pages of the diary might be thought of as a kind of mirror before which the diarist stands assuming this posture or that. One might even draw analogies between the process of psychoanalysis and the process of periodic life-writing, where the transference is made to the pages of the journal. But unlike the many oral forms of self-presentation, the self-constructions in the pages of a diary are fixed in time and space, available to the diarist for later viewing. Evidence abounds in all periods that women read and reread their diaries, a reality that renders the self-construction and reconstruction even more complex. Some diarists record comments upon previous entries, some emend them, some copy over entire diaries and edit them. One Amherst, Massachusetts woman in rewriting her diary omits an entire year and comments: "We had such a hard year in 1905 that I destroyed my diary did not want to read it—."[19] Mary MacLane, very aware of the charged experience of encountering past selves in the pages of her journal writes: "I write this book for my own reading. / It is my postulate to myself. / As I read it it makes me clench my teeth savagely: and coldly tranquilly close my eyelids: it makes me love and loathe Me, Soul and bones."[20] As modern psychoanalysis has demonstrated, such dialogue with aspects of the self is a potent process capable of unlocking mysteries of the human psyche and becoming the occasion of profound knowledge, growth, and change.

This power may explain why numbers of diarists record that periodic life-writing becomes addictive. Even in some early diaries we find comments like that of Lydia Smith in 1805: "I find that my idle habit of scribbling interferes so much with all regularity that I have determined to relinquish it, tho not entirely, yet I must so constrain it as to pursue my duties and studies, etc. I must wean myself by degrees for I have not strength to quit at once."[21] For those who do not wean themselves from the writing, diaries may be kept for a lifetime, and in some cases seem to be understood as synonymous with the life itself. In 1899, knowing she is near death, Cynthia Carlton writes: "I am not very well. Tried to straighten diary."[22] And the well-known last entry in Alice James's journal is by her companion Katherine Loring, who writes: "One of the last things she said to me was to make a correction in the sentence of March 4th 'moral discords and nervous horrors.' This dictation of March 4th was rushing about in her brain all day, and although she was very weak and it tired her much to dictate, she could not get her head quiet until she had it written: then she was relieved . . ."[23] For these women it is almost as though the life cannot be ended until the diary is finished. After her death in 1848, Elizabeth Ann Cooley's husband makes this final

entry in her journal: "This journal is done! The author being Elizabeth A. McClure died March 28, 1848. Tho happy in Christ Jesus
being the only consolation left me!! She was 22 years 7 months and
12 days old."[24] In the spirit of the diarist, he does not begin the entry
saying she has died, but that the journal is done.

This conflation of the journal and the life itself may indeed be an
accurate rendering of a complex dialectic. Some evidence exists that
the persona in the pages of the diary shapes the life lived as well as
the reverse. As Mary MacLane comments: "I don't know whether I
write this because I wear two plain dresses or whether I wear two
plain dresses because I write it."[25] The statement makes one ask to
what extent Helen Ward Brandreth "plots" the romantic episodes of
her life in order that they be available to "Fannie Fern" and whether
Alice James views the world as ironic social satirist *because* of the
persona in her journal or vice versa.

Reading a Diary: The Manuscript

The ideal way to study a diary is to have the manuscript itself in your
hand because all the material aspects of a diary create important
impressions. Is the cover ornate? Are the edges gilt? Does it have a
lock? Or was the writing done on the least expensive of notebooks
whose covers have barely survived? Perhaps no notebook at all was
available and the diarist wrote between printed lines of poetry in a
book she owned. Or perhaps the diarist is using a book manufactured
for the purpose; volumes such as "A Line A Day" dramatically influence the form of the written record.

The most intriguing state in which to find a manuscript is the one
complete with all the bits and pieces the diarist placed inside: clip-
pings from newspapers, dried flowers, mementos from friends. Each
detail adds a bit of knowledge or suggests a mystery. Jennie E. Greson's journal of her "grand tour in 1877" stands apart from the numbers of similar accounts with its collection of hotel cards, theater
tickets, and flowers picked "inside the coliseum," "on the grounds of
Hampton Court," and "on the grounds of the Royal Academy, Am-
sterdam."[26]

Handwriting tells stories, too. What do we make of the tiny, almost
invisible because written in pencil script of a mill girl in Easthamp-
ton, Massachusetts, who kept a diary in 1863?[27] Or of the dramatic
changes in handwriting matching changes in tone in the 1901 entry

of Elizabeth Hudson?[28] Would we read the passage where she is angry at her husband in the same way if we had not seen the uncharacteristically large and bold letters and the dark impression of a pen pressed hard against the page? Would the passage in a contemporary journal: "Another goddamn idiot evening with Amy crapping around about going to sleep. . . . I am so pissed I started her to bed at 8 and she is still up at 9:25! No more naps! . . . I have so much to do. SHIT. ANGER. FRUSTRATION"[29] read the same neatly printed on a page as it does scrawled across the pages of a notebook in increasingly larger block letters?

The Edited Diary

But, of course, we most often do not have the advantage of the information contained in the material object as we read a diary. The diaries available to the general reading public are the ones that have been published and the process of publication has almost always involved the process of editing. The editor may or may not be the author herself, but as Arthur Ponsoby, the well-known critic and historian of English diaries, has written, "No editor can be trusted not to spoil a diary."[30] Only a pair of examples, are needed to underline his point. Eliza Frances Andrews, who edited her Civil War diary for publication fifty years after it was written, writes in her introduction:

To edit oneself after the lapse of nearly half a century is like taking an appeal from Philip drunk to Philip sober. The changes of thought and feeling between the middle of the nineteenth and the beginning of the twentieth century are so great that the impulsive young person who penned the following record and the white-haired woman who edits it, are no more the same than were Philip drunk with the wine of youth and passion and Philip sobered by the lessons of age and experience. The author's lot was cast amid the tempest and fury of war, and if her utterances are sometimes out of accord with the spirit of our own happier time, it is because she belonged to an era which, though but of yesterday, as men of ages count history, is separated from our own by a social and intellectual chasm as broad as the lapse of a thousand years.[31]

Andrews's sense of the sharp discontinuity of the past and present, including past and present selves, is not the only force shaping the published document. As have many diarists, Andrews destroyed a large part of the diary she kept over a ten-year period "in those periodic fits of disgust and self-abasement that come to every keeper of an honest diary in saner moments." A relative who expressed an interest in the Civil War portion of her diary saved that volume from a similar fate. But Andrews admits, "So little importance did the writer attach to the documents even then, that the only revision made in changing it from a personal to a family history, was to tear out bodily whole paragraphs, and even pages, that were considered too personal for other eyes than her own. In this way the manuscript was mutilated, in some places, beyond recovery." Such lessons learned, however, are rarely learned forever, and in preparation of her manuscript for publication, Andrews states that she omitted "Matters strictly personal," explaining "a natural averseness to the publication of anything that would too emphatically 'write me down to an ass.' "[32]

The diary and letters of Maria Mitchell, Nantucket astronomer and educator, edited by her sister Phebe M. Kendall, met a similar fate. Of her sister, Kendall writes: "She had no secretiveness, and in looking over her letters it has been almost impossible to find one which did not contain too much that was personal, either about herself or others, to make it proper; especially as she herself would be very unwilling to make the affairs of others public."[33] The contemporary reader, living in an age that values "the personal" in ways that neither Andrews nor Kendall would have understood, will find such editorial decisions unforgivable.

Indeed, even small changes that are nothing like such major butchering can change the impression of a passage. Punctuation marks where there were none or inconsistent capital letters regularized all alter the record of the diarist. Even spaces on a page can communicate, but few editors of a diary can afford to leave them. Many editors will be tempted to omit repetitious material, but in fact it is precisely in what *is* repeated that we find the preoccupations, the obsessions, the "metaphors of self" of the diarist. So, the first problem for the reader of a published diary is the integrity of the text, and she or he will want to know as much as possible about the editorial history of any given text.

That is not to say that the reader should be entirely cynical about the diary that has been edited. Most published diaries, just like published fiction, have gone through an editorial process in shaping the manuscript for an audience different from the one for whom the record was originally kept. The reader's instinctive suspicion of this process is grounded in the sense of the immediacy and verisimilitude claimed by the genre. But the reader should remember that the original record is itself a reconstruction of reality and not "truth" in any absolute sense. Perhaps then the reader can think of the editorial process as an activity separate and distinct from the production of the life-record, one that may be creative and artistic in its own right.

The challenge to the editor in transforming a manuscript diary to a published one is to render both an accurate and accessible version of the original text and to make known as fully as possible the methods by which those goals were pursued. Most talented editors will operate with a combination of clear guidelines and good instincts that can be subject to scrutiny through comparisons with the original text. Some diaries lend themselves to publication in their entirety with complete verbatim transcription or even facsimile reproduction, but many (because of length, for example) do not. Readers who would object to any changes in an original record must remember that without the editorial process, many diaries that have been made available to a reading public would be resting in archives and read only by research specialists.

Diaries as Literature: The Writer as Protagonist

How, then, do we read a diary, whether an original manuscript or an edited version, with an awareness that it is a verbal construct with important relationships to other forms of literature such as autobiography and even fiction? First, we must attend to the main subject of any diary, the author herself, mirrored directly or mirrored slant in its pages. Here we can test Robert Fothergill's hypothesis about women as protagonists in their diaries:

. . . the need to project an ego-image does not appear to be a leading motive in diaries written by women. This is not to say that the personalities of women are rendered any less vividly or variously in the diary imprint than men's, but that the projection of self as dramatic protagonist is not the mode which the imprint commonly takes. There should be nothing very surprising in this. It is the merest platitude to observe that the position of women in society has tended to preclude the assertion of individual ego. . . . Egotism in men and pre-occupation with an effective self-image have been accepted and rewarded; in women they have been discouraged. A woman cannot easily cast herself as protagonist, when society and the controlling personal relationships of her life demand proficiency in exclusively supporting roles.

Nor does it follow that she might therefore tend to project a more rather than less assertive ego in the diary. . . . Hence one does not find in past centuries women diarists who strut and perform and descant on their own singularity.[34]

Mary MacLane certainly does "strut and perform and descant on her own singularity," and the memorable self-portraits created by Abigail Abbot Bailey, Nancy Shippen Livingston, Charlotte Forten, Alice James, Molly Sanford, Helen Ward Brandreth, to name just a few, suggest that Fothergill's conclusions need further examination in relation to American texts. He may be quite correct in asserting that "ego" in women rests on principles other than contest and dramatic self-assertion. If so, women's diaries will be a rich territory for study of the female construction of self and its literary representation.

In the accumulation of selected detail, particularly in the repetitions, preoccupations, even obsessions of the diarist, we find what James Olney calls the "metaphors of self." In reading a diary we must interrogate such metaphors in order to reveal their principles of construction. What organizing ideas, conscious or unconscious, shape the persona? What symbols come to represent the subject? Rebekah Dickinson, like many eighteenth-century diarists, finds these ideas and symbols in Scripture. She presents herself as a "stranger in a strange land," the entries in her diary echoing each other with the words "lonesome," "alone," "forsaken." Mary Dodge Woodward, a widow building a new life with her adult children on the Dakota plains, finds her self-reference in ordinary flowers. A rose geranium she has brought from home is the frequent subject of a diary entry. "The sitting room is full of sunshine and I am alone with the exception of Roxy, our dog, and my old rose geranium which really seems like a thing of life, it looks so much like home. I tend the plants with the greatest care fearful lest I might lose them." When she is sick, she notes that the rose geranium has "drooped"; when the temperature drops to forty below she writes: "There are still plenty of leaves on the old geranium which, with the help of the big coal stove has braved a Dakota winter." The plant comes from home, is old, and does not grow naturally on the prairie. And when she writes about a peony plant that she brought from her mother's home in Vermont, planted in Wisconsin where she lived with her husband,

and which now blooms in the Dakota Territory, her comment, "anything that can live in this cold country should be reverenced," is about the persistent flower but it is also about herself.[35]

Mary Holyoke's litany of childbirths and deaths, Elizabeth Fuller's accounting of work in her father's household, and Sarah Nichols's record of her walking tours are also such imprints of self. Even a record of the weather may tell us much about the diarist who chose to record it. Elizabeth Dixon Smith Geer, on an overland journey from Indiana to Oregon, sends this report to friends left at home:

Nov. 30 [1847] Raining. This morning I ran about trying to get a house to get into with my sick husband. At last I found a small, leaky concern, with two families already in it . . . My children and I carried up a bed. The distance was nearly a quarter of a mile. Made it down on the floor in the mud. I got some men to carry my husband up through the rain and lay him on it. . . . There are so many of us sick that I cannot write any more at present. I have not time to write much, but I thought it would be interesting to know what kind of weather we have in the winter.

Two months later, her sick husband has died and the weather continues to be the emblem of her condition: "Today we buried my earthly companion. Now I know what none but widows know; that is, how comfortless is that of a widow's life, especially when left in a strange land, without money or friends, and the care of seven children. Cloudy."[36]

Time and Narrative Structures

While the novel and autobiography may be thought of as artistic wholes, the diary is always in process, always in some sense a fragment. That is not to say that diaries do not have distinct shapes, but that their shapes derive from their existence in time passing. Some are shaped by external events in the diarist's life, which, even from the writer's point of view, have a beginning, middle, and end. Courtship diaries ending with a marriage and travel diaries ending with the arrival at a destination are examples of such texts.

Because diaries are periodic in creation and structure, incremental repetition is an important aspect of the structure of most journals, and the dynamic of reading the periodic life-record involves attending to what is repeated. Repeated actions large and small build tension as they advance the "plot." Will beloved Sister Mary Ermeline in the convent school diary of Suzette Pierce be waiting in the hall again today? Will she take her arm again and speak of friendship and love?[37] Will the wagon train in the diary of Amelia Stewart Knight make it across this next, even more dangerous river?

The calendar year provides the structural rhythms of many diaries. Frequently diarists mark the end of each calendar year with repeated rituals; early diaries often end the year with a list of persons who died during that year, later ones with reflections and resolutions. Many women diarists mark holidays and personal anniversaries as does Mary Dodge Woodward:

Thanksgiving Day. This used to be a day of unusual gladness, for on this day Walter was born, and he has proved a great blessing to me. We used to try, after the fashion of New Englanders, to be all at home on Thanksgiving if it were possible. I have been very happy with my family around the table many years—how happy, I did not realize until that sad day on which the father was taken from us and I was left alone with the children. Never since then have all the children been with me on this day. It is our fourth Thanksgiving in Dakota. The turkey is roasted and eaten, and the day has gone; I am thankful.[38]

Time and the Reader

A novel creates a fictional world complete unto itself, while an autobiography or memoir looks back from a fixed point in time which is the terminus of the retrospective. A diary, on the other hand, is created in and represents a continuous present. And as we have seen, many diarists reread previous entries before writing a current one, creating a complexly layered present to which a version of the past is immediately available. From entry to entry, the text incorporates its future as it reconstructs its past.

While analogies may be drawn between the construction of self in a diary and an autobiography, and even between the creation of a persona in a diary and a novel, the unique demands made of the reader of a diary derive from its periodic creation and structure. The writer's relationship to "real time" and representation of "time passing" in the text itself, create formal tensions and ironies not found in texts generated from an illusion of a fixed point in time. What is known as well as what is *unknown* to the writer underscore the unique dynamic of the periodic text. Further, what is known and unknown to the *reader* of the journal text determine the unusually active role demanded of that reader. Again, periodicity is the key phenomenon determining the relationship of the writer and the reader to the text, and to each other, within both real and imaged time.

While diaries may have narrative structures approximating those of other forms of verbal art—action moving toward an end creating anticipation around the question of what happens next—the obvious difference in the "plots" of diaries and those of most other narratives is that the novelist, poet, oral storyteller, or writer of an autobiographical memoir knows what happens next and directs the reader's response at every point. Most diaries, on the other hand, are a series of surprises to writer and reader alike, one source of the immediacy of the genre. For example, eighteen-year-old Helen Marnie Stewart kept a journal on her family's trip to Oregon in 1853. She writes: "it being raining the road is extremely slippy and there is very steep hills to go up and down and that makes it difficult and hard   there was neer us a grave that had been dug open and a women head was layin and a come sticking in her hair   it seems rather hard."[39] Though the last line, indeed the understatement of the entire passage, suggests the extent to which Helen Stewart and her party had become inured to horror, the reader experiences something of the sharp intake of breath in coming unprepared upon the grave in the diary text that Helen Stewart felt in seeing it along the road.

Surprises, Mysteries, and Silences of Diaries

The surprises, the mysteries, and the silences of diaries must all be considered in relation to what is known and unknown to both writer and reader. Though a diary may have been intended for a real audience, it was likely not created for its current reader. Some of the diary, at least on first reading, may mean nothing to the reader. (This is one reason why it is so hard to imitate a diary in fictional form. The temptation of the author to tell too much makes the reader realize immediately, as in *The Diary of a Shirtwaist Striker*, by Theresa Serber Malkiel,[40] for example, that the diary is not an authentic one.) As a result the reader must take a rather active role in the creation of the world within the diary. One source of the engagement of reading a private, periodic record is precisely this activity, which can be akin to putting together pieces of a puzzle—remembering clues and supplying the missing pieces, linking details apparently unrelated in the diarist's mind, and decoding "encoded" materials.

This process is complicated by the fact that while the diarist almost always has more knowledge about her world than the reader has, the reader may have some knowledge unavailable to the diarist. What we know about the outcome of the Civil War creates, in part, the you-can't-put-it down quality of many narratives from that period. What we know about the continuing struggle for women's rights intensifies our reactions to Abigail Bailey's account of kidnapping by her husband and Mary Ann Sims's account of her brother-in-law's attempt to take her property away upon the death of her husband.[41]

All diarists operate within the limits of their own self-knowledge, limits the reader may be able to transcend. As Mary MacLane writes: "I have analyzed and analyzed, and I have gotten down to some extremely fine points—and yet there are still things upon my horizon that go beyond me."[42] The repeated patterns of a life may escape the writer recording them while they do not escape an aware reader. In a very real sense the contemporary reader may know more about the source of anguish felt by Rebekah Dickinson, more about Charlotte Forten's drive to prove she was as capable as any white person, more about the racism of Eliza Frances Andrews than the diarist did herself.

One task for the reader of any diary is to identify the "silences" of the text. What the diarist did not, could not, or would not write sometimes shrieks from the page. Adrienne Rich's poem, "Cartographies of Silence," illuminates:

> The technology of silence
> the rituals, etiquette
>
> the blurring of terms
> silence not absence
>
> of words or music or even
> raw sounds
>
> Silence can be a plan
> rigorously executed
>
> the blueprint to a life
>
> It is a presence
> it has a history a form
>
> Do not confuse it
> with any kind of absence[43]

The task of the reader of a diary is to identify these presences: their technology, ritual, etiquette, plan, history, and form. One of the loudest silences in the diaries of American women surrounds the line written by Mary Holyoke on September 1, 1782: "My Dear Child Died 9 A.M., which makes the 8ᵗʰ Child."[44] This woman, who gave birth to twelve children, three of whom survived, records no grief, no terrified anticipation of childbirth, no mention of pregnancy, no mention (of course) of sex. Only the careful record of babies born to herself and others in her community and of babies dead and buried. Most diaries contain such silences created by choices, conscious and unconscious, made by the writer in her time.

Sometimes the diarist indicates the things she will not say in her written record. Helen Ward Brandreth's last New Year's resolution for 1877 is a wonderful example:

This is my greatest *sin*. O Fan, if I could only stop but it is *so* hard. I have made more good resolutions about it than anything else and when I think I have entirely recovered from it I do it over again. The last time I did it was Dec. 14, 1877, only a little bit of a while ago. I would tell you what it is only it is so horridly awfully vile and then some one *might* read this and O horrors! what would they think of me. I would be disgraced for life.[45]

The diary contains no entry for Dec. 14, 1877, and so the reader is left with only this suggestive mystery.

Another example is the contemporary diarist who writes freely about sex, but adds, "But, I am finding it tricky to write about my attractions to women . . . I will leave that private."[46] Her comment reveals her assumption that somehow the diary, even in an age where it is usually thought to be, is not, in fact, private. Such silences when so identified indicate the presence of an implied or potential audience, who even if not a conscious presence, exerts a powerful shaping influence on the text.

The Reader's Journey

Today's reader of the text, another powerful shaping audience, recreates the journal in the act of reading. The words "journal" and "journey," like the word "diary," have their roots in the French word for "day." So we might think of all diaries as travel diaries and the overriding metaphor of all journals as the journey, a journey from one "place" in time to another. The journey becomes a parallel one for writer and reader in more than one sense. The vividness of the self-created character in many journal pages derives in part from the concrete, distinct, and peculiar detail she reports along her journey. The unique specificity of most journals creates the effect sought by writers of other forms of verbal art—an entire world whose closed borders the reader may enter for a time. For the reader who may never have had thirteen children, or traveled in a wagon to Oregon, or sailed to Africa as a black American, the journey recorded in the diary becomes the reader's journey.

Further, the special demands made upon the reader for active participation in the recreation of the writer's journey affirm the reader's like capacities of imagination. The text created in a continuous presence but now fixed in time, must be re-created by a reader in a new, continuous present. The reader's consciousness of time passing may be, in part, what makes reading the journal a compelling experience. As the journal pages construct continuity out of the apparent discontinuity created by time passing in the writer's life, the act of reading may generate a parallel process for the reader. The participation of the reader means that the writing act has indeed succeeded in defying time; and the text, in turn, grants the active reader the conviction, "they wrote, therefore, I am."

NOTES

1. Less than 10 percent of the diaries listed in William Matthews, *American Diaries: An Annotated Bibliography of American Diaries Written Prior to the Year 1861* (Berkeley: University of California Press, 1945) and Laura Arskey, Nancy Pries, and Marcia Reed, *American Diaries: An Annotated Bibliography of Published American Diaries and Journals*, vol. 1 (Detroit: Gale Research, 1983) are diaries written by women. Of course, this ratio may not accurately reflect who was keeping diaries as it is possible that that family members, historians, archivists, and publishers may have valued more highly diaries kept by men and more often preserved them.

2. From the diary of Mary Vial Holyoke, in *The Holyoke Diaries, 1709–1856*, ed. George Francis Dow (Salem, Mass.: The Essex Institute, 1911), p. 73.

3. *I, Mary MacLane: A Diary of Human Days* (New York: Frederick A. Stokes, 1917), pp. 1–2.

4. See the diary of Eleanor Arms at the Pocumtuck Valley Memorial Association Library, Old Deerfield, Mass.

5. *The Diary of Alice James*, ed. Leon Edel (New York: Dodd, Mead, 1934), p. 125.

6. *Marie Bashkirtseff: The Journal of a Young Artist, 1860–1884*, trans. Mary J. Serrano (New York: Cassell, 1889), p. viii.

7. *Mollie: The Journal of Mollie Dorsey Sanford in Nebraska and Colorado Territories, 1857–1866* (Lincoln: University of Nebraska Press, 1959), p. xii.

8. "The Original Diary of Mrs. Laura (Downs) Clark, of Wakeman, Ohio," *The Firelands Pioneer* (January 1920), pp. 2,311, 2,314.

9. *The Journal of Charlotte Forten,* ed. Ray Allen Billington (New York: Dryden Press, 1953), p. 33.

10. James Olney, *Metaphors of Self: The Meaning of Autobiography* (Princeton: Princeton University Press, 1972).

11. From the manuscript diary of Rebekah Dickinson, 20 August 1787 and 22 August 1787. Used with permission from Betty Billings.

12. *Journal of Charlotte Forten,* pp. 76, 100, 115.

13. From the typescript of the diary of Helen Ward Brandreth, 2 January 1876 and 2 October 1876, pp. 1, 6.

14. From the manuscript diary of Carol Potter. Used with permission.

15. From a manuscript diary loaned to Margo Culley. Used with permission.

16. Brandreth, 27 June 1877, p. 12.

17. *The Story of Mary MacLane* (Chicago: Herbert S. Stone, 1902), pp. 75, 133.

18. Robert A. Fothergill, *Private Chronicles: A Study of English Diaries* (London: Oxford University Press, 1974), p. 119.

19. Typescript of the diary of Eunice Williams Smith, Amherst, Mass.

20. *I, Mary MacLane,* p. 141.

21. "Lydia Smith's Journal, 1805–1806," *Proceedings of the Massachusetts Historical Society* 48 (1914–1915), p. 515.

22. *Cynthia: Excerpts from the Diaries of Cynthia Brown Carlton, 1841–1900, Burton, Ohio, in the Western Reserve,* ed. Margaret Patricia Ford (Privately printed, 1976), not paginated.

23. *Diary of Alice James,* pp. 232–33.

24. "From Virginia to Missouri in 1846: The Journal of Elizabeth Ann Cooley," ed. Edward D. Jervey and James E. Moss, *Missouri Historical Review* 60, no. 2 (January 1966), p. 206.

25. *I, Mary MacLane,* p. 189.

26. The manuscript diary of Jennie E. Greson, 1877. Owned by Margo Culley.

27. The manuscript diary of Anna Pike, 1863. Owned by Margo Culley.

28. The manuscript diary of Elizabeth Hudson, 1901. Owned by Margo Culley.

29. From a manuscript diary loaned to Margo Culley. Used with permission.

30. Arthur Ponsoby, *English Diaries: A Review of English Diaries from the Sixteenth to the Twentieth Century* (London: Methuen, 1923), p. 5.

31. Eliza Frances Andrews, *The War-Time Journal of a Georgia Girl, 1864–1865* (New York: D. Appleton, 1908), p. 1.

32. Ibid., pp. 4–6.

33. *Maria Mitchell: Life, Letters and Journal,* ed. Phebe Mitchell Kendall (Boston: Lee and Shepard, 1896), p. 255.

34. Fothergill, *Private Chronicles,* p. 87.

35. Mary Dodge Woodward, *The Checkered Years,* ed. Mary Boynton Cowdry (Caldwell, Idaho: Caxton Printers, 1937), pp. 24, 35, 224.

36. "Diary of Mrs. Elizabeth Dixon Smith Geer," *Transactions of the Oregon Pioneer Association,* Thirty-Fifth Annual Session (1907), pp. 172–73, 174.

37. The manuscript diary of Suzette Pierce, 1899–1900. Owned by Margo Culley.

38. Woodward, *Checkered Years,* p. 104.

39. "The Diary of Helen Stewart, 1853." Typescript produced by the Lane County Pioneer-Historical Society, p. 6.

40. Theresa Serber Malkiel, *The Diary of a Shirtwaist Striker* (New York: Cooperative Press, 1910).

41. "Private Journal of Mary Ann Own Sims," ed. Clifford Dale Whitman, *Arkansas Historical Quarterly* 35, nos. 2 and 3 (Summer and Autumn 1976), pp. 142–87, 261–91.

42. *The Story of Mary MacLane,* p. 75.

43. From Adrienne Rich, "Cartographies of Silence," in *The Dream of a Common Language, Poems 1974–1977* (New York: W.W. Norton, 1978), p. 17. The aptness of this poem in relation to silences in women's diaries was suggested to me by Leslie Schwalm.

44. Holyoke, *Holyoke Diaries,* p. 107.

45. Brandreth, 31 December 1877, p. 24.

46. Manuscript diary loaned to Margo Culley. Used with permission.

IN THE FATHERLAND

Mary Vial Holyoke

(1737–1802)

Mary Vial was the only child of Boston shopkeepers, but as the second wife of Edward Augustus Holyoke, she gave birth twelve times. Though her husband was a prominent Salem, Massachusetts physician, only three of their children survived to adulthood. Seven of Mary Vial Holyoke's children died at birth or in infancy; one died at age 3, one at age 17. In January 1764, October 1765, November 1766, September 1767, and October 1768 she lost a child. She lost two more in the 1770s and two in the 1780s, her last born dying at 6 months of age when Mary Holyoke was 45. Edward Holyoke outlived his wife, practiced medicine in Salem for eighty years, and died at the age of 101.

Mary Holyoke began her diary soon after her marriage as though it were one of the duties of her new station. Typical of the secular diaries of the period, it serves as a family and community history. In it she records births and deaths as one would write names in the family Bible. She also notes events in the community, large and small, including visits made and received, travel undertaken, and work accomplished. The Revolutionary War remains far in the background, though on February 17, 1776 she writes, "The troops Left Boston. Our People took Possession of it."

1764
[*Mary Vial Holyoke's first child Mary (Polly) was born on September 14, 1760. She appears in her mother's diary during the next three years: "Poll began her shoes and stays" (January 23, 1762); "first went to meeting" (May 22, 1763); and "went to school" (April 18, 1763). In 1764 the child is taken ill.*]

From the diary of Mary Vial Holyoke, in *The Holyoke Diaries, 1709–1856*, ed. George Francis Dow (Salem, Mass.: Essex Institute, 1911) 60, 61, 65, 66, 67, 73, 77, 95, 107. The manuscript of the diary is at the Essex Institute in Salem, Massachusetts. Reprinted by permission.

Jan. 8, 1764. First wore my new Cloth riding hood.

9. My Daughter Polly first confined with the quinsy. Took a vomit.

10. Nabby Cloutman watch'd with her.

11. Very ill. Molly Molton watched.

12. Zilla Symonds watched.

13. My Dear Polly Died. Sister Prissy came.

14. Buried.

17. Small Pox began to spread at Boston.

19. Mrs. Fitch came from Boston for fear of small pox.

21. Town meeting for guarding the town from small pox.

22. Dr. Lloyd Came from Boston to See Stephen Higginson.

24. A violent snow storm. College burnt.

25. Mr. [John] Appleton moved to the pest house with the small pox which proved to be Chicken Pox.

27. First heard of their inoculating at Boston.

29. Dr. Gardiner Came from Boston. Mrs. Vans brought to bed.

31. Mr. Oliver's child taken with Convulsions.

Feb. 3. The Dr. received an invitation from my uncle to be inoculated at his house.

Mar. 9. The Dr. came home [from Cambridge and] brought news of 5 or 600 being inoculated at Boston.

10. Sally Bernard went to point Shirley to be inoculated.

13. Mrs. Brown drank tea here. News of Caleb Ward's death.

14. I made Mr. [Israel] Atherton a Gown for small Pox.

16. Mr. Atherton gone to the Castle to be inoculated for the small Pox.

26. Mrs. Higginson brought to bed.

28. Mr. Appleton returned after his having Small Pox at the Castle.

29. Bought Plaid for the Drs. [small pox] gown of widow Cabot. Molly Appleton came from Portsmouth.

April 1. Mrs. Higginson's Child Baptized Mehitable.

6. The Dr., Susy Higginson, Nancy Cabot & Betsey went to be inoculated at Boston.

3. Sister Kneeland & Prisey inoculated last Monday.

12. Went to Cambridge with Mr. Appleton.

14. The Dr. had some Slight Complaints.

15. He had a very restless night, one pustule appeared.

16. Very ill all day, had a very good night.

17. 3 more appeared very bright this morning.

19. I drank tea at Aunt Glovers.

20. I went to see Prisey, as I did every day while at Boston.

21. I went to see Aunt Winslow with Aunt Holyoke at Mrs. Amory's.

26. Came home with Mr. Atherton.

27. Bought salmon. Cut 37 asparagus, first cutting here. Bought 11 Ducks.

May 4. Mr. Atherton brought the Dr. home from having the Small Pox. 2 in 3 Dies with it in the natural way. . . .

[*After two more daughters, Margaret, born March 4, 1763 and Mary (Polly), born January 9, 1765, who lives only nine months, Mary Vial Holyoke gives birth to her first son on August 12, 1766.*]

[1766]

Aug. 12. I was brought to bed 33 m^r after 7 P.M.

17. The Child Christened Edward Augustus. Mr. [Edward] Kitchen died.

27. Mrs. Higginson Delivered of a Dead Child. Mr. Orne's negro broke his leg.

31. The Doctor went to Cape Ann. Mr. Orne's negro Died.

Sept. 1. Setting up week. Washed.

2. Ironing. Nurse Call^d away.

14. I first went to meeting. The Child taken with a sort of fit, lay very bad for 8 or 9 hours.

30. Mr. Walter married.

Oct. 2. I made the wedding visit with 20 Ladys.

7. Training.

8. Trooping, etc.

16. Father & mother Came. I drank tea at the farm with 22.

17. Father & mother went to the Hamlet.

23. Mrs. Brown sent out for Virginia.

26. The Child taken unwell with the same disorder.

Nov. 2. I was out all day at meeting. The Child taken with another turn, lay till 5° in the morning & then Died.

4. My Dear Child Buried. Mr. Brown went to new port.

14. Training.

20. Opened firkin of butter, 85 lb.

24. Put things in the Closets. Club here.

27. Mrs. Pyncheon Brought to Bed.

Dec. 1. Dr. Cut of[f] Lovets hand back from fingers.

8. Mr. Pinchback Came.

10. Mr. Pinchback & Miss Joe Davis went to Marblehead in the afternoon to Mr. Crowningshields.

11. Mr. Pinchbacke carried Miss Joe home.

12. Colonel Pickman's Family Dined & spent the evening here.

13. Shock of an earthquake, small.

20. Snow very high.

25. Bought of Wm Williams a Doe rabbit to which we gave the name of Sterril. Jan. 26, 1767, She brought forth 6 young ones 3 of which died.

Jan. 1, 1767. I went to the assembly for the first time this winter.

3. Mr. Jackson and [Mr.] Lowell married.

4. Dr. made Mr. Jackson's wedding visit.

5. Mr. Bernard, Mr. Jackson with their Ladys, young Mr. Bernard and Miss Roberts Dined here.

8. Made Mr. Lowell's wedding visit.

9. Went to see Mrs. Jackson.

13. News of Judge Russel's death.

22. Mrs. Ropes brought to bed.

27. At a Dance at Mr. Burnet Brown's.

Apr. 2. Miss Loice Gardiner here.

3. We made two Barrels of Soap.

7. Mantua maker here.

10. Sowed Pease. Seeds up in the hot bed. Began to paint the entry.

11. Sewed radishes, set out turnips & stumps.

May 3. Mr. Mascarene's Boy and furniture Came. Finish'd the entry.

4. Mr. Mascarene & the maid came.

5. Lodged at his house.

9. Scoured furniture Brasses & put up the Chintz bed & hung pictures.

14. Mr. Mascarene Brought his wife and son.

31. Colonel Pickman very poorly.

June 17. Turtle at Jonson's.

18. Capt. Tong Came.

July 8. At the fort. Capt. Tong sailed for Halifax.

14. Mr. Walter, Capt. Cotnam, Mr. Pickman and Ladys, Mr. C. P. and Mrs. Eppes here in the Evening.

18. At the fort with Colo. Brown & others.

28. Betty Herbert buried.

Aug. 2. Old Mrs. Cabot Died.

23. First staid from meeting.

Sept. 5. I was brought to bed about 2°Clock A. M. of a daughter.

6. The Child Baptized Mary.

7. The Baby very well till ten o'Clock in the evening & then taken with fits.

8. The Baby remained very ill all day.

9. It Died about 8 o'clock in the morning.

10. Was buried.

11. Mrs. Woodbridge brought to bed.

Sept. 17. Mrs. Vans & Mrs. Cranch brought to bed.

23. Training. Miss Brandon, Mrs. Brown here.

Oct. 2. Mrs. Mackey's baby Buried.

8. Mrs. Vans Baby Buried. . . .

[*After losing the third daughter named for herself, she chooses another name for the girl born eleven months later, but the child lives only nineteen days. Her seventh-born lives four days.*]

[1770]

May 14. Mrs. Mascarene here & Mrs. Crowninshield. Taken very ill. The Doctor bled me. Took an anodyne.

15. Kept my Bed all day.

17. Brought to Bed at 12 of a son.

19. The Baby taken with fits the same as ye others. Nurse came. Mrs. Vans Died.

20. The Baby very ill. I first got up.

21. It Died at 11 °clock A. M. Was opened. The Disorder was found to Be in the Bowels. Aunt Holyoke died.

22. Training. Mother Pickman here. Mrs. Sarjant yesterday.

23. My dear Baby buried.

28. Mrs. Pickman, Miss Dowse Drank tea here. Mrs. Jones, Lowell, Brown, Cotnam, Miss Cotnam & Miss Gardner Called to see me.

29. Wrote to Boston and Cambridge. Mrs. Savage Brought to Bed. The widow Ward lost 2 children with ye Throat Distemper from May 25th to May 29th. . . .

[Her eighth-born, a daughter, survives infancy but dies later at age seventeen.]

[1771]

Sept. 6. Mr. Marrot's Shoulder Set here. His Sister Lodg'd.

7. I rode up to Mr. Mascarene's.

9. Very poorly. Put up bed.

12. Very ill. Brought to Bed quite alone 11 A. M. of a Daughter. Child very well.

13. 2 Mrs. Pickmans, Mrs. Eppes & Mrs. Rowth here.

15. Mr. Holyoke Christened the Child Elizabeth.

Oct. 7. Sitting up week. Mrs. Eppes, 2 Pickmans, Mrs. Rowth & Miss Dowse here. Club here.

22. Dr. Din'd at Mr. Mascarene's. First got out today.

23. Col. Brown Carried me to ride.

Nov. 5. Polly Cabot Buried. I went to the house.

11. Mrs. Crown^sd here. Mad^m Oliver called to see me.

13. Molly Morgan worked here.

15. Molly finished. Violent pain in my breast.

22. The Dr. opened my Breast.

30. Left off the poultice. Put on a frog Plaister. In a good deal of pain. Col. Higginson & Lady here. . . .

[Judith, born January 20, 1774, is a healthy child; two years later her tenth-born succumbs.]

[1776]

Dec. 4. I had a Bad toothache (taken ill ½ after 4). A. M. Got

5. to Bed Before 8. Mrs. Jones & Mrs. Carwick Spent the Day here. Nurse Came at night.

6. I was very poorly. Mrs. Vans, Debby Higginson, Mrs. C. G. Pickman Call'd to see me.

8. Child Baptized Henrietta. Judy Extrem Bad all night with the quinsey.

26. Violent Storm N. E. News of Gen. Lee's Being taken.

30. My Dear Harriet Died at 9 oClock in ye morning.

31. She was Buried. Mr. Bernard here & Mrs. Carwick. . . .

[Her third child who lives to adulthood is born April 21, 1779. Her twelfth and last is born April 8, 1782.]

[1782]

Mar. 10. Capt. Harriden married.

29. Mrs. Pearson Died this morn^g 4 °Clock.

30. Mrs. Gardner Brought to Bed.

Apr. 8. Sent for Mrs. Jones & Mrs. Carwick. Very Bad till ½ Past 11 A. M. when I was D^d of a son. Mad^m & Mrs. Pickman & Mrs. Derby Called in.

9. Mrs. Goodale & Miss Higginson Called. Miss Minott & her Brother D tea here.

10. Two Mrs. Pynchons Call^d & Mad^m Oliver & her son & Dr. Goodhue Calle^d. Dr. Bernard Called.

14. Child Baptized Edward Augustus.

25. Fast Day. Dr. at Reading. Dr. Goodhue very Bad.

28. Sitting up week.

May 11. News of the Death of Mr. Carwick.

20. Mrs. Higginson arrive^d from Halifax.

22. Nurse went to nurse Mrs. Derby.

June 14. News of Bill Andrews Death.

July 10. Mrs. Goodhue sent for me. He Died at 10°clock A. M.

22. We made Mrs. Fisher wedding visit.

23. My teeth set.

Aug. 8. At Mrs. Goodhue Last time.

13. At Mrs. C. G. Pickman. Her child Died yesterday.

23. Mrs. Goodhue Left Salem.

Sept. 1. My Dear Child Died 9 A. M., which makes the 8th Child.

Abigail Abbot Bailey
[1746–1815]

Abigail Abbot, daughter of James and Sarah Abbot of Concord, New Hampshire, married Asa Bailey when she was twenty-two years old. They established their family, which eventually numbered seventeen children, in Landaff, New Hampshire, where Asa Bailey became a prominent landowner, town selectman, and soldier in the Revolutionary War.

The manuscript recording her struggles with her husband was found among her things after her death. Friends and family who thought her account of her life should be published brought the papers to the Reverend Ethan Smith of Haverhill, New Hampshire, who had known the author during her lifetime. His conviction that "few lives of christians, in modern days, have afforded such rare materials for instructive biography," led him to edit her story for publication. Written in the form of a diary, the document is, more precisely, a retrospective memoir. In both content and tone, the narrative is in the tradition of women's religious autobiography as well as in the tradition of American "captivity narratives."

December, 1788. Mr. B. began to behave in a very uncommon manner: he would rise in the morning, and after being dressed, would seat himself in his great chair, by the fire, and would scarcely go out all day. He would not speak, unless spoken to; and not always then. He seemed like one in the deepest study. If a child came to him, and asked him to go to breakfast, or dinner, he seemed not to hear: then I would go to him, and must take hold of him, and speak very loudly, before he would attend; and then he would seem like one waking from sleep. Often when he was eating, he would drop his knife and fork, or whatever he had in his hand, and seemed not to know what

From *Memoirs of Mrs. Abigail Bailey*, ed. Ethan Smith (Boston: Samuel T. Armstrong, 1815).

he was doing. Nor could he be induced to give any explanation of his strange appearance and conduct. He did not appear like one senseless, or as though he could not hear, or speak. His eyes would sparkle with the keen emotions of his mind.

I had a great desire to learn the cause of this strange appearance and conduct. I at first hoped it might be concern for his soul; but I was led to believe this was not the case. He continued thus several days and nights, and seemed to sleep but little.

One night, soon after we had retired to bed; he began to talk very familiarly, and seemed pleasant. He said, now I will tell you what I have been studying upon all this while: I have been planning to sell our farm, and to take our family and interest, and move to the westward, over toward the Ohio country, five or six hundred miles; I think that is a much better country than this; and I have planned out the whole matter. Now I want to learn your mind concerning it; for I am unwilling to do any thing contrary to your wishes in things so important as this. He said he wished to gain my consent, and then he would consult the children, and get their consent also. I was troubled at his proposal; I saw many difficulties in the way. But he seemed much engaged, and said he could easily remove all my objections. I told him it would be uncertain what kind of people we should find there; and how we should be situated relative to gospel privileges. He said he had considered all those things; that he well knew what kind of minister, and what people would suit me; and he would make it his care to settle where those things would be agreeable to me, and that in all things he would seek as much to please me, as himself. His manner was now tender and obliging: and though his subject was most disagreeable to me, yet I deemed it not prudent to be hasty in discovering too much opposition to his plans. I believe I remarked, that I must submit the matter to him. If he was confident it would be for the interest of the family, I could not say it would not be thus; but really I could not at present confide in it.

He proceeded to say, that he would take one of our sons, and one daughter, to go first with him on this tour, to wait on him; and that he probably should not return to take the rest of the family under a year from the time he should set out. He said he would put his affairs in order, so that it should be as easy and comfortable for me as possible, during his absence.

Soon after, Mr. B. laid this his pretended plan before the children;

and after a while he obtained their consent to move to the westward.
They were not pleased with the idea, but wished to be obedient, and
to honor their father. Thus we all consented, at last, to follow our
head and guide, wherever he should think best; for our family had
ever been in the habit of obedience: and perhaps never were more
pains taken to please the head of a family, than had ever been taken
in our domestic circle.

But alas! words fail to set forth the things which followed! All this
pretended *plan* was but a specious cover to infernal designs. Here I
might pause, and wonder, and be silent, humble, and astonished, as
long as I live! A family, which God had committed to my head and
husband, as well as to me, to protect and train up for God, must now
have their peace and honor sacrificed by an inhuman parent, under
the most subtle and vile intrigues, to gratify the most contemptible
passion! I had before endured sorrowful days and years, on account
of the follies, cruelties, and base incontinency of him who vowed to
be my faithful husband. But all past afflictions vanish before those
which follow. But how can I relate them? Oh tell it not in Gath! Must
I record such grievousness against the husband of my youth?

> Oft as I try to tell the doleful tale,
> My quivering lips and faltering tongue do fail:
> Nor can my trembling hand, or feeble pen,
> Equal the follies of this worst of men!

I have already related that Mr. B. said he would take one of our
sons, and one daughter, to wait on him in his distant tour, before he
would take all the family. After he had talked of this for a few days,
he said he had altered his plan; he would leave his son, and take only
his daughter: he could hire what men's help he needed: his daughter
must go and cook for him. He now commenced a new series of
conduct in relation to this daughter, whom he selected to go with
him, in order (as he pretended) to render himself pleasing and familiar
to her, so that she might be willing to go with him, and feel happy:
for though, as a father, he had a right to command her to go, yet (he
said) he would so conduct toward her, as to make her cheerful and
well pleased to go with him. A great part of the time he now spent
in the room where she was spinning; and seemed shy of me, and of
the rest of the family. He seemed to have forgotten his age, his honor,

and all decency, as well as all virtue. He would spend his time with this daughter, in telling idle stories, and foolish riddles, and singing songs to her, and sometimes before the small children, when they were in that room. He thus pursued a course of conduct, which had the most direct tendency to corrupt young and tender minds, and lead them the greatest distance from every serious subject. He would try to make his daughter tell stories with him; wishing to make her free and sociable, and to erase from her mind all that fear and reserve, which he had ever taught his children to feel toward him. He had ever been sovereign, severe and hard with his children, and they stood in the greatest fear of him. His whole conduct, toward this daughter especially, was now changed, and became most disagreeable.

For a considerable time I was wholly at a loss what to think of his conduct, or what his wish or intentions could be. Had such conduct appeared toward any young woman beside his own young daughter, I should have had no question what he intended: but as it now was, I was loth to indulge the least suspicion of base design. His daily conduct forced a conviction upon my alarmed and tortured mind, that his designs were the most vile. All his tender affections were withdrawn from the wife of his youth, the mother of his children. My room was deserted, and left lonely. His care for the rest of the family seemed abandoned, as well as all his attention to his large circle of worldly business. Every thing must lie neglected, while this one daughter engrossed all his attention.

Though all the conduct of Mr. B. from day to day, seemed to demonstrate my apprehension, that he was determined, and was continually plotting, to ruin this poor young daughter, yet it was so intolerably crossing to every feeling of my soul to admit such a thought, that I strove with all my might to banish it from my mind, and to disbelieve the possibility of such a thing. I felt terrified at my own thoughts upon the subject; and shocked that such a thing should enter my mind. But the more I labored to banish those things from my mind, the more I found it impossible to annihilate evident facts. Now my grief was dreadful. No words can express the agitations of my soul: From day to day they tortured me, and seemed to roll on with a resistless power. I was constrained to expect that he would accomplish his wickedness: And such were my infirmities, weakness and fears, (my circumstances being very difficult) that I did not dare to hint any thing of my fears to him, or to any creature. This may to some appear strange; but with me it was then a reality. I labored to divert his mind from his follies, and to turn his attention to things of the greatest importance. But I had the mortification to find that my endeavors were unsuccessful.

I soon perceived that his strange conduct toward this daughter was to her very disagreeable. And she shewed as much unwillingness to be in the room with him, as she dared. I often saw her cheeks bedewed with tears, on account of his new and astonishing behavior. But as his will had ever been the law of the family, she saw no way to deliver herself from her cruel father. Such were her fears of him, that she did not dare to talk with me, or any other person, upon her situation: for he was exceedingly jealous of my conversing with her, and cautioning her. If I ever dropped words, which I hoped would put her upon her guard, or inquired the cause of her troubles, or what business her father had so much with her? if I was ever so cautious, he would find it out, and be very angry. He watched her and me most narrowly; and by his subtle questions with her, he would find out what I had said, during his absence. He would make her think I had informed him what I had said, and then would be very angry with me: so that at times I feared for my life. I queried with myself which way I could turn. How could I caution a young daughter in such a case? My thoughts flew to God for relief, that the Father of mercies would protect a poor helpless creature marked out for a prey; and turn the heart of a cruel father from every wicked purpose.

After a while Mr. B's conduct toward this daughter was strangely altered. Instead of idle songs, fawning and flattery, he grew very angry with her; and would wish her dead, and buried: and he would correct her very severely. It seems, that when he found his first line of conduct ineffectual, he changed his behavior, felt his vile indignation moved, and was determined to see what he could effect by tyranny and cruelty. He most cautiously guarded her against having any free conversation with me, or any of the family, at any time; lest she should expose him. He would forbid any of the children going with her to milking. If, at any time, any went with her, it must be a number; so that nothing could be said concerning him. He would not suffer her to go from home: I might not send her abroad on any occasion. Never before had Mr. B. thus confined her, or any of his children. None but an eye witness can conceive of the strangeness of

his conduct from day to day, and of his plans to conceal his wickedness, and to secure himself from the light of evidence.[1] . . .

The black cloud, rising like a storm of hail, had rolled on, and had
gathered over my head. I clearly saw that Mr. B. entertained the most
vile intentions relative to his own daughter. Whatever difficulty attended the obtaining of legal proof, yet no remaining doubt existed
in my mind, relative to the existence of his wickedness: and I had no
doubt remaining of the violence, which he had used; and hence arose
his rage against her. It must have drawn tears of anguish from the eyes
of the hardest mortals, to see the barbarous corrections, which he,
from time to time, inflicted on this poor young creature; and for no
just cause. Sometimes he corrected her with a rod; and sometimes
with a beach stick, large enough for the driving of a team; and with
such sternness and anger sparkling in his eyes, that his visage seemed
to resemble an infernal; declaring, that if she attempted to run from
him again, she should never want but one correction more; for he
would whip her to death! This his conduct could be for no common
disobedience; for she had ever been most obedient to him in all lawful
commands. It seemed as though the poor girl must now be destroyed
under his furious hand. She was abashed, and could look no one in
the face.

Among the many instances of his wickedly correcting her, I shall
mention one. One morning Mr. B. rose from bed, while it was yet
dark. He immediately called this daughter, and told her to get up. She
obeyed. And as she knew her daily business, she made up her fire in
her room, and sat down to her work. He sat by the fire in the kitchen.
As my door was open, I carefully observed his motions. He sat

---

1. *Editor,* 1815: The discreet reader will repeatedly wonder that this pious sufferer did
not look abroad for help against so vile a son of Beliel, and avail herself of the law
of the land, by swearing the peace against him. Her forbearance does indeed seem
to have been carried to excess. But when we consider her delicate situation at this
time; her peaceable habits from youth; her native tenderness of mind; her long fears
of a tyranical cruel husband; her having, at no time of her sufferings, seen all that
we now see of his abominable character, as a reason why he should have been brought
to justice; her wishes and hopes that he might be brought to reformation; her desires
not to have the family honor sacrificed; and the difficulty of exhibiting sufficient
evidence against a popular, subtle man, to prove such horrid crimes;—these things
plead much in her behalf. After all, it will be difficult to resist the conviction, which
will be excited in the course of these memoirs, that Mrs. B. did truly err, in not having
her husband brought to justice. The law is made for the lawless and disobedient.

looking into the fire for some time, as though absorbed in his thoughts. It soon grew light. The small children arose, and came round the fire. He looked round like one disappointed and vexed. He sprang from his chair, and called his daughter, whom he first called. She left her work in her room, and came immediately to him. In great rage, and with a voice of terror, he asked why she did not come to him, when he first called her? She respectfully told him that he called her to get up, which she immediately did, and went to her work. But she said she did not hear him call her to come to him. He seized his horse whip, and said, in a rage, he would make her know that when he called her, she should come to him. He then fell to whipping her without mercy. She cried, and begged, and repeated her assertion, that she did not know he called her to come to him. She had done as he told her. She got up, and went to her work. But he was not in the least appeased. He continued to whip her, as though he were dealing with an ungovernable brute; striking over her head, hands, and back; nor did he spare her face and eyes; while the poor girl appeared as though she must die. No proper account could he ever be prevailed on to give of this conduct.

None can describe the anguish of my heart on the beholding of such scenes. How pitiful must be the case of a poor young female, to be subjected to such barbarous treatment by her own father; so that she knew of no way of redress!

It may appear surprising that such wickedness was not checked by legal restraints. But great difficulties attend in such a case. While I was fully convinced of the wickedness, yet I knew not that I could make legal proof. I could not prevail upon this daughter to make known to me her troubles; or to testify against the author of them. Fear, shame, youthful inexperience, and the terrible peculiarities of her case, all conspired to close her mouth against affording me, or any one, proper information. My soul was moved with pity for her wretched case: and yet I cannot say I did not feel a degree of resentment, that she would not, as she ought, expose the wickedness of her father, that she might be relieved from him, and he brought to due punishment. But no doubt his intrigues, insinuations, commands, threats, and parental influence, led her to feel that it was in vain for her to seek redress.

My circumstances, and peculiar bodily infirmities, at that time, were such as to entitle a woman to the tenderest affection and sympathies of a companion. On this account, and as Mr. B. was exceedingly stern, and angry with me for entertaining hard thoughts of him, I felt unable to do any thing more for the relief of my poor daughter. My hope in God was my only support. And I did abundantly and earnestly commit my cause to him. I felt confident that he would, in his own time, and as his infinite wisdom should determine, grant relief. . . .

Sept. 15, 1789. . . . The next morning I took an opportunity with Mr. B. alone to have solemn conversation. My health being now restored, I thought it high time, and had determined, to adopt a new mode of treatment with Mr. B. I calmly introduced the subject, and told him, plainly and solemnly, all my views of his wicked conduct, in which he had long lived with his daughter. He flew into a passion, was high, and seemed to imagine, he could at once frighten me out of my object. But I was carried equally above fear, and above temper. Of this I soon convinced him, I let him know, that the business I now had taken in hand, was of too serious a nature, and too interesting, to be thus disposed of, or dismissed with a few angry words. I told him I should no longer be turned off in this manner; but should pursue my object with firmness, and with whatever wisdom and ability God might give me; and that God would plead my cause, and prosper my present undertaking, as he should see best. I reminded Mr. B. of my long and unusually distressing illness; how he had treated me in it; how wicked and cruel he had been to the wife of his youth; how unable I had been to check him in that awful wickedness, which I knew he had pursued; that all my inexpressible griefs and solemn entreaties had been by him trampled under foot.

I therefore had not known what to do better than to wait on God as I had done, to afford me strength and opportunity to introduce the means of his effectual control. This time I told him had arrived. And now, if God spared my life, (I told Mr. B.) he should find a new leaf turned over;—and that I would not suffer him to go on any longer as he had done. I would now soon adopt measures to put a stop to his abominable wickedness and cruelties. For this could and ought to be done. And if I did it not, I should be a partaker of his sins, and should aid in bringing down the curse of God upon our family.

By this time Mr. B. had become silent. He appeared struck with some degree of fear. He, by and by, asked me what I intended or expected to do, to bring about such a revolution as I had intimated? whether I knew what an awful crime I had laid to his charge? which he said could not be proved. He wished to know whether I had considered how difficult it would be for me to do any such thing against him? as I was under his legal control; and he could overrule all my plans as he pleased. I told him, I well knew I had been placed under his lawful government and authority, and likewise under his care and protection. And most delightful would it have been to me, to have been able quietly and safely to remain there as long as I lived. Gladly would I have remained a kind, faithful, obedient wife to him, as I had ever been. But I told Mr. B. he *knew* he had violated his marriage covenant; and hence had forfeited all legal and just right and authority over me; and I should convince him that I well knew it. I told him I was not in any passion. I acted on principle, and from long and mature consideration. And though it had ever been my greatest care and pleasure (among my earthly comforts) to obey and please him; yet by his most wicked and cruel conduct, he had compelled me to undertake this most undesirable business—of stopping him in his mad career; and that I now felt strength, courage and zeal to pursue my resolution. And if my life was spared, he would find that I should bring something to pass, and probably more than he now apprehended.

As to what I could prove against him, I told Mr. B. he knew not how much evidence I had of his unnatural crimes, of which I had accused him, and of which *he knew he was guilty*. I asked him why he should not expect that I should institute a process against him, for that most horrid conduct, which he had long allowed himself to pursue, and with the most indecent and astonishing boldness? I told him I well knew that he was naturally a man of sense; and that his conscience now fully approved of my conduct.

Mr. B. seeing me thus bold and determinate, soon changed his countenance and conduct. He appeared panic-struck; and he soon became mild, sociable and pleasant. He now made an attempt, with all his usual subtlety, and flatteries, to induce me to relinquish my design. He pretended to deny the charge of incest. But I told him I had no confidence in his denial of it; it was therefore in vain! Upon this he said, he really did not blame, or think hard of me, for believing him guilty of this sin. He said, he knew he had behaved foolishly; and had given me full reason to be jealous of him; and he repeated that he did not at all think hard of me for entertaining the views which

I had of him. He then took the Bible, and said, he would lay his hand upon it, and swear that he was not guilty of the crime laid to his charge. Knowing what I did, I was surprised and disgusted at this impious attempt. I stepped towards him, and in a resolute and solemn manner begged of him to forbear! assuring him, that such an oath could not undo or alter real facts, of which he was conscious. And this proceeding, I assured him, would be so far from giving me any satisfaction, that it would greatly increase the distress of my soul for him in his wickedness. Upon this he forbore, and laid his Bible aside.

Mr. B. now said, he was very sorry he had given me so much reason to think such things of him; and that he had so far destroyed my confidence in him as a man of truth. He then begged of me to forgive all that was past; and he promised that he would ever be kind and faithful to me in future, and never more give me reason to complain of him for any such conduct. I told him, if I had but evidence of his real reformation, I could readily forgive him as a fellow creature, and could plead with God to forgive him. But as to my living with him in the most endearing relation any longer, after such horrid crimes, I did not see that I *could,* or *ought* to do it! He then anxiously made some remarks upon the consequences of my refusing to remain his wife, and seeking a separation from him. These he seemed unable to endure. I remarked, that I well knew it was no small thing for a husband and wife to part, and their family of children to be broken up; that such a separation could not be rendered expedient or lawful, without great sin indeed: and that I would not be the cause of it, and of breaking up our family, for *all the world.* But, said I, you have done all in your power to bring about such a separation, and to ruin and destroy our family. And I meet it as my duty now to do all in my power to save them from further destruction. . . .

[*Abigail Bailey determines to seek a separation from her husband, and rather than be brought to trial, he agrees. He also agrees to a 50/50 property settlement to which end he arranges to sell his farm to Captain Gould of Granville, New York, for 500 pounds. To complete this bargain, Abigail Bailey consents to travel with her husband to Granville, a journey that should take three days.*]

Monday, March 19 [1792]
After we had proceeded several miles, Mr. B. threw off the mask at once, and kept me no longer in the dark, at least relative to what

was *not* the object of his journey, that it was not what he had ever said. He told me, we are now in the State of New York, and now you must be governed by the laws of this State, which are far more suitable to govern such women as you, than are the laws of New Hampshire. He added, that he was not going to Granville; nor had he ever intended to go thither, or to trade with Capt. Gould. But all this plan, he said, he had laid, to lead me off from home, that he might get me away from the circle of the Abbots, and Brocks, and my connexions; and then see if he could not bring me to terms, that would better suit himself. And now, if I would drop all that was past, and concerning which I had made so much noise; and would promise never to make any more rout about any of those things; and to be a kind and obedient wife to him, without any more ado; it was well! If not, he would proceed accordingly. He said, unless I would thus engage, he would drive on among strangers, till that sleigh, and those horses were worn out! He went on conversing in this way. Sometimes he would speak of carrying me to the Ohio; sometimes of taking me among the Dutch people, where, he said, I could not understand a word of their language. And then he would talk of taking me to Albany, or where he could sell me on board a ship. He assured me that I should never return home again. He said he had been cunning enough to get me away from home; and now he believed he should be crafty enough to keep me away. I might *cry,* he added, as much as I pleased; but I could not help myself. If I should try to escape from him, he said, he was as long headed as I was; and I might well expect that he could outwit me. Mr. B. said that his brothers, D. and F. and also E.F., were all confederate with him in this plan. And if I should by any means escape from him, and get home, he had empowered his brother D. to keep all the interest out of my hands, and to advertise me in his name, forbidding all persons harboring or trusting me.

[*In New York, Abigail Bailey contracts smallpox and the illness brings her near death. Mr. B. leaves her in this condition and returns to New Hampshire to sell his farm. Left on her own, Abigail Bailey decides she must, even in her weakened condition, attempt the 270 mile journey back by herself. She leaves on horseback on May 24 and finds food and lodging at taverns and homes along the way. Those who are shocked to find a woman traveling alone are quick to offer assistance when they hear her story. After a series of "kind providences," she finds herself six days later almost out of New York state.*]

The next morning I crossed the river; not as a captive, or in fear of falling through the ice, as when I came over it before. I well remembered the wormwood and the gall, when I was dragged over it by the man who vaunted over me, and seemed to rejoice in the imagination, that no power could take me out of his hands. I now saw it is safe trusting in that God, who, when the wicked deal proudly, Is above them. Finding myself safely on the east side of the North river, I felt a confidence that God, who had thus far delivered, would, in due time, bring me out of all my distresses. . . .

This day I must get my horse shod. I had set out from Unadilla with less than one dollar in money. While I was thinking of this subject, a young gentleman rode up and went on with me with naked hands. I told him I thought he needed a pair of gloves. He said he did, and meant to have a pair as soon as he could find them. I took a good pair out of my saddlebags, which I had provided on purpose to help bear my expenses in the way. They just fitted his hand. He paid me a generous price for them, and some refreshment beside. Now I had plenty of money for shoeing my horse. I called and got it done. The blacksmith asked but a moderate price; and gave me dinner. Thus I lived on a series of mercies. From Sabbath morning till Wednesday night, I had been kept, nights and days, without cost, for me or my horse. Wednesday night I put up in a tavern near Salem court house. Here they were so kind as to take for my reckoning such articles as I had to spare.

Thursday, May 31, I set forward. I crossed the line of the state, into Vermont. I remembered the terrors of my mind, when I was told, that now I was in the state of New York, and was threatened with horrid treatment. I rejoiced that God had thus far broken the rod of the oppressor: and I gave him thanks for his great goodness. . . .

[*After arriving home, Abigail Bailey enlists the aid of her brothers and swears a warrant against her husband. Before he is arrested however, he is able to persuade an associate, Captain White, to flee with the Bailey children and property. White is intercepted in his attempt. Asa Bailey, under the threat of a public trial for his crimes, agrees to a property settlement. He is allowed to depart with his three oldest sons (who later return to their mother), leaving the other children with her.*]

I was at Gen. B.'s, when Mr. B. was brought there under keepers. It was indeed a solemn sight to me. Here was the man, who had been the husband of my youth, whom I had tenderly loved, as my companion, in years past, now a prisoner of civil justice, and at my prosecution. But his most obstinate and persevering wickedness had rendered it necessary. And I thought I might hope that the situation of my family might now be altered for the better. . . .

Thus I have sketched some of the most important events of my life, through which God, in his deep and holy providence, caused me to pass, from the time I entered the family state, A.D. 1767, in the twenty-second year of my age,—till A.D. 1792, when I was in my forty-seventh year. Great trials, and wonderful mercies have been my lot, from the hands of my Heavenly Father.

[*Abigail Bailey was eventually granted a "bill of divorcement" and Asa Bailey left Landaff. After arranging for her children to be "put out in regular and good households," she joined the family of a minister in a neighboring town. In the last years of her life, she lived with various of her children and died of "lung fever" while with the family of her son Asa in Bath, New Hampshire.*]

Elizabeth Sandwith Drinker
[1735–1807]

Persecuted as a religious nonconformist, Elizabeth Sandwith's Quaker father left Ireland for Philadelphia where he married Sarah Jervis and became a prominent merchant. Both parents died when Elizabeth was young, and in 1761 she married Henry Drinker, also a Quaker and successful Philadelphia businessman. They had nine children, four of whom survived to adulthood.

As Quakers, the Drinkers refused to participate when the Revolution broke out. Suspected of Loyalist sympathies, Henry Drinker, along with nineteen prominent Philadelphia Quakers, was arrested in 1777 and taken to prison in Virginia. That fall, the British, after defeating George Washington at Brandywine and Germantown, occupied Philadelphia, where they remained for the winter (while Washington withdrew to the ill-fated Valley Forge). Elizabeth Drinker had a literal eyewitness view from the family mansion overlooking the Delaware River of the contests between the British and the American patriots for control of that crucial waterway.

Sept. 12 [1777]. . . . A part of Washington's army has been routed, and have been seen coming into Town in great numbers; the particulars of the Battle I have not attended to; the slain is said to be very numerous. Hundreds of their muskets laying in the road—which those that have made off have thrown down.

I was a little fluttered by hearing a Drum stop at our door, and a hard knocking succeed; it proved to be men with orders for H.D. to appear, or find a substitute. There has been a meeting this afternoon at the State House, on what account I know not. 'Tis supposed that

From *Extracts from the Journal of Elizabeth Drinker, From 1759 to 1807*, A.D., ed. Henry D. Biddle (Philadelphia: J.B. Lippincott, 1889). The manuscript of the diary is at the Historical Society of Pennsylvania in Philadelphia.

G. Washington is in Town this evening. The wounded have been brought in this afternoon, but to what amount I have not learnt. . . .

Sept. 15. I have heard no news from abroad this morning, but Carriages are constantly passing, and the inhabitants going away. Last night I heard of several friends having lost their Horses—taken from the stables—for which reason I ordered our Horse and Cow to be put into the washhouse, where they at present remain. . . .

Sept. 19. Jenny awoke me this morning about 7 o'clock, with the news that the English were near; we find that most of our neighbors, and almost all the Town have been up since one o'clock in the morning. The account is, that the British army crossed the Swedes-Ford last night, and are now on their way hither. Congress, Council &c. are flown; Boats, Carriages and foot pads going off all night. Town in great confusion. But just now (about noon), I am informed that the above report arose from 2 or 3 of the English Light-horse having been seen reconnoitering the Ford.

Sept. 20. The Town has been very quiet all this day. It is said that Washington's army has crossed the Ford, and are at present on this side. Some expect a battle hourly, as the English are on the opposite side. . . .

Sept. 23. . . . Many have had their horses taken from them this afternoon; some going one way, and some another. It is likely from the present prospect of things that we shall have a noisy night, tho' at this time (9 o'clock), I hear nothing like it, but we, living back and retired, escape many hurries that others are exposed to. All the bells in the city are certainly taken away, and there is talk of Pump handles and Fire-Buckets being taken also—but that may be only Conjecture. Things seem to be, upon the whole, drawing towards great confusion. May we be strengthened and supported in the time of trial.

Sept. 24. . . . The report continues of the English approaching us, but I know not what to believe. . . . There is talk of the city being set on fire. . . .

Sept. 25. This has been so far a day of great confusion in the city, tho' with respect to ourselves we have experienced no injury, and but little fright, (set aside the consideration of the situation of him we love). . . .

Sept. 26. Well! here are the English in earnest; about 2 or 3000 came in through Second street, without opposition or interrution—no plundering on the one side or the other. . . .

Sept. 27. About 9 o'clock this morning the Province and Delaware Frigates, with several Gondelows came up the River, with a design to fire on the Town. They were attacked by a Battery which the English have erected at the lower end of the Town. The engagement lasted half an hour, when many shots were exchanged. Nobody that I have heard of hurt on shore, but the people in general, especially downwards exceedingly alarmed. The Cook on board the Delaware, 'tis said, had his Head shot off, another of the men wounded. She ran aground, and by some means took fire, which occasioned her to strike her colors. The English immediately boarded her—the others sheared off. They took Admiral Alexander and his men prisoners. It seems he declared that their intentions were to destroy the Town. Part of this scene we were spectators of from the little window in our loft. . . .

Oct. 1. . . . Several fire rafts which were sent down the River to annoy the Fleet, ran ashore and were burnt. . . .

Oct. 3. . . . 'Tis reported to day that Gates has beaten Burgoyne, also that Burgoyne has beaten Gates; which is the truth we know not —perhaps neither.

Oct. 4. . . . This has been a sorrowful day at Philad^a, and much more so at Germantown and thereabouts. It was reported in the forenoon that 1000 of the English were slain, but Chalkley James who lodges here to night, as Henry is out on guard, tells us—that he has been to day as far as B. Chew's place, and could not learn of more than 30 of the English being killed, tho' a great number were wounded, and brought into the City. He counted 18 of the Americans lying dead in the lane from the Road to Chew's house. The House is very much damaged, as a few of the English troops had taken shelter there, and were fired upon from the road by great numbers of the others. The last account toward evening was that the English were pursuing Washington's troops, who are very numerous, and that they were flying before them. The Americans are divided into three divisions —one over the Schuylkill, another near Germantown, and the third, I know not where; so that the army that was with us are chiefly called off, and a double guard is this night thought necessary. It is thought it was the intention that one division should enter the city, while the troops were engaged with the others. The apprehension of their entering, and fears of the Gondelows and other vessels in the River, will render this night grievous for many. Washington is said to be wounded in the thigh. Friends, and others in the Jerseys, and indeed almost all around the country, are suffering deeply. 'Tis now past 12 o'clock, and all in the House except myself are I believe asleep; the watchman has cried the hour, and all seems quiet. Fine starlight. . . .

Oct. 14. Much talk of Washington endeavoring to enter the city; a number of people greatly alarmed on that account. . . .

Oct. 18. The Troops at Germantown are coming within 2 or 3 miles of this city to encamp. Provisions are so scarce with us now, that Jenny gave ⅖ pr. lb. for mutton this morning. The people around the country dare not come near us with anything; what little butter is brought is ⅞ per lb. The fleet not yet up, nor likely to be soon, I fear. Jenny and Billy went this afternoon with coffee and whey for the soldiers.

Oct. 19. First day. The troops have come this afternoon within a mile of us. . . .

Oct. 20. . . . There has been a skirmish this morning between Germantown and Philadª, the particulars of which I have not learnt, and there was very heavy firing below a great part of the afternoon, I know not yet upon what occasion. Last night 16 or 18 flat bottom boats came up, and got safely by the Gondelows and Battery, but were fired upon by some of the English who did not know them, and one man was killed.

If things don't change ere long, we shall be in a poor plight; everything scarce and dear, and nothing suffered to be brought in to us. Tom Prior is taken up to day, on suspicion, as 'tis said, of sending intelligence to Washington's army. . . .

Oct. 23. This day will be remembered by many. The 2500 Hessians, who crossed the River, the day before yesterday, were last night driven back 2 or 3 times, in endeavoring to storm the fort on Red bank; 200 were slain and great numbers wounded. The firing this morning seemed to be incessant from the Battery, the Gondelows, and the Augusta man-of-war, of 64 guns. She took fire, and after burning near 2 hours, blew up. The loss of this fine vessel is accounted for in different ways. Some say she took fire by accident; others that it was occasioned by red hot Bullets from Mud-Island Battery. Another English vessel, somewhat smaller, it is said is also burnt. Many of the inhabitants of this city are very much affected by the present situation and appearance of things—while those on the other side of the question, are flushed, and in spirits. Count Donop is said to be among the slain. It was between 11 and 12, near noon, when the Augusta blew up—many were not sensible of any shock—others were. It was very plain to those who were at meeting, as this is fifth day, and appeared to some like an earthquake. . . .

Nov. 15. The firing to day has been like thunder, comparatively speaking—from the Vigilant and Somerset Men-of-war, on the formidable Mud-Island Battery, which is not yet conquered, tho' greatly damaged. . . .

Nov. 19. . . . G. Cornwallis left this city the day before yesterday at 2 o'clock in the morning, with 3000 men, as it is said. He was fired at from a house near Darby, when some of his men rushed in, and put 2 men to the sword, and took several others prisoners. He designs for the Jerseys. . . .

Nov. 21. I was awakened this morning before 5 o'clock by the loud firing of canon—my Head was aching very badly. All our Family were up but little Molly, and a fire was made in the Parlor more than an hour before day. All our neighbors were also up, and I believe most in Town. The Americans had set their whole Fleet on fire, except one small vessel, and several of the Gondelows, which passed the city in the night. The firing was from the Delaware, which lay at Coopers Point, on the Gondelows—which they did not return. Billy counted 8 different vessels on fire at once, in sight; one lay near the Jersey shore opposite our House; we heard the explosion of 4 of them when

they blew up, which shook our windows greatly. We had a fair sight
of the blazing Fleet from our upper windows. . . .

[*In Quaker tradition, Elizabeth Drinker kept her diary for almost fifty
years and it is much more than a "war diary." It is among the most
complete records we have of life in eighteenth-century America and includes chilling records of the recurring smallpox epidemics of her lifetime.*

*Like many of their white Philadelphia neighbors, Drinker's parents had
owned slaves. The fate of one black woman in particular preoccupies
Elizabeth Drinker and on two different occasions (it is always of interest
to note what a diarist repeats) she records the following account in her
journal.*]

July 22 [1799]. Black Judy was here today. She is now about 52 or
53 years old. My sister and self sold her when 9 years old into the
country. We did not think we were doing wrong, for we did not
know what to do with her, as our parents were dead, and we were
going to board out. We loved the child, and after a few week's
consideration took a ride to her mistress's habitation, and offered her
40 pounds for the child; they gave us 25, promising to use her very
kindly. She said that she would not part with her for 100 pounds—
she thought Providence had directed her to the child, and she meant
to treat her with kindness—we came away disappointed. She was
afterwards sold again, but has been many years free, and her children
are free when of age. We had formerly some uneasy hours on her
account, tho' nothing to accuse ourselves of as a crime at that time,
except parting with a little child we loved, to be a slave, as we feared,
for life.

Oct. 12 [1807]. Our black Jude, whom we sold 51 years ago when she
was a child, was here this afternoon. I thought she was dead, as we
have not seen her for many years; she is now not far from sixty years
of age. When we sold her, there was nothing said against keeping or
selling negroes; but as we were going to board out we knew not what
to do with her. Some time after, we were more settled in our minds,
and were very sorry we had sold the child to be a slave for life, and
knew not what would be her fate. We went to Springfield to repur-
chase her, but her mistress, a very plausible woman, refused to sell
her, tho' we offered her £40, and had sold her 2 months before for
£25. Some time afterward, her mistress sold her to Parson Marshall.

It was several years after she had grown up, and when there was much talk of the iniquity of holding them in bondage; my husband called upon her master, and had some talk with him, who did not see the matter in the same light as we did, but at his death, he left her free.

Nancy Shippen Livingston
[1763–1841]

Nancy Shippen, daughter of William Shippen and Alice Lee Shippen, was born the eldest child into one of the most prominent families in colonial America. Her mother was a Lee of Virginia and her father was a physician in a Philadelphia family. When the Revolution broke out, he was appointed chief of the medical department of the Continental Army. During the war, the Shippen home in Philadelphia became the center of the revolutionary forces and, in particular, of the international delegations supporting the war. It was there at age sixteen that Nancy Shippen, one of the city's most eligible debutantes, met and fell in love with Louis Guillame Otto, Compte de Mosley, secretary to the French Minister to America. Alarmed at the prospects of his daughter's desire to marry a man with nothing but "honorable expectations," William Shippen hastily arranged his daughter's wedding to another of her suitors, Henry Beekman Livingston, heir to a great family fortune in New York.

Nancy agreed to a marriage that she regretted almost immediately, not only because she continued to love Louis Otto, but because her husband turned out to have a tyrannical temper fueled by jealousy. She also learned of his numerous mistresses and several illegitimate children. Pregnant herself almost immediately, she returned to her home in Philadelphia to have her child, a daughter, named after her husband's mother, Margaret Beekman Livingston.

Nancy Shippen Livingston never returned permanently to the family estate in New York. In Philadelphia she began a journal in which the most significant people in her life are named as follows: Lord and Lady Worthy (her parents), Leander (Louis Otto), Lord B. (her husband), The Old Lady (her husband's mother, Margaret Beekman Livingston).

April 10*th* [1783]—After Breakfast rode out with Lord Worthy. Had a conversation about Lord B. & dear Leander. His sentiments corresponding with mine made me extremely happy—wou'd to God it was a happiness that wou'd last—but the die is cast—& my life must be miserable! Lord Worthy sees the consequences of my unhappy choice too late—it is well for me that he sees it at all.

April 11*th*—Saw Leander—spoke to him—he praised my sweet Child—good man! . . .

April 18—This day spent entirely alone, enjoying my own meditations—they were not unpleasant—I feel calm & composed, & please myself with the reflection of having conform'd to the will of my parents in the most important action of my life—O! may I reap the benefit of it! I'm sure I shall! I have the sweetest Child that ever was born—in her I shall be most blest. . . .

April 27—heard from Lord B.—obdurate man! he still continues to persecute me with his reproaches—God knows that I do not deserve them. How miserable shou'd I be if it was not for my dear Child.— Wou'd to Heaven he cou'd but see it perhaps it perhaps wou'd soften him & make him relent. . . .

May 10. 10 *at night.*—Miserable all day—in consequence of a letter from Lord B. He tells me—O what is it that bad he does not tell me! but what affect[s] me most is his accusing me of infidelity. Wretched Unhappy man—Nothing but your being jealous, & treating me ill in consequence of that jealousy, shou'd have tempted me to leave you —& now you say I left you because I loved another.—Had you not deceived me by so often swearing you loved me to distraction I shou'd not have been the wretch I am. O I'm wretched indeed! & the father too of my sweet baby—I'm almost distracted— . . .

May 15—10 *in the morning*—I sit down to write now what I intended to write the day before yesterday. I hope I shall not be disturb'd. My baby lies assleep in the Cradle before me—I will write till she awakes—

From *Nancy Shippen: Her Journal Book,* ed. Ethel Armes (Philadelphia and London: J.B. Lippincott, 1935). © 1935 by Ethel Armes. Reprinted by permission of Harper and Row. The manuscript of the diary is at the Library of Congress.

Do not hope for perfect happiness; there is no such thing in this sub-lunary state. Your sex is the more exposed to suffer, because it is always in dependance: be neither angry nor asham'd of this dependance on a husband. . . .

Do not hope that your union will procure you perfect peace: the best Marriages are those where with softness & patience they bear by turns with each other . . .

Do not expect the same degree of friendship that you feel: men are in general less tender than women; and you will be unhappy if you are too delicate in your friendships.

Beg of God to guard your heart from jealousy: do not hope to bring back a husband by complaints, ill humor, or reproaches. The only means which promise success, are patience & softness: impatience sours & alienats hearts: softness leads them back to their duty. In sacrificing your own will, pretend to no right over that of a husband: men are more attach'd to theirs than Women, because educated with less constraint.

They are naturally tyrannical; they will have pleasures & liberty, yet insist that Women renounce both: do not examine whether their rights are well founded; let it suffice to you that they are established; They are masters, we have only to suffer & obey with a good grace.

Thus far Madame de Maintenon must be allow'd to have known the heart of man. I cannot agree with her that Women are only born to suffer & to obey—that men are generally tyrannical I will own, but such as know how to be happy, willingly give up the harsh title of master for the more tender & endearing one of Friend. Equality is the soul of friendship: marriage, to give delight, must join *two minds,* not devote a slave to the will of an imperious Lord.

9, *at night*—Spent this Even^g at Mrs Gadsdens; a Carolina Lady. She is an Elegant woman & very Chatty & agreable. Found a good deal of Company.

May 16—Papa told me this morn^g at breakfast that I must send my darling Child to its Grandmama Livingston; that she had desir'd Mrs Montgomery to request it of me, as a particular favor. I told him I cou'd not bear the Idea of it, that I had sooner part with my life almost than my Child. He told me it was for the future interest of my baby, that its fortune depended on the old Lady's pleasure in that particular—beg'd me to think of it, & to be reconciled to it. If I know my own heart I never can. When will my misfortunes end! I placed my happiness in her! She is my all—& I must part with her! cruel cruel fate—

May 17—10 *oclock at night*—I have been so unhappy all day that I have not stir'd out of my room except to dinner. Mamma then ask'd me if I had thought of Mrs L's proposal. I told her, I had thought of nothing else—she ask'd me my determination—I told her I wou'd not part with my Child if I cou'd possibly help it. she then told me Mrs M.—y did not go to the Manor till the middle of June; that Papa had determin'd that the Child shou'd go at any rate—that he cou'd not be answerable for the Childs losing her fortune which she wou'd certainly do, if I kept her from her Grandmother. I cried all the time she was speaking & then retir'd to my room—which I have not left since. I feel pleased however that I have a month to determine in, & be with my angel Child.—I have kiss'd her a thousand times since. —& find I love her as well as myself. I must think of some thing in order to keep her with me, & yet secure her fortune.

May 18—Spent the day at home—Papa has not mentioned that dreadful subject to me since. I begin to flatter myself that with a little persuasion I may keep her with me—at least some time longer. My sweet Child! my whole soul is wrapp'd up in *you!* if I am oblig'd to part with you (O! dreadfull Thought!) I will look upon myself as the most miserable of woman kind. Why was my heart made so susceptible, since I am to experience nothing but misery?

May 19—I Visit'd Miss E Livingston this morn^g I like her extreamly. I had a long conversation with her. I think her very sensible—was much affected at a little annecdote I heard this morn^g of a young Lady who was sacrificed to the avarice & ambition of her parents to a man she hated—& her death was the natural consequence of her misery. She had a soul form'd for friendship—she found it not at home, her elegance of mind prevented her seeking it abroad; & she died a meloncholy victim to the Tyranny of her friends & the tenderness of her heart. It is a painful consideration, that the happiness or misery of our lives are generally determin'd, before we are proper judges of either.

May 20.—To-day wrote to Eliza—told her my misfortune—told her it was the greatest but one I had ever experienced. But I have not yet experienced it. I know not yet how much I shall suffer when the time comes.—O! what a separation! how much I dread it! but I will if possible stay with her. Ah! It will be impossible I'm affraid, because it depends on the *disposition* of her father.—Alass! he will never change.

May 21—This morn^g I sent Betsy out with the Child to give it an airing—then set down to work at the Tambour. I was working a work-bag for my mamma. It is very pretty work—& I am fond of it —my Brother read to me while I work'd—he read Gill Blas. It diverted me & made me for a time forget my unhappiness. When the child return'd I allmost devour'd it with kisses.

May 22—I spend so much of my time in caressing & playing with Peggy that I allmost forget I have any thing else to do—I forget to read—to write—to work—in short I neglect the business of the day. At night I sit down to unfold my thoughts on paper—I love it much —me thinks it is allmost as pleasing as telling them to a friend. My child sleeps—I am sitting close by her—I feel happy at present be- cause I put off the future prospect from my thoughts—I hope for the best—& enjoy the present moment.

May 24—Afternoon—I thought seriously this Morn^g about my sweet Childs education. I form'd many schemes which I believe it would be very difficult to put in execution. I wish in some particulars that it may differ from mine. In some respects I wish it may be as good. I have her wellfare at heart more than any earthly object. God grant she may be in every respect what I wish her.—I have met with sentiments on that head that please me. I will insert them here that I may not forget them:

SOME DIRECTIONS CONCERNING A DAUGHTERS EDUCATION

1st.   Study well her constitution & genious.
2d.   Follow nature & proceed patiently.
3d.   Suffer not Servants to terrify her with stories of Ghosts & Goblins.
4th.   Give her a fine pleasing idea of Good, & an ugly frightful one of Evil.
5th.   Keep her to a good & natural regimen of diet.

6th. Observe strictly the little seeds of reason in her, & cultivate the first appearance of it diligently.

7th. Watch over her childish Passions & prejudices, & labour sweetly to cure her of them.

8th. Never use any little *dissembling* arts, either to pacify her or to persuade her to anything.

9th. Win her to be in love with openness, in all her acts, & words.

10th. Fail not to instill into her an abhorance of all "serpentine" wit.

11th. If she be a brisk witty child do not applaud her too much.

12th. If she be a dul heavy child, do not discourage her at all.

13th. Seem not to admire her wit, but rather study to rectify her judgment.

14th. Use her to put little questions, & give her ready & short answers.

15th. Insinuate into her the principles of politeness & true modesty, & christian humility.

16th. Inculcate upon her that most honorable duty & virtue SINCERITY.

17th. Be sure to possess her with the baseness of telling a Lye on any account.

18th. Shew her the deformity of Rage & anger.

19th. Never let her converse with servants.

20th. Acquaint her in the most pleasant & insinuating manner, with the sacred History, nor let it seem her lesson, but her recreation.

21st. Set before her the gospel in its simplicity & purity, & the great Examples of Antiquity unsophisticated.

22d. Explain to her the nature of the baptismal san[c]tion.

23d. Prepare her in the best manner for confirmation.

24th. Animate, & instruct her for the holy communion.

25th. Particularly inform her in the duties of a single & married state.

26th. Let her be prepared for the duties & employment of a city life, if her lot should be among citizens.

27th. See she be inform'd in all that belongs to a country life.

28th. Discreetly check her desires after things pleasant, & use* her to frequent disappointments. *Ro[u]sseau

29th. Let her be instructed to do every thing seasonably & in order, & what ever she is set to do let her study to do it well, & peaceably;

30th. Teach her to improve everything that nothing may be lost or wasted, nor let her hurry herself about any thing.

31st. Let her always be employ'd about what is profitable or necessary.

32d. Let nothing of what is committed to her care be spoil'd by her neglect.

33d. Let her eat deliberately, chew well, & drink in moderate proportions.

34th. Let her use exercise in the morning.

35th. Use her to rise betimes in the morning, & set before her in the most winning manner an order for the whole day.

When wisdom enters into her heart, & knowledge is made pleasant to her soul, "discretion shall preserve her, & understanding shall keep her."

May 24—8 at night. There is such a sameness in my life at present that the particulars of it are hardly worth the pains of writing, tho' it is very agreable to look back upon ones life & see whether our actions & thoughts alter for the better. My past life has been chequer'd with misfortunes. I will write every particular occurrence some future day when I have a great deal more time than I have at present —tho' I cou'd never make a better use of my time. I cannot have a more pleasing task than takeing care of my precious Child—It is an amusement to me preferable to all others. . . .

May 27—I received an invitation this Morn^g to spend the Even^g with Mrs Bland—but I was engaged—& I spent the Afternoon & Even^g with Maria. . . . I never was more happy—I kept my lovely Child with me all the time. The dear angel was the life of the company—Leander went past the window while we were at Tea—he look'd in—& his Eyes told me he wou'd be happy to join us—but I did not ask him —prudence forbid it—Why shou'd it? he is my friend—& I am his —but because he was once my lover I must not see him—Cruell custom—I have read or heard, I forget which, "that the best friendship is the child of love"—why am I not at liberty to indulge that friendship? Why? because it wou'd displease my husband.

[Nancy eventually agrees to the plan devised by the Livingstons and her parents for her daughter's future and yields her child to the care of her

mother-in-law with the understanding that she may visit Peggy when she wishes. Nine months after giving up her child, Nancy prepares to visit her in New York.]

[*April*, 1784]
Saturday 10—Busily employ'd all day packing up for my jaunt to N. Y. I expect to go on Monday. How happy I feel in the thought of clasping my beloved child once more in my fond arms, & pressing her to my bosom—but alass! I shall be obliged to part with her again in a few days after I have seen her as I can't leave my mamma longer & my father won't permit me to take her from her good Grandmother. Indeed prudence forbids it also, as upon her must my dear Child depend. O! may I be enabled to bear all my trials with patience & fortitude.

Sunday 11—Papa inform'd me last night that Mr Willing cant go tomorrow. Again disappointed! said I—when shall I go to see my Child? If he can said my dear father he will go on Thursday. This morning about one oclock I recieved a note from Mr Willing informing me that he cou'd not possibly go before Monday week. I bore it as well as I cou'd, & as I knew then of no other opportunity resolved to wait with patience. Went to meeting in the afternoon & brought Cleander & his Emelia home with me to Tea & one of their lovely Children. After Tea we all went to Even^g Meeting except Cleander who staid to converse with Lady Worthy.

Monday 12—Writ this morn^g to Mrs Livingston to inform her that I was disappointed & to let her know that I should set of[f] on Monday. About half an hour after I had sent & thou't it was gone Papa came in with it in his hand & told me it shou'd not go. I started—he put on a stern countenance & told me to get drest immediately, that Col. Duer wou'd wait on me in half an hour & take me to N. Y. tomorrow. I was so delighted that I jum^d about the room for joy. Col. Duer came & we settled the plan for setting out on Wednesday, & he had politely invited me to stay at his house while I am in N. Y. I shall be very busy till the day comes. Cleander & Emelia dined with us & partook of my happiness. . . .

Tuesday 14—Tomorrow & Tomorrow & one day more, & then I shall see my Lovely Child. The Thought alone makes me happier than I can express. My heart has been as light as a fly all day. & I have thought of nothing else hardly all day. Lady Worthy rid out to Mount Peace, & Lord W [orthy] went to see his farm, so I have been all alone. At my return I shall begin the second book of my journals.

Wednesday 15—My dear friend Louisa staid with me last night; at nine o'clock this morning I took leave of her & my dear Parents, & set off in the Stage with Mr Duer for New York, dined at Bristol, & arrived at Princeton at 7 this Evening; eat a very hearty supper of oysters & retired to my room.

Thursday 16—Arose at 6 this morn'g & went as far as Brunswick to breakfast, & arrived at Elizabeth Town to Dinner; we cou'd proceed no farther this afternoon the weather being very bad. A stage arrived here about 8 this Even'g with Company in it that I was acquainted with, So we proceeded together as far as Newark & arrived about 10 oClock.

F. 17.—Set off after breakfast with the same company & after crossing 3 ferrys arrived at Powles Hook where we dined, & after dinner tho' the wind was very high crossed over to New York. It was about 4 in the afternoon when we reach'd the City. I parted with my fellow travellers at the landing & proceeded with Mr Duer to his house in Broad Way. There I tarry'd for a few minutes, & adjusted my dress, & then walk'd to the Old Ladies, in queen street accompanied by Miss Susan Livingston & her B^r Brockhurst L[ivingston] children of the Governors. When first I enter'd the room I cou'd scarce see any body in it my Eyes so eagerly search'd every part of it for the dear object of my affections, but she was not there so I paid my respects to the family as well as I cou'd, & seated myself; M^rs L[ivingston] arose immediately after & said she wou'd go & fetch the Child. My heart leap'd for joy; & I was in such an agitation that I cou'd hardly answer the questions of the family concern'g my health & that of my Parents, with any tolerable propriety. At length in came Mrs L. with the dear Baby in her arms, but so much alter'd I should not have known her, had I seen her any where else; so much grown, so much more beautiful; I got up instantly that the door open'd, & ran to meet her & clasp'd her in my arms, but she had quite forgot me & told me to "get long."

I beg'd her to come [to] me & call'd her my darling Child & try'd to take her, by force. All wou'd not do, she wou'd not take ye least notice of me, nor let me take her from her grandmother; it was more than I cou'd bear, I was distress'd & mortified, & burst into a flood of tears. Mrs L. & the rest of the family did all in their power to prevail on her to come to me, but in vain; I walk'd to the window to hide my tears, & thought of some trinkets I had in my pocket which I had brought for her. I set down and display'd them upon my lap, & called her to me, the sight of them made her come instantly. I took the dear creature upon my lap, & she sat with me contentedly for near an hour; I spent the remainder of the Even'^g there. Some part of it she was quite sociable with me & in high spirits. About ten I took my leave of the family & went home with Lady Kitty Duer: I took the Child with me & her maid Kitty who she is very fond of.

Saturday 18—She has been contented all this day, & some part of it appear'd more reconciled to me than I cou'd have expected.—Several Ladies of this City & 2 of my sisters in law waited upon me this morn'g;—& one of them Mrs Tillotson has politely offer'd me her house for my home while I stay here. I believe I will accept her invitation as it will look better for me to lodge with one of the family. Mrs L. made me a very good apology for not asking me to lodge with her. O! the racking thought that I must part with all my soul holds most dear. Eliza L.[ivingston] call'd on me the day before yesterday, Early in the morn'g before I was up, as she heard I was to set off that day, but as it was a mistake we walk'd out together to pay some visits. Now I am really going & she dont know it; she is the best female friend I have here. She is possess'd of very shining quallities and has a mind well turn'd & much improv'd, has a great deal of tenderness in her disposition, & sympathizes with the distresses of every one. She receiv'd a packet the other day while I was with her from my friend Leander. I did not before know they corresponded tho' I knew of their friendship. She shew'd me the letter in confidence, as illeberal custom prevents a correspondence between the sexes. It was writ in the most friendly manner. His style is elegant. At my return to P. Eliza L is to correspond with me.

[*In 1785, Henry Livingston suggests a reconciliation with his wife which, given the prospect of being reunited with her daughter, Nancy is willing to try.*]

February 24th 1785—This is my Birth day. I intend from this time to continue my journal, which I have neglected doing for these (near) four Months past. I heartily pray that I may so spend my time as to make me here after happy in the reflection. But O! may I have a better motive for trying to act well. O that my principal aim may be to please God, & appear good in his sight. May I from this time never offend "Him" in act, word, or deed! May I be duly mindful of every duty so as to be acceptable to God & approved of by virtuous people. Within these last three months my time has passed in a continual round of insipid amusements, & trivial occupations. I have however in the meantime, not long since, seen my husband, after an absence of three years; he came to this City upon business. I contrived however to see him, and thank God am reconciled to him. I have now a prospect of living happily with him & my darling Child.

[*But without explanation, Henry Livingston writes that he has changed his mind. After showing his letter to her father, Nancy writes: "he sees it will never do for me to return to my inflexible husband. . . ." In September 1785, Louis Otto returns to Philadelphia.*]

[*September 6, 1785*]
I have lived as usual with my dear indulgent Father trying to be happy, & to make him so, since I wrote the journal of last June. This Morn'g I was disturbed again in my mind, by hearing that my Friend Leander is arrived from France in the honorable character of Secretary to the Embassy & chargé des affairs of France. Now must I be wretched in the reflection of what I have lost. O! had I waited till the obstacles were remov'd that stood in my Fathers way, then had I been compleatly happy. Now they are removed, but what is my unfortunate situation!—A wretched slave—doom'd to be the wife of a Tyrant I hate but from whom, thank God, I am separated. My amiable & still sincere friend writ me an account of his arrival & appointment. I answer'd his letter by an opportunity I heard of today. I wish'd him happiness! I sincer[e]ly wish it him tho' I am deprived of it. What have I not suffer'd in my mind since his arrival; all my woes revived afresh. . . .

Sep[tr] 15—The strangest alteration has taken place in my feelings that can be conceived; my tranquility is fled, I am absent, thoughtfull &

unhappy; I make a thousand mistakes in a day. This last week what miseries have I not suffer'd in my mind; my dear Father too observes it. Alass! my behavior does not please him. I appear discontented. I neglect my duties—I seek in the charms of disipation for happiness. I find none—I return home more unhappy than before, displeased with every thing I have said or heard—I will for the future stay more at home, see less company; for two reasons, my Father wishes it, & I feel more than ever that retirement *suits me best.*

Ah! me where shall I seek for consolation? My darling Child! If I had but her; I shou'd not be quite unhappy, she wou'd serve to console me, but she is taken from me, for I know not how long. O! my God teach me resignation to thy divine will, & let me not suffer *in vain!* I staid at home all this day till the Even'g, I then went with my Mamma to harrowgate springs. I return'd early & drank Tea alone with Papa. He is now gone out & I am alone. My Mother is gone to bed—what shall I do—it is two hours before my bed time—I wont go out. I can't fix my attention to read. Had I but my Child with what care I'd watch *over her.*

October 15th—Another Month is pass'd & no alteration has taken place in my situation; I am however more reconciled to it than ever I was. I find an infinite pleasure in trying to improve myself & my mind is much more composed since I have determin'd to employ every hour of my time usefully, except those destin'd by every body to amusement & relaxation. Music & reading & writing fill up half the day; work, family duties & dressing, the other; the evening I devote to seeing my friends either at home or abroad. Thus I enjoy at present a negative happiness—disturb'd it is occasionally, by some few cross accident[s] & disagreable reflections. Now & then I hear of my Child —& some times form plans of having her with me, & as often am disappointed. My Husband (what misery, alass to me, that I have one) lives in his old way trying to deprive his wife & lawful heir of their property by throwing it away on miserable undeserving objects. I have another new scource of woe, for the authoriz'd separation that I have been so long expecting to take place, is given over entirely. Thus am I situated differently from all the human race, for I am deprived of all hope of ever being more happy in this world—the next I leave to HEAVEN.

[*When Louis Otto announces his intention to marry Nancy Shippen's close friend Eliza Livingston, Nancy Shippen wishes them both well. But within a year, Eliza dies giving birth to their first child. At this point Nancy and Louis resume a warm correspondence based on their long friendship.*

In 1789, Nancy Shippen Livingston decides to sue for divorce from her husband, which could only be granted by passage of a special bill in the New York legislature. Nancy is encouraged by no one in this except her mother-in-law. Henry Livingston refuses to cooperate and does what he can to damage the reputation of his wife and Louis Otto. Knowing her greatest vulnerability, he also threatens to assume official custody of their child, remove her to the South, and take charge of her education himself, thus preventing further visits between mother and daughter. When the divorce petition ends in defeat for Nancy Livingston, she is at least assured that her contact with her daughter will continue.

In April 1790, Louis Otto marries Fanny de Crevecoeur. The next year, Henry Livingston sues his wife Nancy for divorce on the grounds of desertion and wins his case in a Connecticut court. Nancy Shippen lives the rest of her life in Philadelphia, where her daughter Peggy joins her when she becomes sixteen in 1797, thereby giving up claims to the Livingston fortune. Peggy Livingston remains permanently with her mother and never marries.]

Elizabeth Fuller
[1776–1856]

*Born in Princeton, Massachusetts three months after the signing of the
Declaration of Independence, Elizabeth Fuller was one of ten children of
the Reverend Timothy Fuller and his wife. The family was a very close
one and all ten children are reported to have gathered twenty-five years
after their father's death at the site of the family home—then only a cellar
hole—to sing hymns learned in their childhood.*

*The obvious preoccupation of Elizabeth Fuller in her diary is the work
she performed as her contribution to the family economy. All aspects of the
manufacture of cloth—including carding, picking and combing, spinning, weaving, and dyeing—were typically the responsibilities of the
unmarried daughters of a colonial household. Elizabeth Fuller seems to
have been the primary "spinster" of the family, though she does share the
work with a sister and her mother. After logging days, weeks, and months
at her task, she writes: "I think I might have spun up all the Swingling
tow* in America by this time."*

1791

April   1—I wove two yards and three quarters & three inches to-
         day & I think I did pretty well considering it was April
         Fool day. Mr. Brooks & Mr. Hastings here to get Pa to
         do some writing for them.

         2—I wove three yards and a quarter.

---

*The coarse part of flax separated by a swingle, a wooden tool used to beat the flax
or hemp to cleanse it of these rough particles.

From Francis Everett Blake, *History of the Town of Princeton, In the County of
Worcester and Commonwealth of Massachusetts, 1759–1915* (Princeton, Mass.: Published
by the town, 1915). Reprinted by permission of the town of Princeton.

3—Sabbath. I went to church.—an anular eclipse of the sun, it was fair weather.

4—I wove five yards & a quarter. Mr. Cutting here this eve.

5—I wove four yards. Mrs. Garfield & Mrs. Eveleth who was once Caty Mirick here a visiting.—The real estate of Mr. Josiah Mirick deceased is vendued to-day.
(eve) Timmy has got home from the vendue Mr. Cutting has bought the Farm gave 255£ Sam Matthews has bought the part of the Pew gave eight dollars.

6—I got out the White piece Mrs. Garfield warped the blue, came here & began to draw in the Piece.

7—I finished drawing in the Piece & wove a yard & a half. Sam Matthews here to-day.

8—I wove two yards & a quarter.

9—I wove two yards & a quarter.

10—Sabbath. I went to church in the A.M. Mamma went in the P.M. she has not been before since she came from Sandwich.

11—I wove a yard & a half. Parmela Mirick here to see me.

12—I wove to-day.

13—Mrs. Brooks here a visiting. I wove.

14—I got out the Piece in the A.M. Pa carried it to Mr. Deadmans. Miss Eliza Harris here.

15—I began to spin Linnen spun 21 knots. I went to Mr. Perrys on an errand. Pa went to Mr. Matthews to write his will & some deeds. He has sold Dr. Wilson 20 acres of Land & given Sam a deed of some I believe about 25 acres.

16—Pa went to Mr. Matthews again.—I spun 21 knots.

17—Sabbath I went to church all day Mr. Davis Preached Mr. Saunders is sick.

18—I spun two double skeins of Linnen.

19—I spun two double skeins.

20—I spun two double skeins.—Ma went to Mrs. Miricks for a visit was sent for home.—Revd. Daniel Fuller of Cape Ann here to see us.

21—Revd. Mr. Fuller went from here this morn. Ma went to Mrs. Miricks again.—I spun two skeins.—Sukey Eveleth & Nabby here to see Nancy.

22—I spun two double skeins O dear
   Quadville has murdered wit, & work will do as bad,
   for wit is always merry, but work does make me sad.

23—I spun two skeins. Nathan Perry here.—Wareham Hast-
   ings at work here.

24—I went to church. Mr. Thurston Preached.—Mr. Saunders is sick.

25—Leonard Woods here all this forenoon, brought Holyokes singing Book. Left it here.

26—Pa went to see Mr. Saunders. I Pricked some tunes out
   of Holyokes Singing Book.

27—I spun five skeins of linnen yarn.

28—I spun five skeins of linnen yarn. Pa went to Sterling.

29—I Pricked some Tunes out of Holyokes singing Book. I
   spun some.

30—I spun four skeins to-day.

1791
May   1—Sabbath I went to Meeting to-day.

2—I spun five skeins to-day.

3—I spun five skeins to-day.

4—I spun two skeins to-day finished the Warp for this Piece.
   —Nathan Perry worked here this P.M.

5—I spun four skeins of tow for the filling to the Piece I have
   been spinning. Pa went to Worcester to get the newspaper. Nathan Perry here this eve.

6—I spun four Skeins to-day.

7—I spun four Skeins to-day.

8—Sabbath. I went to church A.M. Mr. Thurston preached.
   Mr. John Rolph & his Lady & Mr. Osburn her Brother
   & a Miss Anna Strong (a Lady courted by said Osbourn)
   came here after Meeting and drank Tea.

9—I spun four skeins. Mr. Thurston here this P.M. a visiting
   he is an agreeable Man appears much better out of the
   Pulpit than in.

10—I spun four Skeins to-day.

11—I spun four skeins.

12—I spun four skeins. Lucy Matthews here.

13—I spun four skeins.—Ma is making Soap. Rainy.

14—I spun four skeins. Ma finished making soap and it is very good.

15—I went to church A.M. Mr. Thurston Preached   he is a——
—.—Mr. Rolph drank Tea here.

17—I spun four skeins to-day.

18—I spun four skeins of linnen yarn to Make a Harness of.
—Ma is a breaking.

19—I spun two skeins and twisted the harness yarn.

20—Mrs. Garfield came here this Morning to show me how to make a Harness, did not stay but about half an Hour.
—Mrs. Perry & Miss Eliza Harris here a visiting.

21—I went to Mrs. Miricks and warped the Piece.

22—I went to church in the A.M. Mr. Saunders preached gave us a good sermon his text Romans 6th Chap. 23 verse. For the wages of Sin is Death.

23—I got in my Piece to-day wove a yard.

24—Wove two yards & an half.

25—Election. I wove three Yards to-day.—Mrs. Perry here a few moments.

26—I wove three Yards to-day. The two Mrs. Matthews here to Day. I liked Sam's Wife much better than I expected to.—Miss. Eliza Harris here about two Hours.

27—I wove five Yards to-day.

29—Pleasant weather. Pa went to Sterling. My Cousin Jacob Kembal of Amherst came here to-day.

30—General Election at Bolton.—Mr. Josiah Eveleth & Wife & Mrs. Garfield here on a visit. . . .

1792
Apr.   1—Sabbath. no Meeting in town.

5—I wove. Pa went to sterling.

6—I wove. Parmela Mirick here. Elisha Brooks here.

7—I finished weaving the linnen Piece, there is Thirty Yards of it. Nathan Perry here this evening.

8—Sabbath. very pleasant.

9—I drawed in a Piece of coarse Wool & wove four yards.

11—I wove half a Yard, got out the Piece. There is eleven Yards & an half.

12—I drawed in a Piece of blue Worsted.

15—Sabbath. I stayed at home

20—I got out the Piece there is sixteen Yards & an half. I got in the Piece for rag Coverlids. I wove four Yards.

22—Sabbath. Mr. Davis preached. I went to Church.

24—I wove five Yards got out the Piece, there is 25 Yards of it.

25—I spun four Skeins of tow.

26—I helped Sally alter my dark Callico Gown.

27—I began to draw in a Piece of linnen.

28—I finished drawing in the Piece & wove five Yards.

29—Sabbath. Mr. Davis Preached. I went to Church all day. Nathan Perry came home with me at night to get the Newspaper.

30—I wove eight yards.

1792
May

1—I wove eight Yards.

2—I wove eight yards.

3—I wove two & a half Yards. Got out the Piece, there is thirty one Yards & an half; have finished my weaving for this year I have woven a hundred and forty Yards since the ninth of March.

4—I sewed.

28—I wove six yards & an half to-day.

29—Sabbath. I went to church in the A.M. Mr. Saunders Preached from Matthew 15th Chap. 28th verse. "Then Jesus answered and said O Woman great is thy faith: be it unto thee even as thou wilt."—Exceeding Hot to-day.

30—Mr. & Mrs. Hobbs & Mr. Saunders here a visiting to-day. Mr. Saunders is a very agreeable pretty Man. I wove three yards to-day.

31—I wove six yards & a half to Day. Silas Perry here a few Moments.

1792
June

1—I wove five yards to-day got out the Piece, there is thirty six yards of it. Welcome sweet Liberty, once more to me. How have I longed to meet again with thee. . . .

1792
Aug.   1—I washed.

2—I spun four skeins of linnen Yarn.

3—I spun five skeins.

4—I spun three Skeins & scoured the best Chamber Floor. Lt. Mirricks Lady Capt. Gills Lady & Mrs. Brooks here a visiting. Pa went to Shrewsbury to see Mr. Morse with Mr. Adams. Sally is nineteen years old to-day.

5—I spun four skeins. Nathan Perry here.

7—Sabbath. I went to church A.M. Mr. Adams Text Proverbs 3rd Chap. 8th verse She shall bring thee to Honour when thou dost embrace her. Mr. Thomas Mason & Lady dined here.

8—I washed to-day.

9—I spun four skeins.

10—I spun four skeins of linnen. Uncle & Aunt Dwight & Sally came here, we rejoice exceedingly to see Sally come home.

11—Uncle & Aunt Dwight went from here about one o'clock. I love Uncle & Aunt exceedingly. Aunt gave me a lawn Handkerchief. Pa & Ma went as far as Rutland with them.

12—I did not do much, spent chief of my time with Sally very much against her inclination, for she sent me out of the Room fifty times in a minute but I did not care any more than our white chicken does when we drive it out of the House.

13—I made a Cheese. Mr. Adams here to-day.

14—Sabbath. I went to meeting A.M.

15—I washed. Mrs. Garfield here a visiting.

16—I picked blue Wool.

17—I broke blue Wool.

18—I finished breaking the Wool & carded some.

19—I carded blue Wool. Ma spun.

20—I carded.

21—Sabbath. I went to church all day Mr. Davis preached.

22—I washed.

23—Silas Perry here this morning.

24—Ma and Sally went to Mrs. Miricks and warped the Piece.

25—Mrs. Garfield here.

26—I drawed the Piece into the Harness & Sley & wove a yard.

27—I wove five yards of Cloth. Revd. Mr. Morse & Miss Tamar Beaman came here & drank Tea.

28—Sabbath. I went to church Mr. Davis Preached.

1792

Sept. 1—I began to spin the white Wool.

2—I spun three Skeins of Warps.

3—I spun three Skeins.

4—Sabbath. I went to church Mr. Rice of Westminster Preached.

5—Rainy. Trooping & Training in this Town to-day.— Sally & I went to see them.

6—I spun three skeins.

7—Fidelia Mirick here a visiting to-day.

8—I spun three Skeins to-day.

9—I spun three Skeins. Pa & Ma went to Mr. Richardson's a visiting.

10—I spun three skeins.

11—Sabbath dull weather. I stayed at home all day. Pa preached at Leominster.

12—Sis came home.—Lucretia Mirick here.

13—Timmy cut the stalks to-day.—Ma & Sally went to Lieut. Miricks.

16—Esqr. Gill's Lady & her sister Becky here a visiting.

17—Pa went to Daniel Cheever's.

18—Sabbath. Mr. Sanders Preached. Put in the white Piece.

19—Mr. Russell here.

20—Pa & Ma went to Mr. J. Rolph's on a visiting.

22—I wove. Put in the white wool.

23—I wove to-day.

24—I wove.

25—Sabbath. Wet weather. Mr. Goodridge preached.

26—I wove.

27—I wove to-day.

28—Mr. Rolph & his Lady here a visiting this afternoon.

29—I wove to-day.

30—I got out the woollen Piece. There is 19 yards & half of it. I drawed the linnen piece through the Harness.

1792
Oct.   1—Sabbath Mr. Goodridge preached.
        2—I wove to-day.
        3—Cold. I wove.
        4—I wove to-day. Pleasant.
        5—I wove to-day.
        6—Muster at Lancaster. John Allen here.
        7—I wove.
        8—I wove.
        9—Sabbath. I went to church.
       10—I wove to-day.
       11—I wove A.M. Miss Polly Mirick & Miss Polly Baxter here P.M.
       12—I wove got out the Piece before night 27 Yards of it.
       13—My birth day. I am sixteen Years old   How many years have been past by me in thoughtlesness & vanity.

THE JOURNEY OUT

Margaret Van Horn Dwight (Bell)

[1790–1834]

Though "well-connected"—her father, William, was a brother of the President of Yale University and her mother, Margaret, was a granddaughter of Jonathan Edwards—Margaret Van Horn Dwight had an unsettled childhood. When she was six her father died and her mother remarried. At this time she was sent to live with her grandmother in Northampton, Massachusetts, where she spent the next eleven years. When her grandmother died in 1807, she was sent to the family of an aunt, Elizabeth Dwight Woolsey (whose son Theodore was a later president of Yale), in New Haven, Connecticut. After three years, she left to join cousins in Warren, Ohio, where she met and married William Bell the next year. Most of their married life was spent in Pittsburgh, Pennsylvania, where he was a merchant. They had thirteen children.

Margaret undertook the wagon trip to Ohio in the company of the parsimonious Deacon Wolcott and his wife and daughter. They set out in October of 1810 for a journey of about six weeks over rough roads through Connecticut, New York, New Jersey, Pennsylvania, and Ohio. Accommodations along the way were most often the busy, sometimes raucus, public inns and taverns.

It was common for women to keep travel diaries such as the one below. This form of diary resembles a long letter written in installments for someone left behind. Such diaries begin and end with the journey and are usually sent to the audience upon arrival at the destination. Margaret kept her journal as a promise to her cousin Elizabeth Woolsey, and the author's heightened sense of audience contributes much to the liveliness and humor of her record.

[1810]

October 22—Monday—Cook's inn——

County West Chester—

I never will go to New Connecticut with a *Deacon* again, for we put up at every byeplace in the country to *save expence*— It is very grating to my pride to go into a tavern & furnish & cook my own provision— to ride in a wagon &c &c— but that I can possibly get along with— but to be oblig'd to pass the night in such a place as we are now in, just because it is a little cheaper, is more than I am willing to do— I should even rather drink clear rum out of the wooden bottle after the deacon has drank & wip'd it over with his hand, than to stay here another night—— The house is very small & very dirty— it serves for a tavern, a store, & I should imagine hog's pen stable & every thing else— The air is so impure I have scarcely been able to swallow since I enter'd the house— The landlady is a fat, dirty, ugly looking creature, yet I must confess very obliging— She has a very suspicious countenance & I am very afraid of her— She seems to be master, as well as mistress & storekeeper, & from the great noise she has been making directly under me for this half hour, I suspect she has been "stoning the raisins & watering the rum"— All the evening there has been a store full of noisy drunken fellows, yet Mr Wolcott could not be persuaded to bring in but a small part of the baggage, & has left it in the waggon before the door, as handy as possible— Miss W's trunk is in the bar-room unlock'd the key being broken today— it contains a bag of money of her father's, yet she could not persuade him to bring it up stairs—— I feel so uneasy I cannot sleep & had therefore rather write than not this hour— some one has just gone below the stairs after being as I suppos'd in bed this some time— for what purpose I know not— unless to go to our trunks or waggon—the old woman, (for it was her who went down,) tells me I must put out my candle so good night—— Tuesday Morn——I went to bed last night with fear & trembling, & feel truly glad to wake up & find myself alive & well— if our property is all safe, we shall have double cause to be thankful—— The old woman kept walking about after I was in bed, & I then heard her in close

From *A Journey to Ohio in 1810 as Recorded in the Journal of Margaret Van Horne Dwight*, ed. Max Farrand (New Haven: Yale University Press, 1912). Reprinted by permission. The manuscript of the diary is at the Western Reserve Historical Society in Cleveland, Ohio.

confab with her husband a long time——— Our room is just large
enough to contain a bed a chair & a very small stand— our bed has
one brown sheet & one pillow—the sheet however appear'd to be
clean, which was more than we got at Nash's— there we were all
oblig'd to sleep in the same room without curtains or any other screen
— & our sheets there were so dirty I felt afraid to sleep in them—
We were not much in favor at our first arrival there; but before we
left them, they appear'd quite to like us— & I don't know why they
should not, for we were all very clever, notwithstanding we rode in
a waggon——— Mʳˢ Nash said she should reckon on't to see us again
(Miss W & me) so I told her that in 3 years she might expect to see
me—She said I should never come back alone, that I would certainly
be married in a little while— but I am now more than ever determin'd
not to oblige myself to spend my days there, by marrying should I
even have an opportʸ——— I am oblig'd to write every way so you
must not wonder at the badness of the writing— I am now in bed
& writing in my lap— Susan has gone to see if our baggage is in order
——— I hear the old woman's voice talking to the good deacon— &
an "I beg your pardon" comes out at every breath almost——— Oh I
cannot bear to see her again she is such a disgusting object——— The
men have been swearing & laughing in the store under me this hour
— & the air of my room is so intolerable, that I must quit my writing
to go in search of some that is *breathable*— I don't know how far I
shall be oblig'd to go for it— but there is none very near I am certain
——— Having a few moments more to spare before we set out, with
my book still in my lap, I hasten to tell you we found everything
perfectly safe, & I believe I wrong'd them all by suspicions——— The
house by day light looks worse then ever— every kind of thing in the
room where they live— a chicken half pick'd hangs over the door—
& pots, kettles, dirty dishes, potatoe barrels— & every thing else—
& the old woman— it is beyond my power to describe her— but she
& her husband & both very kind & obliging— it is as much as a body's
life is worth to go near them——— The air has already had a medicinal
effect upon me——— I feel as if I had taken an emetic— & should stay
till night I most certainly should be oblig'd to take my bed, & that
would be certain death——— I did not think I could eat in the house
— but I did not dare refuse— the good deacon nor his wife did not
mind it, so I thought I must not——— The old creature sits by eating,
& we are just going to my great joy so good bye, good bye till to
night———

Tuesday Noon— Ferry House near
State Prison—
It has been very cold & dusty riding to day——— We have met with
no adventure yet, of any kind——— We are now waiting at the ferry
house to cross the river as soon as wind & tide serve— The white
waves foam terribly how we shall get across I know not, but I am in
great fear— If we drown there will be an end of my journal———

Hobuck, Wednesday Morn—
Buskirck's Inn———
After waiting 3 or 4 hours at the ferry house, we with great difficulty cross'd the ferry & I, standing brac'd against one side of the boat
involuntarily endeavouring to balance it with my weight & groaning
at every fresh breeze as I watch'd the side which almost dipt in the
water— & the ferrymen swearing at every breath— M^r, M^{rs} & Miss
Wolcott viewing the city and vainly wishing they had improv'd the
time of our delay to take a nearer view——— At length we reach'd
this shore almost frozen— The Ferry is a mile & a half wide——— I
was too fatigued to write last night & soon after we came retired to
bed— We were again oblig'd all to sleep in one room & in dirty sheets
— but pass'd the night very comfortably——— If good wishes have any
influence, we shall reach our journey's end in peace— for we obtain
them from everyone——— The morning is pleasant & we are soon to
ride——— Mrs Buskirck the landlady, I should imagine is about 60
years of age & she sits by with a three year old child in her lap— She
wears a long ear'd cap & looks so old I thought she must be Grandmother till I enquir'd——— . . .

Peach Orchard, P— Thursday night—
Phelps' Tavern———
I do not feel to night, my dear Elizabeth, as if I should ever see you
again— 3 mountains & more hundreds of miles part us; & tho' I
cannot give up the idea of returning, I cannot think of traversing this
road again— If I live to return I will wait till the new turnpike is
finished——— We cross'd the last brother this morning, & found the
greater part of it, better than the other two— but about 60 rods near
the top it was excessively steep——— We found a house at the foot of
the steepest part— A woman & her 2 sons live there & keep cakes &
beer——— The woman told us she had no husband at *present*———I

suppose she has one in expectation——On the first mountain, I found some sweet Williams—— We stopt at noon, at a dismal looking log hut tavern— The landlady (I hate the word but I must use it,) talk'd about bigotry, bigotted notions, liberty of conscience &c— She did not look as if she knew the meaning of conscience, much less of bigotry—— All this afternoon we have been walking over young mountains, distant relations of the 3 brothers, but not half as clever — I was so lame & so tir'd that for an hour I did not know but I must set down & die— I could not ride— the road was so bad, it was worse than walking— I would not tell you all this, if you were to receive this before it is all over—— It rain'd a very little all day, but just at night it began to rain very fast, & I expected we should all catch our death, walking thro' mud & mire, with no umbrella, or but one that would not cover us all — We were wet thro before we reach'd this dreadful place where we now are—— The Woman is cross & the Man sick— ——

Friday night— It rain'd all day yesterday, & such a shocking place as this is, I never saw— A dozen Waggoners are here, some half drunk & no place for us to stay in but our waggons or a little chamber with 3 squares of glass in it— with scarcely room to sit or stand——

Saturday morn— — I am now in despair, it continues raining faster than ever— The house full of drunken prophane wretches, the old woman cross as a witch— We have nothing to eat & can get nothing but some slapjacks at a baker's some distance off, & so stormy we cannot get there—— — Mrs Jackson frets all the time, I wish they would go on & leave us, we should do as well again— — Mr Beach & his wife & child & the woman who is with them, are here, & the house is full— Mrs Beach rode in all the rain Thursday, but took no cold & bears it well as any one— It rains most dreadfully & they say it is the clearing off shower— Oh, if it only proves so— —— "Oh had I the wings of a dove, how soon would I meet you again"— We have never found the wretches indelicate till last evening, but while we were at tea, they began talking & singing in a most dreadful manner— — We are 4 miles from Sidling hill, the next mountain, & a mile & a half from this, there is a creek which we must cross, that is so rais'd by the rain, as to render it impossible to pass it——

Saturday night— Our "clearing up shower" has lasted all day with unabated violence,—— Just at sunset we had a pretty hard thunder shower, & at dusk there was clear sky visible & the evening star shone bright as possible, but now it is raining fast again—— After giving an emetic I would take a long journey with my *intended,* to try his patience— — mine is try'd sorely now— I wish you could just take a peep at me— my frock is wet & dirty a quarter of a yard high, only walking about the house— I have been in my chamber almost the whole day, but was oblig'd to go down just at night to eat, & look at the sky— I was very much frighten'd by a drunken waggoner, who came up to me as I stood by the door waiting for a candle, he put his arm round my neck, & said something which I was too frighten'd to hear— It is the first time the least insult has been offer'd to any of us— One waggoner very civilly offer'd to take Susan or me, on to Pitts^g in his waggon if we were not like to get there till spring— It is not yet determin'd which shall go with him—— One waggon in crossing the creek this afternoon, got turn'd over & very much injur'd —— We have concluded the reason so few are willing to return from the Western country, is not that the country is so good, but because the journey is so bad—— Mr W. has gone to & from there, 5 times, but thinks this will be the last time— Poor Susan groans & sighs & now then sheds a few tears— I think I exceed her in patience & fortitude————Mrs Wolcott is a woman of the most perfect equanimity I ever saw— She is a woman of great feeling & tenderness, but has the most perfect command over her feelings— She is not *own* mother to these children, but she is a very good one— —— — — I have learn'd Elizabeth, to eat raw *pork* & drink whisky—dont you think I shall do for a new country? I shall not know how to do either when I end my journey, however— We have almost got out of the land of dutchmen, but the waggoners are worse— —— The people here talk curiously, they all reckon instead of expect— — Youns is a word I have heard used several times, but what it means I don't know, they use it so strangely—— Mr Rees used to exclaim at any thing wonderful, "Only look at that now"—— "I reckon you are going into the back countries" is now our usual salutation from every one— — —— Susan is in bed for want of some employment & I will join her, after telling you, it has really clear'd off now, & the moon is shining in full splendor.— I hope to-morrows sun will deign to smile upon us— It is long since we have seen it— —— I expect to be oblig'd to go thro' a process of fire & brimstone at my journeys end & shall feel thankful, if that will remedy all the evils arising from dirty beds &c—— I find no necessity for even that yet, but I fear I shall soon——good night——

Sunday 2 oclock P M— We left the Inn this morning in the hope of getting a *little piece* on our way, but have only reach'd the baker's, half a mile from where we set out— The creek is so high we cannot cross it yet— An old man & his wife live here, & appear to be very kind clever people, & what is more than we have found before, they appear to regard the Sabbath— They are Methodists— This is a small log hut, but clean & comfortable— There are no waggoners here— — I shall be oblig'd to colour my frock I believe, for it attracts the attention of those creatures so much, that I dare not go in sight of them scarcely— I often think of the 2 lines your Mama repeated to us "In Silk, &c"

Sunday night.

About sunset, we left the baker's & came down to the Creek, but found it was impossible to get over the waggon, & the road was so intolerable between the place we had left & the creek, that we could not go back, & what to do, it took a long time to determine; but at length M^r W concluded we had better come over to a dirty tavern this side, & let Erastus sleep in the wagon—— The stream runs so fast, that we did not dare cross it alone, as there was nothing but a log to cross on; so the waggoners & our own party, were oblig'd to lead & pilot us, over the stream & thro' a most shocking place as I ever saw— The men were all very civil— they are waiting with their waggons, like the rest of us—— —— We fare worse & worse, & still M^r W— & his wife, tell us this is nothing to what will come— I do not fully believe them, for we cannot endure much more & live—— Susan & young Mrs Jackson have been quite unwell all day—— I never felt in better health, & my spirits are pretty good, considering all things—— We are not able to get beds here, & are to sleep on the floor to night— There is another family here, with several little children—— They say there has been a *heap* of people moving this fall;— I don't know exactly how many a heap is, or *a sight* either, which is another way of measuring people—— I would be *apt* to think it was a *terrible* parcel, to use the language of the people round me—— I have such an enormous appetite the whole time, that I have been in some fear of starving— for food of every kind, is very scarce with us— Money will not procure it, & nothing else I am sure, will— for they love money better than life, if possible——   4 Sabbaths we have pass'd on the road, & I suppose 2 or 3 more will pass before we get among people who "remember the sabbath day to keep it holy"—— We find no books to read, only at the bakers to day I found part of a bible, a methodist hymn book & a small book containing an account of the progress of Methodism throughout the country; in letters from Ministers & others—— —— We left Mr Beach & family, at the tavern we left to day—— I hope tomorrow to write you from a comfortable place 6 or 8 miles at least from the next mountain——

Monday morn— We have now I think met with as bad as can befal us—— Never, never did I pass such a night— — — We could get no bed & for a long time expected to be oblig'd to set up all night — but we could get no room nor fire to stay by, & the landlady was so kind as to give up her bed to us; so M^rs W & Susan went to bed there, while I went to bed with Mrs Jackson in another room— I took off my frock & boots, & had scarcely lain down, when one of the wretches came into the room & lay down by me on the outside of the bed— I was frighten'd almost to death & clung to Mrs Jackson who did not appear to mind it— & I lay for a quarter of an hour crying, & scolding & trembling, begging of him to leave me— At last, when persuaded I was in earnest, he begg'd of me not to take it amiss, as he intended no harm & only wish'd to become acquainted with me —— A good for nothing brute, I wonder what he suppos'd I was— I don't know of any thought word or action of mine that could give him reason to suppose I would authorise such abominable insolence — — The man & his wife, who are here, & their family, John Jackson & his wife, & Mrs Jackson, were all in the room—The moment he left the room, I put on my frock & was going in to M^rs W & Susan, but I could not get to them without going thro' the room where all the waggoners were, & Mrs Jackson did not think it safe, so I got on another part of the bed where none of them could come near me, & had been there about 10 minutes when M^rs W & Susan came into the room both crying, & as much frighten'd as I had been, for one of the creatures had been into their room, & they could scarcely get him out — M^r W — was in the waggon, & the landlord was so afraid of these wag^gs that he did not dare stay in his own house, for they threaten'd to put him into the creek, if he did not continue giving them liquor

— I wish they had put him in— a mean sneaking fellow!—— His poor wife was then oblig'd to bear it all, & she was very much distress'd on our account— She was not to blame for any thing that happen'd, for as long as her husband suffer'd it, she could not prevent it— At last M^{rs} W —— went to bed with Mrs Jackson & me, & Susan lay down with John & his wife— We lay but a few minutes, when one of them came into our room again crawling on his hands & knees — M^{rs} W & I sprung & run out into the mud in our stocking feet & were going to call Mr W.— but the creatures came out to us & begg'd us not to, & pledg'd their honor (of which you may suppose they possess'd a great share) that we should not be disturb'd more— & tenderness for M^r W— who we knew would be sick to day if depriv'd of rest, at length determin'd us to go back; but we did not go to bed again till just morning, when some of us slept nearly or quite an hour— which was every wink of sleep we could obtain during the whole night— The fellows were all but one, very still afterwards— Indeed there was but 2 who made any disturbance, & only one of those was very bad— but one, was a complete child of the evil one— the vilest, worst, most blasphemous wretch, that ever liv'd—— M^r W — came back to the house before 2 oclock, & this morning, threaten'd them with a prosecution— They are quite angry — they are in the employ of this man who is moving; he is a merchant & they carry his goods to Pitts^g——

Nov^{br}—12th Monday night— Nail Shop—
on the 4th Mountain

We have got 8 1-2 miles on our journey to day, & now it rains again —— If I could describe to you our troubles from roads, waggoners & creeks, I would,— but it is impossible—— The waggoners set out just before we did & the bad one being foremost has taken all the pains in his power to hinder our progress, by driving as slow as possible & stopping every other moment— The road was too narrow to pass them, unless they would turn out for us— all but one did, but he swore he would not— We came by them as they stopp'd at noon, & put up to night at an inn on the mountain, out of the direct road, where we should peaceably pass the night— but the waggoners have follow'd us, & the house is full— They are not in our room—— Our party now consists of Mrs Jackson's, Mr Beach's & M^r W's familys —— The woman who is with Mr Beach, is such a foolish old creature, that we are all out of patience with her— — She is aunt to them, I believe— —— If I were to choose, I would never have company on a long journey— such company at least— Our chairs here are taken from us for the Waggoners— —— Our road over the mountains, has not even a good prospect to render it pleasant— I have been repeating to Susan all day, "Comfort damsel &c"— Mrs Jackson is scolding because she has no chair to set on.— M^r W — tells her, "Fret not thyself because of evil doers"— — There is another impassable creek a head, & a hundred waggons waiting to cross it— Our prospect brightens fast— dont you think so? good night——

Sarah Peirce Nichols
[1804–?]

The twenty-nine-year-old unmarried daughter of George and Sally Nichols of Salem, Massachusetts, Elizabeth Nichols used her diary to record her extraordinary daily exercise. After rising each morning, usually before 3:00 A.M., she sets out for a walk averaging twelve miles per day. She walks in the rain, in the snow, and when the thermometer reads ninety-six degrees. One morning she records walking to the burying ground in the next town (about eight miles) "in moonlight." These feats of perambulation must have taken most of every morning, for only in the afternoon does she record other activities such as visiting or dressmaking. Sarah Nichols seems to have suffered from chronic ill health including severe stomach pain and "tic douloureux," intense pain of nerves in the face. Apparently the walking was undertaken for reasons of health as in one place she refers to her daily trek as "my usual remedy."

[*April* 19, 1833]

Friday, I took my usual walk twelve miles. At night I was taken with a pain in my stomach, which deprived me of a great part of my rest and seemed to unfit me for the duties of the next day but with considerable of resolution, and the blessing of Providence I was enabled to perform my twelve miles walk and felt much better. It is the anniversary of my birthday; I am twenty nine years old; I desire to be grateful for the blessings of the past year.

Monday, I took my usual walk in the morning. We heard a few days since that Ropes Leach had a severe gale of wind at sea, in which

From "Journal of Sarah Peirce Nichols of Salem," *Essex Institute Historical Collections* 82 (1946), 213–17. Reprinted by permission. The manuscript of the diary is at the Essex Institute in Salem, Massachusetts.

he lost one of his masts, and was obliged to put into Cork. Uncle Henry Peirce came from Boston, to pass the night with us.

Tuesday, I took my twelve miles walk; spent the afternoon at Grandma's with E. Pierce and Susan Lawrence.

Wednesday, I took my usual walk twelve miles and three quarters; spent the afternoon at Mr. Thompson's.

Thursday, Mr. Brazer set out for Richmond this morning. I took my twelve miles walk, spent the remainder of the day at home. Aunt Peirce sent me a present of a ribbon.

Friday, I received two more presents today, a large shawl from John, and a small one from Henry, God grant that I may be able to make some returns to all my dear friends.

Sunday, tolerable pleasant till evening, when it clouded up and looked very much like rain; I had my twelve miles walk in the morning, attended public worship in the afternoon; Mr. Walker preached.

Monday, very warm and pleasant! I took my usual walk in the morning. Grandma, Elizabeth Peirce and Susan took tea with us.

May 1st. Not very pleasant, I had my twelve miles walk.

May 2d. Cloudy, I took my usual walk.

5th I had my usual walk, attended public worship in the forenoon. Mr. Palfrey preached; after the usual exercises, the sacrement was administered.

6th Very pleasant but cool, I took my walk of twelve miles.

7th E. Peirce set out this morning for N. York. I took my usual walk. George passed the night with us.

8th I took my walk in the morning of twelve miles. George left Salem for Cambridge this afternoon.

9th I set out on my journey little after four in the morning: everything appeared to be alive after the rain. 10.13 miles walk this day. Pleasant but cool. I took tea at Susan's with Mrs. T. Ropes, the Miss Miller's and the bishop.

11th Pleasant till the latter part of the afternoon when it clouded up. Susan took tea with us. Mr. and Mrs. Johonnot passed the evening with us, twelve miles walk this day.

12th I attended public worship in the afternoon. Mr. Putnam preached. Dr. Pearson returned from Europe this evening. Thirteen miles walk this day.

13th I took my usual walk in the morning, drank tea at Mrs. Johonnot's.

16th & 17th I took my usual walk each day. Miss Lehee, a niece of Mr. Forrester's died on Thursday; her death was occasioned by taking arsenick.

18th Uncle Ben Nichols and B. Pierce came in town this evening, to pass the sabbath with us. Twelve miles walk this day.

19th I had my usual walk in the morning, attended public worship in the afternoon. Dr. Follin preached.

24th I rose at twenty minutes before four, set out on my journey at little after 4, which is my usual hour at this season. Susan and Elizabeth Treadwell took tea with us.

26th In the morning I walked four miles only, after which I took Miss Darling's class at the sunday school, it was very interesting. I attended public worship all day. Dr. Follin preached.

27th I took my usual walk in the morning, spent the afternoon at Grandma's. Mr. Brazer returned from his journey this evening, his health is much better.

28th Tolerable pleasant; I took tea at Aunt Leach's; called at Mrs. Brazer's where I met Mr B.   13 miles walk this day.

31st Mr and Mrs Johonnot took tea with us this afternoon. I had my usual walk this morning.

June 1st. Very fine weather. 12 miles walk. Five years from this day I have travelled 15,961¼ . I have received two handsome presents this week a bonnet and belt ribbon.

2nd I took my usual twelve miles walk in the morning attended public worship in the forenoon. Mr Brazer preached.

3d I walked 12 miles this morning, took tea at grandma's, called upon Mrs. E Lander this afternoon.

6th I took my usual walk this morning. We are called this day to lament the death of Dr Treadwell, he was out this morning about 6 o'clock, he came in and died very soon, his complaint was of the heart. God is continually reminding us of the uncertainty of life; may this lesson teach us to have our treasures in heaven, that we may be ready to meet our God, when he shall see best to call us.

7th Dr. Treadwell was buried this afternoon, it is not true, he had been out in the morning; he died very sudden before he got up. Twelve miles walk this day.

9th I attended public worship in the afternoon. Mr. Loring preached. Twelve miles walk this day.

12th I took my usual walk this morning. God has seen best to afflict me for this fortnight past, every night with my old pain the ticdolerue, but far be from me every murmuring thought, my heavenly Father will order every thing right, let his will be done.

14th 12 miles walk this morning. I took tea at grandma's, where I met Aunt and U Saunders, who came from Andover last evening.

17th I had my usual walk. Susan took tea with us this afternoon.

19th I walked fourteen miles this day.

20th Aunt Betsy is quite sick. Twelve miles walk today.

21st I took tea at grandma's. Twelve miles walk today.

22nd I took my usual walk this morning. George came this forenoon to pass a few days with us. Aunt Betsy is getting well fast.

23d I took my usual walk in the morning of twelve miles, and one mile after tea; attended public worship in the forenoon at Mr. Thompson's, George preached. The afternoon I went in to read to grandma.

24th I took my usual walk in the morning; part of the afternoon I spent into grandma's, about 7 o'clock I was obliged to come home, on account of a bad pain in my face. Elizabeth met with quite an accident, as she was sweeping her school, one of the benches fell on to her foot, and hurt it very much.

26th great preparations are making for the president, dressing arches, raising the flags, every one must seem to be doing something for his majesty, who is expected here this afternoon. 12 miles walk today.

27th The president went round town this morning, the bells rung and all Salem seemed to be in confusion. I took my usual walk.

28th I took tea at Mrs. H. Ropes'. I walked 13 miles this day.

29th I took my usual walk of 12 miles this morning. We are expecting the Miss Emerys, and Miss Gay to tea this afternoon.

July 1st I took my usual walk this morning of 12 miles. In the afternoon I went to grandma's.

4th Father is 55 years old; may that kind Being who has preserved his life through another year, ever watch over him, and pour down upon him, and all my dear friends, heavens richest of blessings. I took my usual walk this morning. Mrs Treadwell and her children took tea with us; Susan passed the day here. Uncle Henry Pierce likewise spent the day with us.

6th after my usual walk, I called to see Mrs. Johonnot, who returned from her journey last evening.

8th Henry Nichols and Sarah Atthurton, took tea with us. We were very much alarmed, at hearing the cries of a woman, who appeared to be in distress; on inquiry, we found it was a Mrs. Tunnison, whom they were trying to bind, in order to carry her off to jail, for an outrage she had committed on her son, in one of her drunken fits, by draging him out of bed by his hair, and he in trying to extricate himself broke a blood vessel. Thus we see the dreadful effects of sin. Twelve miles walk this day.

Rebecca Cox Jackson

[1795–1871]

Seventy-five years before the Civil War, Rebecca Cox was born a free black woman near Philadelphia to parents whose names are unknown. Both before and after her marriage to Samuel S. Jackson, she was a member of her oldest brother's household. When Joseph Cox, a prominent member of the Bethel African Methodist Episcopal (A.M.E.) Church, became a widower, Rebecca, who had no children of her own, assumed responsibility for raising his children.

During a thunderstorm in July of 1830, Rebecca Jackson experienced an intense religious conversion. Here began her extraordinary career as a controversial revivalist preacher, healer, prophet, and religious visionary. Her call to a new-found celibacy led to a break with her husband. And a decade of itinerant preaching as a Holiness Methodist, which took her throughout Pennsylvania, New York, Connecticut, and Massachusetts, led eventually to a break with her revered brother.

In 1842, she visited the Shaker community in Watervliet, New York, and immediately felt an affinity with this plain-living group given to ecstatic religious worship and committed to celibate living. She was also strongly drawn to the Shaker belief in the female presence in the Godhead. When Rebecca Jackson joined this religious community, she did so with another black woman, Rebecca Perot. The "two Rebeccas" had become friends and companions, and remained living and working together until Rebecca Jackson's death. In 1851, the two women, after some differences with Shaker leadership, left Watervliet to found a black Shaker sisterhood in Philadelphia. This community became the focus of their religious mission and ministry for the rest of their lives.

At the time of her conversion in 1830, Rebecca Jackson could not read or write. Though she had insistently urged her brother to teach her, he had resisted. He did function, however, as her scribe, but it was a source of anguish for her that he took editorial liberties with her dictations. A year after her conversion, she found one day that she could read the Bible—she had received the gift of literacy as an answer to prayer. Now she was able to transcribe her religious visions and dreams and has, thus, left a remarkable record of her ecstatic inner life.

Journals kept for religious purposes often gave American women "permission" to focus attention on the self and on the inner life when they otherwise would not have found such "self-centeredness" appropriate. Urged by their religious leaders to do so, great numbers of women and men, from the earliest Puritan settlers to the Mormons of today who still practice this tradition, kept regular records of the progress of their spiritual lives. Rebecca Jackson stands in this tradition but her religious autobiography also goes beyond it. Though her writing was not published until one hundred years after her death, it places her among the great women visionaries who wrote (or dictated) autobiographical accounts, including Juliana of Norwich, Margery Kempe, Teresa of Avila, Sor Juana Inez de la Cruz, and Ann Lee, founder of the Shakers of which Rebecca Jackson was a member.

March 11, 1843. In the morning I found myself under great power of God. An angel came in the room, and I found my body under strange feeling. I thought I was dying. I was seized with a trembling within and without my body, and I was then carried away. The earth trembled and a great storm came from the south. The house that I was in began to shake, and the people all ran out. I stood still. The house began to sail on dry ground. It went eastward and southward, and then it brought me back to the same place again safe. And then I was all alone, and my vision ended, and I was very happy.

Sunday, 12th of March, after midnight, I laid down, fell asleep and dreamt I was in a house in the north. I went out at the east door and looked up into the air, saw wonderful strange colored clouds coming

From *Gifts of Power: The Writings of Rebecca Jackson, Black Visionary, Shaker Eldress,* ed. Jean Humez (Amherst: University of Massachusetts Press, 1981). © 1981 by the University of Massachusetts Press. Reprinted by permission. The text is based on a manuscript in Jackson's handwriting at the Berkshire Athenaeum in Pittsfield, Massachusetts, with material collated from a version dictated by Jackson to Rebecca Perot and held by the Western Reserve Historical Society in Cleveland, Ohio; excerpts from the latter are marked [W. R.]. Wording in brackets is from a copy made by Alonzo G. Hollister in the 1870s and 1880s as indicated by Jean Humez.

from the east. And I then looked into a cloud and saw a company in it coming north where I was. I then came into the house again, came in the same door I went out at. This house had three doors, one east, one north, one south. The windows, one north, one west, one south. After I came in, it began to rain, as it were cotton, until the earth was covered.

I stood in the middle of the floor with my face toward the west. There was a man with his children, in great distress about his wife and acrying, "It is the Day of Judgment," He stood in the south door. He did not find his wife.

The house tilted three times toward the east. I stood still in secret prayer, for I spoke not a word during the whole scene. After the house tilted, it then stood firm and moved no more in the time of this raining of cotton, and the moving of these strange clouds, and the coming of this army of people.

All the house, trees, and everything else disappeared. And then the rain changed from cotton to sweet-smelling flowers. There was one clap of thunder and a great noise in the heaven.—I should have mentioned that before all things disappeared, the people were in great distress, running to and fro seeking a place to go, but could find none. They were all lost in the storm.

This was a little white flower. They fell in bunches, the flower in between two beautiful green leaves. I stepped to the door, picked some up, tasted them. Their taste was sweet just like the smell. I then put some in my bosom, but I am not able to tell what they smelt like. The whole air was perfumed with their odor, yea, with their heavenly smell.

Then there came a sound from heaven which had never been heard before. And in that storm came streams of light. And they came in the form of hoops, white as snow, bright as silver, passing through the shower of flowers. They went like the lightning. They were moved by female angels, and they were beyond the tongue of mortals to describe their heavenly appearance. I wondered where Mary was, for I saw her not. I then awoke, and went right to sleep again.

I was in the same house again and saw Mary. I told her I had a dream, and then I called her to the south window to show her where I saw the armies coming north. And when I got to the window, I saw the armies in the south coming north. I then said, "Oh, Mary! Why, it ain't a dream! It is true! Here they are! Come see them!" She came to the window, but could not see them, though she tried hard.

And while I looked at these armies, under them I saw three mountains, one in the east, one in the south, one in the west—Yet they were all south, though they laid southeast, south, and southwest. They were about a half a mile apart. And before these mountains lay a great many people in the earth, with their heads to the south. And while I was trying to show Mary all these things, the people by the west mountain got up and shook themselves. And I saw that their bed was dirt and their cover dry sods, and it fell all off, and in a moment, as it were, they were all in the west mountain. And it became a [baiting] house for the poor. And I stood in their midst. And there was an Irish girl about ten years old, ateasing them. And they were unwilling to bear with her. I told them to bear it, for her time was short. So they heard me, and I comforted them with the words that was given to me for them. They were all colored people, and they heard me gladly. . . .

Then I woke and found the burden of my people heavy upon me. I had borne a burden of my people for twelve years, but now it was double, and I cried unto the Lord and prayed this prayer, "Oh, Lord God of Hosts, if Thou art going to make me useful to my people, either temporal or spiritual,—for temporally they are held by their white brethren in bondage, not as bound man and bound woman, but as bought beasts, and spiritually they are held by their ministers, by the world, the flesh, and the devil. And if these are not a people in bondage, where are there any on the earth?—Oh, my Father and my God, make me faithul in this Thy work and give me wisdom that I may comply with Thy whole will." . . .

P.M. May 16, 1844. After a heavy thunderstorm, I read the sixtieth chapter of Isaiah and was greatly comforted in the gospel of truth, after which I lay down, late at night, under the instruction of my heavenly Father and Mother. After laying some time in this happy state, I fell into a little doze, and found myself standing at the west window. I looked out in the elements and saw a woman in the air. Her head leaned toward the northeast, and she was coming east, toward me, as I was looking in the direction from whence she came. The sky was clear, and I saw all distinctly. She wore a white garment, and a crimson scarf which was brought over her right shoulder and loosely tied under her left arm, and the two ends hung down to near the bottom of her garment. She was bare headed, bare footed, and bare handed. Her hair was black, loosely falling over her shoulders, and she was beautiful to look upon. She appeared pensive and looked upon this city like one bemoaning her only child.

At her right side, awaiting her commands, was a large body of something which I was not permitted to see—only in a body, like a pillar or a mountain. But it was with her and was her possession. She looked upon me, and from the northeast, the direction in which her head leaned, there came forth to her black clouds, which were full of judgment, to be poured out upon this city. I called upon a woman to come and see her, but I found I had done wrong, for the clouds covered her from their sight. I looked into the yard beneath the window and there saw two Irish women and one man. And they cried, "Oh, the Judgment! the Judgment!" They saw the woman. In this time, my eyes were operated upon in a wonderful manner, and I awoke. But the scene remained, and I continued under instruction. Such lightning I think I never before witnessed. The thunder shook the earth, and it continued all night over the city. The city appeared to be so wrapped in sheets of lightning that the citizens were alarmed. . . .

Friday morning, January 14, 1848, between half past four and five o'clock, I thought I was in Philadelphia and Rebecca Perot was with me, in bed. I lay with my head to the west, and my face to the south, and Rebecca was behind me.

As I was going to sleep I thought someone might come in while we slept. And I said, "Rebecca, go and get three forks, and fasten the doors."—There was one in the east, and two in the south side of the room. Rebecca rose immediately, and as she put the fork over the latch, a man rushed against the door. I then arose and ran to the southeast door. And as I placed the fork over the latch, the man that used to be my husband rushed in, and I ran out.

In a moment I stood in the upper door, in the southwest corner, which opened south. I looked down in the dooryard and saw a well. Then it was a tub with a pump in the middle. I then saw one of our brethren standing at the lower door, out of which I had fled, having a watermelon in his hand. He tossed it into the tub and it splashed. He tossed another and it splashed more than the first. He tossed a third, and they moved around and stood up on end in the south side of the tub. And when they began to move, I saw many in the tub. He then tossed the fourth, which was larger than all the rest, and it plunged to the bottom, a great distance below the top of the ground. I then perceived it was a well. And as the melon rose to the top of the water, it shook the whole earth.

I looked east and saw a river of ice which ran north and south, and three ice rocks in it, and three men upon the rocks with their faces toward me. And the shaking of the earth caused the river, the rocks, and the men to move up and down, and the men moved their hands like a person shooting.

On the south side of these rocks, I saw a man coming on a white horse. The man, the horse, the rocks, the river, and the elements over them, were all one transparent brightness—white as snow and bright as silver, when the sun's rays are reflected from its surface. The man and the horse were small. Rays of light emanating from the man's head formed a beautiful circle. And I thought in my heart, the sight was magnificent. As the man came toward me, I awoke.

It was five o'clock. It struck four just before I went into my vision.

March 20, 1848. I dreamed that Rebecca Perot and I were in a house upon a rock together, and a storm arose, which made us feel that we were in great danger. A storm arose also in the west, and both met together and came with great force upon the house. A stream of water ran north and south upon the east side of the house. And I thought the storm would dash the house into the water and it would carry us down to New York, and then our friends would see our good home, and our destruction also. I felt not to go out, and I said to Rebecca, "We will stay in the house," though the storm was heavy. And the house stood firm, because it was on a rock. [W. R.] . . .

February 9, 1849. After a spiritual conversation with Brother P. about departed spirits, I felt a strong desire to know something about the condition of my natural mother. I earnestly entreated my Heavenly Parents to let me know how it was with her. I went to bed, and dreamed that I was going west, to bear testimony, and I was called into a garden south. The gate opened north. A sister led me through the garden southward, and in the southwest corner was a [flower] bed on which lay a woman. The sister told me that she owned the garden, and was asleep. But I perceived that she saw me. The garden was full of all manner of sweet flowers in full bloom, and the perfumes thereof was beyond description. The sister picked me some flowers, and told me to pick some, which I did. And she led me out of the north gate, [and with a smile bade me farewell].

The eyes of the woman that lay on the bed of flowers followed me until I passed out [with an endearing look that I never shall forget]. Then I went and bore testimony. [After I came out of the vision, it was made known to me that the woman in the bed was my mother, and that she was a caretaker of children. That young sister told me she helped her take care of the flower garden.] [W. R.] . . .

February 14, 1850. I earnestly prayed to God that He would give me something the next day, that would encourage me in His holy work, as that is my birthday. [W. R.]

On the morning of the 15th, I dreamed that I was housekeeping in Philadelphia, and had around me a little family of spiritual children, and among them was Susan Thomas and Rebecca Perot. I was busy at the table, preparing something to eat, and somebody came and told me they wished me to take a young child and care for it until it was four years old, and then somebody else would take it and keep it until it was eight. For its mother was a poor girl.

While they talked, I heard the child crying. And I wanted Susan and Rebecca to hasten and get their work done, and go out and bring the child. I felt ashamed of them, because they did not do their work. At length the child ceased crying, while I was talking to some who wished to hear what I was saying. When I considered how long the child had ceased crying, I started off in a hurry, just as I was, with my hands from the dough, thinking the child had cried itself to death.

I went up 7th Street to Spruce Street and up Spruce to 8th. And on the right hand, going down 8th, stood a box about four feet long, on four legs, and in it was the child. When I went to it, it looked at me and smiled. I took it up and pressed it to my bosom, and it nestled its little face in my neck. Oh, how I loved it! I said, "Keep it four years! My! I will keep it forever!—It shall be my own child." It was a darling boy, yea, a proper child. I brought it home and took care of it. And oh, how I loved it! So healthy a child in every respect, I have not seen for many a day.

I then awoke, and after I awoke I loved the child still. In the evening of February 15th, as I went to draw down the curtain, I thought I would look out first and see if there was a new moon. And

I saw the new moon over my right shoulder. Oh, I thought, that was good! Then I recollected it was the evening of my birthday, and what I had prayed for the day before, and how the Lord had this morning encouraged me in my dream, and I loved my darling boy still.

This is indeed a spiritual dream, which greatly encourages me. I am fifty-five years old today. Nineteen years of this I have spent in the service of God, in obedience to my call to the Gospel. Thirteen years thereof, *I have dedicated my soul and body to the Lord in a virgin life,* for which I do this day lift up my heart, my thought, my mind, my soul, with all my strength, in thanksgiving to God, who in His unbounded mercy has looked upon me, the least of all His people, and has shown me such great things, and has given me such great faith to patiently wait upon the Lord, and to know His voice from all others. Glory! Glory! Glory! to God the Father, and to Holy Mother Wisdom, and to my Blessed Savior, and to my Blessed Mother Ann Lee, who in mercy thus looked upon poor helpless me. [W. R.] . . .

March 20, 1850, I dreamed that Rebecca Perot and I were in a garden, and a sister was with us. She suddenly disappeared, and in a moment I understood that the people designed to kill us. I wanted Rebecca to make haste, and we would fly to Philadelphia, but she hindered me a long time. At last we went. And as we went, we met the people. The men had killed all the women and children, and were dragging them like dogs through the street. I flew westward above them all until we came to a street that ran north and south. Rebecca went south, and I kept on west.

Directly I perceived they were locking a large door behind me, and by looking I found that I was in a large building, and they were pursuing with intent to kill me. I continued to fly above them until I found an open place at the top in the northeast corner of the building, out of which I flew, and found myself in another, and heard them lock the gate behind me. In this way, I passed through three places. And from the last place I was let out by a little boy. He led me through a room in which an aged woman was sitting. She looked at me but did not speak.

He led me through a hall and then into a room where there was a large bulldog, and a lion. They were both at the door through which I was agoing to pass out into the street. The dog rose to his feet and looked at me, and then at the lion, as if to ask the lion whether or no he would let me pass. I had to pass between them if I passed at all. My all was at stake—if I stayed I would be killed, and if I went, I could only be killed. So I prayed, and passed through, and they had not power to touch me.

I came out into the street. The day was clear, and the way was beautiful, and just as I was agoing to fly, I awoke. [W. R.] . . .

March 27, 1851, I dreamt that Rebecca and me lived together. The door opened west, and there was a river that came from the west and it ran eastward, passing our house on the south side and one part came front on the west—a beautiful white water. I stood in the west door looking westward on the beautiful river. I saw Rebecca Perot coming in the river, her face to the east, and she aplunging in the water every few steps, head foremost, abathing herself. She only had on her undergarment. She was pure and clean, even as the water in which she was abathing. She came facing me out of the water. I wondered she was not afraid. Sometimes she would be hid, for a moment, and then she would rise again. She looked like an Angel, oh, how bright! R. J. [W. R.] . . .

January 6, 1856. I dreamt that Rebecca and me were together, and Sally Ann Parker came in. I got up, after speaking to Sally Ann, and went out of the room. I was gone a few minutes, and when I came in, I found that Sally Ann had combed all Rebecca's hair out. And her hair was black, sleek, and short. I put my hand upon it with great sorrow, and said, "Oh, you have combed all her hair out!" She made light of it. I said, "I would not have had it done for nothing! I have took so much pains, and had got it so long." "Long?" she said. "Yes, I had," I replied.

She then took a large bun of hair from somewhere. And holding it in her right hand, turning it over, "Long?" she said. "Yea," I said. And she began to pull it out in locks. "Why, I did not know it was so long."

All this time, Rebecca was making light of it. And when I looked again, the hair on her head had become gray and stubby and curly and hard. I put my hand on it. And oh, I did lament over it! [W. R.]

February 14, 1856. I desired that I might receive something on my birthday that would strengthen me in my pilgrimage.

In the morning of the 15th, when I came down stairs, Rebecca said to me, "Mother, the door was open all night." I stood for some moments like one amazed. I knew not what to say. When I collected my senses, these words were spoken. "You asked me to give you something that would strengthen you in your pilgrimage. What else could I give you, that would have strengthened you more than that? All that you had, your own life and the life of Rebecca also, was exposed to murderers, and the people's goods, that you have in the house, to thieves. And who but I, the Lord your God, have preserved you and all your house? Then be faithful."

This was the answer to my prayers. My heart was humbled within me, and Rebecca and I poured forth our souls to God in prayer, with tears and strong cries, that He would strengthen us in all things and at all times, to do His holy will. Rebecca Jackson and Rebecca Perot. [W. R.]

February 19, 1856. After I laid down to rest, I was in sweet meditation. And a beautiful vision passed before my spirit eye. I saw a garden of excellent fruit. And it appeared to come near, even onto my bed, and around me! Yea, it covered me. And I was permitted to eat, and to give a portion to Rebecca Perot, and she ate, and was strengthened. Rebecca Jackson. [W. R.]

Wednesday, February 27, 1856. While Rebecca and I were sitting at our work and conversing about our home in Zion, and about the kindness of our beloved brethren and sisters, and about one sister in particular who left the form soon after we came away, Rebecca said, "Mother, have you never seen her?" "Nay," I answered.

And the word had no sooner passed my lips, than I saw her coming toward me from the east, descending a beautiful hill which appeared to slope from north to south. She came down the west side, with a beautiful heavenly smile on her countenance. She looked me in the face with an endearing look of heavenly love, and gave me a bunch of grapes, and a book for Rebecca and a gold chain to place around her neck. She said, "Mother says this will help you to overcome your nature, and give you strength to conquer all your enemies, and that book will give you understanding. Be faithful." She then gave a bunch of cherries, a basket of apples, and a bright sword to cut her way through all opposition. Such was the mighty power of God attending these heavenly gifts, that we continued to feel its divine influence for many days. That beautiful hill where I first saw our beloved sister was all light, and glistened with a silver bright mist, which was all the time moving through the air, and on and through the trees, and among the grass. . . .

January 7, 1857, was a day of deep meditation and of heartfelt sorrow for my sins and my many shortcomings in the sight of a just and holy God, who will reward every soul according as their work shall be.

While I was reading in Holy Mother Wisdom's Book, where She was giving Her holy heavenly counsel to the daughters of the children of men, it was there, yea, it was there I saw my unholiness before a pure and holy God, and before Holy and Ever-blessed Mother Wisdom. It was there I saw Her tender loving Mother's care for all Her poor helpless daughters. It was there I saw Her everlasting care, and unchangeable love and kindness, which She bestows upon all. After I laid the Holy Book away, I received counsel in the most feeling and tender manner, from Holy, Ever-blessed Mother Wisdom.

Oh, Her loving and heavenly counsel was indeed the dew of Heaven to my poor thirsty soul! Truly the reproof of a friend is better than the kiss of an enemy. And where, oh, where is there one that is better able to be a friend to poor helpless souls than Holy Mother Wisdom, the Mother of men and angels—yea, the Mother of Christ the Bridegroom, and the Mother of the Bride, the Lamb's wife? It is Her of whom Solomon wrote, saying, "Wisdom has builded Her house. She has hewn out Her seven pillars. She has sent forth Her maidens." And when I think that I am blessed to live in the day that Solomon wrote of, I am happy, I am thankful, I am little, I am humble, I am meek and lowly in heart and in mind and spirit. And I will be good, I will be faithful, I will forsake all for Christ's sake and the Gospel, and I will be one of Mother's little, humble children. R.J. [W. R.] . . .

Wednesday, February 14, 1857. I dreamed that a large mastiff dog was trying to hold Rebecca and I, with intent to kill us or have us killed. I shot him in the forehead, between his eyes. [W. R.]

Carolina ("Linka")
Keyser Preus
[1829–1880]

Agnes Louise Carlsen and Christian Nicolai Keyser of Christiana, Norway had eight children—a son followed by seven daughters, of whom "Linka" was the oldest. After the death of both parents, the seven girls were placed in a grandmother's care in a household where Linka assumed domestic responsibilities at a young age. As her father had been a pastor and professor of theology, no one was surprised when Linka announced her engagement to Herman Preus, also a Lutheran minister and a cousin she had known all her life. When Herman Preus received a call to become the new minister at the Norwegian community at Spring Prairie, Wisconsin, the couple decided to marry and the newlyweds sailed for America in 1851. After arriving in New York, the couple traveled by steamer up the Hudson River to Albany, by train to Niagara Falls, by steamer on the "inland sea" to Detroit, by train to New Buffalo, Michigan, by steamer to Chicago and Milwaukee, and by wagon to their final destination of Spring Prairie. There they settled permanently and raised two sons and two daughters.

Linka and Herman Preus thus became part of the millions who have immigrated to the United States since 1607. Linka and Herman Preus traveled in 1851, one of the peak periods of immigration from Europe. They were among the early settlers from Scandinavia, most of whom followed later in the century and many of whom, like the Preuses before them, settled in the Midwest. For Linka, as for many young women in her situation, marriage was synonymous with departure to a new homeland.

May 4, 1851. And so the time has come when I shall take leave of Girlhood and say a wistful "I thank thee" for cherished companionship. What thou hast meant to me, I know full well, but what Wifehood may have in store for me is a mystery.—But Thou, O God, wilt be with me and all will be well; in this hope I face the future with confidence and good cheer.—Adieu, sweet Girlhood, we have always been good friends; I recall no occasion when I wearied of thee; and still I have decided to part company with thee.—There must, indeed, be something attractive about being a wife since I have decided to become one; but what is it?

"Tell me, my cousin Independence, do I enjoy thee more as wife or as maiden?"

"Indeed, as wife you become nothing but a slave."

"Dear me, then I dare not marry—"

"Indeed, that is what you ought to do. Very likely you will never feel the slavery of wifehood; rather you will be giving thought to woman's calling in life, and then your love and your common sense will teach you to heed its voice, and as you say, you will no longer remember me, your cousin Independence; and that is all to the good, for in reality I do belong to the husband."

"How could I ever forget thee, Independence, whom I so dearly love!—Yet, this evening I shall take leave of thee also, but with the conviction that thou art not resentful because as a maiden I made thee my companion. That a spark of affection for thee will always smoulder within my heart, I have no doubt."—But since it is so ordered that it must be subdued, I pray God to help me set it aside.

"In the meantime I am too stubborn to agree with thee that the maiden shall give no thought to Independence. A human being is a free and independent creature, and I would recommend that every woman consider this, and I insist that every maiden owes it to herself to do so. Circumstances may arise where it will be of no essential benefit to her, but rarely will it be to her disadvantage if she combines it with determination and self-confidence."—Oh, but that I must not do; for it is this very determination which frequently has caused me distress throughout my girlhood years.

From *Linka's Diary: On Land and Sea, 1845–1864*. trans. and ed. Johan Carl Keyser Preus and Diderikke Margrethe Brandt Preus (Minneapolis: Augsburg, 1952). © Augsburg Publishing House. Reprinted by permission.

Here I find myself writing a regular dissertation, and one which perhaps does not even make sense. That is because I am deeply moved at the thought of saying "Fare-thee-well" and "I thank thee, sweet Girlhood." "This, I know, thou wilt understand. What stronger proof of friendship can I give thee than this, that at our parting I say: 'Though as a wife I attain the highest degree of earthly happiness, my girlhood days shall never be forgotten.' " I have a feeling that every happy hour I spend as a wife shall be placed in the balance over against my girlhood days. Should sorrow be involved, the same would be true; and now in recognition of man's need of sorrows I would say: "May Wifehood, when placed in the balance, never suffer in comparison with Girlhood!" . . .

The 10th of July, Thursday, 1851. Seven weeks to the day since we left Norway, we are rapidly approaching New York; only a few miles remain; and if the wind continues and the fog does not thicken, we should be there in a few hours. . . .

Since seven o'clock this morning we have sighted land. I am not looking forward to the landing, though I am glad that we shall again have our feet on firm ground. A strange depression of spirit has yesterday and today come over me; I seem unable to master it.

The 16th of July, 1851. Already I feel like a resident of New York, and with what have I busied myself since my last effusion? That was late afternoon on the tenth of July. It was then we dropped anchor just off Staten Island after making our way through storm, lightning, and thunder showers into the great jaws of the harbor. Not at any time during our voyage have we encountered such violent thunder storms as those with which America greeted us. In a moment all sails were struck, and still the ship careened mightily. Thunder, lightning, and a heavy downpour—it made me shudder. Still, there was no time to become frightened; the land was right ahead and absorbed our attention completely. After seven weeks at sea, we naturally were delighted at the sight of land; and from our hearts did we thank our heavenly Father for guiding us across the sea to the new country.— Without Thee, O God, we can do nothing, wretched sinners that we are!

It was hardly a pleasing reception America accorded us; just as contrary winds had harassed us during the voyage, so now the heavy squalls, in demonstration of their power, seemed to be putting us to the test, as to whether we could face it—almost as though the purpose were to turn us back. Still, it was to no avail that Norway sent us contrary south wind just as we were weighing anchor—we did not return to the land which so reluctantly let us go; nor was it to any avail that America sent against us the west wind—it could not turn us back.—Indeed no power is great over against Thy will, O God. If Thou be for us, who can be against us? Thou great and good Ruler, Creator of the world, without whose will not even a leaf falls to the ground! Thanks be to Thee for bringing us all, one hundred and sixty-nine human beings, safely to shore. Sincere are our thanks, and from grateful hearts—or are we perchance such evil creatures that the word "sincere" may be false? No, no, we cannot possibly be that selfish.—Our hearts are deeply stirred; they stammer forth their prayers of thanksgiving. Of Thy mercy, O Father, hear our prayer for Christ's sake!

It was amazing to observe the innumerable ships, sailing out and countersailing in the harbor, and it excited our admiration to see the speed with which they were able to lower their sails—and there we all lay, like plucked chickens! The instant a squall had passed, up went a couple of sails, only to be hauled down for the next one. But the countryside, how beautiful! The entrance to the harbor was pleasing to the eye; but how surprising to see the fields already out, the haycocks enjoying their surroundings! The other passengers have recovered sufficiently to join us in marveling at the things we see.

There we dropped anchor—"Captain, thank you, thank you, for bringing us safely into port!" said I, as I gripped his hand with a trusty handshake.

The Pilot was odd. He sat in an easy chair and issued commands. I did not like him. He left the ship with the customs official who had come aboard and I did not say goodbye to him.

We were not permitted to go ashore, nor was anyone allowed to come on board. An immigrant swindler did sneak up and try to persuade the Captain to turn crook. In this he failed; Falchenberg, our Captain, is a man of honor and would play no one false; with scorn was the swindler sent on his way.

Next came the Doctor. He permitted us to go ashore. The Captain, Ziølner, Herman, and I rowed over to Staten Island and spent some time sight-seeing. As we passed the home of the Doctor, he treated oranges, offered us through the window of his home; the Captain had told him I was a minister's wife; we appreciated the kindness. As we were about to return to our ship, we were delayed by thunder, lightning, and squalls for about one and one-half hours; by the time we were again on board, it was midnight.

During the night three sailors stole the best boat on the *Columbus* and made their getaway—the scoundrels! Since that night the Captain and the Chief Mate have alternated in standing watch, and no one has escaped, though attempts have been made.

Friday, July the eleventh, we were taken by steamer to New York. We had previously by row boat visited Staten Island where the Captain was surrounded by agents from various concerns. We reached New York in a very short time. On the pier we stood; but how desolate and dreary in spite of the noise on every hand. We could hardly draw a deep breath. In all that mass of humanity there was not a familiar face; no one to be seen but shouting hucksters and peddlers, or tradesmen, breathless in their hurry of business, and scurrying to get aboard some bus which in the shortest possible time could bring them to their office. Today we visited the Bureau of Exchange and also the Consulate, where we met several of our countrymen. We had a table-d'hote dinner with some Danes.

My head was in a whirl and I was extremely tired in the evening when we returned to the *Columbus.* I gave my fellow travelers a description of New York which was not very complimentary. One of a group of immigrants who had gone ashore helped me in my description by exclaiming: "And you ought to see their horses, great big beasts they are, and would you believe it, they have white and red woven covers on their ears!" By this he meant a netting in which the whole horse was inclosed, network adorned with fringes and spread out to protect against horse-flies. It is used on draught horses and carriage horses; some have straps across the back and tassels on the ears.

On shipboard, life had been relatively quiet; the people had made little noise, save as they sang, danced, and chatted as they walked back and forth between the galley and their living room, carrying with them their lunch pails and frying pans. Throughout our seven weeks' voyage our ears had become adjusted to all this, to the accompaniment of the roar of the sea and the unsteady bluster and whistling of winds, together with shouted commands of the ship's officers. No wonder we were now confused by the noise of innumerable wagons, horses, and people, trying to make their way across every street. At street corners we frequently had to wait fifteen minutes before we could cross, and if we tried to pass the time by conversing, we were compelled to shout at the top of our voices, and still we could rarely hear what was said.—What a relief to be back on the *Columbus!*

The same busy activity which prevailed in the city was in evidence also in the harbor. Countless steamboats, some small, others larger, chugged and scurried out and in between Staten Island and New York. They came from many surrounding points: Hoboken, Jersey, Long Island; many of them carrying only people, with which they literally swarm even though they touch at the same places every half hour. Others are engaged in towing ships and their crews in or out of the harbor.

Ships are passing back and forth; many beautifully constructed sloops, schooners, and brigs daily passed us while we were living on the *Columbus.*

Emigrant ships lay at anchor alongside of us and according as the tide moved the ships, we had occasion to greet one another. An indescribable confusion exists in the harbor, corresponding perfectly to the city with its railroads, omnibuses, cabs, and dray wagons.

That people who live daily in such tumult and noise have the appearance of consumptives is not surprising. Rather it strikes me that all the people look poorly. The ladies resemble china dolls which readily could be toppled by the mere touch of a breath or a finger. The men are tall, gaunt, pale figures, whose frail pelican-legs are in danger of breaking off at every step—how, pray, do they fare when they shall bow in order to help a lady? For it is evident that when the opportunity is at hand, the American plays the chevalier; women have an honored place among them and exercise great power.

Amelia Stewart Knight
[N.D.]

On September 18, 1834, Boston-born Amelia Stewart married Joel Knight,
who had come with his family from England as a young man. A hatter
by trade, Knight had come to Boston to study medicine, and when these
studies were completed, the family moved to Iowa where they remained
for sixteen years. In 1853, the Knights decided to join the many Americans
who were moving further West. They were the parents of seven children
when they left by wagon train on the five-month journey. At the time of
their departure, Amelia was four months pregnant with their eighth child,
a fact she never mentions until the child is born outside of Troutdale,
Oregon, as they near their destination.

The Knights were part of an extraordinary movement of people that
saw 250,000 Americans cross the continent from 1840 to 1870. The com-
mon practice of keeping a journal record of the trip makes the westward
expansion one of the best-documented periods of American history. One of
the most vivid accounts of life with a wagon train, Amelia Knight's diary
conveys both the excitement and the extreme hardship of the transcontinen-
tal trip.

[1853]

Tuesday, July 19th—Came 15 miles. Crossed Rock Creek about
noon in the midst of all the dust; we had a nice little shower, which
laid the dust and made the traveling much better. Camped about three
o'clock close to a canyon on Rock Creek.

Wednesday, July 20th—Dry traveling today. No grass; water is
very scarce. Stopped at noon to water at a very bad place on Snake

From Amelia Stewart Knight, "Diary of an Oregon Pioneer of 1853," *Transactions
of the Oregon Pioneer Association, Fifty-Sixth Annual Reunion* (1928), pp. 38–56. The
manuscript of the diary is at the University of Washington Library.

River, one and a half miles or more down a steep bank or precipice. The cattle looked like little dogs down there, and after all the trouble of getting the poor things down there, they were so tired they could not drink, and were obliged to travel back and take the dusty road again. We are still traveling on in search of water, water.

Thursday, July 21st—Very warm, traveled 25 miles yesterday and camped after dark one-half mile from Snake River. Crossed Salmon River about noon today and are now traveling down Snake River, till we reach the ferry. Afternoon—Came 12 miles and have camped close to the ferry. Our turn will come to cross in the night. Have to pay 4 dollars a wagon, cross on a ferry boat, and swim the stock, which is a very hard job, on such a large river. Indians all around our wagons.

Friday, July 22nd—Crossed the river before daybreak and found the smell of carrion so bad that we left as soon as possible. The dead cattle were lying in every direction. Still there were a good many getting their breakfast among all the stench. I walked off among the rocks, while the men were getting the cattle ready; then we drove a mile or so, and halted to get breakfast. Here Chat had a very narrow escape from being run over. Just as we were all getting ready to start, Chatfield, the rascal, came around the forward wheel to get into the wagon, and at that moment the cattle started and he fell under the wagon. Somehow he kept from under the wheels, and escaped with only a good, or I should say, a bad scare. I never was so much frightened in my life. I was in the wagon at the time, putting things in order, and supposed Francis was taking care of him. After traveling 6 miles, we have encamped for the day, to rest the cattle; plenty of good grass. Afternoon, rained some.

Saturday, July 23rd—We took a fresh start this morning with everything in order, for a good day's drive. Travel about 5 miles and here we are, up a stump again, with a worse place than we ever had before us to be crossed, called Bridge Creek. I presume it takes its name from a natural bridge which crosses it. This bridge is only wide enough to admit one person at a time. A frightful place, with the water roaring and tumbling ten or fifteen feet below it. This bridge is composed of rocks, and all around us, it is nothing but a solid mass of rocks, with the water ripping and tearing over them. Here we have to unload all the wagons and pack everything across by hand, and then we are only on an island. There is a worse place to cross yet, a branch of the same. Have to stay on the island all night, and wait our turn to cross. There are a good many camped on the island, and there are camps on each side of it. There is no chance to pitch a tent, and this island is a solid rock, so we must sleep the best way we can, with the water roaring on each side of us. The empty wagons, cattle, and horses have to be taken further up the river and crossed by means of chains and ropes. The way we cross this branch is to climb down about 6 feet on rocks, and then a wagon bed bottom will just reach across, from rocks to rocks. It must then be fastened at each end with ropes or chains, so that you can cross on it, and then we climb up the rocks on the other side, and in this way everything has to be taken across. Some take their wagons to pieces and take them over in that way.

Sunday, July 24th—Crossed the river this morning and got loaded up; then traveled 16½ miles without water; then we came to a creek of poison water in the bottom. Did not dare to stay there. Came on a mile and a half to a spring in the bottom, and have camped. Have to keep watch all night.

Monday, July 25th—Bad luck this morning to start with. A calf took sick and died before breakfast. Soon after starting one of our best cows was taken sick and died in a short time. Presume they were both poisoned with water or weeds. Left our poor cow for the wolves and started on. Evening—It has been very warm today. Traveled 18 miles and have camped right on top of a high, round sand hill, a fine mark for the Indians. We have also got on to a place that is full of rattle-snakes. One of our oxen sick.

Tuesday, July 26th—Very warm and terribly dusty. We ascended a long and tedious mountain this forenoon; crossed one little creek about noon, all the water we have seen today. It is near night and we are still traveling on, and urging our poor, tired cattle on till we find water. It looks as though it never rained in this region, it is so dry and dusty. We have been jumping and jolting over rocks all day and are now about to camp near a creek of clear, cold water. Traveled 17 miles.

Wednesday, July 27th—Another fine cow died this afternoon. Came 15 miles today, and have camped at the boiling springs, a great curiosity. They bubble up out of the earth boiling hot. I have only to pour water on to my tea and it is made. There is no cold water in this part. (Husband and myself wandered far down this branch, as far as we dare, to find it cool enough to bathe in. It was still very hot, and I believe I never spent such an uneasy sleepless night in my life. I felt as if I was in the bad place. I still believe it was not very far off. I was glad when morning came and we left).

Thursday, July 28th—Filled all the empty vessels last night with water to cool for the stock. Have traveled 12 miles today and have camped in the prairie 5 or 6 miles from water. Chat is quite sick with scarlet fever.

Friday, July 29th—Came 18 miles over some very rocky road and camped by a spring. Chat is some better.

Saturday, July 30th—Traveled 16 miles over a very hilly, but good road and camped by a stream of water and good grass. It has been very warm today.

Sunday, July 31st—Cool and pleasant, but very dusty. Came 12 miles and camped about one o'clock not very far from Boise River. We will stay here a day or two and rest and revive our cattle.

Monday, August 1st—Still in camp, have been washing all day, and all hands have had all the wild currants we could eat. They grow in great abundance along this river. There are three kinds, red, black, and yellow. This evening another of our best milk cows died. Cattle are dying off very fast all along this road. We are hardly ever out of sight of dead cattle on this side of Snake River. This cow was well and fat an hour before she died. Cut the second cheese today.

Tuesday, August 2nd—Traveled 12 miles today and have just camped about one-half mile from the river. Plenty of good grass.

Thursday, August 4th—We have just crossed Boise or Reed's River. It is deep fording, but, by raising the wagon beds about a foot, and being very careful, we are all landed safe and about to camp not far from the bank of the river. Have traveled 20 miles today. Have also seen a good many Indians and bought fish of them. They all seem peaceable and friendly.

Friday, August 5th—We have just bid the beautiful Boise River, with her green timber and rich currants; farewell, and are now on our way to the ferry on Snake River. Evening—Traveled 18 miles today and have just reached Fort Boise and camped. Our turn will come to cross some time tomorrow. There is one small ferry boat running here, owned by the Hudson's Bay Company. Have to pay three dollars a wagon. Our worst trouble at these large rivers is swimming the stock over. Often after swimming half way over the poor things will turn and come out again. At this place, however, there are Indians who swim the river from morning till night. There is many a drove of cattle that could not be got over without their help. By paying them a small sum, they will take a horse by the bridle or halter and swim over with him. The rest of the horses all follow and by driving and hurrahing to the cattle they will almost always follow the horses, sometimes they fail and turn back. This Fort Boise is nothing more than three new buildings, its inhabitants, the Hudson's Bay Company officials, a few Frenchmen, some half-naked Indians, half breeds, etc.

Saturday, August 6th—Got all safe across the river by noon, and it being 15 miles to the next water, we are obliged to camp here, near the river, till morning. Camps all around us.

Sunday, August 7th—Traveled 15 miles, and have just reached Malheur River and camped. The roads have been very dusty, no water, nothing but dust and dead cattle all day, the air filled with the odor from dead cattle.

Monday, August 8th—We have to make a drive of 22 miles, without water today. Have our cans filled to drink. Here we left, unknowingly, our Lucy behind, not a soul had missed her until we had gone some miles, when we stopped a while to rest the cattle; just then another train drove up behind us, with Lucy. She was terribly frightened and so were some more of us when we found out what a narrow escape she had run. She said she was sitting under the bank of the river, when we started, busy watching some wagons cross, and did not know we were ready. And I supposed she was in Mr. Carl's wagon, as he always took charge of Francis and Lucy and I took care of Myra and Chat. When starting he asked for Lucy, and Francis said "She is in Mother's Wagon," as she often went there to have her hair combed. It was a lesson to all of us. Evening—It is near dark and we are still toiling on till we find a camping place. The little ones have curled down and gone to sleep without supper. Wind high, and it is cold enough for a great coat and mittens.

Tuesday, August 9th—Came into camp last night at nine o'clock, after traveling 19½ miles, with enough water in our cans to make tea for supper; men all tired and hungry. I groped around in the dark and got supper over, after a fashion. We are now on our way to Birch Creek, which is two and a half miles from our camp. Halted at Birch Creek and got breakfast, then started on and traveled as far as Burnt River—17 miles—and camped.

Wednesday, August 10th—Traveled 12 miles; crossed Burnt River 5 times and have camped on the bank of it, about 4 o'clock in the afternoon to repair the wagons. Evening cold.

Thursday, August 11th—Frost this morning. Three of our hands got discontented and left this morning, to pack through. I am pleased, as we shall get along just as well without them and I shall have three less to wait on. Evening—Came 10 miles today and crossed Burnt River four times and have camped near a small spring, about three miles from the river.

Friday, August 12—Came 12 miles today. Crossed Burnt River twice. Lost one of our oxen. We were traveling slowly along, when he dropped dead in the yoke. We unyoked and turned out the odd ox, and drove around the dead one, and so it is all along the road, we are continually driving around the dead cattle, and shame on the man who has no pity for the poor dumb brutes that have to travel and toil month after month on this desolate road. I could hardly help shedding tears, when we drove round this poor ox who had helped us along thus far, and have given us his very last step. We have camped on a branch of Burnt River.

Saturday, August 13th—Traveled 5 miles this morning, then stopped to water at a spring; it is near night. We are still traveling on, through dust and sand and over rocks, until we find water. Had none since morning.

Sunday, August 14th—Camped last night after dark after traveling 15 miles, in a large bottom, near some puddles of very poor water.

Found out this, that it needed straining. Afternoon—After traveling 10 miles we have camped on the bank of Powder River about one o'clock. Another ox sick. We will rest here until morning.

Monday, August 15th—Traveled 11 miles (Powder River is a small, clear stream), and have camped on a small creek, 12 miles from the Grand Ronde Valley.

Tuesday, August 16th—Slow traveling on account of our oxen having sore feet and the roads being very rocky. Passed the Sylvest Springs. Traveled 12 miles and now we have a long steep, rocky hill to descend into the valley. It is a mile long, very steep and very rocky. From the top of this hill, we could see a band of Indian horses in the valley below, and being mostly white, they looked like a flock of chickens. After reaching the bottom of this hill with a good deal of difficulty, we find ourselves in a most lovely valley, and have camped close to a spring, which runs through it. There are also two or three trading posts here, and a great many fine looking Cayuse Indians riding around on their handsome ponies.

Wednesday, August 17th—Crossed the Grand Ronde Valley, which is 8 miles across, and have camped close to the foot of the mountains. Good water and feed plenty. There 50 or more wagons camped around us. Lucy and Myra have their feet and legs poisoned, which gives me a good deal of trouble. Bought some fresh salmon of the Indians this evening, which is quite a treat to us. It is the first we have seen.

Thursday, August 18th—Commenced the ascent of the Blue Mountains. It is a lovely morning and all hands seem to be delighted with the prospect of being so near the timber again, after the weary months of travel on the dry, dusty sage plains, with nothing to relieve the eye. Just now the men are hallooing to their echo rings through the woods. Evening—Traveled 10 miles today and down steep hills, and have just camped on the banks of Grand Ronde River in a dense forest of pine timber—a most beautiful country.

Friday, August 19th—Quite cold morning, water frozen over in the buckets. Traveled 13 miles, over very bad roads, without water. After looking in vain for water, we were about to give up as it was near night, when husband came across a company of friendly Cayuse

Indians about to camp, who showed him where to find water, half mile down a steep mountain, and we have all camped together, with plenty of pine timber all around us. The men and boys have driven the cattle down to water and I am waiting for water to get supper. This forenoon we bought a few potatoes from an Indian, which will be a treat for our supper.

Saturday, August 20th—Cold all day. Came 11 miles and camped about two o'clock in a pine and fir forest close to a small stream of poor water. Grass very scarce. Fifteen miles more and we will leave the Blue Mountains.

Sunday, August 21st—Cold. After a great deal of trouble to find all our cattle, we got started about 11 o'clock and traveled 4 miles, then stopped to noon, not far from a spring; then traveled 3 or 4 miles and turned out to let the cattle feed an hour. Feed very scarce. Evening —We are descending a long mountain. It is nearly dark. Came 12 miles and still traveling.

Monday, August 22nd—I began to think last night that we would never get to the foot of the mountain. It was 4 miles long. However, we came into camp after nine o'clock at night and find ourselves in the Umatilla Valley, a warmer climate, more like summer. No feed for the poor stock. We are now traveling on the Nez Perce plains. Warm weather and very dusty. Came 12 miles and camped at a spring one-half mile from Umatilla River. Grass all dead, but the stock eat it greedily. For fuel, willows and some little sage brush.

Tuesday, August 23rd—Very warm. Grass all dead. The dust is worse than ever today. I can hardly see the tongue cattle.

Wednesday, August 24th—Traveled 20 miles yesterday and came into camp after dark on the banks of the Umatilla River. Numbers were camped around us. No feed for the poor stock. It is quite warm. Came 5 miles this morning and have just stopped at the Indian Agency to fill our cans at the well. Evening—After filling our cans with water, we came on and stopped at noon, and let the cattle pick dry grass, as it is too warm to travel in the middle of the day, then came 10 miles and crossed Butter Creek, then came a mile up the creek and have encamped near a good spring and as there is no feed near the road, the men have driven the stock a mile and a half out, to dry bunch grass.

Thursday, August 25th—We will remain in camp today to wash, and rest the cattle. It is 18 miles to the next water. Cotton wood and willows to burn. We will start this evening and travel a few miles after dark. It is too hot and dusty to travel in the heat of the day. Camped about nine o'clock in the dry prairie.

Friday, August 26th—Came 6 miles last night and 12 today, and have just reached a small spring, where we can only water one ox at a time by dipping up buckets full. This spring seems to rise out of the ground and then fall again right off. We will camp here and drive the cattle a mile to feed; a good many Indians camped around us. Bought salmon of them for supper and breakfast. Sage brush to burn.

Saturday, August 27th—Came 5 miles and stopped at the well spring about noon and watered the stock, then drove them out to grass. This well spring is not much better than a mud hole. We will remain in camp until evening. Our cattle are weak, and in order to save them, we travel slowly and rest during the heat of the day. Fifteen miles to the next water.

Sunday, August 28th—Started last night about sun down and drove 5 miles and found tolerably good grass to turn the cattle out to. Started very early this morning and drove as far as Willow Creek, 10 miles, and camped again till evening. Plenty of willow to burn, but no running water. It is standing in holes along the creek and very poor. It will be 22 miles before we get water again.

Monday, August 29th—Traveled 10 miles last night and 12 today, and have camped about one o'clock on Rock Creek. Weather very warm and dust bad.

Tuesday, August 30th—Traveled 7 miles this morning. Crossed Rock Creek 4 times and have just crossed John Day River and encamped on the bank of it about one o'clock, not far from a trading post. Here husband sold an ox that was unable to work for 25 dollars. We will make the best of this river, as it is 25 miles to the next. Our camp is in a very p[r]etty valley or glade, surrounded by hills, and our cattle and horses are feeding among the hills. A mile or two distant and close to us lies the river, a beautiful, clear stream running over a gravelly bottom.

Wednesday, August 31st—Still in camp. It was too stormy to start out last evening, as intended. The wind was very high all the afternoon, and the dust and sand so bad we could hardly see. Thundered and rained a little in the evening. It rained and blew very hard all night. Is still raining this morning, the air cold and chilly. It blew so hard last night as to blow our buckets and pans from under the wagons, and this morning we found them (and other things which were not secured) scattered all over the valley. One or two pans came up missing. Everything is packed up ready for a start. The men folks are out hunting the cattle. The children and myself are out shivering around in the wagons, nothing for fires in these parts, and the weather is very disagreeable. Evening—Got a late start this morning. Traveled about a mile, and were obliged to stop and turn the cattle out on account of rain. At noon it cleared off. We ate dinner and started. Came up a long and awful rock hollow, in danger every moment of smashing our wagons. After traveling 7 miles, we halted in the prairie long enough to cook supper. Split up some of the deck boards of our wagons to make fire. Got supper over, and are on our way again. Cloudy and quite cold all day.

Thursday, September 1st—Traveled 8 miles last night and encamped in the prairie without wood or water. Afternoon—After traveling 11 miles and descending a long hill, we have encamped not far from the Columbia River. Made a nice dinner of fried salmon. Quite a number of Indians were camped around us, for the purpose of selling salmon to the emigrants.

Friday, September 2nd—Came 5 miles this morning, and are now crossing Fall (or Deschutes it is called here) River on a ferry boat, pay 3 dollars a wagon and swim the stock. This river is very swift and full of rapids. Evening—Traveled 5 miles this afternoon. Ascended and descended a long steep hill; crossed Olney's Creek and have camped on the hill close to it. Cold weather and no wood. Pretty good grass.

Saturday, September 3rd—Cool and pleasant. Had a fine shower last night which laid the dust and makes the traveling much better. Here husband (being run out of money) sold his sorrel mare (Fan) for a hundred and twenty-five dollars. Evening—Traveled 17 miles today. Crossed Olney's (or the 15-Mile Creek) 7 times and have encamped on the banks of it. We are near timber once more.

Sunday, September 4th—Clear and bright. Had a fine view of Mount Hood, St. Helens and Jefferson. Traveled 15 miles today; water. After descending a long, steep, rocky and very tedious hill, we have camped in a valley on the bank of Indian Creek, near some Frenchmen, who have a trading post. There are also a good many Indians encamped around us. No feed for the cattle tonight. 15 miles more will take us to the foot of the mountains.

Monday, September 5th—Passed a sleepless night last night as a good many of the Indians camped around us were drunk and noisy and kept up a continual racket, which made all hands uneasy and kept our poor dog on the watch all night. I say poor dog, because he is nearly worn out with traveling through the day and should rest at night; but he hates an Indian and will not let one come near the wagons if he can help it; and doubtless they would have done some mischief but for him. Ascended a long steep hill this morning, which was very hard on the cattle, and also on myself, as I thought I never should get to the top, although I rested two or three times. After traveling two or three miles over some very pretty rolling prairie, we have turned our cattle out to feed a while, as they had nothing last night. Evening—Traveled about 12 miles today, and have encamped on a branch of Deschutes, and turned our cattle and horses out to tolerably good bunch grass.

Tuesday, September 6th—Still in camp, washing and overhauling the wagons to make them as light as possible to cross the mountains. Evening—After throwing away a good many things and burning up most of the deck boards of our wagons so as to lighten them, got my washing and cooking done and started on again. Crossed two branches, traveled 3 miles and have camped near the gate or foot of the Cascade Mountains (here I was sick all night, caused by my washing and working too hard).

Wednesday, September 7th—First day in the mountains. Came 16 miles today; crossed Deschutes, or a branch of it, 4 times and have encamped on the bank of it. Bought flour at 20 cents per pound to feed the stock.

Thursday, September 8th—Traveled 14 miles over the worst road that was ever made, up and down, very steep, rough and rocky hills, through mud holes, twisting and winding round stumps, logs and fallen trees. Now we are on the end of a log, now over a big root of a tree; now bounce down in a mud hole, then bang goes the other side of the wagon, and woe be to whatever is inside. There is very little chance to turn out of this road, on account of timber and fallen trees, for these mountains are a dense forest of pines, fir, white cedar or redwood (the handsomest timber in the world must be here in these Cascade Mountains). Many of the trees are 300 feet high and so dense to almost exclude the light of heaven, and for my own part I dare not look to the top of them for fear of breaking my neck. We have camped on a little stream called Sandy. No feed for the stock except flour, and by driving them a mile or so, they can get a little swamp grass or pick brush.

Friday, September 9th—Came eight and a half miles. Crossed Sandy 4 times; came over corduroy roads, through swamps, over rocks and hummocks, and the worst road that could be imagined or thought of, and have encamped about one o'clock in a little opening near the road. The men have driven the cattle a mile off from the road to try and find grass and rest them till morning. We hear the road is still worse ahead. There is a great deal of laurel growing here, which will poison the stock if they eat it. There is no end to the wagons, buggies, yokes, chains, etc., that are lying all along this road. Some splendid good wagons just left standing, perhaps with the owners names on them; and many are the poor horses, mules, oxen, cows, etc., that are lying dead in these mountains. Afternoon—Slight shower.

Saturday, September 10th—Pleasant. Noon—We have just halted in a little valley at the foot of Big Laurel Hill to rest ourselves and poor, weary cattle an hour or so. We dare not rest long in these mountains, for fear of a storm, which would be almost certain to kill all of our stock, although the poor things need it bad enough, after what they have gone through with this forenoon. It would be useless for me with my pencil to describe the awful road we have just passed over (let fancy picture a train of wagons and cattle passing through a crooked chimney and we have Big Laurel Hill). After descending several bad hills, one called Little Laurel Hill, which I thought is as bad as could be, but in reality it was nothing to this last one called

Big Laurel. It is something more than half mile long, very rocky all the way, quite steep, winding, sideling, deep down, slippery and muddy, made so by a spring running the entire length of the road, and this road is cut down so deep that at times the cattle and wagons are almost out of sight, with no room for the drivers except on the bank, a very difficult place to drive, also dangerous, and to make the matter worse, there was a slow poking train ahead of us, which kept stopping every few minutes, and another behind us which kept swearing and hurrying our folks on, and there they all were, with the poor cattle all on the strain, holding back the heavy wagons on the slippery road. The men and boys all had their hands full, and I was obliged to take care of myself and little ones as best I could, there being no path or road except the one where the teams traveled. We kept as near the road as we could, winding round the fallen timber and brush, climbing over logs, creeping under fallen timber, sometimes lifting and carrying Chat. To keep from smelling the carrion, I, as others, holding my nose. (Must quit, as all hands are getting ready to travel again.) Evening—Came 10 miles today. Crossed Sandy River once and have camped by it about dark. Fed the stock flour and cut down alders for them to browse on. Nothing else for them, poor things. Kept them yoked and tied all night (there I was sick all night and not able to get out of the wagon in the morning).

Sunday, September 11th—Traveled 12 miles today. Crossed Sandy (or Zigzag) River once and have encamped close to a spring branch and drove the cattle one-half mile from the road to feed on swamp grass. The road has been a very little better today, although we came down some very bad hills, also through mud holes.

Monday, September 12th—Came 12 miles today. Crossed Sandy once, ascended three very steep hills, passed over the (they call it here) Devil's Backbone. We also passed over some very pretty country today. We stopped to noon at a very beautiful spot. It was prairie interspersed with strips of pretty fir timber, with their branches sweeping the ground. To the left of us was a deep ravine, with a clear stream of water meandering through it (this pretty place was along toward the end of the old fellow's backbone). Passed one new made claim this evening, and have encamped near a small stream of water. It is three miles to the first farm.

Tuesday, September 13th—Ascended three steep, muddy hills this morning. Drove over some muddy, miry ground and through mud holes, and have just halted at the first farm to noon and rest awhile and buy feed for the stock. Paid $1.50 per hundred for hay. Price of fresh beef 16 and 18 cts. per pound, butter ditto, 1 dollar, eggs 1 dollar a dozen, onions 4 and 5 dollars per bushel, all too dear for poor folks, so we have treated ourselves to some small turnips at the rate of 25 cents per dozen. Got rested and are now ready to travel again. Evening—Traveled 14 miles today. Crossed Deep Creek and have encamped on the bank of it, a very dull looking place; grass very scarce. We may not call ourselves through, they say; and there we are in Oregon, making our camp in an ugly bottom, with no home, except our wagons and tent. It is drizzling and the weather looks dark and gloomy. Here old man Fuller left us and Wilson Carl remains.

Wednesday, September 14th—Still in camp. Raining and quite disagreeable.

Thursday, September 15th—Still in camp and still raining. I was sick all night.

Friday, September 16th—Still in camp. Rain in the forenoon and clear in the afternoon. Washed some this forenoon.

Saturday, September 17th—In camp yet. Still raining. Noon—It has cleared off and we are all ready for a start again, for some place we don't know where. Evening—Came 6 miles and have encamped in a fence corner by a Mr. Lambert's, about 7 miles from Milwaukie. Turn our stock out to tolerably good feed.

A few days later my eighth child was born. After this we picked up and ferried across the Columbia River, utilizing skiff, canoes and flatboat to get across, taking three days to complete. Here husband traded two yoke of oxen for a half section of land with one-half acre planted to potatoes and a small log cabin and lean-to with no windows. This is the journey's end.

(Finis)

Helen Marnie Stewart (Love)
[1835–1873]

Helen Marnie Stewart was eighteen years old when she, along with her father, mother, and two of her sisters, joined Mrs. Margaret Love and her three sons in a journey from Pennsylvania to Oregon in 1853. The Stewart/Love party traveled the same route described by Amelia Stewart Knight (about ten days behind them) until they decided to try a new trail from Fort Boise to the Willamette Valley. Helen's diary breaks off before this fateful decision which led them, along with hundreds of others, to become lost in eastern Oregon. Here, as part of the "Lost Wagon Train of 1853," they endured extremes of hardship and deprivation before reaching their destination in the late fall. In Oregon, Helen married David Love and with him joined the "gold rush" in Oregon in the 1860s. Helen Stewart Love died at age thirty-eight, the mother of seven children.

In this excerpt from her diary, she describes her encounters with the Sioux Indians near Fort Laramie.

[*June* 1853]
fry 17
we started this morning at the usual time   we got to court house rock   we eat dinner neerly opisite to it and in site of chimney rock
to day we hear great word of the indians   they say that there is five hundred of them going to fight   we hear that they have laid down blankets   that is the sine for the emigrants not dare govern them   we shall see when we come up to the place whether it is true or not and that they have sent over the river to gether up more
there was one old bachlier poor old fellow that was dreadful afraid

From "The Diary of Helen Marnie Stewart," a typescript prepared and copyrighted by the Lane County Historical Society in Eugene, Oregon. Reprinted with permission. The manuscript of the diary is at the University of Oregon Library in Eugene.

he looked as if he wished his eyes might go ahead a peace to se if it was true or not　I had to laugh at him　while his legs were running backward for he said that if the emigrants was stopt untill more would come up he thought it would be best just to have enough men with the wagons to mind them and the rest to go and kill every one men weamon and children and he would kill little sucking baby so he would for if they could not fight not they would kill white peoples babys when they got big enough so they would by G swearing all the time at a great rate　poor little soul　he has a toleable big body but a very little soul but old bachaliars ought to be excused a little all ways for they are not always accountable

but the great army that frightened him so proved to be an Indian camp and in deed they were very friendly with us for they was one come first and shuck hands with us all showed us a peace of paper that had the name of evry thing he wanted such as tobacco flower coffe and whole lot of other things　he told to that his was the best family among them and that he had ten children　I saw some of the prittyist girls to and they ware drest so nice after their own fashion of course though I do not know wether old John has got over his panic yet or not

sat 18
we have had good luck so far　one of our oxen was sick last night but better this morning　the indians followed us so far today　oh it is beautiful　there is such romantic screeneary　we can see scots bluffs and a rang on the opste side that is far more beautiful　o deare me it is so warm the dust is flying in a cloud

sabeth 19
it is a fine day extremely windy　the dust is flying　the poor oxen I do pity them so　I wish they had goggles　we come to an exslent spring of water but required some diging out　it i[s] runing out of a very mountain　neer this spring is the hill that if you go up on it you can larimie peak　I went up but it was such a dull dusty day we could not see any distance

mon 20
it is warm　the cattle is travling with there toungs hanging out there are so warm and tiard　there is a storm comeing up

tews 21

this morning is a beautiful after the rain   the road is leavel and good   we past three dead oxen no a great distance apart   what death they died I know not poor things   we are nearing for laramie   it is about five miles to it yet there is so many that is there before us waiting to get across that there is no grass neer it so we have to wait here awhile

wed 22

this is my birthday   my eighteenth birthday   I feel myself geting older but not any wiser   it is a cold bleak day   the wind blows extremely hard;   we are washing and bakeing and fixing ma[n]y little things   there is lots of camps all around us   some is moveing on and others are moveing in ther places   we had some what of snow storm on my birthday the 22 of June 1853

thirs 23

we start to the ford and stops awhile on the above it   there is some wagons there yet   Mary Ag and I took a walk up some of the high hills and as we was comeing back we met in two Indians one of them was dressed fine he had a brod stripe of beads sowd in the middle of his blanket and his shoulders was just covered with them   he had two peaces of some kind of fur and a long plated consurne it looked like a whip fastened to the back of his head and a black bird on the place where they ware fasend   he had a small loocking glass set in wood string round his neck   some thing to smell also it had a very pleasant smell   I cannot begin to discribe all the fixings he had on   the other one had nothing nice only his legins and shoes   ther ware just covered with beads   the drest one was very talktive and wanted me to get on his horse behind him and wride to where the wagons was

Eliza Frances Andrews
[1840–1931]

When the Civil War broke out, Eliza Frances Andrews lived on the family plantation of her parents, Garnett and Annulet (Ball) Andrews, near Washington, Georgia. Her father, a prominent lawyer and owner of over two hundred slaves, opposed secession and remained a staunch Unionist throughout the war. His position was unpopular in the community and the family (three sons fought for the Confederacy), but Garnett Andrews, proud that his father had fought in the Revolution at Yorktown, felt that division from the Union meant death for the South.

Eliza Frances Andrews never married, and after the Civil War became a teacher of botany and achieved some prominence as a writer. She published on scientific and social topics and wrote fiction under the pen name "Elzey Hay." In 1908 she edited and published the journal she had kept during the war. By this time she had read Karl Marx, considered herself a socialist, and the journal is introduced with a discussion of how "wage slavery" has replaced "chattel slavery" in the American economy.

The Civil War rivals the westward expansion for the event that "produced" the most American diaries. Women and men of the North and South, both participants and observers, kept journals and many of these have been published in whole or part (see Bibliography). During the period of Andrews's journal entries, she and a younger sister have been sent for protection to an elder sister's home near Albany, Georgia, where life continues largely untouched by the war. She then describes their return home at the point when her father feels it is safe for them to travel.

[1865]

   Jan. 11, *Wednesday.*—I am just getting well of measles, and a rough time I had of it. Measles is no such small affair after all, especially

From Eliza Frances Andrews, *The War-Time Journal of a Georgia Girl, 1864–1865* (New York: D. Appleton, 1908).

when aggravated by perpetual alarms of Yankee raiders. For the last week we have lived in a state of incessant fear. All sorts of rumors come up the road and down it, and we never know what to believe. Mett and I have received repeated letters from home urging our immediate return, but of course it was impossible to travel while I was sick in bed, and even now I am not strong enough to undertake that terrible journey across the burnt country again. While I was ill, home was the one thought that haunted my brain, and if I ever do get back, I hope I will have sense enough to stay there. I don't think I ever suffered so much before in all my life, and dread of the Yankees raised my fever to such a pitch that I got no rest by night or day. I used to feel very brave about Yankees, but since I have passed over Sherman's track and seen what devastation they make, I am so afraid of them that I believe I should drop down dead if one of the wretches should come into my presence. I would rather face them anywhere than here in South-West Georgia, for the horrors of the stockade have so enraged them that they will have no mercy on this country, though they have brought it all on themselves, the cruel monsters, by refusing to exchange prisoners. But it is horrible, and a blot on the fair name of our Confederacy. Mr. Robert Bacon says he has accurate information that on the first of December, 1864, there were 13,010 graves at Anderson. It is a dreadful record. I shuddered as I passed the place on the cars, with its tall gibbet full of horrible suggestiveness before the gate, and its seething mass of humanity inside, like a swarm of blue flies crawling over a grave. It is said that the prisoners have organized their own code of laws among themselves, and have established courts of justice before which they try offenders, and that they sometimes condemn one of their number to death. It is horrible to think of, but what can we poor Confederates do? The Yankees won't exchange prisoners, and our own soldiers in the field don't fare much better than these poor creatures. Everybody is sorry for them, and wouldn't keep them here a day if the government at Washington didn't force them on us. And yet they lay all the blame on us. Gen. Sherman told Mr. Cuyler that he did not intend to leave so much as a blade of grass in South-West Georgia, and Dr. Janes told sister that he (Sherman) said he would be obliged to send a formidable raid here in order to satisfy the clamors of his army, though he himself, the fiend Sherman, dreaded it on account of the horrors that would be committed. What Sherman dreads must indeed be fearful. They say his soldiers have sworn that they will spare neither man, woman nor child in all South-West Georgia. It is only a question of time, I suppose, when all this will be done. It begins to look as if the Yankees can do whatever they please and go wherever they wish—except to heaven; I do fervently pray the good Lord will give us rest from them there. . . .

March 8, *Wednesday.*—I went up to Americus yesterday, with Flora and Capt. Rust, to see Cousin Bolling about my eyes, expecting to return to Gopher Hill on the afternoon train, but Cousin Bessie insisted that we should stay to dinner, and her attempt to have it served early was so unsuccessful that Capt. Rust and I got to the station just in time to see the train moving off without us. Flora had another engagement, that caused her to decline Mrs. Pope's invitation, so she made the train, but the captain and I had nothing for it but to spend the night in Americus and kill the time as best we could. I was repaid for the annoyance of getting left by the favorable report Cousin Bolling gave of my eyes. He says it is nothing but the effects of measles that ails them, and they are almost well. I occupied Flora's room that night. Cousin Bessie lent me one of her fine embroidered linen nightgowns, and I was so overpowered at having on a decent piece of underclothing after the coarse Macon Mills homespun I have been wearing for the last two years, that I could hardly go to sleep. I stood before the glass and looked at myself after I was undressed just to see how nice it was to have on a respectable undergarment once more. I can stand patched-up dresses, and even take a pride in wearing Confederate homespun, where it is done open and above board, but I can't help feeling vulgar and common in coarse underclothes. Cousin Bessie has brought quantities of beautiful things from beyond the blockade, that make us poor Rebs look like ragamuffins beside her. She has crossed the lines by special permit, and will be obliged to return to Memphis by the 2d of April, when her pass will be out. It seems funny for a white woman to have to get a pass to see her husband, just like the negro men here do when their wives live on another plantation. The times have brought about some strange upturnings. Cousin Bolling is awfully blue about the war, and it does begin to look as if our poor little Confederacy was about on its last legs, but I am so accustomed to all sorts of vicissitudes that I try not to let thoughts of the inevitable disturb me. The time to be blue was five years ago, before we went into it. . . .

April 17, *Monday. Macon, Ga.*—Up early, to be ready for the train at seven. The Toombses met us at the dépot, where Capt. Greenlaw, Mr. Renaud, and a number of others came to see us off. When the train arrived from Eufaula it was already crowded with refugees, besides 300 volunteers from the exempts going to help fight the Yankees at Columbus. All sorts of wild rumors were flying, among them one that fighting had already begun at Columbus, and that a raid had been sent out towards Eufaula. Excitement on the train was intense. At Ward's Station, a dreary-looking little place, we picked up the train wrecked yesterday, with many of the passengers still on board. They had spent the night there in the cars, having nowhere else to go. Beyond Ward's, the failure of this train to appear had given color to all sorts of wild rumors about the advance of the Yankees into South-West Georgia. The excitement was intense all along the route. At every little station crowds were gathered to hear the news, and at many places we found a report had gone out that both our train and yesterday's had been captured. The excitement increased as we approached Fort Valley, where the Muscogee road (from Columbus) joins the South-Western, and many of the passengers predicted that we should be captured there. At the next station below Fort Valley, our fears regarding the fate of Columbus were confirmed by a soldier on the platform, who shouted out as the train slowed down, "Columbus gone up the spout!" Nobody was surprised, and all were eager to hear particulars. I was glad to learn that our poor little handful of Confederates had made a brave fight before surrendering. The city was not given up till nine last night, when the Yanks slipped over the railroad bridge and got in before our men, who were defending the other bridge, knew anything about it. We had not enough to watch both bridges, and it seemed more likely the attack would be made by the dirt road. Then everybody blundered around in the dark, fighting pretty much at random. If a man met some one he did not know, he asked whether he was a Yank or a Reb, and if the answer did not suit his views he fired. At last everybody became afraid to tell who or what they were. It was thought that our forces had retired towards Opelika. When we reached Fort Valley the excitement was at fever heat. Train upon train of cars was there, all the rolling stock of the Muscogee Road having been run out of Columbus to keep it from being captured, and the cars were filled with refugees and their goods. It was pitiful to see them, especially the poor little children, driven from their homes by the frozen-hearted Northern Vandals, but they were all brave and cheerful, laughing good-naturedly instead of grumbling over their hardships. People have gotten so used to these sort of things that they have learned to bear them with philosophy. Soldiers who had made their escape after the fight, without surrendering, were camped about everywhere, looking tired and hungry, and more disheartened than the women and children. Poor fellows, they have seen the terrors of war nearer at hand than we. As our train drew up at the dépot, I caught sight of Fred in the crowd. He had been in the fight at Columbus, and I concluded was now on his way to Cuthbert to find Metta and me. I called to let him know that we were on board, but he did not hear me, and before I could make my way to the opposite window, the train moved on a few hundred yards and he was lost in the crowd. I was greatly disturbed, for it was said that the train we were on was the last that would be run over the South-Western Road. While I was in this dilemma, Col. Magruder and Marsh Fouché came out of the crowd and hailed me. They said they were on furlough and trying to make their way to Uncle Fouché's plantation in Appling County. I told them my troubles, and they went to hunt up Fred for me, but must have gotten swallowed up in the crowd themselves, for I never saw either of them again. At last I sent for the conductor to unlock the door so that I could get out of the car and begin a search on my own account. Just as I had stepped out on the platform Fred himself came pushing through the crowd and sprang up beside me. He said that some of the passengers who had come with us from Cuthbert, happened to hear him say that he was going to South-West Georgia to get his sisters, and told him that we were there.

From Fort Valley we traveled without interruption to Macon, where the excitement is at its climax. The Yankees are expected here at any moment, from both north and south, having divided their forces at Tuskegee, it is said, and sent one column by way of Union Springs and Columbus, and another through Opelika and West Point. I saw some poor little fortifications thrown up along the line of the South-Western, with a handful of men guarding them, and that is the only preparation for defense I have seen. We are told that the city is to be defended, but if that is so, the Lord only knows where the men are to come from. The general opinion seems to be that it is to be evacuated, and every preparation seems to be going forward to that end. All the horses that could be found have been pressed for the removal of government stores, and we had great difficulty in getting our baggage from the dépôt to the hotel. Mr. Legriel's nephew, Robert Scott, was at the train to take us out to Lily's, but Fred thought it best for us to stay at the hotel, as he wants to leave in the morning by the first train over the Macon & Western. Mulberry Street, in front of the Lanier House, is filled with officers and men rushing to and fro, and everything and everybody seems to be in the wildest excitement. . . . In the hotel parlor, when I came from Lily's, whom should I find but Mr. Adams, our little Yankee preacher! I used to like him, but now I hate to look at him just because he is a Yankee. What is it, I wonder, that makes them so different from us, even when they mean to be good Southerners! You can't even make one of them look like us, not if you were to dress him up in a full suit of Georgia jeans. I used to have some Christian feeling towards Yankees, but now that they have invaded our country and killed so many of our men and desecrated so many homes, I can't believe that when Christ said "Love your enemies," he meant Yankees. Of course I don't want their souls to be lost, for that would be wicked, but as they are not being punished in this world, I don't see how else they are going to get their deserts.

April 18, *Tuesday.*—The first train on the Georgia R.R., from Atlanta to Augusta, was scheduled to run through to-day, and we started off on the Macon & Western so as to reach Atlanta in time to take the next one down, to-morrow. There was such a crowd waiting at the dépôt that we could hardly push our way through, and when the ladies' car was opened there was such a rush that we considered ourselves lucky to get in at all. Jenny and Jule were with us, and we were fortunate enough to get seats together. Fred and Mr. Toombs had great difficulty in getting our trunks aboard, and were obliged to leave us to look out for ourselves, while they attended to the baggage. Many people had to leave theirs behind, and some decided to stay with their trunks; they contained all that some poor refugees had left them. The trains that went out this morning were supposed to be the last that would leave the city, as the Yankees were expected before night, and many predicted that we would be captured. There was a terrible rush on all the outgoing trains. Ours had on board a quantity of government specie and the assets of four banks, besides private property, aggregating all together, it was said, more than seventeen million dollars—and there were somewhere in the neighborhood of 1,000 passengers. People who could not get inside were hanging on wherever they could find a sticking place; the aisles and platforms down to the last step were full of people clinging on like bees swarming round the doors of a hive. It took two engines to pull us up the heavy grade around Vineville, and we were more than an hour behind time, in starting, at that. Meanwhile, all sorts of rumors were flying. One had it that the road was cut at Jonesborough, then, at Barnesville, and finally that a large force of the enemy was at Thomaston advancing toward the road with a view to capturing our train. I never saw such wild excitement in my life. Many people left the cars at the last moment before we steamed out, preferring to be caught in Macon rather than captured on the road, but their places were rapidly filled by more adventurous spirits. A party of refugees from Columbus were seated near us, and they seemed nearly crazed with excitement. Mary Eliza Rutherford, who was always a great scatter-brain when I knew her at school, was among them, and she jumped up on the seat, tore down her back hair and went off into regular hysterics at the idea of falling into the hands of the Yankees. Such antics would have been natural enough in the beginning of the war, when we were new to these experiences, but now that we are all old soldiers, and used to raids and vicissitudes, people ought to know how to face them quietly. Of course, it would have been dreadful to be captured and have your baggage rifled and lose all your clothes, but if the Yankees had actually caught us, I don't think I would have gone crazy over it. So many sensational reports kept coming in that I finally lost patience and felt like saying something cross to everybody that brought me a fresh bit of news. Before we left Macon, Mr. Edward Shepherd gave me the worst fright I almost ever had, by telling me that my trunk and Jenny Toombs's had been thrown out of the baggage car and were lying on the track, but this proved to be a false alarm, like so many others. Then somebody came in and reported that the superintendent of the road had a dispatch in his hand at that moment, stating that the enemy was already in Barnesville. The statement seemed so authoritative that Fred went to Gen. Mackall himself, and was advised by him to continue his journey, as no official notice had been received of the cutting of the road. At last, to the great relief of us all, the train steamed out of Macon and traveled along in peace till it reached Goggins's Station, four miles from Barnesville, where it was stopped by some country people who said that the down train from Atlanta had been captured and the Yankees were just five miles beyond Barnesville waiting for us. A council was held by the railroad officials and some of the army officers on board, at which it was decided that the freight we were carrying was too valuable to be risked, although the news was not very reliable, having been brought in by two schoolboys. There was danger also, it was suggested, that a raiding party might mistake such a very long and crowded train, where the men were nearly all forced out on the platforms, for a movement of troops and fire into us. I confess to being pretty badly scared at this possibility, but the women on board seemed to have worked off their excitement by this time, and we all kept quiet and behaved ourselves very creditably. While the council was still in session, fresh reports came in confirming those already brought, and we put back to Macon, without standing on the order of our going. Helen Swift, a friend of the Toombses, who had joined us at Macon, lives only fifteen miles from the place where we turned back. She was bitterly disappointed, and I don't blame her for nearly crying her eyes out. Mr. Adams undertook to administer spiritual consolation, but I don't think Helen was very spiritually-minded towards Yankees just at that time.

Excited crowds were waiting at all the stations as we went back, and the news we brought increased the ferment tenfold. The general impression seems to be that the Yanks are advancing upon Macon in three columns, and that they will reach the city by tomorrow or next day, at latest. We came back to the Lanier House, and Fred hopes to get us out by way of Milledgeville, before they arrive. When our train got back to Macon, the men on board had gradually dropped off on the way, so that I don't suppose there were more than 200 or 300 remaining of all that had gone out in the morning. The demoralization is complete. We are whipped, there is no doubt about it. Everybody feels it, and there is no use for the men to try to fight any longer, though none of us like to say so.

Just before we reached Macon, the down train, which had been reported captured, overtook us at a siding, with the tantalizing news that we might have got through to Atlanta if we had gone straight on. The Yankees were twelve miles off at the time of its reported capture, and cut the road soon after it passed. There was an immense crowd at the dépot on our return, and when I saw what a wild commotion the approach of the Yankees created, I lost all hope and gave up our cause as doomed. We made a brave fight but the odds against us were too great. The spell of invincibility has left us and gone over to the heavy battalions of the enemy. As I drove along from the station to the hotel, I could see that preparations were being made to evacuate the city. Government stores were piled up in the streets and all the horses and wagons that could be pressed into service were being hastily loaded in the effort to remove them. The rush of men had disappeared from Mulberry St. No more gay uniforms, no more prancing horses, but only a few ragged foot soldiers with wallets and knapsacks on, ready to march—Heaven knows where. Gen. Elzey and staff left early in the morning to take up their new quarters either in Augusta or Washington, and if we had only known it, we might have gone out with them. I took a walk on the streets while waiting to get my room at the hotel, and found everything in the wildest confusion. The houses were closed, and doleful little groups were clustered about the street corners discussing the situation. All the intoxicating liquors that could be found in the stores, warehouses, and barrooms, had been seized by the authorities and emptied on the ground. In some places the streets smelt like a distillery, and I saw men, boys, and negroes down on their knees lapping it up from the gutter like dogs. Little children were staggering about in a state of beastly intoxication. I think there can be no more dreary spectacle in the world than a city on the eve of evacuation, unless it is one that has already fallen into the hands of the enemy. I returned to the hotel with a heavy heart, for while out I heard fresh rumors of Lee's surrender. No one seems to doubt it, and everybody feels ready to give up hope. "It is useless to struggle longer," seems to be the common cry, and the poor wounded men go hobbling about the streets with despair on their faces. There is a new pathos in a crutch or an empty sleeve, now, that we know it was all for nothing. . . .

May 6, Saturday.—The mournful silence of yesterday has been succeeded by noise and confusion passing anything we have yet experienced. Reënforcements have joined Wilcox, and large numbers of Stoneman's and Wilson's cavalry are passing through on their way to Augusta. Confederate soldiers, too, are beginning to come by this route again, so Washington is now a thoroughfare for both armies.

Our troops do not come in such numbers as formerly, still there have been a great many on the streets to-day. About noon, two brigades of our cavalry passed going west, and at the same time a body of Yankees went by going east. There were several companies of negroes among them, and their hateful old striped rag was floating in triumph over their heads. Cousin Liza turned her back on it, Cora shook her fist at it, and I was so enraged that I said I wished the wind would tear it to flinders and roll it in the dirt till it was black all over, as the colors of such a crew ought to be. Then father took me by the shoulder and said that if I didn't change my way of talking about the flag of my country he would send me to my room and keep me there a week. We had never known anything but peace and security and protection under that flag, he said, as long as we remained true to it. I wanted to ask him what sort of peace and protection the people along Sherman's line of march had found under it, but I didn't dare. Father don't often say much, but when he does flare up like that, we all know we have got to hold our tongues or get out of the way. It made me think of that night when Georgia seceded. What would father have done if he had known that that secession flag was made in his house? It pinches my conscience, sometimes, when I think about it. What a dreadful thing it is for a household to be so divided in politics as we are! Father sticks to the Union through thick and thin, and mother sticks to father, though I believe she is more than half a rebel at heart, on account of the boys. Fred and Garnett are good Confederates, but too considerate of father to say much, while all the rest of us are red-hot Rebs. . . .

May 7, Sunday— . . . But even if father does stick to the Union, nobody can accuse him of being a sycophant or say that he is not honest in his opinions. He was no less a Union man in the days of persecution and danger for his side than he is now. And though he still holds to his love for the Union—if there is any such thing—he has made no indecent haste, as some others have done, to be friends with the Yankees, and he seeks no personal advantage from them. He has said and done nothing to curry favor with them, or draw their attention to his "loyalty," and he has not even hinted to us at the idea of paying them any social attentions. Poor father, it is his own house, but he knows too well what a domestic hurricane *that* would raise, and though he does storm at us sometimes, when we say too much, as if he was going to break the head of the last one of us, he is a dear, good, sweet, old father, after all, and I am ashamed of myself for my undutiful conduct to him. I know I deserve to have my head cracked, but oh! I do wish that he was on our side! He is too good a man to be in the same political boat with the wretches that are plundering and devastating our country. He was right in the beginning, when he said that secession was a mistake, and it would be better to have our negroes freed in the Union, if necessary, than out of it, because in that case, it would be done without passion, and violence, and we would get compensation for them—but now the thing is done, and there is no use talking about the right or the wrong of it. I sympathize with the spirit of that sturdy old heathen I have read about some-where, who said to the priests who were trying to convert him, that he would rather stick to his own gods and go to hell with his warrior ancestors, than sit down to feast in heaven with their little starveling band of Christians. That is the way I feel about Yankees; I would rather be wrong with Lee and his glorious army than right with a gang of fanatics that have come down here to plunder and oppress us in the name of liberty. . . .

June 27, Tuesday— . . . I consider that flag a personal insult to Cora and me, who made the first rebel one ever raised in Washington. And such a time as we had making it, too, for we had to work on it in secret and smuggle it out of sight every time we heard any one coming, for fear father might find out what we were at and put a stop to our work. But we got it done, and there it floated, while the bells were ringing for secession, just as that horrid old Yankee banner floats there now, the signal of our humiliation and defeat. Poor, dear, old father, my conscience hurts me to think how I have disobeyed him and gone against his wishes ever since the war began. We are all such deter-mined Rebs that I sometimes wonder how he can put up with us as well as he does—though we do have awful family rows sometimes. We barely missed one this evening, when I came in and commenced to tell the news, but luckily the supper bell rang just in the nick of time, though father was so upset he wouldn't say grace. That old flag started it all. We children were so incensed we couldn't hold in, and father reproved us for talking so imprudently before the servants. I said I hated prudence—it was a self-seeking, Puritanical sort of virtue, and the Southerners would never have made the gallant fight we did, if we had stopped to think of prudence. Mother turned this argument against me in a way that made me think of the scene in our house on the night when that first rebel flag was raised. We try to avoid politics at home, because it always brings on strife, but a subject of such vital and general interest *will* come up, in spite of all we can do. I am afraid all this political turmoil has something to do with father's illness, and my heart smites me. I don't want to be disrespectful to him, but Henry and I are born hot-heads, and never can hold our unruly tongues. In the beginning, I think a great many people, especially the old people, felt, way down in the bottom of their hearts, just as father did. Cora says that her grandpa was ready to crack anybody on the head with his walking stick that talked to him about dissolving the Union, and she never dared to open her mouth on the subject in his presence, or her father either, though he and all the rest of them believe in Toombs next to the Bible. I felt differently myself then. Before Georgia seceded, I used to square my opinions more by father. I could see his reasons for believing that secession would be a mistake, and wished that some honorable way might be found to prevent it. I loved the old Union, too—the Union of Washington and Jefferson —as much as I hate the new Union of compulsion and oppression, and I used to quarrel with Henry and Cora for being such red-hot secessionists. Even after the fight began, though my heart and soul were always with the South, I could still see a certain tragic grandeur in the spectacle of the Great Republic struggling desperately for its very existence. On looking back over the pages of this diary, I cannot accuse myself of unreasonable prejudice against the other side.

Its pages are full of criticisms of our own people all through the war. I could see their faults, and I would have done justice to Yankee virtues, if they had had any, but since that infamous march of Sherman's, and their insolence in bringing negro soldiers among us, my feelings are so changed that the most rabid secession talkers, who used to disgust me, are the only ones that satisfy me now. And I am not the only moderate person they have driven to the other extreme. Not two hours ago I heard Garnett say that if they had shown one spark of magnanimity towards us since we gave up the fight, he would be ready to enter their service the first time they got into a foreign war. "But now," he says, "I would fight in the ranks of any army against them."

The next war they get into, I think, will be against the negroes, who are already becoming discontented with freedom, so different from what they were taught to expect. Instead of wealth and idleness it has brought them idleness, indeed, but starvation and misery with it. There is no employment for the thousands that are flocking from the plantations to the towns, and no support for those who cannot or will not work. The disappointed ones are as much incensed against their "deliverers" as against us, and when they rise, it will not be against either Yankee or Southerner, but against the white race. Unfortunately, many of them have been drilled and made into soldiers. They have arms in their hands, and when the time comes, will be prepared to act the part of the Sepoys in India, thanks to Northern teaching. At the beginning of the war I was frightened out of my senses, when I read the frightful story of Lucknow and Cawnpore, for fear something of the kind would happen here, but the negroes had not been corrupted by false teachings then, and we soon found that we had nothing to fear from them. Now, when I know that I am standing on a volcano that may burst forth any day, I somehow, do not feel frightened. It seems as if nothing worse could happen than the South has already been through, and I am ready for anything, no matter what comes. . . .

July 21, *Friday*— . . . The streets of Washington are crowded all the time with idle men and women who have no means of support. They are loitering in the shade of every hedge and tree, and gossiping in every cabin doorway. Where they lodge, Heaven only knows, but how they are fed, the state of our orchards and cornfields can testify. Capt. Cooley hung up two by the thumbs the other day, for robbing father's orchard, but the discipline was of no avail, for we have not gathered a full-grown peach or pear this season. Roasting-ears are pleasant food, and to be had for the—taking; our early corn gave out before we had used it a week. Ben Jones shot a negro the other night, for stealing in Mr. Waddey's garden, and it is a miracle that he escaped being put in jail. Fortunately the negro wasn't hurt. Negroes may kill white men whenever they please, provided the white man wears not a blue coat, but woe to the white man that touches a negro! . . .

That murder case into which Gen. Wild and Dr. French have been prying for the last week has wrought these apostles up to a state of boundless indigation, and father is afraid it will bring their vengeance upon the town. He is counsel for the defense, and I don't think he feels any too much respect for his clients, though it is his duty, as their lawyer, to make out the best case he can for them. He don't say much about the case because conversation on such subjects nearly always brings on a political row in the family, and we are all so afraid of starting a fracas that we are constrained and uneasy whenever anything touching on politics, no matter how remotely, is mentioned. However, from the little I have heard father tell, I am afraid this murder is a very ugly affair. It seems his clients are accused of having killed an old negro woman because she left her master's plantation to go off and try the blessings of freedom. She certainly was an old fool, but I have never yet heard that folly was a capital offense. One of the men is said to have shot her, while the other broke her ribs and beat her on the head with a stone till she died. They left her unburied in a lonely place, and the body was not discovered till ten days after. In spite of the stench, father says Gen. Wild examined the body with ghoulish curiosity, even pulling out the broken ribs and staring at them. And all the while the old woman's son stood looking on with stolid indifference, less moved than I would be over the carcass of a dead animal. Gen. Wild was bred a doctor and didn't seem to mind the most sickening details. Father says he would rather have the sharpest lawyer in Georgia as his opposing counsel than these shrewd, painstaking Yankees. Capt. Cooley was sent out to collect evidence, and even brought back the stone which was said to be the one with which the poor old creature was beaten on the head. There is only negro evidence for all these horrors, and nobody can tell how much of it is false, but that makes no difference with a Yankee court. Father thinks one of the men is sure to hang, and he has very little hope of saving the other. The latter is a man of family, and his poor wife is at Mrs. Fitzpatrick's hotel, almost starving herself to death from grief. She has left her little children at home by themselves, and they say that when the Yankees went there to arrest their father, they were so frightened that two of them went into convulsions; they had heard such dreadful things about what the Yankees had done during the war. The younger of the two accused men is only twenty years old, and his poor old father hangs around the courtroom, putting his head in every time the door is opened, trying to catch something of what is going on. He is less privileged than our dog Toby, who follows father to the courthouse every day, and walks about the room as if it belonged to him, smelling at the Yankees, and pricking up his ears as if to ask what business they had there. Father says he would not, for millions, have had such a case as this come under the eyes of the Yankees just at this time, for they will believe everything the negroes say and put the very worst construction on it. Brutal crimes happen in all countries now and then, especially in times of disorder and upheaval such as the South is undergoing, but the North, fed on Mrs. Stowe's lurid pictures, likes to believe that such things are habitual among us, and this horrible occurrence will confirm them in their opinion.

Another unfortunate affair took place the other night, in Lincoln County. The negroes were holding a secret meeting, which was suspected of boding no good to the whites, so a party of young men went out to break it up. One of the boys, to frighten them, shot off his gun and accidentally killed a woman. He didn't mean to hurt anybody, but the Yankees vow they will hang the whole batch if they can find them. Fortunately he has made his escape, and they don't know the names of the others. Corrie Calhoun says that where she lives, about thirty miles from here, over in Carolina, the men have a recipe for putting troublesome negroes out of the way that the Yankees can't get the key to. No two go out together, no one lets another know what he is going to do, and so, when mischievous negroes are found dead in the woods, nobody knows who killed them. All this is horrible, I think. If they want to bushwhack anybody, why don't they shoot Yankees? The poor negroes don't do us any harm except when they are put up to it. Even when they murdered that white man and quartered him, I believe pernicious teachings were responsible. Such things happen only in places where the negroes have been corrupted by the teachings of such wretches as this French and Wild.

Annie Holmes Ricketson
[1841–?]

Women married to men in the whaling industry often endured separations from their husbands for three, four, or five years. Communication by letter during those years was sporadic at best, and months might pass before spouses learned of the most momentous events of life at home or at sea—the death of a parent, the birth or death of a child, indeed the death of the spouse him/herself.

By the 1870s women married to whaling captains increasingly chose an alternative to separation and joined their husbands at sea. In doing so, they left behind the community they had been a part of to become the only woman on board ship. Their quarters on the ship were confined, their responsibilities limited. Vast oceans, strange ports, extremes of weather became the commonplaces of life among companions chosen "for their qualities as whalemen not as gentlemen."* Meeting another woman in port or at the "gamming" (visiting at sea) of two ships was always an occasion for celebration.

Annie Holmes Ricketson left New Bedford, Massachusetts on May 2, 1871, for a three-and-a-half-year voyage with her husband in the Indian Ocean and South Atlantic. Their ship, the A.R. *Tucker, was ninety feet long and twenty-three feet wide. When they departed, Annie Ricketson was thirty years old; she had lost her first child at birth four years earlier, and was six months pregnant with her second child (though she never mentions it).*

An enthusiastic chronicler of all aspects of the whaling life, Annie Ricketson accompanied her husband on at least three voyages, including one in 1885–88 when her husband died of a fever before their return. She remarried two years later, and after her second husband's death, married for the third time.

*Emma Mayhew Whiting and Henry Beetle Hough, *Whaling Wives* (Boston: Houghton Mifflin, 1953), p. 7.

[1871]

August 25th: We have had It very rugged to day. I have had to lay abed most of the day. Their has been a very heavy sea washing across deck all day. At dinner the vessel gave a roll and away come my cup of tea in my lap and the victuals went in every direction! Of course I had to have a good hearty laugh. I have tried sitting on my trunk and on a box and the floor, but I find one place about as good as another for she will pitch and roll in spite of every thing. Daniel seys It is about as bad a sea as he ever saw for It seems to be all in heaps going every which way. I think I am getting to be quite a sailor for I have not been sick at all.

August 26th: I wanted to go on deck yesterday but could not for such a sea coming across deck. After breakfast I began to pick up things and make myself ready to go ashore, about eleven o clock they put our trunks in the boat and every thing being ready we started for the shore. A gentleman they called the doctor was standing on the end of the pier and before we could land he wanted to know what the name of the vessel was, where from, how much oil, what ports we had touched to, If the was any sickness aboard, and if we had any passengers aboard? Then he asked Daniel if he had his papers. Then we started for the landing where the was a great many portugese men and women standing at the landing. Their were dozen or twenty stone steps but jest as I was going to step on these steps their came a heavy breaker and completely covered us. If I had not had on my water proft I should been wet through. My Husband lifted me up and some gentleman on the pier hauled me on the steps. I was very much frightened and very weak. I went with Daniel to the docters office where I rested while my Husband did some writeng. Then a gentleman offered to escort me to the Hotel. It was not far from the landing but I was so weak I could hardly walk, but we reached the Hotel at last and of all the gloomy places that I ever saw I think that Hotel seemed the worse. When I went in the long entry with stone floor and walls and a long heavy door to the head of the stairs we had to knock and the door to be unlocked before we could enter. All I could

From *The Journal of Annie Holmes Ricketson on the Whaleship A.R. Tucker, 1871–1874* (New Bedford, Mass.: Old Dartmouth Historical Society, 1958). Reprinted by permission. The manuscript of the diary is at the Kendall Whaling Museum in Sharon, Massachusetts.

think of was a prison. But after we got inside it seemed pleasanter. The gentleman Introduced me to the Hotel Keeper and I liked his appearance very much. He and his wife are Inglish. He showed me into the parlor where I meet with a lady from New York. I layed aside my wet rappings and made myself as Comfortable as I could. In a short time Mr Bourne our mate came in and brought me a good package of letters from home which I prized very highly. I dont think I ever realized so much pleasure receiving any letters as I did this package. After a while the servant girl showed me up to my room. The lady of the House not being well, did not see her for several hours after I arrive. She came to my room and we had a pleasant chat, I liked her very much and guess I shall enjoy myself very well while here. We did not dine till 2 o clock and I felt very faint before we had dinner as we have breakfast so early aboard the ship. We had a very nice dinner, a plate of soup first, always, for that is their Custom in all Foreign places, then we have fowl and meats of different kinds and also fruits of all kinds. I have a nice room on the first floor fronting the street and we can look right out of our window on the Harbor which makes It very pleasant seeing the vessels come and go. After dinner I layed down and read the rest of my letters. After getting a good rest I got up and dressed for tea at seven o clock. Went to bed quite early as we were both very tired.

August 28th: This afternoon Capt Gifford and his wife come ta the Hotel. Had not been here long before they preposed a walk so we all started and went up to the Dabneys garden and found it to be a very pretty place. It was laided out very pretty but I began to grow tired so we turned our steps toward the Hotel. After we got back to the Hotel we went up to our rooms and before long Daniel come up seying that a Capt Tabor and his wife and child was below in the parlor and she wished to see m[e] very much, so I went down Immediately. She was very much overcome when she meet me although we had never meet before, but she was in very trying Condition as well as my self and her Husband was not going to stop ashore with her and she was feeling very bad about It. After tea we all went into the parlor where our Husbands joined us after they had their smoke where we we had a pleasant chat till quite late. I was very tired and feeling pretty bad but I had to have a box opened that came from Home. It was well filled with nice things. I have got such a kind father and mother to think of me when so far away from them. I felt so bad that Daniel sead he would put them back for me and I retired.

August 29th: I had a poor nights rest and to day I cannot get up. Called the docter about six o clock and twenty minutes past nine our little one was born which proved to be a little girl which of course we were very proud of. A Lady by the name of Mrs. Graham stoping here at the Hotel came in and dressed the baby and stoped all night with me which was very kind of her for Daniel was very tired.

August 30th: I felt very proud and happy this morning when I awoke and see our baby laying on my arm. When my Husband went down to breakfast they treated and congratulated him. After breakfast Daniel come up to my room and could not stay away from the baby long for he carried it round the room as proud as a father could be. My nurse come this morning a Portugese woman but could not make her understand much of any thing. They all think here at the Hotel that my baby is very pretty. Of course we do. Who ever saw a father and mother that thought their baby a homely one if It was ever so plain looking. We have got along after a fashion to day. One or two has droped in to see the baby. It is such a tiney little thing, only weighed three pounds.

August 31st: This morning I woke as happy as ever, little thinking that before night I should be in sorrow. My little baby was sick all day. It would cry out with pain all day and towards night I noticed that Its cry was weaker. About four o clock my Husband went and layed down to get a little rest and a nap if he could and the nurse went down stairs for some thing. I lay looking at my little one and all to once It gave a loud cry. I lifted up the little blanket that was over Its and I see its hands looked very white. I tryed to make Daniel hear but could not. The nurse came in jest then so I got her to call him and he came in. He looked at our little one and I see what he thought right away. I shall never forget how he looked up at me. Our little darling did not breath but twice after Daniel come in the room. It did seem to me that I could never give It up. They took it away from me and put it in the next room. Daniel came in and wanted some little clothes to put on It as they were going to lay it out, so he got my little trunk out that Its little clothes was in while I was trying to find some of the smallest garments for It. Miss Beaver came in and she helped me look them over and sead she would see that every thing was done right and she helped lay It out. But o how hard it was to give that little thing up! I had some narrow pink ribbon which I told daniel to give them and they tied It around its waist and and tied Its sleeves up with It. They brought It in and let me see It. It looked jest as though it was asleep, looked to nice to lay away in the Ground.

September 1st: I have not felt as well to day. They carried my little one to the picture room this afternoon and had Its picture taken. It looks like It some bot not so much as I wish It did. Had to pay five dollars but I do not begreidge the money for It is all I can ever have of my little one. It was put in the coffin this forenoon, a little white satin casket. They do not make their coffins here as they do at home but it was a pretty one, the nicest we could get. At four o clock this afternoon the Hack come that Daniel spook for and Mr. Dabney and Capt Burke went to the grave with Daniel. They layed it in a pretty green spot daniel seys with trees round it that shade it. Now my little one is an angel with the angels in Heaven. It is much better off then it would be here in this wicked would of ours. I must try to be reconciled as I know that Jesus has it safe with him.

September 12th: Mrs Tabor called this Afternoon. I shall not have the pleasure of a call from her right away for about ten o clock they had to call the docter she has got another little daughter, a fine baby weighing seven pounds.

September 19th: To day about one o clock Mrs Tabors baby died. It brought up everything so fresh about my little one that I felt very bad indeed. One thing we have to console us, they are a great deal better of[f] th[a]n they would be here for they have gone to their Heavely Home. It is hard for us but better for them. Today Mrs Tabors baby was buryed. The Hack came about five o clock and my Husband with Capt Williams and the Councel who he envited to go with him went to the grave. I felt so bad for Mrs Tabor that I thought I would try to go in and see her although her room was right next to mine, only a few steps. I was very tired, I find I am not very strong yet.

September 26th: This morning I went down to breakfast and after Breakfast Daniel ordered a Hack and we went to ride and I dont know when I have enjoyed any thing as I did that ride.

September 27th: I see one of the portugese woman pass the hotel today with an armful of wood. My Husband tells me that they buy it by the dossen sticks all cut ready to burn. O dear, they do have things so strange here at Fayal!

October 3rd: This morning on getting up and looking out of the windows we see a Bark which looked very much like the *A. R. Tucker* and after looking through the glasses It proved to be her. She came in quite unexpected. Did not think of seeing her under two weeks. Mr. Bourne come to the Hotel and sead he got in near and thought he would come in and see if we were ready to go out, if not he would cruse round the Island. But I had got quite strong and Husband was glad enough to see him come for he was very anxious to be on his way. Mr. Bourne and I went out shoping and had a plesant walk and a good deal of fun trying to make them under stand what we wanted and making change.

October 5th: Got up this morning and went to packing. It seemed as though I should never get all my things put up. We had accumulated quite a number of things together while in here. After I got aboard I got up on the stern of the vessel and I see my Friends up on a hill where they went so to see me on board the vessel, I waved my handkerchief and they returned it. I expect It will be a long time before I have the pleasure of womans society again. But I am content if I can have my Husbands society.

Helen Ward Brandreth
[1862–1905]

Helen Ward Brandreth, daughter of Virginia Gasby Ward and George Brandreth, was born into a large, wealthy, prominent family in Ossining (Sing Sing), New York. Her mother died when she was nine, and the socialization appropriate to a young lady of her "position" was taken over by older sisters and aunts. She attended the Morristown Seminary in Morristown, New Jersey in 1878, made her debut at West Point in 1879, and married Frederick Potter in 1884. Her journal, a "courtship diary," chronicles her life and the affairs of her heart from January 2, 1876 to September 1885. She names the diary "Fannie Fern" after the popular novelist of her time, Sara Parton (Willis), who wrote under that pen name (spelled "Fanny")—an appropriate audience for her romantic adventures. With the goal of her narrative accomplished, the journal closes with a newspaper clipping describing the lavish wedding: "The present of the bride's father to the bride (a share in the Porous Plaster Company) . . . is worth $50,000."

When Helen Brandreth Potter died at age 43, leaving her husband and five children, her obituary praised her as "one of God's noblest creatures . . . the ideal wife and mother." Carol Potter has written an essay about her great-grandmother's diary, " 'Good-bye Spooney Sunday': Fanny Fern and the Diary of Helen Ward Brandreth," in To Live a Woman, *ed. Leonore Hoffmann and Elizabeth Hampsted (New York: Modern Language Association, 1981).*

January 2, 1876
Sunday

I have determined to keep a journal. I shall call it Fannie Fern.

From "The Diary of Helen Ward Brandreth." Printed by permission of Carol Potter and the Potter family.

My name is Nellie Brandreth. I have a low forehead, light hair and eyes and will be 14 in February.

My Mama is dead, she died March 5, 1871, so my eldest sister May takes care of me and is housekeeper. Lillie, my next sister, is 19. Fannie is 17. I am the youngest and have no brother.

We live at Sing Sing in the village, but Grandpa has a large place near the river. I am staying there for a few days with Bella for Grandma and the girls have gone away. . . .

June 27, 1877
Wednesday

Dearest Fannie,

Aunt Beatrice gave a German last night and it was just splendid. . . .

Mr. Erwin led the German with Aunt B. He took me out first. O the delight of having his arm around my waist and the joy of holding his hand. I danced with him about six times; then he asked me to go out on the stoop with him. Of course I went and when we got out there he took off his glove and wanted to hold my hand. I resisted the temptation for awhile but, O Fan, I am *so* ashamed; at last I yielded. My hand trembled so that I was afraid he would notice it. O Fan, Fan!! I will die if he marries Birdie, for he does like her more than anybody else. At present.

I shall never forget the happiest five minutes of my life. It did not seem more than a second before we had to go into the house.

Some of the girls have come up. I thought Jim had come too but he stayed home with Birdie. O dear, O dear, O dear.

Now good bye, Deary, Lovie, *Petsie*, Lamb. . . .

Dec. 31, 1877

. . . I must turn over a new leaf tomorrow and behave myself more properly. I shall write down a list of all the things to remember.

1. Not to be so affected.
2. Not to be so conceited.
3. Not to be so selfish.
4. To remember my prayers in the morning.
5. To devote myself to my lessons.
6. To be more religious.
7. Not to gossip!!!!!

8. Not to tell *all* I know.

9. Never, under any circumstances, to mention a certain person's name.

10. Not to be so cross to the family in general and my dear little Fanny in particular.

11. This is my greatest *sin*. O Fan, if I could only stop but it is *so* hard. I have made more good resolutions about it than anything else and when I think I have entirely recovered from it I do it over again. The last time I did it was Dec. 14, 1877, only a little bit of a while ago. I would tell you what it is only it is so horridly awfully vile and then some one *might* read this and O horrors! what would they think of me. I would be disgraced for life.

It is almost twelve. It makes me feel so queer to be sitting here all alone on the last night of the year.

Good bye, my darling.

Your own
Nell

• • •

West Point
Aug. 28, 1879

. . . After supper we had a hop. I was dreadfully tired so I did not dance much. I was sitting in one of the windows when Jim suddenly appeared and jumped in the window. He sat and talked for a while then left, saying that he would be back by the sixth dance. By and by he came and I went off with him. We walked up and down and then we went down Flirtation. We wandered along until Jim suddenly stopped and took both my hands. I am not going to tell you all he said but he drew me into his arms, bent his head and kissed my lips. We stood there a long time. With both his dear arms about me and his kisses on my cheek do you wonder that I did not doubt him or his love? We walked back slowly until we came to the edge of Flirtation, then he stopped and quietly asked me to kiss him. For a moment I hesitated; then I leant forward and our lips met. And I can truly say that kiss has bound me to Jim as if the marriage service had been read over us. . . .

Class Day
June 20th [1881]

These two pages at least shall hold what no one else shall ever know. Dear Book, what a comfort you have always been. Need I tell you my forlorn little story in words? Do not these three things speak all too plainly? [Attached small bunch of flowers labelled, "This was his graduating bouquet given at the commencement," and small gold ribbon labelled, "And this his badge."] Ah, where now is my peace of mind? My rest in Jim's love? *Gone, gone,* everything but a mad, crazy longing to be with "him". Am I miserable? Yes, utterly so at times, for to my shame let me confess it—he *does-not-care*-for-me. What shall I say to excuse myself? *Nothing,* for what is there to say? I was utterly blind and when I saw my danger I would not stop— *no,* nor shall I stop *now.* I shall see him every chance I have and *afterwards* bear *twice* the pain I am bearing now. I will tell you part of the story, then close these two pages forever. I met him in Princeton on the 2nd of May. I liked him from the first moment we met. He is so bright and full of fun, yet withal so dignified and manly. When I again visited A.J. I saw quite a great deal of him. But it was not until our drive that I forgot myself so utterly as to *give love* where it was not *asked.* I need not say how I *hate* myself for it. I know that no one suspects, thank Heaven. Even if he cared for me what should, what could I do? I *never could break* my engagement with Jim; that is out of the question. How could I marry anyone else? After he has *kissed* me and we have been engaged *two* years. Oh, why did I ever meet Mr. Loney? I was happy before and now I am *miserable.* I pray that this is but a *passing fancy;* how could I be so *dishonorable;* and when Jim trusted me so, too. Oh, why did I become engaged when I was *seventeen;* it was utter madness. Perhaps I may get entirely over it and care for Jim once more. We were so happy together last summer. If I was not in love with Jim then I never will love anyone. Oh how I hate and despise susceptible people! Now you have the story. I pray that it will be but as a "Tale that is told".

Nellie

• • •

PRIVATE
Vine Cottage
Nov. 25, 1881

. . . I expect Jim home in a few weeks. I am sure I hardly know how to feel, whether to dread or anticipate it. I have almost decided what to do. I have had such a dreadful lesson; I mean the Zete affair; that I think for a year I will break my en—and be perfectly free. I fear that I have not met the right one yet or else I would not be so fickle and silly. I don't know how I will tell *him* for he seems to be contemplating speedy *matrimony!!* I shall not tell anyone. I hardly think it safe to write it here. I fear, dear old book, I will have to burn you in the end for you hold too many dangerous secrets. If I do break it, I will exchange rings with him and wear my own so no one will suspect! If at the end of '82 we both find that we care for each other and cannot be happy *apart*, why then we will renew it, but as no one will know it there will be no talking and wagging of heads over it. During that time I shall not write him or see him. If he comes to S.S. I will see him a few times to avoid suspicion or else I will manage to be far away. But, oh, I dread telling him. I think I will tell him how I felt about Zete, and then perhaps he will say so too. Poor old fellow, I will be glad to see him and I fear during those first days my resolution may falter and shake. I know I am so weak where he is concerned. But I do not think that, after my June trouble, I should marry Jim until we have both had a fair chance. Jim has seen very few women since our engagement and it would be a good thing for him to be free to choose again. And I have never been free for I was engaged while I was in school. I do not think that my decision has been influenced by Zete; for that would be nonsense. I will never see him again. He is in love and perhaps engaged to a lady in his City. I often think that I might as well submit to my fate and marry Jim. I *think* I would be happy but there are some things about him that I *despise* too utterly! Oh, I don't know what to do and no one can help me *either!* . . .

Vine Cottage
Nov. 29, 1881

I rarely write in here so often but lately I have been so worried. I wish I knew my own mind but I don't. One day I think I am in love with Jim and the next I am filled with a desire to get as far away from *him* as possible. Poor old fellow, I don't see why I feel so. If I had only never gone to Princeton—my worst trouble began there. But how foolish and wrong I am to think of him. He has in all probability forgotten even my existence, and for me to waste my heart in vain wishes and longings. It is unwomanly. How could I care for him when he did not care for me? I should have taken stricter care of my heart. But I was so sure I cared for Jim, and then besides this love came to me before I realized it, and then I did not know how hopeless and worse than useless it was. For, to tell you a wee bit of a secret, at one time I thought perhaps he might care just a little for me. He was so kind and he came to see me quite often. I don't mean that he acted in any way but the most honorable, only I deceived myself by a fond belief that faded like the summer roses at the end of June. Oh, woe is me! Am I never to get over it? Will all my life be spent in one great longing? I only heard from him once and I have not seen him since June—almost six months! Perhaps the sight of Jim may revive my love for him, but I doubt it. "Smoldering embers it is easy to fan into a flame, but the ashes of a dead love it is impossible to relight!" I only wish it were over, oh I dread it so. Even if I break off my engagement I cannot be any happier. For I will never see *him* again. For my own peace of mind, I hope not. He is so entirely different from other men. I thought my affair with Jim troublesome enough, but this last has been *misery, misery, misery.*

Fifth Ave. Hotel
(With Aunt Josie)
Dec. 31, 1881

11:30.

As usual, dear book, I have come to you the last thing in the old year. I do not intend to write much, for I am very tired, only a few words, for I could not let this night go without it.

Of all the years of my life, this has passed the most quickly and it has been a happy year too.

Last year I was looking for Jim's return; *now* I hardly know what to expect. No very great changes have come during the past year, thank God. All the ones I love most dearly are still on earth and I have so many blessings for which to be thankful, that it almost frightens me. If they are all well and happy next year I will be content. I have been very happy these twelve months. Somehow I dread to look forward to "82". Some changes will surely come and I fear that a year from now my engagement will be a thing of the past. Ah, well, whatever comes, I pray that it may be for the best.

I am discouraged this year, for I think I have become more careless and wicked every day. It is no use to make good resolutions for I will surely break them. Three things I must try to conquer with God's help; first, my hasty temper, then my wicked thoughts, last my extravagence, which is positively shocking.

I hereby solemnly swear that I will not charge anything at Sterns until my bill is paid. If I do, this must be burned.

I hope I will have strength to stick to that. The year is almost gone. I hope I will improve in body and soul during the next year. . . .

Home
Ash Wednesday
Feb. 22, 1882

Dear me, Lent has commenced and with it so many new responsibilities. I have decided to break my engagement very soon. I am only waiting for an answer to my last from Jim. I want him to be a little *prepared*. It is the only *honorable* thing I can do for there is not the slightest prospect of our ever being married. I cannot bear to break everything for I have grown up with the idea of being *Jim's wife*. I guess I will live and die an old maid now. . . .

Now I must write something that I never expected to chronicle in this book. I received a cool, calm letter from Jim which made me think that he was in a hurry to have my answer. So I wrote him a nice letter and told him I could not renew it at all. Five days after I got a telegram from each of the girls saying that Jim would be down to Spring Lake Wednesday night. Of course I was horribly nervous, but with true female instinct I wore my black lace dress with poppies. He came while we were at supper, hardly spoke to any of us, merely asking for a talk with me. Oscar Wilde was lecturing that night so after the lecture I went with Jim to the end of the piazza. I was trembling so I could not keep still. O! it was so hard to see him; to have every recollection of our happy engagement come rushing to my mind, and yet to end everything. I don't know where I ever found the strength. May I never have such another struggle. I never could do it again. Sometimes I feel that I have made a dreadful mistake but it is too late now, alas!! He was very sweet and kind. But he should have been. I could not help it. If I still love him my faith and trust are gone. I never could feel sure of him again. But it is not my fault. What I have lost I would give worlds to regain. I thought I should die when he took off the ring I gave him. He covered his face with his hands and cried, *"Nell, Nell!"*, with such a bitter cry. I almost gave in; the tears came in my eyes and I felt if I waited he would conquer.

So I rose to go; he took both my hands in his and looked down in my face. Then he said, "Promise me if you ever have confidence in me again that you will send for me?" And I said, "Yes, or if I feel as if I need you". Then he said, "Goodbye and God bless you." I turned and left him standing there alone in the dark.

Ah me! I wonder if his heart was any heavier than mine? O my *Sweetheart!* My lost *Sweetheart!* It will never be the same again. I may love and marry someone else, but it will not be my *Sweetheart,* never again; never again. No wonder that I cried the bitterest tears that night that I have ever shed. O it does not seem possible. I loved him so and I was so sure I would be *his* wife some day. It is all over now. I don't suppose I will ever see him again—.

I saw him on the train Monday night. He stopped me and said he had a chance for the Ordnance; should he take it? I wrote him that night and sent him his ring and Class Album. If he tries for the Ordnance, even if he fails, I will respect him more than any time in the last year, but if he succeeds I don't know what I shall do. O if it could only be as it was a few years ago! Why was he not in business like other men? But I won't say anything more. The silver cord is parted. I am free. But like a bird with clipt wings I can only hover around my cage. . . .

Vine Cottage
Sept. 17th, 1882

Dear Fan,

At the Theatre Party Thursday night I saw Jim and his Mother! O dear, every time I get satisfied without him I meet him again and then I realize what I have lost out of my life. It made me miserable to see him; twice they played, "We sat by the river, you and I, in the sweet summertime long ago!" Poor Sweetheart, it was hard on us both. He came to Sing Sing next day, but I did not see him. Only I was so unhappy! O how I longed to send for him, to put my arms around his neck and be forgiven, but I *could* not. What a mistake my life has been. I wish now I had married him in "80" before I ever saw Zete or mistrusted my Sweetheart or myself. I know I would have made it up if I had been sure of him. Ralph says he is sure he cares for me, but he did act dreadfully with Miss Howard and then he rarely wrote me and never even sent me a line Christmas or my birthday. Little things but they all count. I hope after a time I won't care; only now I am miserable. I don't know what I want for I don't suppose I would marry him even now. The Cavalry is so terribly hard. I have lost faith in everything, myself included. I utterly despise myself! O dear, I am such a *fool!* How could I have been in love with *two* men, and yet I have been miserable about them both. However, I honestly believe I have gotten over my fancy for Zete. I wish I were entirely different. I am so weak. O! I blame myself bitterly for the way I have acted. I never told you much about the way I acted with John Shober. I am so ashamed of it and I knew how wrong it was at the time, but he used to beg me so. He held my hand ever so many times; once he caught me in his arms; and twice, another time, he kissed my hair. But worse than anything else is that one night when his head was close to my arm, I bent and kissed it twice. O it is so dreadful. How could I so far forget myself. I hate fast women and I intended to keep myself pure and free from stain. And yet *how* I have fallen! It must have been because I trusted in my own strength, and did not beg God to help me. O, I have fallen so far short of what I reached after. I have drifted away from God and am growing a wicked, careless woman. I hope and pray I will become different. To think of one of Mother's children doing such a thing! How grieved she would have been. It must be a dreadful sin for I worry so about it. I have made a vow that with God's help I will never let a man so much as touch my hand again.

Nellie

• • •

Vine Cottage
Sept. 25th, 1882

Two years ago today Jim went out West. Ah me, how sad and unhappy I was *that* day. But I thought that I would be married this day—in 1882. Alas, how differently everything is now!! He is so far away and I have not even his rare letters to comfort me. Dear Sweetheart. Sometimes I feel sure that it will come right and that this 25th of September perhaps a few years hence will yet see me "Mrs. Erwin". How strange it looks and yet I was so sure I would be his wife. I have liked other men, have even been spooney on them, but I have always come back to him. All through our engagement we took such real comfort together. I was so happy all the summer of "80" with him. O! dear! I wish people had let me alone. If he could only leave the Cavalry and go in business; for I am as much, if not more, opposed to the Army than ever. I do not hardly realize yet that I am free. No wonder I wrote in here in May that I was happy; for I knew I could renew my engagement at any moment. So I could even now for he wrote me to that effect last Sunday; but no, I must wait. Although I have more confidence in him than I had when he first came on, still I must be sure he can be fully trusted. Let him prove himself, what he says. I shall watch him carefully and myself too, for I blame myself almost as much as I do him. I really think I do love him, but I know I am fond of admiration and I have a very soft spot in my heart for two or three "old beaux". I suppose I need something to bring out my love for him, true and strong. I sometimes wonder how it will turn out. I suppose I would be better off if I cared for someone else for we would be poor, but still he is sweet and loveable, and if I should marry anyone else I would never dare meet *him* or even see him. I am the funniest, and most inconsistant girl, I ever met. When I was engaged I was wild to be free, and now that I am free, I don't know what I want! . . .

[*Newspaper clipping dated Dec.* 23, 1882]
"Announcement is made of the engagement of Lieut. James B. Erwin, 4th U.S. Cavalry, of Fort Leavenworth, Kan. to Mrs. Belle Borup, nee Doan."

Dec. 29th, 1882

Put on your specs, Miss Fannie Fern! There, do you see what I have pasted on the top of the page? Then don't faint from surprise. I can do nothing but laugh. How deep and noble is the love of man! How lasting! How constant! It is beautiful to see! Is it not? When I think how he raved the night I broke the engagement I smile with pity. One remark comes to my mind now: "I will never marry, Nell; marriage with any other woman would be sacriledge"!!! High tragedy! and this the end. What will his Ma say, I wonder; Pa too; old Grandmothers, Aunts and paralytic Uncle? He will be Harry's brother-in-law so, as Hattie says, "In the family at last". I will put the newspaper account of the wedding in here.

I have been very busy lately and have met many nice people, but woe is me, I am still held by one face, one pair of bright, dark eyes. Ah Zete, Zete! If I could meet him once. To think that Aunt Josie and the girls have met him. O dear what a life this is. We meet by accident the ones we do not care to see, but the one we would give our life to see turns another way.

I expect to go to Susie's next week but will write in here the last night of the old year.

Au revoir.
Nell

Dec. 31st, 1882

Dear Fan,

Although I am tired, I must write a few words in here the last night of "82". How many times I have written on the last night of the year in this dear book. What a comfort you have been; now you are worn out, your cover is tattered and your fair pages soiled and stained. It is all like my heart.

Six years ago I was fresh and pure; now my whole life is marred. Ah me. O that I had never seen Jim Erwin's face. To be three years engaged to an utterly worthless man—to have wasted such a wealth of love! I will never be the same. O, I could weep tears of fire to burn out those years from my life. But how foolish I am. It is done, why these mad regrets—rather let me be thankful that I discovered my mistake before it was too late. But sometimes scenes, words, idle vows and *kisses* come to my memory and nearly drive me mad. This year is nearly gone—let me be glad. I am leaving the old life with its tender recollections, first love and dear happiness far behind. It was not my fault that I chose a man utterly unworthy of the love and faith I gave. Ah, greater the pity! What worse than to find at the end of a three years' engagement my idol pushed from the lofty pedestal, lying broken and defaced, crumbling in the dust. . . .

[*Telegram dated Jan.* 23, 1883]
BALTIMORE, MD.
TO H. W. BRANDRETH
  8 E. 56 ST., VIA SING SING
SOME MISTAKE LETTER JUST REC'D IF MY ANSWER IS NOT
TOO LATE ACCEPT WITH PLEASURE ANSWER
FRANK LONEY
THE BREXTON, PARK AVE.

8 East 56th St.
Jan. 23, 1883

O Fannie, Fannie, do you see that? I believe I am too glad and happy to be alive!

I wrote him ten days ago and asked him to come on for the Charity Ball. I never thought he would come, and as the days went by without a line from him I nearly gave up in despair. Imagine my delight when I received this, this morning. The house could hardly contain me. I dreamt of him all last night. Such a horrid dream, too. He was with another girl all the time and only spoke to me in the most polite and distant manner. I never saw him so plainly in a dream before, and when I woke up I did feel so dreary and heart sick. Perhaps I have only had a very bad attack of imagination for the last nineteen months. Anyway, I will know as soon as I see him. He will be here the *day after tomorrow*! Oh, it is too good to be true. But I must act very dignified and subdued.

New York
Jan. 28, 1883

Well, it is nearly over! O, these last few happy days! I do not wonder that Birdie said she would rather be Herbert's wife for a year and die, than live a long life without him. I cannot imagine being Zete's wife; it is almost happiness enough to see him once more. Oh, how glad I am that he came on; the misery of the dreary weeks before me makes me heart sick, but I have had my prayer and dearest wish fulfilled. I have seen him once more. He is not engaged yet—what would I do if he were! God knows, not I. It is hard enough not to have him care for me, but if I knew he loved someone else—what would become of me?

He came Thursday afternoon. I was rather nervous about meeting him for I feared in the first delight of seeing his face I might betray the love that I have no right to feel. But how can I help it. Each day it grows stronger until it is becoming a part of my very life. He has not the faintest suspicion; I believe does not think me capable of any depth of feeling at all. If he knew he would only despise me for it, and doubtless tell me it is a foolish fancy. How strange it is that I should care so much for him; my pride should have saved me, but alas! it has no power where he is concerned. It does not seem possible that one can love *so much* and the other *not at all*. I used to be ashamed of it, but why—I cannot help it; besides it does him no harm, and although it makes me miserable I would rather love *him*, even if he never cares for me than have the love of every other man I know. He is even more dignified and quiet. The first afternoon he hardly said one word, and I had to do all the talking—for once in my life. O, I was so happy all that day. The Ball was charming, of course, we knew so many people, and I danced nearly every dance. He is so different; some of the men took four of my dances without thinking whether it bored me or not, but when Zete took my card he put his name down for two, then asked me if he could have a third. I said, "Yes, of course"; whereupon he closed the card and gave it to me saying in his most haughty tone, "*No,* I will not *trespass* on your kindness". O, darling, why do you always misunderstand me. I should think he would know I would rather be with him than any man on earth. When the 15th dance came we sat on the stairs, and I quietly made him take the 21st. Altogether he had six of my dances. I did have a lovely time. Of course everyone likes him very much indeed, but they all seem to suspect that I care for him. It is all very well to acknowl-edge an unrequited love here, but I cannot stand other peoples' pity —except Susie; I do not care if she does know it. Strange, she does not blame me, either, only seems sorry that I should care so much, and he not at all.

Friday night he came here to dinner. Sue was so good to ask him, but then she is always so sweet to me; besides she likes him very much and so does Cyrus. I am glad of that. They all went upstairs after dinner and left Zete and I alone. And I enjoyed *that* evening more than *any* ball. We sat in the hall in the tete-tete chair, and there was nothing more I could desire. He stayed until half-past eleven! shock-ing, but you see I have *all* the misery afterwards, so I may as well enjoy every moment. I wore my black lace dress with pink roses and *he* said he never saw me look so well! Wasn't it good that I did. He does not think me changed, either. I am so glad! I wish I were perfectly beautiful, perhaps then he might care for me a *little.* He came yesterday morning, but only stayed an hour and a half. I was so happy, but he was rather quiet. I hope I don't bore him, but he is so bright that I suppose he soon tires of my society. *Poor Nellie!* When he was putting on his coat to go I was standing in the hall, and the misery of it came over me so suddenly that I sighed and, leaning my head against the hat rack, looked at him. As our eyes met he said in his most icy tone: "Are you tired?" Perhaps he read my love and misery in my eyes and wished to show me how foolish it was. Then we shook hands quietly and he went away. The parting was nothing to him, unless a relief, but to me it was *bitter, bitter* pain. He has gone with Mr. Landen to John Pitney's in Morristown! I suppose he is happy there without a thought of me; perhaps it is best so, for if he loved me, I might be too happy for this earth. Tomorrow night he is going to take Mr. and Mrs. Field, Mr. Landen and myself to the theatre. Then I must say the final goodbye. Before them all; oh, why does he not care for me! He said he would try to come to Spring Lake this summer. If he does, how happy I will be! Think of living in the same house with him one or two weeks! Life cannot hold much more. He is such a perfect gentleman, so dignified and manly, no wonder I love him as I do. God bless him, make him happy, and keep him safe and strong.

Nellie

Jan. 29th, 1883
Monday Night
12:45

He is gone! Without one word. Now I see plainly that he never has nor ever will love me. Heaven help me with all my life to live.

Vine Cottage
Feb. 4th, 1883

I write here quietly now, for my tears are past and I have settled down to live my life without him. Why cry for the moon when I know I will never possess it! Alas, something is too strong for me— perhaps Fate—and I cannot fight against this love. By this time he is settled in whether he would come down to Spring Lake or not. I only wish he knew what it was to care as much as I do. Whatever he does, I hope and pray he will be very happy and have as good and true a wife as he deserves.

Spring Lake
July 12th, 1883

Dear Fan,

. . . Zete is non est. I have not heard from him or seen him since I was in Annapolis. I did have one short, curt note from him in answer to an invitation to my party which I had in June. Of course, he did not come. Oh I wish I could forget him. It is so ridiculous, too, for I know him so slightly. Mr. Potter has been devoted to our party this summer, and very kind to me. You know he lives in Sing Sing; they have a beautiful place there. I have seen a great deal of him since June. Lately I felt we were approaching a climax, but determined to keep it off, if possible, for a while at least. Unfortunately, today we got in a religious discussion and he said several things that shocked me dreadfully for I have very strong opinions on that subject. So I foolishly said to him: "Take my advice and don't fall in love with a girl who has strong views on religion". *That* stopped him and he grew very sober; then began to laugh and recite poetry in a most melodramatic manner; finally settled back in a doleful humor. Suddenly he told me I had given my advice too late, and before I could stop him said, to my horror, "I must tell you, Nellie, that I love you dearly". Then went on with the rest of that old story, finishing up in the approved fashion with, "You are the only woman I have ever loved". And I, what had I to say. I have wasted love on an utterly worthless man, and again given it to one who never cared for me. Now, now when a really good man loves me I have nothing to give! What could I do but tell him the truth, that I feared I still cared for Zete and until I saw him again I could not give him a decided answer. Never will I forget how kind and sweet he was, that he would wait until Lily's wedding. What shall I do? I never liked him so well as I did this afternoon, but it was not *love.* I know I am capable of loving with all my heart, and marriage is too serious a thing for me to enter into lightly. Besides, Fan cannot be left alone. Oh, if I had only *never* seen Zete. I pray I may get over caring for him, but I tremble when I think of meeting him. I must and shall conquer this love; where is my pride.

O what a fool I am! . . .

Vine Cottage
Sept. 5th, 1885

I am more sorry than I can tell that I have let so many months pass without writing in here. I commenced New Year's Eve, but was called away and never finished.

All last summer Frederick and I were together and gradually I became more and more attached to him. In September Fanny, Mrs. Wakefield and I went to the Catskills for a few weeks. Frederick brought us home. After that we were rapidly approaching a crisis. It is strange how differently things happen from what one would expect. I always intended to get engaged in the moonlight; instead it was in the little room, and not at all romantic. I was not half good enough to my dear boy. We should have been engaged long before. It was on the 22nd of September, Mother's wedding day. I a[m] more than thankful to God that he has added and not taken from our number. George Hyatt is in business; Aunt Mary and Ginger are still here. We could not do without them. The younger Brandreths are rapidly taking our places and we old married people will soon be on the shelf.

Dear old journal, good bye. I will never care for another; as for you, I sign myself with my dear new name:

HELEN WARD POTTER

Mary Dodge Woodward
[1826–1890]

The pioneer life was not new to Mary Dodge Woodward when, as a widow of fifty-six, she accompanied three of her adult children to a land claim in Fargo, Dakota Territory. Twenty-five years earlier, she had left Vermont with her husband to settle in Wisconsin where they raised five children. With her husband now dead, and her two oldest children gone from home, she followed her son Walter (age thirty), her daughter Katie (age twenty-three), and her son Fred (age eighteen) farther West. In the 1880s the Dakota Territory was booming—eight million acres in 1883 alone were transferred from government hands to homesteaders.

What was new to Mary Dodge Woodward were the extremes of climate and the wonders of the Dakota landscape of which she was a keen observer. And the homesickness. This compounded by a growing sense of uselessness as she grows older makes holidays, birthdays, and anniversaries days of poignant reflection for her. Throughout her diary, she refers to her "old rose geranium," which she has brought from home and nursed through brutal winters. It seems the emblem both of her ties to the past and of her insistence on life in the present. In 1889, the Woodwards returned together to Wisconsin (Katie later marries Harry Green from Dakota), where Mary Dodge Woodward died the next year on Christmas day.

[1885]

MAY 31, SUNDAY

The wheat is rising out of the ground. The day is very beautiful and I have been out nearly all of it picking posies. The air is soft and cool. I think there is something fascinating about gathering wild flowers, strolling along, not knowing what you will find. It gives one a child-

From Mary Dodge Woodward, *The Checkered Years*, ed. Mary Boynton Cowdry (Caldwell, Idaho: Caxton, 1937). Reprinted by permission.

ish delight. There is a bright yellow flower in bloom now which looks like a Montana verbena, except in color, and is as fragrant; and there are violets in great numbers, some of them nearly pink. Katie says that down at the Sheyenne the air is fragrant with blossoms. Yet I should not like to live there, for the storms follow the river and the mosquitoes are troublesome.

The river woods are looking green. I stand at the east chamber window—which is my observatory—with the spyglass every day and look at them. They seem as near as Vince's woods at home. There is only a narrow strip, but they are dense and filled with a thicket of underbrush, all tangled together. This has been cleared out in several places and farm houses stand close to the river. Hundreds of pounds of hops, growing wild, are gathered there by the settlers every year. Hops possess the qualities of yeast-making in a high degree. I think this is rightly called the land of bread—the wheat, the yeast, the water, and the coal—the very "staff of life."

JUNE 3

It is hard to cook without vegetables, but I have learned to make use of dried fruits. I put in just enough water to swell the berries, then cool them before putting in the sugar, and they swell to their full size. I make all the bread myself. We like good bread and butter at every meal. I have made all the pies since we came here with the exception of lemon pies which Katie makes better than I.

Walter is painting the sitting room floor. It is useless to try to keep a carpet here. I never believed in making a parlor out of a sitting room where members of the family should feel free to come and go as they please.

I have cut out the dress which Nellie sent me so as to finish it before Daniel arrives. Were I farther west, I should not dare to make it "Mother Hubbard" as the paper says that in Pendleton, Oregon, that type of costume is prohibited unless worn belted. Bills to that effect have been posted in the town, ladies who violate the ordinance being fined heavily. The alleged reason is that such garments "scare horses, cause accidents, and ruin business."

JUNE 7, SUNDAY

There was a terrific thunder and wind storm last night. The boys said the roof of the granary fairly wiggled, and the plows were positively blown out of the furrows. The wind tore my lovely pansies all to pieces, and the leaves on the trees hang in ribbons. Afterward, there was a hard frost which left the ground white. At half past nine this morning the ice was not all out of the watering troughs. The peonies froze so hard that the buds hung limp—what few had not been cut off. . . .

JULY 30

We had a fearful storm this morning at seven o'clock. The sky was black as ink. Then came the rain, wind, thunder, and lightening with terrible force. The wind laid flat everything in the garden, lodged the grain, and blew things around generally. It moved the machine house about an inch. A brood of chickens that I had taken a great deal of pains with was killed. The hen was out about two rods from the barn, too far to get in. She took the chicks under her wing, but she was blown off against the barn.

It seems strange to have Cousin Daniel here. He hitched up Gumbo, and he and Roxy and I rode around the quarter-section after supper. The daisies are blossoming in the sloughs, hundreds in one bunch: pink, purple, and white. They are about the size of a nickel. The fallen wheat and oats and vegetables have lifted. The wheat begins to have a ripe, yellow look.

AUGUST 11

Harvest has started. Now there will be no rest for man, woman, or beast until frost which comes, thank heaven, early here. I was nearly beside myself getting dinner for thirteen men, besides carpenters and tinners, with Katie sick in bed and Elsie washing. I baked seventeen loaves of bread today, making seventy-four loaves since last Sunday, not to mention twenty-one pies, and puddings, cakes, and doughnuts.

The men cut one hundred acres today. All four of our harvesters are being used as well as three which were hired to cut by the acre. Things look like business with seven self-binders at work on this home section. The twine to bind our grain will cost three hundred dollars this year.

One of the farm hands broke the thermometer. Now if we are ever so warm we will not know it. I shall send for one as soon as possible.

AUGUST 16

How beautiful the wheat fields look, long avenues between the shocks, just as straight, one mile in length! The whole country is covered with shocks, heavy ones too. Any time during the past week we could see a hundred reapers with the attendant shockers—six to four reapers. Daniel has been flying here, there, and everywhere. Everybody is rustling, which is what I like.

The boys have gone to the Sheyenne to see if there are any plums. Last year there were great quantities of them, very large for wild ones; and grapes, large ones too. The feathery plumes of the golden-rod are beautiful, growing everywhere. They remind me of home. This morning one of the boys said that this was a God-forsaken country. I told him that the whole of Cass County was covered with No. 1 hard wheat, and the wayside was all abloom with goldenrod and asters which proves that God has not forsaken it. . . .

NOVEMBER 26

Thanksgiving Day. This used to be a day of unusual gladness, for on this day Walter was born, and he has proved a great blessing to me. We used to try, after the fashion of New Englanders, to be all at home on Thanksgiving if it were possible. I have been very happy with my family around the table many years—how happy, I did not realize until that sad day on which the father was taken from us and I was left alone with the children. Never since then have all the children been with me on this day. It is our fourth Thanksgiving in Dakota. The turkey is roasted and eaten, and the day has gone; I am thankful. . . .

[1886]

MARCH 26

There is a blizzard of dust today. The wind has blown a hurricane, great clouds of dust flying through the air and sweeping across the prairies. The fine black soil dries on top of the snow as fast as it thaws. Then the dust flies. Part of the time we cannot see McAuliffe's house, less than a quarter of a mile away. The snow has frozen on top just enough so that the horses would break through, which makes hauling difficult.

The boys have been drawing and piling the wood which came to the sidetrack. The carload contained nine cords, and cost $49.50. We burn more wood in summer than in winter, for in the busy season we have a fire in the cook stove from five in the morning to nine at night. The wood is beautiful: straight, dry, and lively. I feel very proud of it. There is nothing more handsome than a nice wood pile. My husband always kept one. When the boys finally finished their work and came in, they were as black as negroes, their eyes looking strikingly white.

Elsie and Lena Lessing walked down to make a call. They think it a short walk, three miles. I have made two crazy blocks which just suit my addled brain. My writing resembles feather-stitching and French knots.

APRIL 10

Seeding is in full swing, and the country begins to teem with activity. The boys have seeded 400 acres this week, walking 110 miles after their seeders, driving their teams. They are footsore and weary after their long tramp. The ground has never been so dry in seedtime since we have been here. In two former springs the men waded in mud and water with rubber boots on. Now dust fills their faces, and they work sometimes in a terrible gale of dirt. I have been out around the fields, but nothing has as yet come out of the ground. Not even a spear of green grass could I find.

Just between daylight and dark, Walter was out working at the cistern when he saw some wild geese fly over and swoop down towards the slough. He ran in, seized his gun, and shot two splendid ones. Now we will have a feast. He brought in one lonesome little buttercup.

APRIL 14

This is the worst day I have ever seen in Dakota. The wind blows without cessation, and the dust flies in great clouds. The boys went out about noon, but could not endure it and came in, their eyes nearly put out. The house is filled with black dust, tight though it be; window sills piled with it. I swept up a dustpan full, upstairs. Dust is even in the closets where there are no windows. Our faces are black in the house.

APRIL 17

I am still cleaning the black dust out of the house that blew in Wednesday. But I should not complain for the same day there was a terrible cyclone in Minnesota which tore the villages of St. Cloud and Sauk Rapids all to pieces, killing about a hundred persons and injuring about two hundred more. At least, so it was reported in the papers. The storm struck a house in which a wedding was taking place, killing the groom and nine of the party of friends present, and injuring eighteen others. There has never been a cyclone so far north before, although there have been tornadoes. If the hand of divine providence directs all things on this earth, I hope we shall be directed what course to pursue to escape. . . .

JUNE 27

My sixtieth birthday. I can scarcely believe that I am nearing the time allotted to mortals. But I am very glad to think that no one would suffer were I to shuffle off this mortal coil.

After supper we all went to the elevator in a lumber wagon. We found some strawberries, and gathered an immense bouquet of lilies, roses, and yellow daisies. It seemed like the days of long ago.

> Forgotten years of silent tears,
> Remembered days of love's sweet praise;
> The long ago of hearts atune
> To glad and happy days of June.

The carpenters commenced the new addition and got the frame up and partly covered the first day (without cider or rum). The new part will go very rapidly. We will have a sitting room, dining room, kitchen, and a good large storeroom or pantry. Now we shall not have to cook in the room in which we eat. . . .

AUGUST 22

Thirty-nine years ago today I was married. That seems a long time, but although there have been many rough places, the years have passed quickly.

Every person and every horse is at work with might and main to secure the wheat crop from storms. There have been many foggy or drizzly days when it was too wet to work in the fields, and the crew were forced to lie around like fish out of water. There have been eight men along looking for work. Patrick Haines left. He could not stand farm work longer. He was a barber from Philadelphia who had gotten out of money in Fargo. Frank Brady came just after the Fourth, ragged and dirty, with not one cent in his pocket. Now, he has fifty dollars which burns him; so he must strike out for Mapleton where, I fear, he will deposit it in a saloon. . . .

DECEMBER 8

There is more snow than at any time last winter. My house plants look very well, a window full of them, and will remain so all winter unless the coal fire should go out, when they would all go. Green's have already lost all of theirs. Katie and I have done a two weeks' washing, hanging our clothes in the new chamber which is a capital place. Everybody in Dakota should have a covered place in which to hang clothes in winter. It would pay a man as well as anything he could build. It would save the wear and tear on the clothes, besides the health of the ones who hang them out.

Elsie and Lena Lessing are hauling wood with a four-horse team. Elsie stands up on her load and touches up the leaders with her whip like any man. They have done almost all the work on their farm this season: plowing, seeding, and harvesting. I cannot understand how any female can do such work as they do, yet it is plain that they are females. . . .

1887

JANUARY 1

The fifth new year finds Walter, Katie, Fred, and myself still here, and still the same only so many years older. We are well, and although we are sometimes lonesome, we are not unhappy. It was forty-two below this morning at eight. We are completely banked in on three sides with snow. The boys are busy a good share of the time taking care of the sixteen horses, the cow (that gives milk), the fifty hens, and the six hogs; besides bringing in the wood and coal for the stove. Poor old Roxy cries when she goes out, and limps when she comes in. A dog likes a pat on the head no less because she is old.

Walter is making out his quarterly report. He says the new well cost only $260. The others have all cost more. As he has done for the past three years, he has again presented me with a handsome diary which deserves better treatment than it will receive at my hands. He exchanges with me for the old one.

> I closed a closely written book last week,
> A volume which no eye but mine will seek,
>   Among the folios laid away.
> If on each page I did imprint fair flowers
> Of deeds, or naught but wasted hours,
>   No one save God and I can say.

JANUARY 8

Forty-two below at 8 A. M. which is as low as our mercury will go. Forty-eight at the signal service. My frozen finger bothers me. It is peeling and stiff and cold, but all I have to do at present is to feed a small family. Walter went to Fargo as our groceries were getting short. I was afraid he would freeze, for the wind was blowing, and any Dakotan knows what that means in winter. He wore two fur coats, one astrakhan and one buffalo, besides his under coat. The last hour that he was out was a hard one for me. I thought surely he would get lost and perish, but he arrived safely home at last with a good bag of mail. The *Daily Sun,* printed in Fargo, and *Scribner's Monthly* kept us from getting lonely tonight.

JANUARY 14

Yesterday was the first day that the thermometer has registered above zero, and we were all elated. I began washing, and even the chickens came out and crowed in glee. Last night after I went to bed a Jack rabbit came and looked in at my house plants. Katie said he looked beautiful. No doubt poor bunny was hungry and wanted to eat his granny's plants. I have a cluster of fuchsias just opening, and how exquisite they look to us here, in this wintry gloom.

> More precious than a garden full of flowers
>   That bloom in summer's prime,
> Are these, that grace the heavy-winged hours,
>   Of barren wintertime.

JANUARY 19

This is the coldest blizzard since we have been in Dakota. It came on so suddenly that I am afraid someone has perished. The snow has been going by for days. The drifts are immense all around the outside of the buildings and enclosures. The snow is a foot higher than the eaves of the machine house. If it keeps on heaping two months longer, I do not know where it will end. One more storm and we shall have to tunnel everywhere. The boys shovel their way around now to do chores. Fred shovels out the pump every time he gets a supply of water for the house. He has been shoveling snow off the roof of the tool house, sliding down on his scoop shovel, calling it his toboggan.

> All day the gusty north-wind bore
> The loosening drift its breath before;
> Low circling round its southern zone,
> The sun through dazzling snow-mist shone.
>   —WHITTIER, *Snow-Bound.*

JANUARY 27

Walter brought me another pair of woolen shoes, without which I could not get along here; also a Dutch calico gown and a felt petticoat, both very handsome. If I just say I want anything, it is forthcoming the first time he goes to Fargo. He bought *Les Miserables* and has already been reading it. We have one sleigh, which has been of no use the past two winters; but this year our wagons are useless. Harry lost his way after leaving here last night, and turned back. He is often snowed in here for two days at a time. I worry so much when our folks are away. Walter has never failed to get here somehow. He seems to delight in hardship.

FEBRUARY 1

This is indeed a hard winter. People say it is the hardest one for seven years, though Walter thinks all winters might be as bad when there was such a quantity of snow and no thaw to lay it. The weather is so extremely cold to have all this snow to shovel. We have sixteen horses, but they cannot shovel snow. I think we should have a snow-plow. The drifts reach the gable-end of some of the buildings. Fred goes down completely out of sight, where he has a hole in a drift, to pump water for the house. He has a regular tunnel into the cellar house which he shovels out every time he goes after vegetables.

The papers are reporting cases of people and cattle freezing to death. A Fargo girl who went to her claim in Dickey County froze to death there alone. A farmer living two miles north of Mapleton went to Fargo on the train. He came home at eight in the evening, and started to walk from the station in a blizzard. He lost his way, and was found in the morning frozen nearly to death within half a mile of his home. He had on a buffalo coat which probably saved his life; but his hands and feet were so badly frozen that they will have to be amputated.

FEBRUARY 13

The wind blew furiously all night, the snow whirling continually through the air. We suffered with the cold in our bedroom. The snow pelted the windows and the wind came in at every crevice. Katie and I could not sleep nor keep warm though the hot coal stove was close by the door. It seemed to have no effect whatever on the cold. The boys were cold all night the same as we. God pity the people who

live in poor houses! I do not see how they live unless God *does* temper
the wind to the shorn lamb—but I would not risk it in Dakota. If it
would thaw enough to make a crust, the snow blizzard would stop.
I never saw a horizontal snow storm until I came here. The snow goes
straight by until it meets something to impede its progress, when it
flies up in a fury. There is no use trying to live here unless the blizzard
is combated with trees, and that will take a long time.

I am so hoarse that I can scarcely speak aloud, which makes it bad
for me but good for the rest of the family. I seem to have a cold
although I wear a great many clothes, as we all do. I get breakfast in
hood, shawl, and mittens as I have done other cold winters. The
kitchen is not warm until noon. Every one of us has a cough even
to Jake, the Norski. It is night and the blizzard is still howling.
Nothing can be seen anywhere except overhead where the moon and
stars shine brightly as the sun often does in a blizzard.

> The wintry wind extends his blast,
> And hail and rain does blaw;
> Or the stormy north sends driving forth
> The blinding sleet and snaw.
>
> *Winter—A Dirge.*

Burns wrote that a hundred years ago.

FEBRUARY 19

Our horse, Pete, got out this morning and thought, I suppose, to view
the surrounding country as Fred found him on top of the drift which
runs onto the tool house. His feet were on the bare roof and he
seemed afraid to come down. Fred tried to lead him, but he would
not stir until the boys had turned him around and given him a few
vigorous whacks. We were afraid he would break through and go
down at the edge of the roof and be buried in snow. But he came
safely off alone at last.

The drifts are as hard as ice. We cut steps in those we pass over
on the way to the well and outbuildings. I climbed to the top of the
drift which runs to the eaves of the granary, and went all around the
buildings. The boys are trying to get an immense snowdrift out of
the horse yard, so that the horses will not climb the stack. It is like
digging ice, and they get into a great perspiration doing it.

I read in one of the papers that sixty frozen corpses have been found in this country this winter. One poor school-teacher, on her way home from school, was lost in a blizzard. Mr. Reily, who was frozen near Mapleton, died in Fargo. Walter will be lost, too, he is so determined to go when he gets ready. When he comes into view in one of these storms, the horses seem to be flying through the air, there being no background nor foreground—just a shape in the storm. The Lessing girls stopped here today. They have been hauling straw and shoveling snow like men.

> It is shovel, shovel, shovel snow,
> Shovel everywhere you go,
> Shovel high and shovel low,
> Shovel, shovel, shovel snow.

FEBRUARY 27

The storm went down in the night after a forty-eight hour run. The drifts are immense and the farm roads and railroads are all blockaded this morning. The boys get around some on snowshoes. It is a hard task to open the railroads. Walter has seen a train with nine engines bucking through the snowdrifts. The companies hire every man they can get to shovel snow along the rails.

This is the first day that it has really thawed. The eaves run, and tonight is warm and pleasant and the moon shines, bringing peace and cheer to us tempest-tossed Dakotans. We have had a three-weeks' pull with colds. Mine nearly wore me out. I could not get up one morning. Katie and I are very thin. We have had no appetites and there has been little to laugh at in Dakota this winter. It has stormed three months, and we are weary and need a rest.

MARCH 1

> With rushing winds and gloomy skies
> The dark and stubborn Winter dies:
> Far off, unseen, Spring faintly cries,
> Bidding her earliest child arise.
> March!
> —BAYARD TAYLOR, *March.*

March has come in mild and lovely and not one bit like a roaring lion, although I have no notion it will make a difference with its exit. Almost daily the sky has looked black and threatening, dark clouds have rolled up in the west at night, and the winds have never ceased their hammering. But the last three warm days have settled the snow so that it could not fly. The drifts are black. The dark soil mixes with the snow, and a little thaw leaves all the dirt on the surface.

MARCH 17

A bright spring morning. The drifts are settling into curious shapes like those of the Arctic regions. One big drift hangs from the gable-end of the machine shed which resembles a great white bear. Since the thaw it has a Roman nose. Everything is ice-coated. The south sides of all the buildings have rows upon rows of long, pointed icicles hanging from their roofs like fringe.

Our hens are beginning to lay and we will have plenty of eggs from now on. Our new Poland China has one little pig. Shell sent us a kitten from Fargo, a pretty one which I hope we will be able to raise.

MARCH 23

Just zero at seven. This cold wave will stiffen the back of old winter which was getting weak and spongy. There is nothing in this place to herald the approach of spring. I suppose at home my dooryard is already showing the swelling of buds, and perhaps the tulips are peeping out, but Dakota is bare. There must be hundreds of children in this territory who have never seen an apple blossom, and what is worse, I fear they never will. The absence of such things takes all the poetry out of life.

> Up our long river-valleys, for days, have not ceased
> The wail and the shriek of the bitter northeast.
> We wait for thy coming, sweet wind of the south!
> For the touch of thy light wings, the kiss of thy
>   mouth.
>   —WHITTIER, *April.*

• • •

[1888]

JANUARY 24

The wind came up last night and by twelve another blizzard was upon us. This morning I could only now and then see the buildings. Great masses of snow were driven against the windows where they stuck fast. That never happens in a very cold storm. The blizzard finally abated somewhat, and the boys went out and sawed and put in place the two loads of ice which they had gotten in Fargo before the storm. It will fill the ice house and I am very glad. It is two feet thick and clear as crystal, much nicer than the ice from the Sheyenne. Now we will drink Red River water.

Cousin Daniel writes that he is thinking of selling the farm in the spring if a good offer is made. He thinks farming does not pay at the present price of wheat and with no prospect of a rise. He has made so many improvements here, which the average farmer does not take into account and will not pay for, that the place will have to be sold at a great sacrifice. We have been here so long that leaving the farm will seem like again leaving home. Except for the cold winters, I should like this place very much indeed. I like a farm better than a home in town; however, for the rest of my days I do not expect to be considered nor consulted as to where I should rather live. But I'll keep up with the procession as long as I am able.

> I'll swing what way the ship shall swim,
> Or tack about with equal trim;
> Whatever turn the matter takes,
> I'll deem it all but ducks and drakes.

JANUARY 29, SUNDAY

Last night there were six Jack rabbits playing in front of the door. They did not seem at all afraid even when Jack went out. They have lived under the granary for a long time and he has given up chasing them for he knows he cannot catch them. Last summer, after they had eaten off all my string beans, I was almost sorry I had not let the boys shoot them.

I have been thinking how this lovely day must affect those who lost fathers, mothers, sisters, and brothers in the storm which has swept so many human beings off the face of the earth. How the mothers' hearts must bleed whose children went away from home in health and happiness only to be returned to them frozen corpses! Miss Ella Lamar, a school-teacher, and one of her pupils were lost. When they were found, the kind teacher had the little girl clasped to her breast in a vain endeavor to save the child from her awful fate.

The newspaper editors were out of paper and many of them were compelled to print their regular editions on blue, red, brown, or any kind of paper which they happened to have on hand. Some of them ran blizzard editions with casualty columns.

The biggest authentic blizzard story which I found in the papers was as follows: Mr. Eric Johnson went out to water his cattle. Among the drove was a large ox. The cattle, one by one, dropped in the snow from exhaustion; and soon the ox became bewildered and lay down in the snow to die. While the man was floundering around in the snow himself he had an inspiration. Drawing his knife, he killed the ox, disemboweled it, and crawled inside. After drawing the sides of the stomach together, he was perfectly sheltered and was kept alive by the warm carcass. In the morning the hide was frozen completely stiff and he could not get out, but he kept calling for help until someone came to release him. . . .

JULY 28

The temperature was 100 at 3 P. M. and Katie and I nearly melted at our work, but we have to prepare three meals a day no matter what happens. The fog drifted early, as the sun struggled through, and hung on the window screens in beads. It is unhealthy weather: cold fog in the morning and hot enough to boil one's blood later on.

I suppose this is my last summer on this farm, and no doubt it is the last summer that I shall have anyone who needs or wants me. I had hoped never to see that time, but I have come to it. Had it not been for Cousin Daniel's farm, the time would have come sooner than this—I mean the time of the breaking up of the family. We could not all have stayed at home in Kingston these last six years. No letters today from Daniel nor Nellie nor Theron, the three that comprise my outside world.

Fannie Hardy (Eckstorm)

[1865–1946]

Fannie Hardy was the oldest of the six children of Manly and Emmeline Hardy of Brewer, Maine. Her father, a strong influence in her life, worked as a fur trader and taxidermist in the Penobscot River watershed north and west of Bangor.* In the years between her graduation from Smith College in 1888 and her marriage in 1893, she accompanied her father on a number of long canoe trips down the West Branch of the Penobscot River. She was likely the first white woman to travel in this region, let alone canoe down the river where every spring over two hundred million feet of lumber were driven down the powerful and dangerous waters. On and around the river, she developed lifelong interests in the logging industry, the Indian peoples indigenous to the area, local and natural history, and folk song.

Her marriage to a minister took her away from New England, but when her husband died in 1899, leaving her with two young children, she returned to the town of her birth. Here began a prolific publishing career that included two books on birds, three on Indian culture, two collections of folk songs (in collaboration), and one volume of stories about the West Branch logging drives. As a noted ornithologist and authority on Indian language, she was a frequent contributor to periodicals in several fields.

This diary excerpt describes a canoe trip taken with her father in 1889.

---

*See Fannie Hardy Eckstorm, *The Penobscot Man*, ed. Edward D. Ives (Somersworth, N. H.: New Hampshire Publishing, 1972), the source of this biographical information.

[1889]

Wednesday, August 21. We got up early and did what cooking was necessary, so that at 5:20 A.M. standard time we started for the mountain. We had at least a mile to go through swampy land before we reached the foot of the slide. Here the trail grew hard to follow though occasional spots, broken branches, and stones laid on the ledges indicated the way when we were in it. We saw a great many signs where Moose had yarded last winter, and one quite recent track; also fresh Deer tracks. The lower part of the slide is overgrown with birch and spruce bushes. Above, where every year the gravel and granite are swept down, the trees become sparser and finally, in the narrower part of the slide, are swept away altogether. In like manner, the growth of the mountain side changes with the increasing elevation until, near the top of the plateau, there are only a few dwarf bushes, firs and alders, and on the tableland and summit, except in one or two places where dwarf spruces grow, there is neither tree nor shrub. We saw these dwarf evergreens off toward the westerly slide but did not go to them.

We made the ascent easily. The climb was [as] steep as going up stairs, in many places steeper, but we did not find it particularly hard, as good footing could be obtained readily and the rocks were at convenient distances apart. Now and then, we would have to climb over a space of gravel for a short distance where the footing was rather hard to keep. The slide had come down, for the lower part, in terraces which made convenient resting places. On one of these we left my gossamer and other luggage. About a third of the way up, we came upon a spring hidden in alder bushes on the right. From that place there were fewer resting places. I found I was able to walk erect and had no trouble with my breath or with blood rushing to my head —two rather unusual things for me. After the top of the slide was reached, there still remained some four or five hundred feet of broken granite piled in inextricable confusion, very steep indeed and dangerous. These huge boulders lay upon each other so loosely as to leave great holes between, and many of the smaller rocks were loose and treacherous. A few stunted half dead firs filled the crevices, and under

From "Down the West Branch of the Penobscot, August 12–22, 1889, From the Journal of Fannie Pearson Hardy (Mrs. Fannie Eckstorm)," ed. Benton L. Hatch, *Appalachia* 27 (December 1949): 480–98. Reprinted by permission of the Appalachian Mountain Club.

the sides of some we found a few of the red mountain cranberries. When we had almost reached the top of the tableland, the fog began to close in about us. We saw it drift between ourselves and the sun, and sat a while wondering whether it was safe for us to go on. At the slightest encouragement from the sun, we pushed ahead, deciding to see the top of the tableland at least. When there, we fastened up our red flag to a stick and set it up on the first monument, at which we also found two shed Caribou horns (not mates) placed side of the monument. The top of the mountain was bare of everything save brown moss, a dwarf kind of blueberry with a small broad elliptical reddish leaf and a peculiar dark blue ovoid berry. The berries were about the size and shape of this spot [an oval was drawn here, about 6 × 8 millimeters], but frequently were larger. We found also the *Corema Conradii* in fruit. It had a roundish black berry—at this season, not a dead black but more like a half ripe huckleberry. We found also the little pearlwort (?) and *Potentilla tridentata* in flower and fruit. These, with a plant unknown to me, dwarf goldenrod, and the mosses which grow there, are the vegetation of the tableland. We found there a nice spring of very cold water which appeared in various places down the slope. We went from there to the east side out onto a little parapet which jutted over the valley. The fog lifted a little so that we could see some of the larger lakes on the southeast. Below us, we could trace the course of Sandy Stream which flows into Millinocket [Lake] and see two openings each some half mile long where the stream, in the spring, had bent or broken down every tree on the banks. We had almost decided not to go farther on account of the fog when suddenly we saw the monument on the summit and pushed on. The ascent was gradual, but to me not as easy climbing as the slide. Here, I felt a little pressed for breath, and father spoke of the same. When we reached the top, the fog lifted for a while and gave us a good view of the Chimney and the Basin with its five ponds in and near. The view is wonderful. No words can be too extravagant. We thought the trail up from the East Branch fully as difficult as our own, though not so long nor so steep. As we came up to the monument, we saw a Red Squirrel on it. He appeared to be quite at home there, and we left him some hardbread to supply his locker. At 10:00 A.M. we left the top of the mountain, and it took us twenty-five minutes of good walking to reach the spring. Here, we ate dinner and soon after started for the slide. Blow flies and black flies were thick on top of the mountain. Mr. Whitcomb complained that going down tired him more than going up; but, although it was somewhat dangerous and required firm feet and a clear head, I did not have any trouble nor strain my knees. We reached the camp at 1:00 P.M. and cooked a little more dinner, then started out again. The afternoon was very hot, but we traveled out to the stream in an hour and forty minutes including half an hour's rest. We saw, on the way, a great hornet's nest. After loading the canoe, Reed waded her down while father and I walked. The moment we came in sight of the West Branch, we saw a canoe drawn up opposite and soon after another canoe out fishing. On going up, we found six men there, three sports-men and their guides. They had been fishing off the mouths of the two Abols and had caught two trout. We ran down, passed an island, through some quick water which ran very strong between great rocks, with the channel on the left. Then we swung round and worked into the carry [around Abol Falls] on the right, but could make a landing only by backing the canoe up. The carry is rather barren having been "camped to death." It shows a few Norways and is largely sand with granite interspersed. We camped at the lower end; found a good spring and camp wood in plenty. That night it rained hard.

Thursday, August 22. The morning being cloudy we decided to wait a while before starting. While delaying, Reed went up to the carry and found some huge granite slabs at the head of the dry way around the island at Abol Falls. One was a natural obelisk 36½ ft. long, 5⅚ ft. wide at the widest place, 4 ft. 7 inches mean width, 4 ft. 9 in. greatest thickness, 4 ft. mean thickness. Another was a slab 15 ft. 2 inches long, 4 ft. 8 inches deep, 33 inches thick at one end and 25 [inches] at the other. One next [to] it was of the same length and depth (they stood on edge) and 10 inches wide at one end, 9 at the other. Another was 17 ft. 8 inches long, 19 inches wide at one end and 20 at the other. The third dimension could not be obtained.

Abol Falls are not very high but so rocky that driving them is hard. One man is kept all the time on the Gray Rock of Abol to pick off logs. The mouth of the carry at this stage of water is about fifteen rods from the putting-in place. We got started about nine o'clock (very hot) and went down with the current. So far from being dead water where the guide book told us, there is usually a strong current and often considerable quick water. We heard a Deer grunt twice in the bushes, and soon after, coming to quick water where it was shoal, father and I got ashore to walk down to the end of the Pockwockamus Carry. We came to what I called a taking-out place; father thought not; so we went ahead about a half mile. We then saw that the falls consisted of two pitches, the upper of which would be hard to run at the present stage of water. On going back, father found Reed stuck on the upper pitch having misjudged the water. He says that in the spring the driving boats run over after taking out the wangun. We carried by in the heat and made our Partridge stew near the lower end just at the head of the lower pitch. This lower pitch is a heavy fall and the rockiest place I ever saw. It is a marvel how logs ever can be engineered through such a place. The great boulders lie packed so closely that one can walk almost across the river by leaping from one to another. At one place, I counted forty from five to ten feet high and much larger in their other dimensions. These great granite blocks are worn to a rounded form by water and logs.

Above the pitch we saw a pile of logs left on a high landing on the left, and on the head of the falls, a larger jam which had been partly burned out. Two Fish Hawks kept wheeling over us all the time we stayed at Pockwockamus. Here we had to go around the bank for some distance, after the canoe was pushed off, before we could get in again on account of the shallow water. We saw numerous signs of Deer where they had been feeding and walking in the grass.

Below this point, we had a very pretty dead water, the Pockwock-amus Deadwater. There were many islands in it, rather low and wooded, with sandy or hard earth shores and birch and poplar growth. The expanse is a small lake in itself. When we got down to the widest part, we began to hear the roar of Katepskonegan Falls. The water is smooth to the edge, but a jam piled in like jackstraws. On the right above the carry, we saw a Fish Hawk's nest and two birds rose from it. On the end of the carry, we saw two men named York who helped Reed carry the canoe across. They were on their way up-river and had carried all but one load across. They said they saw fourteen Deer in coming up.

The Debsconeag (Katepskonegan) Carry is the best we have seen so far, about a half mile long though the men called it "a short quarter." One of them—the son—who wore a sheath made of a Deer's leg, said our canoe was as "big as the Ark of Safety."

PERSONAL AND POLITICAL

Mary MacLane

[1881–1929]

At the age of twenty in Butte, Montana, Mary MacLane emerged from lonely and introspective teenage years as a literary sensation with the publication of her diary, The Story of Mary MacLane. *Variously hailed as obscene, brilliant, or mad, the book detailed the passionate inner life of this self-consciously outrageous young woman. Buoyed by notoriety and financial success—the book sold 80,000 copies in its first month—she spent the next seven years among the intellectuals and Bohemians of Chicago, Boston, and New York.*

When the reception of her second book was disappointing, MacLane returned to Montana in 1909 to work on I, Mary MacLane, *a book in the same diary format as her first success. After its publication, she traveled again to Chicago and starred there in a film for which she had written the script, "Men I Have Loved." She lived the rest of her life in Chicago, where she died poor and obscure in the face of one of the few things she admitted fearing—"a lonely Hotel room."*

The beloved "anemone lady" in the excerpt below is the only human being important to Mary MacLane in the first volume of her diary. Otherwise only "the Devil," for whom she yearns, shares the stage with Mary herself. The "anemone lady" was Fannie Corbin, an English teacher at Butte High School. When Mary MacLane later arrived in Boston, Fannie Corbin, who was studying at Harvard at the time, advised her against applying to Radcliffe for college. Corbin made her remarks public, saying she felt her former pupil academically unprepared. Whether Mac-Lane applied to Radcliffe and was rejected or whether she never applied is unclear, but she never did attend college. And she remained firm throughout her life in her determination never to marry.

Butte, Montana,
January 13, 1901.

I of womankind and of nineteen years, will now begin to set down as full and frank a Portrayal as I am able of myself, Mary MacLane, for whom the world contains not a parallel.

I am convinced of this, for I am odd.

I am distinctly original innately and in development.

I have in me a quite unusual intensity of life.

I can feel.

I have a marvelous capacity for misery and for happiness.

I am broad-minded.

I am a genius.

I am a philosopher of my own good peripatetic school.

I care neither for right nor for wrong—my conscience is nil.

My brain is a conglomeration of aggressive versatility.

I have reached a truly wonderful state of miserable morbid unhappiness.

I know myself, oh, very well.

I have attained an egotism that is rare indeed.

I have gone into the deep shadows.

All this constitutes oddity. I find, therefore, that I am quite, quite odd. . . .

I was born in 1881 at Winnepeg, in Canada. Whether Winnepeg will yet live to be proud of this fact is a matter for some conjecture and anxiety on my part. When I was four years old I was taken with my family to a little town in western Minnesota, where I lived a more or less vapid and lonely life until I was ten. We came then to Montana.

Whereat the aforesaid life was continued.

My father died when I was eight.

Apart from feeding and clothing me comfortably and sending me to school—which is no more than was due me—and transmitting to me the MacLane blood and character, I can not see that he ever gave me a single thought.

Certainly he did not love me, for he was quite incapable of loving any one but himself. And since nothing is of any moment in this

From *The Story of Mary MacLane* (Chicago: Herbert S. Stone, 1902).

world without the love of human beings for each other, it is a matter of supreme indifference to me whether my father, Jim MacLane of selfish memory, lived or died.

He is nothing to me.

There are with me still a mother, a sister, and two brothers.

They also are nothing to me.

They do not understand me any more than if I were some strange live curiosity, as which I dare say they regard me.

I am peculiarly of the MacLane blood, which is Highland Scotch. My sister and brothers inherit the traits of their mother's family, which is of Scotch Lowland descent. This alone makes no small degree of difference. Apart from this the MacLanes—these particular MacLanes—are just a little bit different from every family in Canada, and from every other that I've known. It contains and has contained fanatics of many minds—religious, social, whatnot, and I am a true MacLane.

There is absolutely no sympathy between my immediate family and me. There can never be. My mother, having been with me during the whole of my nineteen years, has an utterly distorted idea of my nature and its desires, if indeed she has any idea of it.

When I think of the exquisite love and sympathy which might be between a mother and daughter, I feel myself defrauded of a beautiful thing rightfully mine, in a world where for me such things are pitiably few.

It will always be so.

My sister and brothers are not interested in me and my analyses and philosophy, and my wants. Their own are strictly practical and material. The love and sympathy between human beings is to them, it seems, a thing only for people in books.

In short, they are Lowland Scotch, and I am a MacLane.

And so, as I've said, I carried my uninteresting existence into Montana. The existence became less uninteresting, however, as my versatile mind began to develop and grow and know the glittering things that are. But I realized as the years were passing that my own life was at best a vapid, negative thing.

A thousand treasures that I wanted were lacking.

I graduated from the high school with these things: very good Latin; good French and Greek; indifferent geometry and other mathematics; a broad conception of history and literature; peripatetic philosophy that I acquired without any aid from the high school; genius of a kind, that has always been with me; an empty heart that has taken on a certain wooden quality; an excellent strong young woman's-body; a pitiably starved soul.

With this equipment I have gone my way through the last two years. But my life, though unsatisfying and warped, is no longer insipid. It is fraught with a poignant misery—the misery of nothingness.

I have no particular thing to occupy me. I write every day. Writing is a necessity—like eating. I do a little housework, and on the whole I am rather fond of it—some parts of it. I dislike dusting chairs, but I have no aversion to scrubbing floors. Indeed, I have gained much of my strength and gracefulness of body from scrubbing the kitchen floor—to say nothing of some fine points of philosophy. It brings a certain energy to one's body and to one's brain.

But mostly I take walks far away in the open country. Butte and its immediate vicinity present as ugly an outlook as one could wish to see. It is so ugly indeed that it is near the perfection of ugliness. And anything perfect, or nearly so, is not to be despised. I have reached some astonishing subtleties of conception as I have walked for miles over the sand and barrenness among the little hills and gulches. Their utter desolateness is an inspiration to the long, long thoughts and to the nameless wanting. Every day I walk over the sand and barrenness.

And so, then, my daily life seems an ordinary life enough, and possibly, to an ordinary person, a comfortable life.

That's as may be.

To me it is an empty, damned weariness.

I rise in the morning; eat three meals; and walk; and work a little, read a little, write; see some uninteresting people; go to bed.

Next day, I rise in the morning; eat three meals; and walk; and work a little, read a little, write; see some uninteresting people; go to bed.

Again I rise in the morning; eat three meals; and walk; and work a little, read a little, write; see some uninteresting people; go to bed.

Truly an exalted, soulful life!

What it does for me, how it affects me, I am now trying to portray. . . .

January 20.

I have said that I am alone.

I am not quite, quite alone.

I have one friend—of that Friendship that is real and is inlaid with the beautiful thing Truth. And because it has the beautiful thing Truth in it, this my one Friendship is somehow above and beyond me; there is something in it that I reach after in vain—for I have not that divinely beautiful thing Truth. Have I not said that I am a thief and a liar? But in this Friendship nevertheless there is a rare, ineffably sweet something that is mine. It is the one tender thing in this dull dreariness that wraps me round.

Are there many things in this cool-hearted world so utterly exquisite as the pure love of one woman for another woman?

My one friend is a woman some twelve or thirteen years older than I. She is as different from me as is day from night. She believes in God —that God that is shown in the Bible of the Christians. And she carries with her an atmosphere of gentleness and truth. The while I am ready and waiting to dedicate my life to the Devil in exchange for Happiness—or some lesser thing. But I love Fannie Corbin with a peculiar and vivid intensity, and with all the sincerity and passion that is in me. Often I think of her, as I walk over the sand in my Nothingness, all day long. The Friendship of her and me is a fair, dear benediction upon me, but there is something in it—deep within it— that eludes me. In moments when I realize this, when I strain and reach vainly at a thing beyond me, when indeed I see in my mind a vision of the personality of Fannie Corbin, it is then that it comes on me with force that I am not good.

But I can love her with all the ardor of a young and passionate heart.

Yes, I can do that.

For a year I have loved my one friend. During the eighteen years of my life before she came into it I loved no one, for there was no one.

It is an extremely hard thing to go through eighteen years with no one to love, and no one to love you—the first eighteen years.

But now I have my one friend to love and to worship.

I have named my friend the "anemone lady," a name beautifully appropriate.

The anemone lady used to teach me literature in the Butte High

School. She used to read poetry in the classroom in a clear, sweet voice that made one wish one might sit there forever and listen to it.

But now I have left the high school, and the dear anemone lady has gone from Butte. Before she went she told me she would be my friend.

Think of it—to live and have a friend!

My friend does not fully understand me; she thinks much too well of me. She has not a correct idea of my soul's depths and shallows. But if she did know them she would still be my friend. She knows the heavy weight of my unrest and unhappiness. She is tenderly sympathetic. She is the one in all the world who is dear to me.

Often I think, if only I could have my anemone lady and go and live with her in some little out-of-the-world place high up on the side of a mountain for the rest of my life—what more would I desire? My friendship would constitute my life. The unrest, the dreariness, the Nothingness of my existence now is so dull and gray by contrast that there would be Happiness for me in that life, Happiness softly radiant, if quiet—redolent of the fresh, thin fragrance of the dear blue anemone that grows in the winds and rains of spring.

But Miss Corbin would doubtless look somewhat askance at the idea of spending the rest of her life with me on a mountain. She is very fond of me, but her feeling for me is not like mine for her, which indeed is natural. And her life is made up mostly of sacrifices—doing for her fellow-creatures, giving of herself. She never would leave this.

And so, then, the mountainside and the solitude and the friend with me are, like every good thing, but a vision.

"Thy friend is always thy friend; not to have, nor to hold, nor to love, nor to rejoice in: but to remember."

And so do I remember my one friend, the anemone lady—and think often about her with passionate love. . . .

January 26.

I sit at my window and look out upon the housetops and chimneys of Butte. As I look I have a weary, disgusted feeling.

People are abominable creatures.

Under each of the roofs live a man and woman joined together by that very slender thread, the marriage ceremony—and their children, the result of the marriage ceremony.

How many of them love each other? Not two in a hundred, I

warrant. The marriage ceremony is their one miserable, petty, paltry excuse for living together.

This marriage rite, it appears, is often used as a cloak to cover a world of rather shameful things.

How virtuous these people are, to be sure, under their different roof-trees. So virtuous are they indeed that they are able to draw themselves up in the pride of their own purity, when they happen upon some corner where the marriage ceremony is lacking. So virtuous are they that the men can afford to find amusement and diversion in the woes of the corner that is without the marriage rite; and the women may draw away their skirts in shocked horror and wonder that such things can be, in view of their own spotless virtue.

And so they live on under the roofs, and they eat and work and sleep and die; and the children grow up and seek other roofs, and call upon the marriage ceremony even as their parents before them—and then they likewise eat and work and sleep and die; and so on world without end.

This also is life—the life of the good, virtuous Christians.

I think, therefore, that I should prefer some life that is not virtuous.

I shall never make use of the marriage ceremony. I hereby register a vow, Devil, to that effect.

When a man and a woman love one another that is enough. That is marriage. A religious rite is superfluous. And if the man and woman live together without the love, no ceremony in the world can make it marriage. The woman who does this need not feel the tiniest bit better than her lowest sister in the streets. Is she not indeed a step lower since she pretends to be what she is not—plays the virtuous woman? While the other unfortunate pretends nothing. She wears her name on her sleeve.

If I were obliged to be one of these I would rather be she who wears her name on her sleeve. I certainly would. The lesser of two evils, always.

I can think of nothing in the world like the utter littleness, the paltriness, the contemptibleness, the degradation, of the woman who is tied down under a roof with a man who is really nothing to her; who wears the man's name, who bears the man's children—who plays the virtuous woman. There are too many such in the world now.

May I never, I say, become that abnormal, merciless animal, that deformed monstrosity—a virtuous woman.

Anything, Devil, but that.

And so, as I look out over the roofs and chimneys, I have a weary, disgusted feeling. . . .

February 12.

I am in no small degree, I find, a sham—a player to the gallery.

Possibly this may be felt as you read these analyses.

While all of these emotions are written in the utmost seriousness and sincerity, and are exactly as I feel them, day after day—so far as I have the power to express what I feel—still I aim to convey through them all the idea that I am lacking in the grand element of Truth— that there is in the warp and woof of my life a thread that is false— false.

I don't know how to say this without the fear of being misunderstood. When I say I am in a way a sham, I have no reference to the truths as I have given them in this Portrayal, but to a very light and subtle thing that runs through them.

Oh, do not think for an instant that this analysis of my emotions is not perfectly sincere and real, and that I have not felt all of them more than I can put into words. They are my tears—my life-blood!

But in my life, in my personality, there is an essence of falseness and insincerity. A thin, fine vapor of fraud hangs always over me and dampens and injures some things in me that I value.

I have not succeeded thoroughly in analyzing this—it is so thin, so elusive, so faint—and yet not little. It is a natural thing enough viewed in the light of my other traits.

I have lived my nineteen years buried in an environment at utter variance with my natural instincts, where my inner life is never touched, and my sympathies very rarely, if ever, appealed to. I never disclose my real desires or the texture of my soul. Never, that is to say, to any one except my one friend, the anemone lady.—And so every day of my life I am playing a part; I am keeping an immense bundle of things hidden under my cloak. When one has played a part —a false part—all one's life, for I was a sly, artful little liar even in the days of five and six; then one is marked. One may never rid oneself of the mantle of falseness, charlatanry—particularly if one is innately a liar.

A year ago when the friendship of my anemone lady was given me, and she would sometimes hear sympathetically some long-silent bit of pain, I felt a snapping of tense-drawn cords, a breaking away of flood-gates—and a strange, new pain. I felt as if I must clasp her gentle hand tightly and give way to the pent-up, surging tears of eighteen years. I had wanted this tender thing more than anything else all my life, and it was given me suddenly.

I felt a convulsion and a melting, within.

But I could not tell my one friend exactly what I felt. There was no doubt in my own mind as to my own perfect sincerity of feeling, but there was with it and around it this vapor of fraud, a spirit of falseness that rose and confronted me and said, "hypocrite," "fool."

It may be that the spirit of falseness is itself a false thing—yet true or false, it is with me always. I have tried, in writing out my emotions, to convey an idea of this sham element while still telling everything faithfully true. Sometimes I think I have succeeded, and at other times I seem to have signally failed. This element of falseness is absolutely the very thinnest, the very finest, the rarest of all the things in my many-sided character.

It is not the most unimportant.

I have seen visions of myself walking in various pathways. I have seen myself trying one pathway and another. And always it is the same: I see before me in the path, darkening the way and filling me with dread and discouragement, a great black shadow—the shadow of my own element of falseness.

I can not rid myself of it.

I am an innate liar.

This is a hard thing to write about. Of all things it is the most liable to be misunderstood. You will probably misunderstand it, for I have not succeeded in giving the right idea of it. I aimed at it and missed it. It eluded me completely.

You must take the idea as I have just now presented it for what it may be worth. This is as near as I can come to it. But it is something infinitely finer and rarer.

It is a difficult task to show to others a thing which, though I feel and recognize it thoroughly, I have not yet analyzed for myself.

But this is a complete Portrayal of me—as I await the Devil's coming—and I must tell everything—everything. . . .

March 5.

Sometimes I am seized with nearer, vivider sensations of love for my one friend, the anemone lady.

She is so dear—so beautiful!

My love for her is a peculiar thing. It is not the ordinary woman-love. It is something that burns with a vivid fire of its own. The anemone lady is enshrined in a temple on the inside of my heart that shall always only be hers.

She is my first love—my only dear one.

The thought of her fills me with a multitude of feelings, passionate yet wonderfully tender,—with delight, with rare, undefined emotions, with a suggestion of tears.

Oh, dearest anemone lady, shall I ever be able to forget your beautiful face! There may be some long, crowded years before me; it may be there will be people and people entering and departing—but, oh, no—no, I shall never forget! There will be in my life always —always the faint sweet perfume of the blue anemone: the memory of my one friend.

Before she went away, to see her, to be near her, was an event in my life—a coloring of the dullness. Always when I used to look at her there would rush a train of things over my mind, a vaguely glittering pageant that came only with her, and that held an always-vivid interest for me.

There were manifold and varied treasures in this train. There were skies of spangled sapphire, and there were lilies, and violets wet with dew. There was the music of violins, and wonderful weeds from the deep sea, and songs of troubadours, and gleaming white statues. There were ancient forests of oak and clematis vines; there were lemon-trees, and fretted palaces, and moss-covered old castles with moats and draw-bridges and tiny mullioned windows with diamond panes. There was a cold, glittering cataract of white foam, and a little green boat far off down the river, drifting along under drooping willows. There was a tree of golden apples and a banquet in a beautiful house with the melting music of lutes and harps, and mulled orange-wine in tall, thin glasses. There was a field of long, fine grass, soft as bat's-wool, and there were birds of brilliant plumage—scarlet and indigo with gold-tipped wings.

All these and a thousand fancies alike vaguely glittering would rush over me when I was with the anemone lady. Always my brain was in a gentle delirium. My nerves were unquiet.

It was because I love her.

Oh, there is not—there can never be—another anemone lady!

My life is a desert—a desert, but the thin, clinging perfume of the blue anemone reaches to its utter confines. And nothing in the desert is the same because of that perfume. Years will not fade the blue of the anemone, nor a thousand bitter winds blow away the rare fragrance.

I feel in the anemone lady a strange attraction of sex. There is in me a masculine element that, when I am thinking of her, arises and overshadows all the others.

"Why am I not a man," I say to the sand and barrenness with a certain strained, tense passion, "that I might give this wonderful, dear, delicious woman an absolutely perfect love!"

And this is my predominating feeling for her.

So, then, it is not the woman-love, but the man-love, set in the mysterious sensibilities of my woman-nature. It brings me pain and pleasure mingled in that odd, odd fashion.

Do you think a man is the only creature with whom one may fall in love?

Often I see coming across the desert a long line of light. My soul turns toward it and shrinks away from it as it does from all the lights. Some day, perhaps, all the lights will roll into one terrible white effervescence and rush over my soul and kill it. But this light does not bring so much of pain, for it is soft and silvery, and always with it is the Soul of Anemone. . . .

April 11.

I write a great many letters to the dear anemone lady. I send some of them to her and others I keep to read myself. I like to read letters that I have written—particularly that I have written to her.

This is a letter that I wrote two days ago to my one friend:

"To you:—

"And don't you know, my dearest, my friendship with you contains other things? It contains infatuation, and worship, and bewitchment, and idolatry, and a tiny altar in my soul-chamber whereon is burning sweet incense in a little dish of blue and gold.

"Yes, all of these.

"My life is made up of many outpourings. All the outpourings have one point of coming-together. You are the point of coming-together. There is no other.

"You are the anemone lady.

"You are the one whom I may love.

"To think that the world contains one beautiful human being for me to love!

"It is wonderful.

"My life is longing for the sight of you. My senses are aching for lack of an anemone to diffuse itself among them.

"A year ago, when you were in the high school, often I used to go over there when you would be going home, so that my life could be made momentarily replete by the sight of you. You didn't know I was there—only a few times when I spoke to you.

"And now it is that I remember you.

"Oh, my dearest—you are the only one in the world!

"We are two women. You do not love me, but I love you.

"You have been wonderfully, beautifully kind to me.

"You are the only one who has ever been kind to me.

"There is something delirious in this—something of the nameless quantity.

"It is old grief and woe to live nineteen years and to remember no person ever to have been kind. But what is it—do you think?—at the end of nineteen years, to come at last upon one who is wonderfully, beautifully kind!

"Those persons who have had some one always to be kind to them can never remotely imagine how this feels.

"Sometimes in these spring days when I walk miles down into the country to the little wet gulch of the sweetflags, I wonder why it is that this thing does not make me happy. 'She is wonderfully, beautifully kind,' I say to myself—'and she is the anemone lady. She is *wondrously* kind, and though she's gone, nothing can ever change that.'

"But I am not happy.

"Oh, my one friend—what is the matter with me? What is this feeling? Why am I not happy?

"But how can you know?

"You are beautiful.

"I am a small, vile creature.

"Always I awake to this fact when I think of the anemone lady.

"I am not good.

"But you are kind to me.

"You have written me two letters.

"The anemone lady came down from her high place and wrote me two letters.

"It is said that God is somewhere. It may be so.

"But God has never come down from his high places to write me two letters.

"Dear—do you see?—you are the only one in the world.

"MARY MACLANE."

*A crucible of my own making**

To-day

It is the edge of a somber July night in this Butte-Montana.
The sky is overcast. The nearer mountains are gray-melancholy.
And at this point I meet Me face to face.
I am Mary MacLane: of no importance to the wide bright world and dearly and damnably important to Me.
Face to face I look at Me with some hatred, with despair and with great intentness.
I put Me in a crucible of my own making and set it in the flaming trivial Inferno of my mind. And I assay thus:
I am rare—I am in some ways exquisite.
I am pagan within and without.
I am vain and shallow and false.
I am a specialized being, deeply myself.
I am of woman-sex and most things that go with that, with some other *pointes.*
I am dynamic but devasted, laid waste in spirit.
I'm like a leopard and I'm like a poet and I'm like a religieuse and I'm like an outlaw.
I have a potent weird sense of humor—a saving and a demoralizing grace.
I have brain, cerebration—not powerful but fine and of a remarkable quality.
I am scornful-tempered and I am brave.
I am slender in body and someway fragile and firm-fleshed and sweet.
I am oddly a fool and a strange complex liar and a spiritual vagabond.
I am strong, individual in my falseness: wavering, faint, fanciful in my truth.

*From *I, Mary MacLane: A Diary of Human Days* (New York: Frederick A. Stokes, 1917).

I am eternally self-conscious but sincere in it.

I am ultra-modern, very old-fashioned: savagely incongruous.

I am young, but not very young.

I am wistful—I am infamous.

In brief, I am a human being.

I am presciently and analytically egotistic, with some arresting dead-feeling genius.

And were I not so tensely tiredly sane I would say that I am mad.

So assayed I begin to write this book of myself, to show to myself in detail the woman who is inside me. It may or it mayn't show also a type, a universal Eve-old woman. If it is so it is not my purport. I sing only the Ego and the individual. . . .

A deathly pathos

To-morrow

I love the sex-passion which is in this witching Body of me. I love to feel its portent grow and creep over me, like a climbing vine of tiny red roses, in the occasional dusks.

It is no shame or shadow or sordidness: but beauty and sweetness and light.

no token of sin: a token of virtue.

no thing to crush: rather to nurture, to garner.

no thing to forget: to remember, to think about.

no flat weak drawn-out prose: live potent clipped heated poetry.

not common and loosely human: rare and divine.

not fat daily soup: stinging wine of life.

not valueless because born of nothing and nowhere: valuable, priceless, a treasure under lock and key.

Sex-desire comes wandering in dusk-time and gulfs me as in a swift violent sweet-smelling whirlwind. It goes away sudden-variant as it came, out of a region of hot quick shadows.

And for that, for hours and days afterward, oranges and apples look brighter-colored to my eyes: hammocks swing easier as I sit in them: rugs feel softer to my feet: the black dresses lend themselves gentler to my form: pencils slide faciler on paper: my voice speaks less difficultly into telephones: meanings sound super-vibrant in Keats's Odes: sugar—little pinches of granulated sugar—are sharper, sweeter-sweeter in my throat.

And God grows less remote. And my wooden coffin and deep wet yellow clay grave move a long way back from me.

—all from fleeting ungratified wish of sly sex-tissues—

Also in it, and in my life from it, I sense some deathly pathos. . . .

An ancient witch-light

To-morrow

Also I am someway the Lesbian woman.

It is but one phase—one which slightly touches each other phase I own. And in it I am poetic and imaginative and worldly and amorous and gentle and true and strong and weak and ardent and shy and sensitive and generous and morbid and sweet and fine and false.

The Lesbian sex-strain as an effect is reckoned a prenatal influence —and, as I conceive, it comes also of conglomerate incarnations and their reactions and flare-backs. Of some thus bestowed it makes strange hard highly emotional indefinably vicious women, turbulent and brilliant of mind, mystically overborne, overwrought of heart. They are marvels of perverse barbaric energy. They make with men varied flinty friendships, but to each other they are friends, lovers, victims, preyers, masters, slaves: the flawed fruits of one oblique sex-inherence.

Except two breeds—the stupid and the narrowly feline—all women have a touch of the Lesbian: an assertion all good non-analytic creatures refute with horror, but quite true: there is always the poignant intensive personal taste, the *flair* of inner-sex, in the tenderest friendships of women.

For myself, there is no vice in my Lesbian vein. I am too personally fastidious, too temperamentally dishonest, too eerily wavering to walk in direct repellent roads of vice even in freest moods. There is instead a pleasant degeneracy of attitude more debauching to my spirit than any mere trivial *traînant* vice would be. And a fascination in it tempers my humanness with an evil-feeling power.

I have lightly kissed and been kissed by Lesbian lips in a way which filled my throat with a sudden subtle pagan blood-flavored wistfulness, ruinous and contraband: breath of bewildering demoniac winds smothering mine.

Lesbian essence is of mental quality. There are aggressively endowed women whose minds are so bent that they instinctively nurture any

element in themselves which is blighting and ill-omened and calami-
tous in effect. There are some to which the natural inhibition of their
own sex is lure and challenge. There are some so solitary by destiny
and growth that the first woman-friend who comes into their adoles-
cence with sympathy and understanding wins a passionate Lesbian
adoration the deeper for being unrealized. There are some so roiledly
giftedly incongruous in trait that they are prone to catch and hold any
additional twisted shreds afloat in human air-currents.

Each of those influences biases the Mind of me, which is none the less
a clear-visioned mind which rates no thing a truth which it knows
to be a lie: though it batten on the lie.

—often here and there around this human world the twisted and
perverted and strongly false concepts are the strong actual working
facts and the straight road is myth—myth—existent but in visions—
I don't understand why it's so: I know it is so.

Not only so with me: so with millions whose stars jangled.

Not always. But often.—

The deep-dyed Lesbian woman is a creature whose sensibilities are
over-balanced: whose imagination moves on mad low-flying wings:
whose brain is good: whose predilections are warped: who lives always in unrest: whose inner walls are streaked with garish heathen
pigments: whose copious love-instincts are an odd mixture of mirth,
malice and *luxure*.

Its effects in me who am straight-made in nothing, but strongly
crooked, is to vivify tenfold or a hundredfold or a thousandfold in my
shaded vision the womanness of any woman whose inner or outer
beauty arrests and stirs my spirit.

I see in some woman, some girl, any who attracts me—be she a casual
acquaintance, or a Victorian poet dead fifty years whose poetry and
portrait live, or an actor in a play, or a sweet-browed friend, or an
Old Master—I see one such as if all her charm were newly painted
and placed near me shining wet with delicate fresh paint. It is be-
witching to look at: it has a deep seductive fragrance of smell: it is
luxuriantly aromatic to all my known senses—and two senses unknown float from my deeps and rise at it. The Stranger becomes a
dearly poignant fancy to dream over. My Friend turns into a vivid
goddess whose fingers and hair I would touch tenderly with my lips.
Because of it a little flame, pale but primal, leaps from the flattest
details of life. In such a mood-adventure a window-shutter blooms:

a hair-brush glows: a sordid floor has gleams upon it. These bewildering frightful beautifulnesses in this life—.

—withal the same inherence which makes me someway Lesbian makes me the floor of the setting sun—strewn with overflowing gold and green vases of Fire and Turquoise—a sly and piercing annihilation-of-beauty, wonderful devastating to feel—oh, blighting breaking to feel—oh, deathly lovely to feel!—It is the bewitched obliquities that run away with me: grind, gnaw, eat my true human heart like bright potent vitriol.

What God means me to do with such gifts and phases—I don't and don't understand. I never get anywhere as I think it out. I don't know shades of rights and wrongs since that ancient witch-light has found more trueness of human feeling in me than has any simplicity my life knows.

It began, they say, with Sappho and her dreaming students in the long-ago vales of Lesbos. It may be, I daresay. I know it did not stop there. And I know that—Greek, French, Scotch, Indian—Welch—Japanese—*all* women sense its light lyric touch. For myself, I know only it is part and parcel in my tangled tired coil.

I don't know whether I am good and sweet in it or evil and untoward. And I don't care.

Anonymous

"The Day's Work in a Cannery: From a Factory Girl's Diary" appeared anonymously in the November 1912 issue of Life and Labor, *the monthly publication of the Women's Trade Union League (W.T.U.L.). The text accurately conveys the working conditions of the women and children employed in the canning industry in the early decades of the twentieth century. The physical demands of the work were great, the hours long (eleven to fourteen hours a day), and the pay extremely low.*

The authenticity of the journal has not been established and it may be in the tradition of labor organizers imitating the journal form in order to create impressions of immediacy and vivid truth. A better-known text in that tradition is Teresa Malkiel's Diary of a Shirtwaist Striker *(New York: Cooperative Press, 1910), describing a strike in 1909 at the Triangle Shirtwaist Company, where in 1911 a fire killed 146 women and girls in New York City.*

[1912]

Monday Evening, September 11

I sneezed a lot today and tonight have a heavy head and an aching shoulder.

I didn't get to work till 7 o'clock, but the rest had been at it from 6:30.

General hours, 6 or 6:30 to 12 and 12:30 to 5:30, 6 or 6:30.

Our building is large and low, divided into two long rooms, one where labeling is done and cans stored, the other used for cooking and capping. There is also a large room called a wharf, built out over the water, very roughly constructed of boards, unpainted, and it is open most of the time. It has windows, however.

The skinners have their places at long tables which are divided into boxed spaces. There are four sets of them, with eight on a side, making 64 in all. There are six zinc tables for packers, and about ten at each table, eight packers, four on a side, and two weighers.

Women do packing at ten cents an hour, peeling tomatoes at four cents a bucket. They carry the peeled tomatoes to the packers' tables, but the waste is carried away for them. Many of the women bring their children, who stand by them in the same little apartment, and do most, if not all, of the canning.

The tomatoes come in wagons or sail boats, are stacked up in the yard or on the wharf and trundled in on trucks as fast as the machines can scald them. They are scalded in a square wire box with pointed bottom. The cold water runs in from the top and steam is turned on. The water is changed several times a day and runs off through a hole in the floor to the water below. When the tomatoes come from the machines they are carried hot to the skinners.

The buckets to carry the tomatoes are made of papier mache. When full they weigh 34 pounds, when headed up 40 pounds. Twenty-five of the children working here look to be very much under fourteen years of age. None look over twelve and many are tiny. One pasty-faced, solemn, skinny little thing, who looks like death, said she was ill. She does all the lifting for her mother and herself. From 1:15 o'clock to 6:05 she carried twenty-three buckets of tomatoes to my table, and I don't know how many she may have lifted down, carried and lifted up at other tables. Some of the children looked to be only six or seven years of age, and from their strained expressions when they were carrying the buckets, one could see how heavy they found them.

There were four pregnant women who did all their own lifting all day.

A woman past middle age who worked beside me complained of a pain in her side. She had been in the hospital seven weeks. After two months in a packing house she had gone home very tired, but could not bear to see the dirty clothes "set" any longer, so she washed them out. Up on the shed drying them, she fainted from sheer exhaustion. She fell from the shed, injuring her back and right side and "insides." Now she can't lift as much or work as fast, and her side and back pain her most of the time and "something turrible by night."

Another woman had six rubber stalls on her fingers, others had one, two, three and more cut fingers. The cuts have to be deep before they bother with them.

At 11 o'clock the skinners struck for five cents a bucket while the tables were all covered with tomatoes. In twenty minutes the boss gave in.

We waited from 11:20 to 11:30 for work; from 1:30 to 1:45; from 5:15 to 5:40 and then had to work till 6:30. The belt coming off the scalding machine caused stoppage three times, strike and waiting for cans twice. I do not know about the machinery, but the waiting for cans could have been prevented by a little better management.

No seats of any kind anywhere. The dressing room the packers use is a small boiler room cluttered up, untidy and very dirty. It looks as if it had never been cleaned, but it at least has a door and is private. We hang our things on a few nails driven in the wall. There is not enough room for all, so the skinners and some of the packers hang their things on the wall of the main room and have to dress and undress before the men.

The two toilets for women are next each other, built over the water. They are wide, simple and whitewashed. Inside they are untidy and malodorous and unsupplied with paper. One for the men is next these and another opposite, with no pretense of privacy.

The skinners work in slop and slush all day, their feet soaking wet, and in spite of the rubber aprons they wear, they are often wet through and through.

The skins are piled on wheelbarrows and trundled off to be dumped on a space next the toilets, and from there carted away each day. We throw our green tomatoes in a bucket and take turns carrying it to another table, where the green slush is packed and sold as "ends." Someone said they went to the army. After work we wash and clean up the tables, but boys sweep and clean the floors.

Mothers who have one or two children supplementing them make as high as $5 a day, and if fairly busy never make less than $2.

Left off work at 6:30.

I walked part of the way home with a girl of ten who had been peeling since 6 a.m. Her mother also works in the cannery. I asked her about school. She said she was not going while she could work in a cannery.

"Things to eat is so high, we can't go to school, we gotter work," she explained.

Tuesday Evening, September 12

I was in to work at 6. The notice read, "6 o'clock a.m.—Darn sharp." It is hard to get up at 5.

Worked till 12 and then had 50 minutes waiting for work. I am capping. I do it alone and get my own caps. Girls cap at the rate of 65 a minute. Before the cans reach the capper a girl with a wooden puncher pokes the tomatoes down in each one. This work is also ten cents an hour.

A girl leaning up against the brick wall of the engine room had cramps very badly and couldn't stand. A Mrs. . . . was terribly sick all day yesterday. She looked ghastly. She vomited and had to go to the wharf to lie down. She went home and worked there till 11 p. m. She went to bed and waked at 4 a. m. and did not sleep again for fear of over-sleeping, as she lives quite a way from the factory.

One little girl of ten, so small that she is called Tiny, carried buckets all day and skinned between times. She ran a nail in her foot and limped about with one shoe and stocking off, as she took time only to tie it up. A small boy also ran a nail in his foot, making an ugly hole. His mother plastered it with tomato skin and wrapped it up in a filthy rag so that he could keep on working. The wages are not high enough in a cannery to lay off unless for something serious.

One of our scalders, aged sixteen, was sick yesterday. She has been working steadily for three or four months. She did not know she was sick, but fainted when she got up, so stayed at home.

Another scalder, aged sixteen, says her sister was working at G. and A.'s, but she had to start work at 4:30 or 5 there and did not get through till 7 or 8, and this was so hard on her husband that he made her stop it.

Several packers did not come in today, so I was moved to another table, where the sides are shallower, and I got wet through and had to change my underwear at night. My stomach was all wet. We were on tomatoes all day. Everybody tired and cross. I am dead tired and my shoulder aches like toothache.

Elizabeth Ashe
[1869–1954]

*Born of pioneer parents, Richard T. Ashe and Caroline Loyall, who had
arrived in San Francisco in 1848 before the Gold Rush, Elizabeth Ashe
trained as a nurse in New York City before the turn of the twentieth
century. Back in San Francisco, she began her long career in public health,
in which she established visiting nurses programs, clinics and neighborhood
centers, and programs placing public health nurses in the schools. Already
a community activist with special interest in the needs of women and
children when World War I began, she offered her services to the American
Red Cross for overseas relief work as early as October 1914. But, partly
because of her age, she was not accepted until 1917, when she was asked
to head the Children's Bureau of the American Red Cross in France.
Toward the end of the war, with a clinic established in Paris, Ashe and
others traveled in northern France to undertake further relief work and
health education.*

Cambrai, March 20, 1919

Arrived here with Miss Ida Tarbell at 2 P.M. The devastation is
terrible, but not so complete as at Lens, where the town is literally
pulverized, not one stone standing on another. A steady stream of
refugees is pouring into Cambrai. All along the road we pass groups
of men, women and children toiling along with heavy loads on their
backs and in their arms. Passing cars and trucks give them lifts when
possible. When they arrive at their home town they begin to search
for their own habitations and are very fortunate if one room is habit-
able. We lunched at Cambrai in the only hotel, which had been quite
a place of twenty-two bed rooms, only one being left intact. The

From *Intimate Letters from France and Extracts from the Diary of Elizabeth Ashe,*
1917–1919 (San Francisco: Bruce Brough Press, 1931).

Boche occupied the town for four years and destroyed what they could before retreating. Lace making was the industry of the place, as of all the surrounding towns. There were one thousand looms in the vicinity. The majority of these were carefully removed by the Boche but at Cambrai they did not have time to remove them. Just did what damage they could. It will take at least a year to start any again. An Englishman who had set many of them up years ago lunched with us. He was there repairing, but the work goes very slowly, as they can bring only forty kilos (about 85 pounds) over the road a day, the freight is so crowded. No material destruction made one so indignant as the theft of this machinery or its deliberate destruction. It is like Sherman's march through Georgia. "War is hell!"

As one looks over the hopeless ruin of this beautiful country, sees the deep shell holes which have ploughed the bottom clay to the surface, sees the countryside denuded of every tree or shrub, not a hamlet left standing—it looks as if life could never take hold here again and still every now and then a tiny patch of cultivation appears. One sees patient, devoted peasants toiling with hand-made implements over their bits of land, filling in and levelling. I suppose that within a few years it will all seem like some terrible nightmare, but at present, it looks like the destruction of the world, as if the gates of hell had been left open and all the evil spirits had burst forth, to do away forever with the beauty of the earth.

In the tale which we heard in the afternoon at Cambrai of the valiant fight for right which one lone woman had made and how she prevailed, we realized the rout and defeat of the forces of hell. Her name is Mlle. L'Hotellier, directrice of the Hospital General at Cambrai. When the Boche took Cambrai in September in 1914 she was in charge of the hospital. One hundred and seven French soldiers took refuge in her hospital and there she concealed them for two weeks in spite of Boche vigilance. She managed to procure civilian clothes for them, letting them escape one at a time under the guise of bakers, butchers, etc. Then the problem of disposing of their uniforms came up. They were burned at night in a furnace and their arms concealed between the walls. For two years these women (she had ten accomplices) aided men to escape. She was finally arrested, twenty men being found in her hospital. She was tried and condemned to death, but the execution delayed, as they were most anxious to find her accomplices. They tried over and over again to starve her into submission but utterly failed. She is a tiny little woman. At the time of her arrest she was very stout but now is very thin—has a petite appearance. I imagine that the world's horror over Edith Cavell's fate made them hesitate to execute her. She was put in a cell with women criminals and treated with every kind of indignity. Finally her health completely broke down and she was put in a prison hospital at Valenciennes where the Sisters connived at her escape. She walked hundreds of miles, trying to escape, and was finally met by the retreating Boche army who were too much in a hurry to question her. She just lost herself with the refugees. This woman went directly back to her hospital, where we found her. She says that her experience has given her the priceless gift of freedom, that no one knows what freedom is who has not been deprived of it; that she is now free from everything; that she realizes that before she was a slave to certain habits, slave to her clothes and to her possessions, but that now that she is free she realizes how little all of these are worth if we are deprived of the freedom of body or soul. She wrote on a card for me, "Vivre libre au mourer."

I was very much impressed by her free, happy attitude toward life in spite of all the terrible sufferings she had been through. I know so many people who are slaves to their possessions. I realized the insignificance of material things at the time of the San Francisco earthquake. My relief at learning that all my loved ones were safe was so great that the loss of my hitherto precious possessions seemed small. My books which had seemed indispensable, seemed to have no value and their loss meant most of all. In fact, we all have too many possessions. Life is very much and very unnecessarily complicated by them.

Lille, March 22, 1919.

We motored all day to Ypres. We went over the Messine Bridge which the British so successfully mined and blew up. The ruin and devastation in this region is worse than near Arras and Lens, if possible. It has not been as much cleaned up. By the way, the only satisfaction one has is the sight of Boche prisoners cleaning up the havoc they have wrought. It really does seem like poetic justice. The English get much more work out of them than either the Americans or French. They look well cared for and content. . . .

We finally arrived at Ypres. I believe that ruin will be a lasting monument to war barbarity. If any one is inclined to forget this world tragedy let him go to Ypres; not one stone left standing on another except for a few wonderful carved pillars which still stand as a witness of the former glory of the Cathedral. The only other thing left standing in Ypres is the side wall of a church and on this side wall a huge crucifix is suspended. The figure of Christ is left there looking over the ruin spread out before Him, ruin wrought by the hand of man. The result of two thousand years of His teaching of love and every day the world seems to become more involved in hatreds and jealousies, both at home and abroad.

We hear that all efforts to unite nations in a common bond of good fellowship and mutual understanding is being bitterly fought at home by men such as Lodge, who are a disgrace to humanity. They are allowing low party politics to stand in the way of the one chance the world has to bring some order out of this chaos. It is heartbreaking and discouraging to a degree. I feel much less hope after this exhibition of low standards and ideals at home for the future than I did in the midst of the war. Each nation too seems most suspicious of each other. All confidence is lost. We even hear that France is suspicious of America's motives.

Edith K. O. Clark
[1881–1936]

In her early fifties, Edith Clark established a homestead on six hundred acres in the Big Horn Mountains of Johnson County, Wyoming. With the help of friends from the neighboring homestead, she felled trees, dragged them out by horseback, peeled the logs, chinked them, raised the ridge pole, laid the floor, and ultimately moved into her cabin. Before coming to her mountain residence, she had led an active public life. After leaving Washington, D.C. early in the century, she accepted a teaching position in a Wyoming school two days' ride by stagecoach from the railroad. Here began a long effort to improve conditions in these rural schools. In 1908, she ran for and was elected County Superintendent of Sheridan County, and in 1914 she became Wyoming State Superintendent of Public Instruction. In the early 1920s, she accepted an overseas position with the Y.W.-C.A., but returned to Wyoming in 1922 to open the Gables Tea Room and Gift Shop in Cheyenne.

Edith Clark kept a journal for thirty years and used it during this period to describe her homesteading experiences for a friend. She died two years after the events recorded below, of cancer.

THE SUMMER OF 1933

August 8, 1933

Now to be honest . . . were you just a little facetious in suggesting I keep a "log" of my homesteading adventures? "Log" . . . that's the most constant word in my vocabulary right now. Log, logger, logging . . . from the crack of dawn till bedtime, and then I dream it till the sun strikes the rocky ledge that I can see from where my bed is

From "The Diary of Edith K. O. Clark," *Annals of Wyoming* 39, no. 2 (October 1967): 217–44. Reprinted by permission. The manuscript of the diary is at the University of Wyoming in Laramie, among the papers of Agnes Wright Spring.

rolled out on the ground. For the chief interest I have in life just now is getting my young cabin put together . . . logs, of course.

We've actually started. And even though I had to abandon my original plans for a house when I found that they would involve more cash than I could command this summer . . . this revised version is going to be a lot of fun.

Today . . . August 8 . . . the first trees for it were felled. I have a unique souvenir. The very first tree that was cut, crashed down across the big rock where I had parked my hat and little white enamel drinking cup. It made no visible difference to the hat, but from now on I'll have a lop-sided cup to remember the occasion. . . .

September 2

When you read my exultant shout that the ridge log was in place, perhaps you visualized my mountain home as practically ready for occupancy. Did you? Well now, just let me wise you up a bit.

At that stage of the game the structure resembled a rather high pole corral as nearly as anything, with two ends rising a bit higher than the sides. True, the men did cut out one log at the places that were to be the windows and door, just to make it possible to get their saws in later to cut the openings. Now I can brag that that has been accomplished, so you can see how I'm going to get in, and look out. And thereby hangs a funny tale! I find that the door and windows are going to be ridiculously low for one of my vertical dimensions! How come? I take all the blame. I had counted logs in other cabins, and ordered the same number high for mine, not realizing that these lodge pole pines on my place are slimmer, and hence would not make for height as they were laid up! Then too, my cabin is faced down hill. The foundation rocks raise the front fairly well off the ground. The building did not look low as it was being put up. But when the floor gets in, it surely will be. I'll have head clearance and that's about all at the sides, and even the ridge won't be out of reach. So, we'll just say, "How quaint and picturesque," and I'll pretend it was meant to be that way. Anyone over five feet tall will have to duck to enter.

Right now I am busy chinking. Does that mean anything to you? Chinking is the process of fitting slim poles into the cracks between the logs. (I have generous "cracks" due to amateur workmanship of the notching). Then later, when the logs season, these cracks will be daubed with cement and the chinking will help hold it in. See? . . .

You see, I have no road into my park. I'm in virgin forest country as far as dwelling or building is concerned. Nothing has ever trod my soil, except on hoofs. And it just happens that there's no natural approach to me for anything on wheels. Some day I'll have to have a road gouged out around the hill to the north, but since this season has been so dry, we can safely cross below the outlet of the group of springs that normally make a marshy place down at the lower end of the little draw west of me. Only, we had to improvise a temporary culvert. We used rocks and willows and brush and chunks of sod on top. That was one rainy day job. I might add that it proved practical. The truck bounced across the next day without mishap. So, came the lumber that would mean a roof for my domicile, and window frames, and door and floor. It looked very grand and interesting. I realized more thoroughly than before that I was building a house! It is the first one I have ever built, you know, so I deserve a thrill, I think! And I like the idea of my first building being this primitive little cabin, in its primitive setting. I can't seem to remember up here that I have been dependent upon electric conveniences and modern plumbing. I am quite content to dip water from my cold running spring, and write this log by candlelight.

As for plumbing, wait till you see what I accomplished *without* Chic Sale! I left the bark on, (protective coloring) as It stands a little back in the edge of the timber. The view, from the seat, is entrancing. I don't remember that even The Specialist ever included a beautiful view in the assets of his handiwork. 'Nuf sed.

September 15

. . . Yesterday was "September Morn" at my camp . . . the first time I have enjoyed a complete bath . . . out of doors! (My others since moving up have been managed at the Gibbs cabin) But yesterday was bright, warm and inviting. I proceeded to fill my scrub pail and largest kettle with water, heated them over my camp fire in front of the tent and . . . really you've no idea what an exhilarating sensation it is to bathe in the open! I think next summer I shall indulge in sun baths. I know now how good they feel. And I have an ideally se-cluded spot for the experiment. But perhaps it would be just as well not to advertise the fact.

Also the same day in the same manner, but partially "draped", I had a glorious shampoo. For it I used my primitive wash stand which is a piece of board nailed onto a convenient tree stump. On it I set my scrub pail and into it I ducked my head. That was really a gymnastic feat . . . in fact, almost a contortion! The pail, as you may guess, was slightly high. To make a contact with the suds within took some arching of all my length. If I'd been six inches shorter I'd never have made it.

Then I made a discovery. I had to laugh aloud up there in the woods by myself. I found, as I bent over, that I had the most gorgeous view while I was standing on my head! Everyone around here teases me about the thrills I get from views. Did you ever try looking at a sunset upside-down? . . . I mean bending over as you stood with your back to it, and looking at it between your knees (or under your chin, if that seems more modest!) That angle seems to intensify the colors, somehow. Try it.

Well, my shampoo pose gave the same effect. So, with soap suds dripping, I got another thrill.

This morning Shorty returned with the truck. The broken spring had been replaced with a good one. He decided that it would be safe to risk the bumpy trail up to my place so he brought the automobile cushions which I had bought to serve as a bed. They are installed in the cabin, resting crosswise on the poles that are the floor joists. (I have no floor as yet!) Tonight I shall sleep beneath my own *roof* for the first time! Selah! . . .

October 5

. . . When I think back to the next morning, October 3, I laugh almost aloud, all by myself. It was spent, most of it if you please, in my toilet, doing carpenter work. I put the hole in the seat! . . . and it took hours, as well as much effort. I bored five feet, three inches of perforation with a brace and bit that didn't have any knob to hold to! I had to wad up an old glove and bear down with it while I ground away, around the outline of the holé space, yes, sixty-three times through that one inch board! Then with a hammer and an old butcher knife I hacked out the center. And after that, well, if I had stopped there, the effect on the anatomy (one part of it) of a sitter might have been rather terrible. I can visualize scallops, something like the rim of a pie! Besides, with such a gorgeous view right from the seat of the toilet, it would be cruel to make it torture to sit and enjoy (?) it.

So, after chopping out the center of the hole, there was much whittling and sand-papering before I could look upon my handiwork and call it good. Do you wonder that it took most of the morning? . . .

October 17

. . . It was just the next Sunday morning after I wrote last, October 8th, that three beautiful deer greeted me from right below my lovely golden aspens as I opened my cabin door! They were the first I had seen so close, though I had found fresh tracks often. They looked up so surprised, as surprised as I was, and then darted back into the timber. I shall look for them again. But with the snow on the ground they won't come down to water at my little stream.

My place is on the State Game Preserve so there won't be hunting close to me. The season is open now and with these fresh light snows, many of the gay young animals will fall prey to the man with a gun. My one hope is that any wounded creature will be killed outright. It is so terrible to think of a deer or elk, or anything being shot and crippled, and escaping to suffer. The game is very plentiful around this region. It does not seem wrong to shoot a deer for meat occasionally when it is used for food and not a pound is wasted. But I always fear during the open season, that unskilled shots may only cripple, and then the waste is cruel.

Another thing I want to write about, though I despair of adequately describing it, is the sunset I watched in the rain up on my favorite lookout rocks. Have I ever mentioned my Sunset Rocks? They aren't actually mine, for they are beyond the boundary of my forty acres, but I claim them many evenings and often other parts of the day. They are an outcropping of granite, great, rough, huge, that jut from one of the hills sloping toward my favorite view. From these rocks I can see not only the rugged outline of my Hazelton Peaks, but across the expanse of open bull camp to the towering rim rocks on the east, and also west across Powder River. From those rocks the panorama is superb. Almost every sunset is worthwhile, but this one in the rain was unusually spectacular.

There was a driving shower that afternoon. I put on my leather jacket and trusty beret and launched forth for a refreshing hike. The clouds were only overhead. Around the horizons, the sky was clear.

Of course I landed on my Sunset Rocks, speculating as to what sort of picture would be offered with that sort of combination. Until the sun dropped low enough to peek under the grey lid that covered most of the sky, the only contrast was the bright rim of light on the western horizon. Then, it happened so suddenly I was startled. Color shot horizontally across the world. The sun threw its evening beams out the under side of that heavy blanket of grey rain cloud and it was rose and violet and amethyst. The rim rocks caught the shaft squarely and seemed to rise taller in the direct light. They reminded me of a Belasco stage setting. I can't describe the intensity of the color, something like a rich salmon, but more vivid with a touch of gold in it. And a great broad swath of rainbow stood straight up from one end of those rocks.

Soon the sun dropped below the sky line and the rose and violet and amethyst turned to a burnished copper that fairly sung. And the rim rocks gradually melted into dull blue. I stood there with the rain drops spattering against my leather coat and watched the color creep up to the summits of Hazelton Peaks. They had stood out a rich purple with accents of magenta. Their rocky points rising above timber line were the last to catch the good night caress of the sinking sun. In a moment they were silent grey and even the little fringe of cloud over the canyon where the sun had stopped, straightened out and grew cold. The curtain was down, the stage a monotone. It seemed almost unbelievable that all that glory had been, and was gone. I wondered how many had seen it. I was alone on the rocks in the rain. Never shall I forget that sunset, the setting and the unbroken expanse that was all mine for the hour. . . .

[*In the summer of* 1934, *Clark is celebrating the Fourth of July with friends at her "other house," the Bar V Ranch on Young's Creek when she learns of a forest fire near her cabin.*]

Sunday, July 15
. . . She told me that a long distance telephone message from Buffalo earlier in the day reported a forest fire raging so near my little mountain home that neighbors feared for my cabin! They had taken everything movable out of the house and piled it in the clearing away from the timber. It seemed inevitable that the little log house would go, perhaps had already been destroyed.

Can you think how I felt? No, strange as it may seem, my first grief was not for the happy little home I had left only about two weeks before, where I had planned so much for this summer and other summers to come. It hurt to think that perhaps it was now only charred black sticks or a pile of ugly ashes. But it wasn't the loss of the cabin that seemed so terrible. Some day I might be able to put up another. Cabins can be built in two or three weeks and mine did not represent a great outlay of expense, even though I would not be able to pay for another very soon.

But the glorious standing timber on those hills! Acres of pine forest that had taken generations to grow to their great green height! To be swept away in a cruel blazing moment ... that was the real tragedy. It haunted me far into the night.

In the morning I drove over to Buffalo. From the valley I could see the great clouds of smoke rolling up from the top of the mountains in the region of my camp. In town several people greeted me with the rumor that everything had been destroyed in the path of the fire that had swept straight across my range. One man who had been up the day before, Sunday, told me that when he was there the fire was at its height in the strip just back of my cabin, that it had not yet caught the building, but was so close, right in the nearest pines, that by now it must surely be gone. Pretty grim prospect, I admit. No one knew anything positive as to the extent of the devastation that might have been wrought in the 24 hours since the last report had reached town.

I wondered about Dorothy and her family. They were up there . . . somewhere.

As quickly as possible I got together a few camp utensils from friends, food and some bedding, and borrowed the 14-year-old daughter of Dorothy's sister. The child was wild to go up with me and I was mighty glad to have her.

When we topped the last divide and began the final 15 miles of the way, the sight we faced was breath-taking. I shall never forget it. Most of this part of the drive is directly toward my camp. The rim rocks back of the cabin site are clearly defined. It has always been fun to watch them showing nearer from each bend in the road. That day they placed the fire only too definitely. The sinister white and grey and black smoke rolled up from all sides of that skyline, sometimes blotting it out, sometimes silhouetting it against their ugly, mocking mass. I knew then that there was nothing left of mine. But we drove on.

The last gate I pass through in going to my camp is at the edge of the Gammon bull camp. It is on the hill across a deep draw from the sloping park in front of my cabin. I used to watch it from the house when people drove through it, and usually looked back for a farewell glimpse of my little place as I went away. It was about the last spot from which I could see my house in taking the road down the mountain, and the first place to see it coming in.

As we neared that gate I wanted to shut my eyes. There was smoke pouring out from the timber on all sides of my little park. Only the rim rocks showed where the cabin had been built. It seemed rather futile to go farther, but there appeared to be no fire down toward the Gibbs place so my young friend "Mike" (short for Mary Frances) and I passed through the gate and onto the point of the hill to take the trail for Dorothy's. I stopped to take a picture. It would show to friends who had seen the views of my location, just how the fire had swept my particular corner of the mountains.

And then I saw my cabin roof! The sunlight played up its light grey-green surface through a rift in the smoke, and below the roof the log walls, still yellow instead of black and charred. Mike saw it too, so I knew I was awake.

We stopped the car at the foot of the hill, across the draw from my slope and walked closer. The fringe of timber in the foreground was not burning. The sloping park was safe to enter. There stood the brave little shack facing us, but oh, so close to the flames behind it! Red, crackling blazes mocked us from the pines such a little way back from the edge of the park. Everything was so parched and dry that just the faintest breeze in any direction would spread the ruin. It seemed a forlorn hope. And we were helpless to avert its inevitable fate. I wondered how much longer the house could stand.

Then we drove down to Dorothy's. The Gibbs home had escaped and the fire had left its vicinity. The family was still settled there, so Mike and I moved in with them. Dorothy told us of the terrible hours they had spent since the fire started on Saturday afternoon. It must have been ghastly. I won't go into its repetition now.

That night we all piled into my car and drove up through the Gammon gate and onto one of the higher hills back away from the timber.

Here is where words are helpless. I cannot hope to describe what we gazed upon. The whole world seemed on fire. In a great semicircle, following the curve of the timbered ridges perhaps ten miles in extent, the forests burned. Flames leaped up in vicious glee consuming tall, age-old pines in one snarling roar, stabbing high into the tinted smoke that rolled up and up against the night sky.

We sat and watched it for an hour and wondered how many more hours and days the destruction would spread unchecked. It seemed utterly beyond control by human effort. From where we looked, it was easy to locate my cabin site. Of course at night we could see nothing of the house, or just where it had stood . . . only the deep red flames on all sides and the lighter red smoke all above.

Mike and I slept on the Gibbs porch that night, but much of the time I lay awake and watched the sinister glow in the sky beyond the high ridge back of their house, and smelt the smoke in the air.

This chapter of my log is getting so lengthy that I really should make another installment of the rest of my forest fire adventures. Can you stand it any longer now? It is hard to break off before telling you how we spent that week. Perhaps I can cut it short, for all the days were very much the same.

In the morning Mike and I went horseback up to my camp, wondering what we would, or would not, find. The miracle still held. The cabin had survived the night. So we rode back and reported. Then Shorty's brother Paul and their sheep herder went back with us, armed with axes and shovels. We worked all day. Wherever there was a patch smoldering or blazing under brush or old logs, we chopped and shovelled and dug and scraped away the carpet of pine needles that had not yet caught. We tried smothering the embers with wet sacks. But there were so many, many such patches on all sides that it seemed a hopeless task. Even though the fury of the fire had subsided from the immediate surroundings of my cabin site, almost the whole forest floor was hot and smoking, which meant real danger. A whiff of wind would fan the sparks into another blaze. In vain we watched for the hope of a cloud which might mean rain. But the only blot against the July sky was the mounting billows of heavy smoke, now just back of my rim rocks.

I shall never cease to be grateful to my good neighbors. It would have been practically impossible for me to have made any progress alone. Some days I did work alone. I don't know how much good

I did, but I could not be content to rest from my task while there was one vicious spark unrebuked in my nearer timber. So every day for all that week I shovelled and raked and chopped and smothered and buried.

And the fire raged a little farther away.

The sky still showed red and angry at night, but just a shade more faintly as the week passed. We began to feel that the danger was more remote, unless the wind changed. That was great anxiety. People drove up from the valley on several different days, sight-seers curious for a closer view of the fire. Every one tried to encourage us with the assurance that we surely were now safe . . . unless . . . the wind changed. So how could we feel at ease? We all knew that real security could come only from a drenching rain. And every day was fair and hot and dry.

By Friday there were no more mocking white spirals curling up from any very near parts of the forest, but we had extended our activity to an isolated bit of burning down-timber in a growth of pines a little to the northeast. The standing trees between it and mine were still unscathed. Even though they might not be a real menace to my own safety, should the fire in them spread, I hated to feel that they might be lost for want of a little effort. So Friday and Saturday I worked there, part of the time with the help of the willing men from the Gibbs outfit. They could wield the ax much more effectively than I.

When that threat had been subdued, there was no real reason for me to linger. I could not safely move back into my cabin, for the forest was still burning furiously off to the east and south. Crews of men were fighting it night and day striving to control its course and check the awful damage it was doing. Everyone seemed to think it would not return to us, unless the wind . . . and in that event we would be utterly helpless. There would be danger all summer, from deeply hidden smoldering sparks until the rain definitely quenched them. It might be weeks.

So, leaving all my *lares et penates* still piled in the clearing, covered over with canvas, Mike and I drove back to Buffalo on Saturday afternoon. It was a week I shall never forget.

Just one thing more in this connection I must tell you.

You are probably wondering how the fire started and why it gained such headway before it was finally put under control.

The blaze started from the Gibbs stove pipe. Dorothy was baking bread on Saturday afternoon. There was a strong wind. Suddenly she heard a crackling in the timber on the slope just back of their cabin and looked out thinking it was deer. Often they had seen game close to their house.

She was horrified to see some pines ablaze and the burning branches blown in great leaps up toward the rim rocks above. In just a few moments the flames had swept over the top in spite of all that she and her limited helpers could do.

They knew that the virgin forest over the ridge was tinder. The fire was sweeping straight for my location, away from the Gibbs home which was safe. So all hands from their place rushed up to mine to save it if they could. Other neighbors, the rider from Gammon's and another man who happened to be there joined the valiant group: They chopped down some of the trees nearest to my house and when they saw that even this would probably not save it, they carried out even the door and windows.

Meanwhile Dorothy drove as fast as she could to the nearest telephone . . . Caribou Camp . . . 16 miles away, and called for help from the forest service. It seems unbelievable, but what do you think the response was? . . . That they could do *nothing* . . . because they "had no authority to go off the Forest Reserve!!!" Can you conceive of anything more narrow and contemptible?

So our glorious timber was sacrificed.

If help, trained help, could have been secured that first day, or even the next day, the damage would have been restricted to a comparatively small area. True, it would have made no difference to my own location. But miles and miles of the forest further away would have been spared. Instead, it burned and burned, with just a handful of nearby men doing what they could to fight it, working against hopeless odds.

Then, after ruin had spread unchecked for five days, the Forest Service finally revised their book of rules and came to the aid of the exhausted homesteaders and ranchers. By then it required ten times the men and hours to get results. I cannot understand why printed rules have to govern in an emergency such as we faced last week. I don't know how long it will take to actually get the fire under control now. It is still raging. And we are still praying for rain.

Juanita Harrison
[1891–?]

At the age of thirty-six, Juanita Harrison, a Mississippi-born black woman, set out alone to travel around the world. With little formal schooling, she had begun her working life as a domestic servant and soon became known as a skilled "ladies' maid." Able to find employment as she traveled, Harrison used this mobility to create an independent and original life. An adventure-loving woman of imagination and resolution, she let nothing prevent her from fulfilling her life's plan: "I will sail far away to strange places. Around me no one has the life I want. No one is there for me to copy, not even the rich ladies I work for. I have to cut my life out for myself and it won't be like anyone else."

With a small amount of money saved, she left New York in June of 1927 and before settling in Hawaii eight years later, she had lived in twenty-two countries. She worked as she went, staying only long enough with each employer to save the money needed for the next step in her odyssey. Her travel journal records enthusiastic appreciation of the peoples and cultures of Europe, the Middle East, Africa, India, Russia, China, and Japan. Entitled "Epilogue," the following passage is the last entry in her journal. The editors of The Atlantic Monthly, *where her narrative first appeared, preserved the spelling and phrasing of the original manuscript.*

[1935]

That cheque from the Atlantic Monthly for my article gave joy. I got it on a Sat. and gave up my weekly job. This is what I am during with the money as I want to enjoy every penny. I had a Tent made to order of course This was my plannes before I left Cap D'Antibes so they have been carried out perfect.

From Juanita Harrison, *My Great Wide Beautiful World* (New York: Macmillan, 1936).

Then I went around Waikiki looking for a privat Yard to Put my Tent So that I could be in a privat Place yet free good and cheap. I asked several just to see no one Knew of any place but I was only Testing that alway give encouragement. I choosed the best from several right here at Waikiki in the front Lot of a nice Japanese Family They have a Cottage in the rear and the Show bath and W.C. are in the Yard and I am right at the front gate so do not trouble any one freedom is my main point.

My grown for my Tent cost $2.50 a month and am in the best neighbor hood in frount is the Beautiful perfect Hawaiain St. Augustine Church with its large yard. Trees bright flouers. all the time I alway long to live in the Showad of a Catholic Church not a Protstant that look alway like a Jail as They open it only on Sundays.

At night Waikiki is more gay and beautiful than in the City and in a half block is a nice resturant with my Kind of Wholesome food fresh daily meals from 15 cents to 35. and there are two places Where I get the best ice cream. just back of me are the Beautiful Hawaiain Village so I get plenty Hula musice and dancing free. when there is a Ball in the Garden of the Royal Hawaiain Hotel facing the Sea we swim or wade and look right on the dancers and all the other things of Pleasure right near where I set up my Tent.

At six A.M. every morning I put on my red bathing suite rap a black flouerd Satan piece around my hips and have a swim take my soap and Towls and have my bath right there under the Show on the Beach. so I didnt need to remain at Cap D'Antibes to have a happy Home.

I meet a sweetheart just as I steped off the Pres. Lincoln and a nice sort. He have seen me just twice since because I move so fast and never trouble to tell and each time He have just by accident seen me going along with a bundle on my head at the time I make a move and so it happen when I was moving from my room to my Tent and He moved me in His car I had planed that Tent to be Taboo but the first minute in it I had to let Him Kiss me.

I had the Tent put up two days before I was ready to go in so that the Children in the neighborhood could go in and out and enjoy it so They would watch after it for me and They do. It was great fun there was about 25 Children the man said When you get through having your House Warming we'll finnish puting it up. Now They never Trouble me. I had a 7 × 7 orange Tent made just as I wanted it I had it that size so I can take up my house and walk at any time without any help or experinces. A fat German where I got it was so Kind and let the Chinese Girls that Sew for him do all the little extra work.

It have Two windows at one end and one at the other and one pocket to stick my flouer vase it open at each end the same way like what are used on sport shirts instead of laped over or laced up and on Each wall which are 4 feet are a pocket for my cloths and a strip over the pocket for to hang a pretty bright Curtain.

I found a boy that made me a floor for a dollar but use His Father's lumber. he lives on my street. the floor is good but light so I can carry it on my head when I want to move. I have a green linolien on the floor with two small rugs I have a good army cot and a fine mattrews made to order. a beautiful bright Chinese blanket a good pilla bright ticken and two Sheets and one pilla case made of outen flannel bright print. It is furnished nothing like a home never any cloths hanging about. it looks like a poch.

Well never in all my life have I slept so wonderful as in my Tent the 4 holes in each of the windows where the ropes drow up the Shade make 12 holes and when the light is out and the door and Windows closed the lights of the street shine through the holes and on to the Top of my Tent and it look just like the Stars.

I'll get a serfe boad and Take a few Hula lessons just to add gayness to that list of things the check bought. I want alway to be where wealth health youth beauty and gayness are altho I need very little for myself I just want to be in the midst of it. I have reversed the saying of Troubles are like Babies the more you nurse them the bigger They grow so I have nursed the joys. Well you have bring out your moth ball smelling cloths and no doubt feel very pleased with the world to be in a caged up Building looking out on others more caged up. I have gone through the same and how greatful I am to myself.

This is my first and only Home. Villa Petit Peep are The name of my Tent as I let my callers sit on a seat in the yard and Peep in so I gave it this True name.

Eslanda Goode Robeson
[1896–1965]

Eslanda Goode was born in Washington, D.C., grew up in New York City, and met Paul Robeson when they were students together at Columbia University. When they married in 1921, Eslanda Robeson became a promoter of the extraordinary vocal and theatrical career of her husband. She also became known as a writer, lecturer, and political activist; in 1930 she became her husband's biographer with the publication of Paul Robeson, Negro *(New York and London: Harper and Brothers, 1930).*

The Robesons lived in England from 1928 until the end of World War II and during this period, Eslanda developed a deep interest in Africa. She studied anthropology with a focus on Africa at London University and the London School of Economics and later at Hartford Seminary in Connecticut. As an anthropologist, she traveled to Africa in 1936 with her only child, Paul, Jr. The selections below are from the journal she kept of that trip.

As enormously important public figures, the Robesons maintained their political activities throughout their lives, addressing in many forums the issues of racism, fascism, and colonialism. Their criticism of the United States and their sympathetic views of the Soviet Union led to years of persecution for the Robesons. Both were the subject of investigations conducted by Senator Joseph McCarthy and both were denied passports during most of the 1950s. At the time of her death, Eslanda Robeson was an active supporter of the Civil Rights Movement in the United States.

[1936]

May 30. On board the S.S. *Winchester Castle.* All day today in the Bay of Biscay. The sea looks calm but there is a lot of underneath

From Eslanda Goode Robeson, *African Journey* (New York: John Day, 1945). © Paul Robeson, Jr. Reprinted by permission of Paul Robeson, Jr.

motion. Pauli is ill, and I am certainly uncomfortable. We spend most of our time on deck out in the air. We keep ourselves very much to ourselves, and are entirely self-sufficient. I brought lots of good books, games, and jigsaw puzzles, so we manage to have a very good time together. The passengers seem friendly enough, but I am taking no chances. They are mostly South Africans, whose attitude toward the Negro I find very familiar, very like that of our "Deep South" Southern white folks in America, only more so. So I will be extremely cautious socially.

Our double first-class stateroom with private bath is pleasant and comfortable. The food and service are excellent, so it looks like a good trip. Our only stop before we reach the bottom of Africa will be Madeira. . . .

June 4. We are off Dakar, Senegal, West Africa. The air is very heavy, the sea gray and hot and calm, the sky lead colored. And it is a gray and heavy thought that between 1666 and 1800 more than five and a half million kidnaped Africans, my ancestors, began the dreadful journey across the Atlantic from this very stretch of coast, to be sold as slaves in the "new world." I say began the journey, because records show that more than half a million of them died en route. No wonder the sea and sky and the very air of this whole area seem sinister to me. . . .

June 10. We have run into the "Cape Rollers" and believe me they are most uncomfortable. They are said to be caused by the meeting of the Indian Ocean with the South Atlantic, and the great difference in their temperatures causes currents and swells. Often it is very, very rough around the cape and far up on both sides as well. Thank heaven the ship is steady, and I can manage, although I took to my bed when we first ran into the rollers yesterday.

Mrs. G. was telling me about Julius, her Native servant ("boy" as they are called) who has been with her for years. He drives her car and is general houseman, I gather. It seems he fell in love with one of her maids, Native of course, and Mrs. G. became interested in the romance. "I gave her a lovely wedding dress, and they were married right in my own parlor. And Julius said a white bride could not have looked as lovely as his black one did." I could almost feel I was at home again, listening to a white Southerner from our own Deep

South. I think it will be easy for me to understand the South Africans: Their attitudes, especially their patriarchal attitudes, are entirely familiar.

I have been asking the passengers, discreetly I hope, about the Cape Colored people. Everyone seems a bit interested in the Cape Colored, but very worried and shy about the Natives. I gather they feel rather safer with the Colored, because they are "more like the Europeans," and their ideal is to become European. They are given just enough encouragement to make them feel themselves "above" the Native and "different" from him. Then too, their numbers are comparatively few: They are less than half the number of the European population. The Natives are so much stronger numerically than the Europeans, and so entirely different, that they are frightening. And they have no desire whatever to become European, which makes them more frightening. . . .

I find myself recognizing the tone of voice, the inflection of these South Africans. "Native" is their word for our "nigger"; "non-European" for our Negro; "European" means white; and "South African" surprisingly enough does not mean the millions of original black people there, but the white residents born there, as distinguished from the white residents born in Europe who are called "colonials" or "settlers". . . .

June 26. . . . All through this spacious country there are European farms: neat, well-built white farmhouses nestling in the most sheltered spots in the wide valleys, with the equally neat, well-built white outbuildings near by for cattle, fowl, and for storage. Definitely and considerably removed from the group of buildings are the dirty, ramshackle huts which house the farmer's Native labor. Always the cattle, chicken, and dogs are far better housed than the African worker.

Once we skirted a small branch line of a railroad for a few miles. Beside the tracks at regular intervals we noticed little shelters made of corrugated iron, shaped like tents. The Natives working on the railway beds live in these, sometimes three or four to a shelter. I have never seen anything more primitive, not even in the shantytowns in America during the depression.

And then we saw our first "mine train," filled with Africans going up to Johannesburg for a term in the mines. These are the lucky ones who do not have to walk at least part of the way. They have been recruited from all over the countryside, and are now hanging out of windows, filling their eyes with a last picture of their home area, which they are leaving for nearly a year.

In the Orange Free State ("What's free about it?" asks Pauli) the locations are quite different from those we saw in the Cape. They are a little nearer the white towns and villages, and are small and crowded, with no gardens and no cattle, because there is no land for planting or grazing. The Africans here have no interest or recreation of any kind. They have only their work in domestic service, on the farms, or on the railway beds. . . .

The idea of individual and private ownership of land is wholly foreign to African thought. Land is to be *used,* not to be *owned.*

This fact has created grave misunderstanding all over Africa. If white men came as friends to the territory of a chief, and he decided to make them welcome and allow them to remain, he gave the white man the *use* of houses and land. This was merely customary traditional African hospitality.

If the white men gave the chief some present, large or small, money or gadgets, in return for his hospitality, this too was merely customary. The chief was sure he had given the guests only the *use* of the houses and land. In fact, that was all he could give. The land belonged to the tribe and could never be alienated, in whole or in part, from the tribe. The white man was equally sure he had *bought* the land, had paid for it (paid very, very little, to be sure), and therefore *owned* it.

This was one of the great differences in thought and intention which has wrought such havoc to African society. . . .

July 2. . . . This traveling about Africa reminds me of traveling through the Deep South in America: You are passed from friend to friend, from car to car, from home to home, often covering thousands of miles without enduring the inconveniences and humiliations of the incredibly bad Jim Crow train accommodations and lack of hotel facilities for Negroes. . . .

The gorgeous incredible sunsets, so spectacular that I always think of a cyclorama at the back of a theater: brilliant gay scarlet, flame, liquid gold skies turning to dull gold, then fading to pastel pinks and blues, blues and grays, then luminous blue-gray, then the swift darkness. No twilight. Just that clarity of light, silhouette, and the sudden night.

The night skies are lovely too: clear vault of blue immediately overhead—not distant as in Europe or at home. Enormous glittering stars and the fleecy clouds, all very, very near.

We saw a mine train, this time coming up from Johannesburg with its tragic burden of Africans who have served their term in the mines. Some broken in health, some coughing, some with the beginnings of the dreaded phthisis. All exhausted, "worked out." Many hanging out of the train windows drinking in the sun and air. All with the pathetic little cash which will be eaten up by taxes and fees.

We pass the now familiar corrugated tents of the railway workers, beside the rare railroad tracks.

And the European farms, widely spaced in their miles of valleys. And always the heartbreaking sight of African families on the road, on foot, trying somehow to escape from the slavery of these farms. The father often leads the small child by the hand, in front, followed by other children and the mother, who has all their worldly possessions on her head: perhaps a crude stove, blanket, a few clothes, a little food. They are friendly, kindly, patient, stubbornly moving on, hoping to find the next place more reasonable, more human. But of course the next place is just as bad. . . .

Our handsome Buick rolled along beautifully until we came into Kroonstad, and there, right in the middle of the main street, one of the elegant balloon tires blew out. While Dr. Xuma and the young driver changed the tire, Pauli and I strolled through the town in search of the post office and Yergan's wire. It was blazing hot. We were stared at all the way by the porky, pie-faced Boers with their small eyes set close together in mean faces. The sight of the undernourished little African nursegirls carrying those overstuffed Boer children on their backs sickened me.

Arriving at the post office, we found separate windows for Europeans and Non-Europeans, but the *Poste-Restante* was general. The ratty-faced clerk asked rudely what I wanted, staring meanwhile at Pauli. Sensing his attitude, I asked respectfully for a telegram for Robeson.

"No telegram for you," he answered immediately, without looking in the lettered boxes behind him.

I could see the yellow envelope in the box under R.

I thought, If Yergan says he'll send a wire, he'll send it.

I said, still respectfully, "But I'm expecting a telegram. If it hasn't come yet, I'll just sit and wait for it."

Taking Pauli by the hand, I went over to a bench and sat down, prepared to wait forever. The clerk glared at us, his mouth hanging open, his face slowly reddening. He flung himself over to the boxes, pulled out the yellow envelope, looked at it first on one side then on the other (I really don't think he could read), and thrust it through the window.

"Here, is this it?" he asked.

I went back to the window, read my name on the envelope, and said: "Yes, it is, thank you very much," and smiled at him. Again he glared at us, and his neck seemed to swell as the scarlet of his face slowly turned to purple. Still with Pauli's hand in mine, we left the post office.

We know this same kind of thing in our own Deep South. If Pauli and I had been ragged and black, and had said a lot of "Yes, Sirs" and "No, Sirs" and "Thank you, Sirs," the clerk would have been condescending and pleasant and helpful, if he had felt in the mood. But we were well dressed and confident, respectful only of his government position—not of his white skin—and that made him furiously uncertain socially, and very angry. And worse, I could read. We didn't "know our place," which to the "cracker" is the unforgivable sin. Our place, of course, is at the very bottom, and very, very definitely under *him!* . . .

July 3. . . . Saw the mine dumps by daylight. They are everywhere on the outskirts of the city, beyond the beautiful European residential suburbs: Great, depressing mountains of slag—whitish looking ashy dirt and clinkers washed clean of all gold dust, and just piled up and left.

In the early evening going home we saw the dreaded pick-up vans everywhere in the streets, in the outskirts of town, and on the roads leading to the locations. The van is a cross between a dog-catcher's wagon and a police patrol wagon. Africans call it, simply, "Pick-Up." If they cannot show a pass or permit to be out on the streets, they are seized, loaded into these vans, and taken to jail. No European can be arrested without a warrant, but none is necessary to arrest an

African. The accusation is decided upon *after* the arrest. They tell me it is easier to plead guilty when picked up, pay the fine, and thus avoid the return trip to court for a hearing and perhaps a much larger fine and a prison sentence.

I can certainly follow their thinking when Africans tell me it is easier to plead guilty than to return to court for a hearing. I would hate to find myself as a Native in a court anywhere in South Africa. The African has no important legal rights. In many parts of the Union, African births and deaths are not recorded. Deaths of African workers in the mines are not published. . . .

July 4. *Sunday.* In the early afternoon we drove through Friedasdoorp, said to be the roughest section around Johannesburg. It reminded me very much of Lenox Avenue in Harlem on a summer Sunday afternoon. The streets were thronged with Africans, all colors, all sizes, dressed in all kinds of clothes, strolling in the sun. Indians, Malays, Colored, and Africans live in this section. There is a sports ground—for Indians and Colored only—where a football game was in progress.

Farther along we came to another sports ground—this one for Africans—and decided to go in to watch this football game. An African street vendor was selling hot roast sweet potatoes just outside the gate and doing brisk business. Inside the place was jammed. Both teams were African, and they played very well indeed. The audience was good-natured, vocal, and enthusiastic. Pauli especially enjoyed it all.

After watching the game for a while, we went along to the mine compound, which was nearly adjoining the sports ground. We watched the Zulu miners dancing, and took pictures. The dancing was interesting and the costumes colorful.

Then we went on to the mine, called Robinson Deep. It being Sunday, the white superintendent was away, and the Induna or Native superintendent showed us around. There are 5,400 Natives working in Robinson Deep, and more than 2,000 additional Natives working in the next mine about a thousand yards away: Swazis, Pondos, Basutos, and many Portuguese East Africans. Pauli and I were soon able to distinguish the Swazis, who wear their hair long, dressed with red-brown clay and brushed right back from their dark faces, giving them a curious red-haired look. And the Pondos, with their hair in regular "corn-rows," sometimes "wrapped"—a style which Negroes in our own Deep South would recognize immediately. Of course we could tell the Basutos by their typical colorful blankets.

The mine kitchens were a revelation: soup, porridge (cooked thick and shoveled out in great solid slabs onto the plates), samp; the meat was "cow shanks," which we found in examination to be cow feet. On workdays the men are usually given raw meat, which they cook themselves over fires built on the ground outside their rooms.

The compound is the living quarters for the Native miners only. The white workers live in their homes outside the compound, in the suburbs, or in the city. The compound is a barren dusty square surrounded by brick barracks, "rooms," and the whole enclosed by a high strong fence; very like a prison. The barracks, or rooms, are high one-story buildings, with a door but no windows. The light and air come through ventilators placed high in the walls, just under the metal roofs.

Pauli and I went inside one of the rooms and saw the double row of stone bunks ranged round the walls—eighteen bunks in the first tier, eighteen bunks in the second tier. The Induna explained that the bunks were made of porous concrete; some of them have boards laid across them. Each man has a bunk on which he sleeps and on which he keeps his few personal possessions. Formerly fifty miners were housed in each of these rooms, but there was so much illness and ensuing loss of labor time that the mine officials reduced the number to the present thirty-six per room. . . .

July 5. I thought I was shockproof. But I found I wasn't when I visited Nancefield, a location of Johannesburg, today. Nancefield is something special, even in locations, and must be seen to be believed. It is a village made up of a peculiar kind of hut, constructed by bending a nine-by-six-foot sheet of corrugated iron into a semicircle over the ground so that both of the six-foot ends anchor in the ground and are fixed there. Sheets of the metal are then placed over the front and back of the openings, leaving just enough space for entrance and exit. The occupants have to bend low or crawl, in order to go in and out of these huts. No windows, no door, no water, no privacy inside. Nancefield is like a village of dog kennels. . . .

July 16. In the train. I have been thinking back over our trip up the east coast. Leaving South Africa we saw fewer and fewer Europeans. In Beira everyone we saw was African except the storekeeper. In Dar-Es-Salaam there were a number of Europeans, but many more Indians and Arabs, as well as Africans. Zanzibar was quite different, almost oriental, with many Indians, Arabs, and Moslem Africans. Mombasa was rather cosmopolitan, with European tourists and settlers, Indians, and Arabs, and a great variety of Africans—Moslem, Christian, and traditional.

We woke at dawn in the train, hoping to get a view of Kilamanjaro, the famous mountain peak 19,320 feet above sea level on the Kenya-Tanganyika border. We were lucky. At first the peak seemed to merge with the clouds which surrounded it. Gradually we made out the snow-covered plateau-like top. Then the sun came out and the mists cleared, and Kilamanjaro stood revealed, towering majestically in the distance.

All this part of Kenya is very high. We have been climbing steadily since we left Mombasa and the heat of the coast, for the cool green of the highlands. The great baobab trees are everywhere; there are mango trees, coconut palms, and great seas of green hills. There are occasional small villages, and people on the roads and in the fields. Climbing still higher, we passed mountain range after mountain range, all covered with a wealth of green.

After breakfast this morning we began to see lots of game. We are now passing through game reserves: many gnu, with their delicate coloring and dainty horns, speed along and give great leaps in which they seem to coast through the air. Pauli watches them spellbound and makes careful mental notes. He says when he is old enough he wants to broad-jump and high-jump, and these performances of the gnu are very instructive! Herds of zebra graze leisurely, fat and gentle, clean looking with their white stripes. Gazelles, wildebeest, and ostriches are everywhere. Pauli is enthralled.

These uplands are great rolling grasslands with sparse umbrella bushes—admirable cover for game, and perfect protection from the sun. When the animals are still, it is hard to distinguish them from the scenery. Our eyes soon became accustomed to their shapes and colorings, and we learned how to watch for motion.

We have to wear sunglasses even in the train, because of the glare. When we stopped at a village called Athi-River, I noticed three separate retiring rooms in the little station, all clearly marked: Europeans, Asiatics, Africans. It always strikes me as amusing, pathetic, and a bit silly when I see Europeans taking so much trouble to segregate themselves in public places, when I know these same Europeans fill their homes with all kinds of Native servants, who come into the most intimate contact with their food, clothing, and especially with their children. . . .

July 17. . . . Mr. Bowers and I got on very well together until we came to the question of salaries for teachers. Here in Uganda, as everywhere else in Africa, the salaries for Europeans—officials, teachers, clerks, and all workers—are royal when compared to the infinitesimal wages paid to Africans for exactly the same work, even though, as often happens, the African is better trained and more efficient at the job. Mr. Bowers, who until then had seemed to me quite reasonable, took this great difference in salaries as a matter of course, quite normal and right, and seemed surprised when I questioned and pressed the matter.

"Why, surely you realize the European has a higher standard of living than the Native, and therefore needs more salary?" he asked.

I said no, I didn't see that at all. I said I thought he was putting the cart before the horse. The European pays himself higher salaries, and therefore is able to maintain a higher standard of living. The European pays the African much lower salaries, and therefore the African must inevitably have a lower standard of living.

So far I have come across many Europeans here in Africa who I am sure are living at a much higher standard than they were accustomed to in the home country. Africans tell me they themselves—the vast majority of them—are living at a much lower standard now than before the coming of the European.

It looks to me as though the African has been forced to lower his own normal standard in order to make possible the often unjustifiably high standard which the European arbitrarily insists upon maintaining for himself. . . .

July 22. I felt better today. The Mukama's sister, Komuntale, came to see me. Her title is Rubuga, which means Queen Sister. She is big, handsome, a very pretty smooth brown color, very shy but delightfully friendly, and speaks English. We got on immediately. When she felt sure I was strong enough, she took me in the car to the local market, which was most interesting. She made me take my camera along, and I blessed her for that. I never bring it out unless I am sure no one will mind.

In one far corner of the market was a place where fish—dried vile-smelling stuff—was sold to the Nubians. Nyabongo says the Nubians, soldiers and their wives, were brought down by Lord Lugard some years ago and remained here, preferring Uganda to their own country. The women wore rings in their noses.

I was interested in the women's corner of the market where toilet articles were sold: bundles of perfuming sticks, soap cakes which look like stones, wire bracelets, bark cloth. In other parts of the market there was produce: coffee, millet, casava, mushrooms, tobacco, beans, the very important salt, locusts, etc. Nyabongo says the locusts are eaten by the Bamba and the Bakonjo, the tribes which live on the slopes of the mountains.

The market is held on a sort of common—an open space outside the village. It was crowded and business was brisk. I bought a lot of things and paid for them with East African silver (which is almost identical with English silver). It was interesting to watch my purchases being wrapped in banana leaves. I then bought a grass shopping bag to hold them.

When we got home Queen Sister explained my purchases to me. The soap ball (asaboni) is used a great deal for shampoo; it leaves the hair very clean and very black. The soap stone is a flat cake of medicinal clay found in river beds or in the mountains. The women take up the wet clay, work it into a very thick pancake, and dry it very hard in the sun; it is called orusasa. To use it you dip the cake into water, rub it in the palm of the hand into a sort of mud, and rub the mud over a small surface of the arm well into the skin; it dries and rubs off, bringing all the dirt and skin trash with it, leaving the skin dry, clean, and sweet-smelling; in this way you go all over the body in sections, cleaning and scenting it.

The bundle of perfume sticks is made up of branches from a tree called ebibaya, which grows in the valley; the people put the sticks in a small fire vessel and let them burn very slowly, put the fire under the chair in which the lady is sitting, and cover her well with blankets; she thus gets a kind of scented smoking, which leaves her clean and fresh and smelling very sweet. . . .

July 23. Went to pay our respects to the Mukama of Toro this morning. He sent his car for us at nine-thirty, and we drove through a locust storm to the palace. Pauli said it was like the movies. (It is strange, when one comes to think of it, that natural phenomena should seem like fiction or films, and not vice versa, to city-bred or highly civilized people.)

When we left the house the sky was clear and the sun brilliant. Five minutes later the air was thick and dark with locusts: They were swarming everywhere, forming a dark gray moving blanket over everything green; over the ground, over the trees, over the car inside and out. They abandoned us and the car immediately when they found we weren't the green stuff which they had come to eat. Clouds of them filled the sky blotting out the sun. Pauli said it was just like a "rainstorm without the water." In less than twenty minutes they had gone, leaving the countryside stripped bare of green. Nyabongo says they don't stay long in Toro because it is too cold here near the mountains.

The palace is built on the highest hill in Kabarole, commanding a splendid view of the surrounding country. It is simple but impressive; white, and strongly built, standing within a series of spacious and beautiful courtyards, the whole enclosed by a high handsome reed fence. Nyabongo tells me these reed fences are typical of Uganda, and the intriguing woven designs have meaning; important chiefs and royalty have certain definite designs; some patterns indicate kitchen, bath, private, or ordinary enclosures.

We drove through the gate into the outer courtyard where we were met by the King's secretary, who ushered us at once to the royal sitting room. The Mukama is a big well-built handsome brown man, about six feet tall and very broad, very well groomed in a well-cut tropical suit. He is young, in his late twenties I should guess, and speaks English very well. He was cordial and friendly, entirely informal, and we liked him immediately.

Pauli had taken great pains to learn the formal royal greeting. He and Nyabongo had gone into a huddle the night before to be sure he was letter perfect. So Pauli, confident, stood to attention after the first greeting and said, in perfect Rutoro (Ru-Toro, the language of Toro): *"Zo-na Okale!"* (Hail to the King!) Mukama smiled in delighted astonishment, and then we all sat down. Pauli then went right over to the King, climbed into his lap, touched his forehead and chin with the tips of his fingers and said, *"Orairata waitu?"* (Did you sleep well, Ours?). I was startled, and hoped he knew what he was doing. But it seems this is the traditional royal greeting. Mukama answered him gravely in Rutoro, then laughed with pleasure and hugged him. "This small one has a gift for languages," he said. "Not only the words, but the accent, the inflection is perfect." He then welcomed us very warmly to Toro, we had a pleasant chat, and he said he was looking forward to a long talk with us very soon. We then took our leave. . . .

July 25. . . . After a while we went back to the house, and Nyabongo again held council. Then we had lunch; millet cooked to a thick mush and very starchy, goat meat, and our first taste of *sim-sim* prepared with mushrooms—which was very good indeed. After lunch Nyabongo put Pauli to bed, then went out and held further council with the men, while I talked with the women through an interpreter. They first welcomed me and thanked me for coming to their obscure village. They wanted to know what kind of work women did "outside," how they brought up their children, how their men treated them, how they dressed, whether they went to school with the men. They wanted to know if I thought our black children will have a place in the world, a real place, or will "they only be told what to do?" "We are tired of being told what to do. Our children will be more tired of it." . . .

July 29. . . . Both Pauli and I have been very ill. The wild indigestion developed into something quite serious. The bananas formed into hard lumps which very nearly gave him intestinal obstruction.

Nyabongo's sister, who is the nurse in the Kampala Hospital, and Queen Sister came over to help Nyabongo nurse us. Pauli had violent spasms of the stomach, couldn't keep anything down for three days, and got quite thin. He was pretty scared, poor lamb, but not half so scared as I was. I couldn't imagine what I would tell Big Paul and Mother if anything happened to him. I dared not think what I would tell myself. Finally we got him cleared out, and then he broke out in a banana rash—great welts on the skin of hands, arms, legs, face, and neck. We massaged the welts with a tropical ointment, which made him comfortable, and they eventually disappeared.

Then I went down with a terrific fever and was in bed three days

—very faint, couldn't even sit up. I was too low to worry about our being such a nuisance to our hosts. I must say it gives one a feeling of confidence to see how the people mobilize for illness, take it in their stride as part of the ordinary business of living, and know just what to do and how to make you comfortable.

Medicine plants and medical knowledge are almost entirely women's work. The young ones get information from their mothers and grandmothers (from "the old ones") and learn the roots, plants, leaves, medicinal clays, and their uses. A man doctor is never called except for extreme or very serious illness. All the minor general ailments are women's work. You call in another woman if you don't know yourself. Royal women especially know a great deal about these things. It is considered one of their accomplishments to know medicine. Queen Sister knows far more than her contemporaries....

The schoolteachers came in from the surrounding districts to see me this evening, to talk and listen and to ask questions. How I longed for Paul to help me. There were about fifty of them, most of them young, eager, and intelligent. They wanted to know all about schools in England and in America: Do black and white people go to the same schools, or do governments waste money by maintaining separate schools? May black people study medicine, economics, law, and the classics, as well as agriculture and crafts? Is education expensive, or do one's taxes cover it? Are there black teachers? How do black people earn money? Are they allowed to do every kind of work, skilled as well as unskilled—do they work side by side with white workers? Do they get the same pay? Will I please tell them about the so-called "backward peoples" of Russia, and what are they doing now? (Africans have been disposed of so long as "backward" that they are eager to hear what is happening to other "backward" peoples.) They were heartily encouraged by what I could tell them about the successful integration of nomads like the Yakuts into the highly industrialized modern Soviet society.

"How long did it take, this integration?" they asked anxiously.

"Ten to twenty years," I said.

A long sigh went through the crowd: "Not the thousand years they say it will take us! Though we are not 'backward' in any sense of the word. What do they mean by this 'backward'?"

Before I could answer, or try to answer, a fellow teacher said:

"They mean people they have kept back, and continue to keep
back." . . .

August 1. I have been working with the herdswomen in the dairy,
learning a lot about custom and tradition. Everything connected with
the handling of the milk after it is collected from the cattle is called
bisahi (dairy) and is women's business. *Bisahi* is considered elegant
work for ladies, and they take great pride in their knowledge and
expertness. Experience in any branch of *bisahi* is definitely an accom-
plishment.

The ladies are delightful, intelligent, companionable, and have a
great sense of fun. They think it a bit silly for me to learn all about
bisahi, when I have no cattle and no hopes of getting any. But they
like me, and I like them. They feel there must be some good reason
for my learning, so they have settled down to doing their utmost to
teach me. They are also pleased with my interest in and respect for
their customs. Some of them speak a little English, I have been
accumulating a few words of Rotoro, and we all understand gestures
and inflection of voice, and so we are able to manage.

We often went off into gales of laughter over misunderstandings,
and we all agreed after the second day that one of the most important
words in any language is "why?" We enjoyed a lot of gossip while
we worked, became very good friends, examined each other's hair,
skin, clothes. We each found out how the other managed her husband, home, and children.

It was a wonderful experience for me. I learned a great deal about
the very important business of living, and as a result have rearranged
my sense of values to some considerable extent. The leisurely approach, the calm facing of circumstances and making the most of
them, is very different from the European hustle and hurry and drive,
and worry and frustration when things don't go well. The African
gets things done, gets a great deal done, but gets it done without the
furious wear and tear on the nervous system. Because the European
doesn't see his own hustle and bustle he says the African is lazy, in
spite of the fact that the African gets the work done.

When things go wrong the African does what he can about them,
then philosophically goes on to something else. Because he does not
waste his nervous energy bewailing what cannot be helped, the European says he is stagnant, indifferent, sluggish. I have always thought

myself very energetic and ambitious, and am called "dynamic" by my friends, yet I find myself continually impressed with the ambition, energy, and capacity for work of the African. The European seems unable to recognize these qualities because their manifestations are in patterns unfamiliar to him.

Bisabi is carried on in a special hut beautifully built and immaculately kept. The dried-grass floor is kept fresh and sweet, and all the milk bowls and calabashes are spotlessly clean. The hut is fumigated at regular intervals. I learned about the making of butter and buttermilk, and there was a lot of teasing laughter as the women explained how every young herdswoman, when engaged, always drinks lots of buttermilk to make her fat and beautiful. Only women and children drink buttermilk; men never drink it. Children up to seven years of age drink sweet milk in the morning and evening, and plenty of buttermilk at noon. When seven years old the children begin to eat plantains, meat, and other things. The children on a diet of milk are always cleaned out regularly and thoroughly once a week.

The women deplored the fact that the herds of cattle are fast dwindling. They say that as recently as 1933 Nyabongo had a herd of 2,000 cattle, and that even the ordinary person had 20 to 50 head. "Then the government began to inject all cattle with needles, and the cattle died. We understand that needles are helpful for some diseases. One must study and understand needles on the one hand, but one must also study and understand cattle on the other. Our cattle were healthy. We had no milk or cattle disease. Yet all our cattle were given the needle, and many of them died. This civilization business," they sighed, "can be very destructive. Now we have little or no cattle, and must return to the soil."

This return to the soil is acutely felt by the herdspeople because their wealth and prestige, traditions and customs are associated with the possession of cattle. The herdspeople were the high caste, the aristocrats, and the agriculturists the lower class, the common men. . . .

August 5. . . . At the hotel, which was a very sad affair, we sat in the lounge while a great deal of conversation went on between the Belgian hotel owner and our D.C. There was a lot of *"noir, noir"* in very rapid French, and we tried to look blank as though we did not understand the language. (I believe every Negro would understand

and recognize the word "black" in any language. He would certainly
recognize the tone of voice which goes with the word!) After considerable pressure from our D.C., and a lot of *"distingué"* and "important" on his part against the *"noir, noir,"* the owner finally gave in
and showed us to our rooms. When we saw them we wondered what
all the discussion had been about. They were scarcely fit for animals.

Nyabongo and Kaboha had a room at the end of the corridor; there
was an apparently occupied room next, then came Pauli's and mine.
Pauli said: "This is what we get when we are black and important.
Wonder what we'd get if we were unimportant." We were soon to
find out. The D.C. called for Nyabongo, who later reported that the
owner had refused to let our "boys" sleep in the hotel, but had said
they could sleep in the huts at the back. Nyabongo found them filthy
and, fearing vermin and disease, made them sleep in the car.

The owner reluctantly consented to give us our meals, "but not
those boys." So Nyabongo quietly made arrangements with the cook
and the waiter, who gave them meals in the car. We ate in the lounge,
part of which was used as dining room, part sitting room, and part
reception desk. The meal was terrible. All through dinner the owner
kept muttering in French: "If I have blacks in my hotel no white
people will come." Pauli finally asked: "Mamma, here in the Congo
where nearly everybody is black, what white people does he mean?"
We were to find out before the night was over.

In the sitting-room part of the lounge two young Belgians were
listlessly playing backgammon, and smoking and drinking steadily.
They were thin and heavy eyed, with the familiar "Congo pallor."
They seemed very pathetic.

After dinner we took a short walk along the road. The moon was
up, enormous and blood red, and the sky was full of lightning—
brilliant and frightening—and low rumbles of thunder. After we
went to bed it rained a "big rain," the downpour making a terrific
clatter on the metal roof, and sounds of water flooding everywhere.

In the midst of all this uproar two Belgians, possibly the two young
backgammon players, brought two women into the room between
Nyabongo's and mine, and they quite noisily and unmistakably slept
together. It was disgusting: the chatter in French between the two
men, the conversation in pidgin French between the men and the
women, and the giggly chatter in some Native dialect between the
two women.

After about an hour of this, through which Pauli slept soundly, thank heaven, I heard the owner rush into the room shouting: "People come, people come!" He swept the young men and their ladies-of-the-night out of the room, the ladies protesting and making a great fuss.

All this noise eventually woke Pauli. We could hear the owner hurrying round the room probably tidying it up. Then we heard two heavy men enter and go to bed. They coughed and spit and murmured drunkenly the rest of the night. I said to myself in answer to Pauli's earlier question: "What white people?" "Oh, *those* white people!" . . .

August 12. Kabarole. We slept late this morning, tired out from our long drive from Hoima last night. In the early afternoon I was working on my notes, when I heard a rhythmic singing and sent Pauli to investigate. He came tearing back, shouting excitedly that the Bamba had come down from the mountains to dance for us. We hurried out to stand on the veranda and watch their arrival. Everyone from all over the house and grounds came to join us.

The Bamba, who are quite small in stature, came into the courtyard singing, dancing, leaping. They danced up to us shaking their spears in greeting, then backed and separated into two groups, one group with shields and spears facing the opposite group with branches and leaves. They danced a mock fight which was very exciting, some from each side falling dead so realistically that Pauli was alarmed.

We thanked them warmly as they left and gave them salt which we had brought from Katwe. They had walked seventy miles to dance for us!

This afternoon we went to see Nyabongo's grandmother, a remarkable old lady who is thought to be about 120 years old. Nyabongo says she has always seemed to him as old as she is now—always on the couch—since he was a baby. He says she used to be fat, now she is thin and her eyes are glazed with a film of age, but her mind is clear and she is aware and intelligent. She was very much interested in Pauli, and said: "That boy belongs to us—see his mouth, eyes, nose, the shape of head—pure African. Oh, yes, that boy belongs to Africa, to us." She said my hair, eyes, nose, and "especially my spirit" are African. . . .

August 13. . . . The ladies came out—the Chief's wife and daughters. It is a great pleasure to see the women, at last. Word has gone around that I always ask for the women, so contrary to custom they come out now to see me. . . .

August 21. Alexandria. We cross the Mediterranean today by sea-plane, the *Scipio,* via Crete and Athens to Brindisi on the southern tip of Italy. I had a bad night, but I think the long rest has done me good. Anyway I feel able to hold on for another day. If I don't feel better when we get to Brindisi, I'll go into a hospital there and have Pauli telephone big Paul. I'll keep my fingers crossed and see.

The *Scipio* is a handsome craft. We taxied out of Alexandria harbor and rose smoothly over the calm blue Mediterranean.

Some of our fellow passengers in the *Horsa* have gone on to Persia and India, and some of them are continuing with us to Paris.

The charming American family from Wilmington, Delaware, is still with us. And so is the English Colonial from South Africa.

Pauli and I had been extremely cautious with these passengers. The Wilmington people were "southerners," and this typical Colonial was a special brand of poison to us, as Negroes.

By the time the *Horsa* had reached Khartoum we were all on very pleasant speaking terms. When we reached Alexandria we were on much more than speaking terms.

The Wilmington family, in spite of their Southern origin, were charming, friendly, and interesting. The attractive middle-aged man and wife had come with their two stalwart handsome sons (about nineteen and twenty) for big-game hunting in Kenya. They had had wonderful luck, and had enjoyed their trip enormously.

The Colonial was on the elderly side, red faced, choleric, and given to asserting himself. He had spent many years in South Africa, made his fortune, and is now returning to England to enjoy it. He has the utmost contempt for "the blacks," as he calls the Africans, and in fact does not think too well of anything or anybody not British.

It took him quite some time and effort to adjust himself to the fact that Pauli and I—"blacks"—were actually fellow passengers with himself. Finally, as he saw the other passengers one by one become friendly with us, he too broke down and talked with us. (I'm sure it never once occurred to him that *we* did *not* want to talk with *him!*) In the end we had some very interesting conversation.

He was obviously a lonely man, and in spite of himself he was very much attracted to Pauli. When he came to know us better he made a curious remark:

"Son of yours a fine boy, fine boy. Incredible he is only nine years old. So intelligent."

I said Pauli had been around grownups a great deal, and perhaps was informed beyond his years because of that.

"No, *intelligent,*" insisted the Colonial gruffly. "Pity he's got that handicap."

"What handicap?" I asked, my feathers ruffling.

"Pity he's black. Pity. Could go far."

"He'll go far *because* he's black," I said. "His color, his background, his rich history are part of his wealth. We consider it an asset, not a handicap."

He was surprised and interested. "Don't understand," he said.

"Of course you don't," I said pleasantly, and let the conversation drop.

But I continued the conversation in my mind.

Soaring in the clouds, with the strange distant toy world spread out below, I felt removed from earth-bound things.

Why am I really glad and proud to be Negro? Why am I sorry for this pitiful "superior" European? Why do I actually feel superior to him?

This poor man doesn't know what it's all about. He has no important or useful knowledge about more than a billion of his fellow men —Negroes, Africans, Indians, Chinese, probably Jews, and probably Russians. Most likely he has simply dismissed them contemptuously as "primitive," "oriental," or "Red." He has built himself into a very small, very limited world of his own, behind a towering, formidable wall of ignorance, prejudice, and "superiority."

This typical Colonial seems to me weak, uncomfortably self-conscious, lonely, pathetic, and frightened.

Certainly he is weak, else why must he carry and maintain armed force—and plenty of it—everywhere he goes, always?

Certainly he is uncomfortably self-conscious, else why need he insist—loudly, constantly—that he is superior? Really superior people take their superiority for granted.

Certainly he is lonely and pathetic. Has he not arbitrarily walled himself off from more than two-thirds of his fellow men, the non-white peoples of the world?

And certainly he is frightened. One has only to watch him when he rants about the "rising tide of color," about the "yellow peril," etc., to realize he is frightened. Only fear can explain much of his irrational behavior toward his non-white brother.

On the other hand we, as Negroes, at least know what it's all about. We know our white brothers—know a great deal about them. They have shown us all their strengths and all their weaknesses.

We have not built any walls to limit our world.

Walls have been built against us, but we are always fighting to tear them down, and in the fighting, we grow, we find new strength, new scope.

We look at slavery—personal, economic, and social slavery—and we know that it has done us grave injury. But we have always fought that slavery, resisted it everywhere, continuously; and in the fighting, in the resistance, we have survived and grown strong.

In fighting a just cause, in resisting oppression, there is dignity.

We look at those who have enslaved us, and find them decadent. Injustice and greed and conscious inhumanity are terribly destructive.

Yes, I am glad and proud I am Negro.

Crete, Athens, Brindisi, Paris, London.
All a dream and a nightmare, because I was ill.

August 25. London. I made it home. With Pauli's sturdy help, I made it.

It seems that Mother arrived in London more than a week ago from her summer in Russia, had prepared the flat and sat down to wait for us. Paul had joined her a few days later.

Paul picked up the paper four days ago, and read that our plane, the *Horsa,* was overdue at Karachi and was thought to be lost somewhere in the Persian desert. (It was found in the desert several days later, with the passengers, pilot, and the nice steward, hungry and parched with thirst, sheltering under the great wings of the plane.) Frightened, Paul called the airways office, and they assured him we had changed at Alexandria from the *Horsa* to the *Scipio,* for the flight across the Mediterranean.

Two days later he picked up an evening paper and read that the *Scipio,* in landing at Crete, had gone straight to the bottom of the sea. The passengers and crew and some of the mail had been rescued.

(This was on the return trip from Brindisi to Alexandria, but Paul didn't know that then.)

Frantic, he rushed round to the airways office for news of Pauli and me. They explained that we had been safe aboard the Paris train when the accident happened.

Paul and Mother drove down to the Croydon Airport outside London to meet us. Pauli, with vast relief, turned his Mamma Dear over to Daddy and Grandma.

"She was awful sick, but I brought her home safe," he said proudly.

Nell Giles (Ahern)
[1907–]

Known as the author of etiquette books for teenagers, Nell Giles worked as a feature writer for The Boston Globe *when the United States entered World War II. With the intention of "writing the glamour out of women in war," she applied for work at the General Electric Company in West Lynn, Massachusetts. For two months, she worked in the factory geared for war production, kept a diary, and published her experiences in* The Boston Globe. *Her co-workers, according to her account, were at first suspicious of her college-educated background, but accepted her when they saw her get her "hands dirty in the machine shop."*

This "Rosie the Riveter" was one of some five million women who poured into the paid labor force from 1940 to 1944 in jobs previously closed to them. When the draft removed male workers from the factories, the War Manpower Commission, supported by the urgings of magazines, newspapers, radio, and films, called for women to take their places. By 1945, the percentage of women in the workforce had risen to 36 percent from the 25 percent of five years earlier. When the war ended, these numbers dropped as dramatically as they had risen, with some women gladly leaving paid employment, and many others leaving when they were fired in favor of male workers.

After her stint in the factory, Nell Giles continued her career as a writer. She served as Assistant Editor and feature writer for the Ladies Home Journal *until she married Robert Ahern in 1947. As a free-lance writer, she wrote frequent features on food, fashion, and travel for* The Boston Globe, *contributed widely to popular magazines, and published several successful cookbooks.*

[1943]

Today our training class was divided into two shifts . . . night and day . . . and put to work on the bench, though what we do is just for practice.

My first job was being taught the value of motions. The foreman sat me down before an arrangement of screws, tiny wires and things called "brackets." With a small "jeweler's screw driver" I was to take fifty of the things apart and then put them together again. Then I was to take them apart for the second time, and on the next assembling I would be timed. Putting them together is supposed to take 36 minutes . . . and can be done by the experts in 23 . . . but it took me 45. Getting them back together again is even worse because the wires get tangled up, and you wouldn't believe a screw driver could slip around so!

Then the foreman assigned me to the ratchet screw driver, which is a wonderful way to let off steam. I was a whiz at that. All you do is exert a little pressure with this "ratchet" which hangs on a spring in front of you, and out pops the screw. It makes a big noise and you feel the house is falling down around your ears and you hope it does! If every home were equipped with a ratchet screw driver, how it would clear the air of verbal steam letting-off!

Every move we make in completing one of these "jobs" has been carefully figured out by the methods department and put on a blue print, which is constantly before us. "With the left hand place new block on table as right hand removes completed block . . ." and so forth, through every move. As far as possible, the duties of each hand are the same, though in opposite directions. You see that there is a rhythm in all this. Again we are told how to use finger movements, rather than shoulder, because they are twice as fast. Someone I know gave me a big tin lunch box . . . the black kind with a handle and a thermos bottle inside, and I suppose they aren't tin any more, at that.

Today . . . 4 to 10 shift again . . . I carried my lunch in the new box and I was absolutely hooted down! You would never believe that such a small incident could cause such a furore. But here everyone must do exactly what everyone else does, and it is not the "fashion," I find to my sorrow, for girls to carry lunch boxes.

From Nell Giles, *Punch In*, Susie! *A Woman's War Factory Diary* (New York and London: Harper and Brothers, [1943]). © 1943 by Nell Giles. Reprinted by permission of Harper and Row.

Brown paper bags are all right . . . but black boxes with a handle DEFINITELY NOT! It's true that it's more convenient, that it would make it possible to bring hot soup or milk or whatever else you'd want, but it's just not done. For the men—yes. Almost to a man they come through the factory gate carrying lunch boxes. But for the girls —NO.

And I can tell you right now that I haven't the courage to buck that line! It's back to the brown paper bag for me.

Some of the girls carry lunches in those flat straw envelope bags . . . you know the kind. One slips over the other. It looks quite like a handbag. But on the whole, there's not much effort to disguise the fact that you're carrying your lunch. For one thing, you go to work either so early or so late that you live in a little world of your own. Everyone else on the subway or bus is going where you're going.

There's a lot of laughing and talking and I have yet to overhear any "military secrets" given away.

That may be because the factory is well posted with signs about the "enemy is listening" . . . or "what he knows will hurt YOU" . . . or it may be something much simpler, such as the people who put these screws and things together just not being crazy enough about them to talk screws ALL the time!

In our training class right now, we feel very "new" and stared at by the experts and old-timers, but there are so many new ones . . . about forty-five a week in this one branch, to judge by the numbers of classes we see coming in . . . that we have plenty of company.

Tonight we all had very sore shoulders and backs . . . we'd probably better brush up on the finger movement!

I am not so crazy about that ratchet screw driver as I was yesterday. I put together fifty things called "blocks" . . . and a whole dozen of them were wrong and the foreman said to do the entire fifty over again . . . taking apart and putting together! This means that I won't have time to learn soldering until I'm assigned to a different part of the factory. I had to do the brackets again tonight and cut down my time to 37 minutes, which is still three minutes over the dead line and I am now the second slowest member of the class!

Except for those blankety-blank ratchet screw drivers, it is very peaceful and quiet to work at night. We are in a long room, everything clean and very cool. Sometimes one of the girls sings (it's the girl who is slower than I am and I am very fond of her!) but for the most part we just sit in our efficiently designed chairs and work.

Without thinking, we try to beat the rhythm of the next girl, if we are doing the same kind of work. There are four screws in the block . . . and I tried to keep one p-r-r with the ratchet screw driver ahead of my chum who used to work in an automobile office. That's probably why I made a dozen mistakes. But I could hear her try to catch up with my p-r-r-s . . . and she did!

The foreman walks up and down the room all the time, watching our work and showing us how to do it a little better. He is a long, tall man who's lived in Texas and has kept the drawl. Every now and then he goes to the room next to this one to take a smoke but he's never had more than a puff without hearing the wrong kind of noise from a screw driver and having to come in again.

He knows by the noise whether you are taking a screw in or out, whether you are pressing down too hard or not hard enough and at what angle you're holding the screw driver! Also, he can tell by one or two "p-r-r-s" how long it will take you to do fifty blocks.

Our windows . . . we are just below street level . . . are covered with a special screen so that we can see out but people on the street can't see in. When we look up from work, we can always see women carrying home groceries, or men coming home from work, and once in a while a very little boy walking that way they do, with stomach sticking out and legs sort of coltishly out of control and awkward. To see these people out the window is a little like seeing *My Sister Eileen* . . . only we haven't had a drunk yet!

Today we were graduated from our training class and assigned to parts of the factory. We are still "in training" but there's quite a difference. This week we were paid a learner's rate per hour for the time we spent in training, but next week we'll be paid according to what we do. I have explained that there is a basic pay per hour. For any pieces you do above a predetermined number you are paid extra, according to the "job." A job is an assignment of work . . . 500 brackets to be assembled, for example. One person does only one operation, though this may entail several parts.

But there is more than a financial difference in our status now. Before today, we have done nothing that will actually be used in aircraft . . . all of it was "practice" and the same material used over again by the next class. But now what we do will go to war. There is no one around to tell us six or seven times how to do something either . . . I found that out before noon today!

My first actual piece of war work started at 7 minutes past 11. The foreman assigned me to a table and said: "Blow the metal chips off these parts." That may sound like Greek to you. Well, it did to me, too. Blow them off . . . you mean just BLOW them off? In the box were about 500 metal gadgets. The nearest description I can give you is that they looked a little like the thing a typewriter ribbon is wound on, only they were more involved. Just as I was trying to figure out how I'd have enough breath to blow metal chips off all those things, I saw a hose attached to the table . . . and of course it was full of compressed air. It looked very simple to press the button and blow off the chips. But the first blast of air blew the gadget right out of my hand! And then somebody walking by said, "Hey, stop blowing that grease out here!" So I learned to hold the hose down. Then a foreman . . . there are several here . . . said don't be so DAINTY . . . take a fistful and BLOW!

We left our training class this morning and were escorted by our instructor to the employment office where our fingerprints were recorded and our pictures made on buttons which we must always wear. Not to the movies, of course . . . only at work!

The pictures were all very funny, just as passport pictures always were, remember? You always look twice your calendar age and one-half your mental age . . . you hope! But unless you wear your button in very plain sight, the policeman at the gate WILL NOT let you pass.

With several other girls from our class, I was assigned to the machine part of the department. This is NOT the lily-white-hand department. It is the dirtiest part of the work done in this factory, but it seems also the most exciting. Where you might say "of the earth earth-y" to describe some things . . . for this you would say "of the dirt dirt-y." There is so much noise you can hear nothing the girl across the table says. Everybody's hands are black . . . black that won't come off.

I've told you about the blowing job . . . Well, in the afternoon I had one that made the first one look like mud pies in the first grade. This was a delightful little box full of small, steel or cast iron (sorry I don't know the difference today, but wait until next week!) . . . things covered with a mixture of grease, kerosene and metal chips.

I was in up to the elbows and it was wonderful! The mixture felt very salty, and I asked the foreman if they put the salt in so the grease would come off our hands quickly, and he looked at me as if I'd just escaped from the sweetness-and-light department and he said NO. It isn't salt, it's finely chipped metal from a cutting tool which makes the gritty feeling. So now you know about that. No one is figuring out what will take the grease off your hands. Also, it isn't grease . . . it's kerosene.

This afternoon I worked at a drill press. I did what is called "spot facing." There is a round aluminum plate with holes in it and paint on one side. Just one . . . a certain one . . . of those holes had to have the paint taken away in a circle around it so that when they assemble it with the other parts, the screw will hold. It is really nice to see what they did with some of our aluminum pots and pans. . . .

Today he called me "Babe."

He is the set-up man who assigns me to jobs and puts in new drills five minutes afterwards. He is the man who calls me a "drill-wrecker." "Helping Hitler again, huh?" he says when I tell him there's a drill on my machine that needs fixing! Sometimes I manage to get another set-up man to fix every other drill . . . but even then, he finds out.

But today he called me Babe!

You have never seen a man so crazy about machinery. He sits you down at one of these Ole Debbil Drills and shows you how to do one piece. He says you can tell by the FEEL of the lever whether or not you've drilled a smooth hole through the aluminum disk.

All I can tell by my feeling is that I am scared stiff. How do you know the disk won't fly out of your hand and hit you? How do you know the chips won't get in your eye? How do you know you won't miss the disk entirely and bore a hole through your hand? That's what I'd like to know . . . let alone that business of boring a smooth hole. Each time I bring down the handle of the machine I wonder if I'll be alive the next minute!

Yesterday I mentioned to him that the aluminum chips burned my hand and couldn't I please wear a glove? I thought he'd laugh himself silly!

Today I did what is called "burring." Somebody else has drilled the holes . . . all I have to do is take off the rough edge. This, I suppose, is to make a smooth place so the screw will fit. I did 1056 pieces . . . one thousand and fifty-six. And I didn't break a drill.

They say it's very hard to break one when you do this job, but anyway I didn't. And that's how it happened that today he called me "Babe." Just walked behind me casually and said "Hi, Babe!"

I am gradually getting my sea legs. Getting up at 4:30 in the morning isn't so bad when you get used to it. The trouble is you have to go to bed at 8:30, and when some innocent friend telephones just as you've dropped off to sleep, you could do murder with your bare hands. . . .

All vacations were canceled today. It was quite a blow to the people who work here the year round, and need relief from the monotony of doing the same thing over and over again.

Many of the girls have husbands in the service, and were planning to visit them before they leave for foreign duty. You can understand, can't you, that all work and no play makes Jane a dull girl? And Jane on the night shift has only a Sunday for recreation, and not always that. If there is extra work to be done, the entire force works on Sunday, too. There are no holidays . . . not even the Fourth of July last week!

But after that first blow . . . all vacations canceled . . . THERE WAS NO GRUMBLING. Everybody understands WHY there is no time for vacations. There was no grouching about working the Fourth, either. And a couple of weeks ago I talked with a girl who had to work on Sunday. She was ill with a cold . . . and you know how a summer cold can give you the miseries . . . but she didn't think of asking for the day off!

I don't want to give you the impression that people who work in a war production factory are all nice and sweet and patriotic, any more than you must think that all soldiers are brave. Money has much to do with how hard people work in a factory, but I honestly think there is an INCREASE in the spirit determined to win this war.

Not a day passes but you'll hear somebody say to a worker who seems to be slowing down, "There's a war on, you know!"

The foreman of each floor gets a monthly quota for production, which he breaks down into weeks and days or nights. At the present time, our factory is two weeks ahead of schedule, but since war doesn't run on schedule, that is not too comfortable a margin.

In spite of the terrific pressure to get things out in a hurry, the first demand is for quality. Everything must be EXACTLY right.

Tonight I got a much deserved call down for drilling a hole in the wrong place. The set-up man gave me a little metal gadget into which

I was to drill seven holes. As usual, there was a fixture to hold the gadget and to indicate where the holes were to go. But unfortunately, the top of the fixture had a pattern for two holes, and I was to drill only one of them. An hour later I began to wonder WHICH one, and of course I'd been drilling the wrong hole.

I said to the man, "Well, maybe these pieces of metal can be used for something else . . ." and he said, "yeah, maybe the Army can use 'em for dust cloths."

Tonight the Chinese girl arranged for me to ride home with a man who works here and lives beyond Boston. He has five passengers, and takes us to and from work for $2.50 a week, which is a great saving in time and money.

He picks up one girl in Dorchester, and the others as we go through Chelsea, Revere, and points north. I'm the second passenger he collects, and my picking up point is the South Station.

All along Atlantic Avenue there are men and girls with lunches and identification buttons waiting to meet their "rides." You seldom see an empty back seat.

These rides are arranged in a number of ways at the factory. In the training department we were asked where we lived and an effort was made to arrange rides with someone driving from the same district. There are also notices put in the employees' paper, "Ride or rider WANTED" . . .

This is just an example of the community spirit that I've found in many ways working in this factory. It's true that each person is working for himself first, but he is also looking out for his fellow-worker. I've noticed this more working at night than while working days, but it's possible because the night shift is smaller.

Each time I start a new job some one of the girls who has been here for a longer time comes up to show me a quicker way to do it, a short cut she's learned by experience. And this isn't because I look green and helpless . . . or is it? Anyway, it happens to the other new people, too.

The college girls, it seems to me, make a good showing. They catch on quickly and they work hard. Most of them consider working in a factory a lark and are doing it to make money for next year. But since college girls seldom wear their hearts on their sleeves, who is to say there isn't a patriotic angle to it, too? . . .

Abigail Lewis

[1923–]

When Abigail Lewis discovered she was pregnant, "The shock was considerable." More than one doctor had told her that because of damage to her Fallopian tubes, she would never have children. They had urged an operation to end the attacks of intense abdominal pain she had been suffering. But she had refused to undergo the operation even though, as the result of her parents' bitter divorce, she was not at all sure she wanted children.

Two years earlier, Abigail had married Nick Lewis, recently returned from the war, and she had begun a career making ceramic sculpture. When she discovered she was about to participate in what was later called "the baby boom," she was more than a little ambivalent: "All around me women were pushing baby carriages, with that blank and foolish look of people who were not doing much of anything, and I pitied and disliked them." Throughout the entire summer of 1948, she kept her secret to herself and thus gained what she called "three more months of freedom."

In August, Abigail Lewis began a journal of her pregnancy. Highly conscious of the passage of time during pregnancy, women have often kept journals during these months, sometimes with the unborn child as an audience. An earlier example of a "pregnancy diary" is Charlotte Teller Hirsch, The Diary of An Expectant Mother *(Chicago: A. C. McClure, 1917).*

Abigail Lewis is the pseudonym of Otis Kidwell Burger, a full-time ceramic sculptor and writer in New York City. She suspects that "Most of the women of my generation (61) have led similarly complicated career/ domestic lives . . ." Today, the daughter in the diary is an environmentalist and teacher. A second daughter born three years later is a singer and actress. Both daughters are also serious rock climbers and recently Otis Kidwell Burger joined the younger daughter in "12 non-stop hours climbing in the High Peaks of the Adirondacks."

[1948]

AUGUST 28, SATURDAY   I haven't had any morning sickness since that two weeks during chemistry class, so I guess I'm getting off easily, but I do feel sort of loathsome and worn out. Nick is getting suspicious too. I told him I would go to see the doctor in September, when he returns from his vacation. It seems a long way off. . . .

AUGUST 29, SUNDAY   Oh God, the black rage that comes over me sometimes, especially at night. The nerve of this creature, the impudence! Placidly leaching food from my body without even an invitation. Who invited it to this feast? Don't they know when they're not wanted? Surely the rush of adrenalin through my blood must be transmitted to it too; if there were only enough, might it not kill it? The only possible way in which anger might kill.

I take a delight in deviling Nick, saying how I loathe children, or rather babies. You can talk to children. We get very cool and bitter about it, which is uncomfortable in so small a space. One cannot really have a satisfactory, blow-up, relieving-feelings quarrel in a two-room apartment. All that happens is that I move out into the other room to sleep, though I feel much more like taking a long walk, or a midnight gallop in the rain. . . .

So many nights I spend on the day bed now. But it hurts to be away from Nick. I can't sleep without my husband's arm under my head, either. And the gritty daylight seeps in through the curtains, the sound of trucks wakes me at dawn. Sleeping and waking become mingled. The year dies and dies, and I want to be away somewhere, but three flights of stairs is such a lot. . . .

SEPTEMBER 5, SUNDAY   The worst thing about all this is that it is so impossible to be objective. To be objective is to stand outside, to have little stake or emotional interest in a matter; either of these abilities is a physical impossibility to the pregnant woman. My very emotions are no longer under normal control but are stirred by unfamiliar hormones. Those who claim that the body is only a vehicle for the soul have obviously never been sick for a long time, or pregnant. One's vision of the world depends very much on the physical condi-

From Abigail Lewis, *An Interesting Condition: The Diary of a Pregnant Woman* (Garden City, N.Y.: Doubleday, 1950). Reprinted by permission of Otis Kidwell Burger.

tions through which one sees it. Now, though I am trying to be logical about my despairs, I am too new to myself, too both inside and outside myself, to be able to say what is nonsense and what is legitimate. And I can't say that I really feel that being objective would help much anyway, since this will go on and happen no matter what I think about it. . . .

The black rages that come over me . . . Yes, they are not pretty. When I am angry I am thoroughly angry, and I have had a lot of practice, in family rows, in saying the things that hurt most. But there is another side to it. I think I will make a good mother. In a way, I resent this most of all, because then I may be tempted to give all my time to the child and save none for my work. But in a way, too, I am glad. I should like to be really good in at least one human relationship, and I have a kind of hunger for the sturdy, independent little bodies of children, the boundless energy, the wonderful uncompromising self-confidence. Perhaps being angry is partly a way of not hoping too much.

SEPTEMBER 7, TUESDAY   Met a boy on the street today with whom I had taken a graduate geology course. He asked if I am planning to go back to school again or if I am "taking my duties as a wife more seriously." Damn men and their conception of duty too! Is it being an irresponsible wife to want to get an education? I got better marks than he did. How much does a wife owe to herself and how much to her husband? I thought I knew, but now I find it takes a lot of thought, time, and effort to make even such a makeshift home as ours. I have often thought of getting a job, but it would probably be in a field very alien to Nick's, and I would be afraid of it splitting my interests. Ceramics at home is a compromise. It gives me time to give Nick criticism on his work when he wants it, and yet keeps me from entirely wasting my own time. I can't imagine not having some outside interest. Perhaps the best possible solution would be a husband-wife team, sharing work they both enjoy; those that I have seen were very successful. I hope, for the sake of society and better marriages, that there will be more of them. Certainly the things that Nick and I can do together, such as trout fishing, criticizing each other's writing, and visiting art galleries, are doubly fine.

SEPTEMBER 10, FRIDAY   The time that I had thought so distant is here; having told Nick that the doctor would be back now, I could no longer put off seeing him. And of course the idea with which I have been playing, like a juggler with a stick of dynamite, is true after all, has exploded in my hands. As I suppose I really knew it would. But it was nice having that doubt in the back of my mind; now I feel as if I'd run into a stone wall. How terrible is the inescapable! To have no way out, no way to qualify or lessen . . . I think even a joyful thing would have some horror if it were inevitable.

Luckily I sold my first and only story this spring, and the money will just cover the expense of a private room. To have a first baby publicly seems impossible, so I reserved a room then and there. It is a relief to be able to do something concrete and on my own. I feel less helplessly pushed around. And the doctor was not as much help in lessening this feeling as I had expected. Though we discussed Birth a little, he did not tell me much, and I was a little distressed to think what my state of mind would have been had I been ignorant of biology, as most women are. How must it feel only to know vaguely that something ineradicable is inside of you that must eventually, and with great pain, come out? I do think doctors ought to take the time to explain childbirth a little to potential mothers, the scientific as well as the practical aspects.

And then home to wait for Nick.

Oh, if only there were some form of telepathy when two people both guess what the other is thinking, but speech seems too crude to express it! Then words lie clumsy and undigested in the mouth, impossible to shape. For a moment, as we stood talking of His Day at the Office, I thought he would not ask and the secret would be safe a little longer. But he did ask, and the words had to be found.

"I've reserved a room at the hospital for the thirteenth of March," I said finally, the least emotional way I could think of putting it. But he put his arms around me. He seemed so happy that suddenly I was glad too; happy for him, happy for having told him. I suppose there is always one of a pair, at least, who is happy at having a child, and I must say it makes it easier for the other. Impossible not to feel some pleasure at the joy of someone you love. . . .

[1949]

FEBRUARY 3, THURSDAY   Time is a curious sensation conditioned by many things. If we faint we may lose all conception of time and awaken not knowing how many years or hours have passed. Why this is not always true of sleep, I don't know. Perhaps sleep is not ordinarily so deep. But surely everyone, at one time or another, has awakened thinking himself in some other place or in some earlier time. The conception of time depends, then, I suppose, upon the perception of continuity, and for this reason a woman's sense of time must be quite different from a man's. Her sense of continuity is internal and natural, not the external and easily interrupted continuity of clocks and calendars. She connects directly to the source of time, and the moon that pulls the tides around the world also pulls the hormone tide within her; her months are marked off without need of calendar. She carries her months, her years, her spring and winter within herself.

How much this internal sense of time is heightened in pregnancy! Were I to lose consciousness for a month, I could still tell that an appreciable amount of time had passed by the increased size of the fetus within me. There is a constant sense of growth, of progress, of time which, while it may be wasted for you personally, is still being used, so that even if you were to do nothing at all during those nine months, something would nevertheless be accomplished and a climax reached. Death has never seemed so far away, because growth, which is life, is so obviously occurring. The sun that rises tomorrow cannot be the sun that rose yesterday, because the fetus is a millimeter and a half larger; and though you may be engaged in repetitive tasks that dull your own sense of time, the fetus is not repeating. It stretches and turns; its movements gain in power and direction. Whatever may be your own doubts about where mankind is heading and what maturity is, the fetus seems to feel no doubt at all as to what it wants; and in all that curious, segregated, seemingly static chunk of a year, you become aware of a new kind of time; the fetus's time, the slow pushing time of growth. . . .

FEBRUARY 10, THURSDAY   Oh, this daylight courage that comes on a sunny morning, when the sparrows are quarreling in the back yard and the big fat cats lie around on the window ledges, asleep, and there are so many things to be done! Then I believe everything will be all right, forget my irritation and despair, prepare to spend the day as if nothing had changed irrevocably in my life, and go forth into the street full of sunlight and peace. Only, after a few blocks the weight becomes a painful pressure, and, like Cyrano, the shadow of my profile on the wall recalls me to myself. Then I remember that last night Nick and I were angry at each other and that, not being able to sleep, I went downstairs to read, until he complained angrily down the stairway how long was this going on, because he could not sleep! There should be a special course for prospective fathers, especially when they are the ones who profess to want the child. I guess men want children, right enough; something to carry on their name and prove that they are not sterile. The smug masculine pride with which men announce to each other that they are about to become fathers! So I imagine stallions talking to each other across a fence. They feel they have conferred quite a favor on their wives, and if the wives do not want the gift, they are angry and amazed. *All* women want children, of course. What else is there for them in life? And if the poor creatures happen to be ill, or despairing, or unable to sleep, the men complain because *their* sleep is spoiled.

No, men are essentially the most conservative of creatures. Though they may pay lip service to the idea of equality of women, let the wife not wash the dishes one night because she is busy with her own work, and they are immediately furious. It is nice for her to have her little interests and bring in a little pin money, but let her become really absorbed in her work, or very successful, and they become indignant and distant and demand that their socks be darned. Nick, if he notices my work at all, always praises the most trivial parts of it. The parts over which I have really worked and which, being the most difficult, are perhaps not the most successful, he brushes off, as if I were foolish to attempt such things in the first place.

And of an evening I come in from some last-minute shopping and find him tight-lipped and sullen because the room is littered with papers. Well, I have been doing some block prints, and they cannot be stacked until they are dry. There is no other place to put them. Does he make any comment on the prints themselves? No.

Or he comes into the kitchen and backs out as if he had just stepped on a toad, exclaiming that the floor is just filthy. Of course it is. I had rather hoped he would notice it and volunteer to wash it of his own accord, because there happen to be a couple of feet in my ribs that keep me from bending over. He replies that he has heard that scrubbing floors is good for pregnant women. (He always has an amazing

number of little knowledges which operate only to bolster his argu-
ments.) Does he notice the new curtains on the kitchen window? No,
though David does. Thank God for friends. I spent five exhausting
afternoons hunting for that fabric, nearly passing out in Altman's at
one point, when the baby decided to turn around.

Well, I don't mention any of these things to him because I, too,
have gotten tired of my complaining, and so we pass a silent and
tight-lipped evening, and I think to myself, Is it for this sullen and
uninterested chap that I am bearing a child?

Oh, the trap of the flesh! No, the placidity is not here today. I feel
like a man building a boat in his basement which he may not be able
to get out through the door. Trapped, frantic and trapped. . . .

FEBRUARY 17, THURSDAY   Took Nick up to meet the doctor, which
he hasn't done before. He becomes rather stiff and pompous, confronted with a doctor; certainly men don't take to doctors as easily
as women do. They don't like to hand their physical problems over
to someone else and don't seem to get that luxurious feeling of Being
Cared For. But a husband is pretty much of a fifth wheel around his
wife's pregnancy, anyway. She has much more trust in the doctor and
is, in a way, more intimate with him. Most men don't bother to find
out about the details of pregnancy because they are bored by them.
This hospital which has been a part of my life for several years did
not seem to interest Nick at all; he lapsed into a rapt contemplation
of *Vogue* ("wonderful photographs") while I went up to get my red
blood count done.

Sitting alone upstairs in the immense corridor, waiting for the
technician, I could hear some large machine close at hand, going on
and on in that overpowering, inhuman way that even the most benefi-
cial machines have, and the loneliness of being a human being came
over me again. Hospitals are so impersonal; they treat the body like
a machine or hand it over to another machine to treat, and no one
really thinks of the poor, helpless little human trapped in the sick
body. One book on childbirth that I read says briskly, "Most young
mothers suffer from acute melancholia the day after the birth of their
baby, but they soon forget this when they see the baby." I expect this
and I think I understand it better than the chap who wrote that. I
wonder if he really knows what goes on inside a young mother's head
or realizes that the melancholia has more behind it than sheer femi-

nine whim? Does he understand the incredible loneliness of giving one's body and risking one's life to create a thing which doesn't really understand what has happened? Neither the baby nor its father can possibly know what the mother goes through; she is quite alone in this, and I think perhaps it is best this way, but I wish babies could be born in a slightly less antiseptic and impersonal atmosphere. People's sense of well-being and faith depend so much on their surroundings. In a strange place I always feel the nervous alertness of a wild animal, forced to pay attention more to external than internal stimuli, and it seems to me that this is the worst possible feeling for giving birth, when all one's attention should be inward.

APRIL 4, MONDAY   Well, I had intended to make a very dramatic little notation when the event occurred, saying something like "Labor has started, off to the hospital," but everything became very crowded. . . . We missed the exit, of course, and had to back down the parkway —a tense moment—and then we had to hunt for the hospital and wait for a couple of very long lights, and by this time I was beginning to be pretty worried and had stopped bothering about our lack of conversation.

As a matter of fact, we were not a moment too soon. There wasn't a wasted moment anywhere, except in being admitted; they couldn't find my name in the book but finally let me go up anyway, and from then on everything happened with great rapidity.

It was then a little after nine-thirty, and I had been more or less in labor for twelve and a half hours. A girl from the admitting office carried my bag and ushered me into a room diagonally across from the elevator, where a pleasant red-haired nurse greeted me and introduced herself. I undressed quickly and got into bed, hoping there was still time to practice Dr. Read's relaxation theory. I hadn't had time before that to worry about whether I was relaxed or not, and I didn't get much of a chance then, either. A truly incredible nurse, a real movie caricature of an old maid, came in to shave me, and in five minutes I was so mad at her that I couldn't possibly relax—or worry, either, for that matter.

"Which do you want, a little boy or a little girl?" she simpered, taking a long stroke with the razor.

I flinched and growled, "I don't really care at this point." She looked a little shocked and took another swipe with the razor. This time she cut me, and I growled, "Take it easy." She ha-haed reassuringly and cut me again. "Damn it, look out," I said, and then I had another pain and asked her please to wait a moment.

"Little Mother is afraid of the razor," she said to the red-haired nurse, who had just come in. "Are you through yet?" she said to me. I was thinking about relaxation and trying to remember that I had had worse menstrual cramps, and I shook my head. There is a secret about pain: if you concentrate on it and divide it into minutes it isn't so hard to bear. It's only when you let the outside world come in, let time begin to carry you onward, that the pain mounts and becomes monstrous.

But apparently inaction was impossible for this nurse; she kept taking little guilty scrapes at me, and I would growl, "*Just* a moment," between clenched teeth, and she would stop and then come back at me again in a surreptitious sort of way, as if pretending she wasn't doing it at all. Then she would sigh and shake her head and say, "You're *so* hairy," so that I felt like a great unclean beast, and I couldn't help giggling. Finally the resident doctor came in while she was out of the room, and I asked him please to take her away; the shaving was over by this time, and whether that was her only function or whether he acted on my suggestion, I don't know, but mercifully she did not reappear.

They asked me to sign a rather sinister little paper authorizing the doctor to give me any anesthetic or perform any operation he thought necessary. I had objections to nitrous oxide and scopolamine, on the grounds that they were emotionally upsetting to some people, and we argued about this for a while. Nitrous oxide is the gas they most frequently use in childbirth; I had had some upsetting experiences with it when it was used as a partial anesthetic for dental work, and I found this rather hard to explain. Finally they agreed to give me something else if possible, and I agreed to take it if necessary, and on this half compromise I signed. I was beginning to feel too much in a hurry to argue, anyway. They offered to give me a painkiller, but I told the doctor I wanted to do without as long as I could; he seemed dubious and left, and two minutes later I was regretting my words, for a really quite unbearable pain came and I felt something flowing. I rang for the nurse, who took one look and sent in a stretcher. As they rolled me off I saw that I had bled and realized things were really beginning to happen.

They wheeled me into the elevator. The pains were quite intense now, and though I could just bear them, I realized I couldn't stand them for any length of time and asked for a mild sedative. It is the wearing-down effect of pain that I dread much more than the individual pain; if I had known it was all going to be over so soon I might not have asked for a sedative. I don't know. Actually, there was one great feature about this pain. It stopped in between. It began in my loins and swelled upward till it seemed to fill my whole abdomen, but just as I began to feel that I couldn't stand it any longer it would all ebb away again, leaving me feeling extraordinarily peaceful and awake. In these brief periods I seemed to see things with a greater clarity than ever before, and I felt strong and light and ready for effort, like a runner before a race. Unfortunately, most of these peaceful periods were occupied throughout by moving on and off stretchers; medical science has devised very comfortable beds and stretchers for patients, but it hasn't invented any sort of crane to move the patient from one to the other, and the patient must make most of the effort himself. I found this the most trying feature of all.

On the seventeenth floor everything seemed dark except the little labor room into which they wheeled me, but I was soon surrounded by a number of young girls with masks, all of whom introduced themselves. (Everyone introduced herself to me this first night; I never saw but two of them again, and I suspect this was just a distracting maneuver.) These student nurses ebbed and flowed around me all during the labor and delivery period; I suspect they had not seen many deliveries, as they seemed quite interested in all the symptoms, although they paid not the slightest attention to me. This annoyed me, rather, since they were not so much younger than I and, I felt, ought to have some spirit of camaraderie. Also, their interest was one I would have shared myself, if I had not been so involved. "Where do you find the fetal heartbeat?" one of them was asking another while poking my stomach with the cold end of a stethoscope. She ignored my feeble attempts to tell her.

An older nurse who had been in and out since I was first admitted popped in again and said, "Well, I expect you'll be out of here by midnight." Since it was then shortly before eleven, I was astonished and asked her what made her think that. "Oh, redheaded women always have babies quickly," she said. It was the first of many peculiarities anent childbearing I was to discover were attributed to my coloring.

A student nurse came in and told me the doctor had ordered an enema. I said I had had an enema that morning and I wanted a sedative. The enema girl said the doctor would prescribe a sedative when he came, and repeated her orders about an enema. I was still feeling pretty argumentative and I said where the hell was the doctor, whereupon the resident came in to tell me he was in New Jersey but that he, the resident, had never known the doctor to take more than eighteen minutes to cross the George Washington Bridge and reach the hospital. (Nick, who was sitting downstairs, told me later that they were frantically phoning all over New Jersey and had finally located the doctor at a party. I suppose I would not have been so calm if I'd known this. There are certain medical reticences I guess I approve of, after all.) So after a little more argument I let the girl give me the enema—quite a painful and uncomfortable process at the stage I was then in, but I felt much better afterward. Also, I became aware almost immediately of a change in the pains; my stomach began to quiver at the end of each one, and I felt an almost irresistible desire to push. Since the Read book said to relax, and since I had had similar impulses during menstruation, when pushing just made things worse, I resisted as best I could. Then suddenly, while I was in the middle of a pain, the doctor appeared, looking rather different from his dapper office self in a white mask and coat. I'm afraid I greeted him rather grouchily too; I was so convinced by this time that I was doing pretty well by myself that I still resented outside interference. He did a brief examination, said the neck of the cervix was almost gone, and told me to bear down with my next pain. I realized that things were happening much faster than I had expected, and with considerable relief I gave way to my natural impulse and did bear down. This changed the character of the pain altogether; in fact, it stopped hurting, and I realized I was in the second stage of labor.

This is a very curious sensation. The impulse to push quite runs away with you; once you start pushing, the push takes hold of you and won't let you stop. It is a tremendous physical effort, and I'm sure my face was horribly contorted in what looked like agony, but I can't remember it as being painful at all. In fact, it was even rather pleasant, a stretching, abandoned sort of feeling, a feeling of getting rid of something and, above all, of being able to make some positive effort and not having just to lie and endure any more. It is also slightly embarrassing, as everything relaxes all at once, but you just have to decide not to worry; childbirth *isn't* neat.

After a few more of these new contractions the doctor reached down and cut the fetal membranes which seemed to be already part way out. I realized that meant that the baby was almost out, too, and was a little disappointed that it would be over so quickly. A little amniotic fluid trickled down, and a couple of student nurses came around to see if they could see the baby.

The moment the membranes were cut, the contractions began in earnest. Three or four student nurses whipped me onto a stretcher and wheeled me into the delivery room, a large bare room next door that looked like any operating room. Here they more or less assisted me onto a table and strapped down my wrists. I protested again. They said it was to keep my hands off the sterile sheets. I privately thought I had enough self-control to keep my hands where they belonged, but I let them strap me down anyway. My legs were lifted onto two metal supports; they were beginning to feel crampy, and I asked the doctor to rub them, which he did. That was my only real discomfort, and it went away as soon as my legs were properly supported.

By this time I knew I could not have a sedative; the doctor had told me there would not be time enough for it to work, and because gas is almost instantaneous, he had called in an anesthetist, a jovial chap who patted my hand and asked me coaxingly if I wouldn't like "just a little whiff." This annoyed me very much, but I realized that everyone thought I was in agony; even the doctor had remarked, "She must be in real pain now," at just about the time the pain stopped.

Someone switched on a dazzling light overhead; there was a mirror diagonally above me in which I could have seen myself if I hadn't been afraid to try. Below this mirror was a ring of bent-over doctors and nurses in masks, just like a movie. For a moment it seemed so unreal I almost laughed. Then there came an enormous contraction; I let go and hung on and pushed, and felt the baby come halfway out —and stop.

"Wouldn't you like just a little whiff now?" the anesthetist pleaded.

"No. Dammit, leave me alone," I said, waiting for the next contraction.

"It's going to hurt," the doctor said.

"It feels fine," I said.

"Take some gas. I have to get this little girl out of here," he said.

"But *it doesn't hurt*," I said.

"It will hurt," he shouted. I remembered that Dr. Read said most unenlightened doctors carried on in just this way, and I stuck to my guns. "Take some gas—it's for the baby's sake," the doctor said finally.

"Just a whiff," said the anesthetist, slipping a mask over my face.

Okay, I thought, if it will please you, just a whiff. As he clamped the mask down I knew he meant to put me out, and I thought to myself, A real sell. I've been had.

". . . Stuck halfway," the doctor said from a distance. . . .

When I came out I was vomiting into a basin held by a nurse who was also pressing my stomach, and my limbs refused to work at all, but I realized I was talking and asking what seemed to me very rational questions, like "Is the afterbirth gone?" And in the background something was screaming—something which, again, I recognized from a hundred movies but had never really heard before. I was rather annoyed at it for being so trite. The hiccuping cry of the newborn. . . . Then a nurse came by holding it—a small red-faced, neckless baby, its face contorted from screaming—and while it didn't seem to belong to me at all, I felt very sorry for it and thought how it looked like my father's oldest baby, and then they wheeled it away down the long corridors, still screaming.

I was still entirely fuzzy, but I began to wonder how I felt, especially my stomach, and then I realized suddenly that I had been expecting it to hurt five inches above where it really was. That was the first time I really believed that the baby had been born. . . .

The whole business, from my entrance into the hospital to the birth of the baby, had taken slightly less than two hours. I had reached the labor room about a quarter to eleven. I didn't look at the clock when the baby started to come, but it couldn't have been much above half an hour later. It certainly didn't seem even that long; I guess there had been too much going on. . . .

FOUR WEEKS OLD   Life is still frantic, certainly, and I am like the very eye of a hurricane, a relatively calm spot surrounded by screaming wind and flying objects. But having now learned certain of the methods, which I rather regret having scorned to learn before, things come more easily. There is not much sleep yet, and I usually don't really get up and get dressed until 2 P.M.; but Mother comes over at three or four, bathes the baby, gives her a feeding or two, and sits with her while I go out to shop, so the day isn't completely shot. I am still shaky and feel, after a long walk, heavier than I ever did when I was pregnant, but it is a relief to get out. There is no real peace in the house, where that dreadful cry may begin at any minute, and an amazing clutter of tiny things piles up in spite of all my efforts at tidying. I haven't been able to settle down to a book or a long thought for what seems years now, and I wonder when I will ever get the time to find out what I really feel about all this.

I suppose it always feels, at first, as if life were never going to be the same and that you will always be surrounded by diapers and howling. Therefore, our first meal out, the first uninterrupted meal in weeks, was very reassuring. I had just bought a new dress. How wonderful to be neat and empty once again! To be out of a house dress! To be able to talk quietly to Nick about matters not involving babies! The curious stunned feeling began to go away from that time; I began to know myself again. The role of mother is too strange to me. I don't think I could ever be primarily a mother without sacrificing a large part of myself, which I am certainly not prepared to do and don't think is really necessary or desirable. But that first dinner showed me I could compromise a little on my motherhood and that my world was not entirely lost. And toward dessert we got around to agreeing that she is, after all, a pretty nice baby. . . .

TWO MONTHS   She is lying on her back with a mouthful of banana, smiling mischievously, and managing to get the banana over everything within reach while she utters little pleased cries. Really, she has a wonderful range of vocal sounds, and sometimes, when I am busy with my ceramics, I think someone has spoken to me. Since these noises reach a pitch of perfect ecstasy when someone is talking to her, I think she must realize that they are a form of communication, although Nick's mother disagrees. But she will also talk to herself for hours when she is lying out in the yard and playing with a contraption of rings, beads, and bells that Steve brought over for her the other day. This gimmick is a blessing, since she is awake much more than babies are supposed to be, and eager to be amused; in the few days she has had it she has played with it almost constantly and greatly improved her skill in grasping.

It is almost summer. The begonias, planted hopefully so many weeks before, are large and sturdy; the Tailor made lawn is a thicket of green grass where the black cat, Inagain, spends hours playing tiger-in-the-jungle. The geranium which Nick brought me on my next to the last day in the hospital is in the middle of its second blooming; scarlet runner beans and rambler roses are reaching thin green shoots toward the sun; the gardenia bush is blooming, pale and luminous at night; and the ailanthus trees cast interlaced whorl patterns across the garden and the baby's face. The scent of blooming privet competes with the smell of chocolate cake from next door. I have just completed two ceramic cats. Surely life cannot be more full and yet be peaceful!

And most of all I am beginning to realize that modern woman is not as lost as many experts seem to think. Surely in her lifetimes a woman has far more opportunity to be creative than the average man nowadays has. She can cook, she can make clothes, she can decorate her house, she can raise children. And in these tasks she is not only her own boss, but she is able to do what few men today can do—perform the whole job from beginning to end, and not just a part of it. Mass production has made civilization, at least on the plane where most men live it, too specialized; a man who spends all day adding a column of figures or performing a single operation on a production line can hardly be said to be doing anything creative. Even men in the more intellectual jobs often find their creative release only in after-hours activities. I know many doctors who write or make sculpture, a few lawyers who act, many businessmen who paint. Only the "housewife" can fit these things into her daily life, for to decorate a home, surely one must know something about art, and in raising a child, is there any field of knowledge that is not useful?

Of course modern life *has* threatened women. Mass production has tended to make the individual artisan, including the housewife, obsolete. Excellent frozen foods, increasingly good-looking ready-made clothes, movies, radio, television, birth control—all these tend to make the "homemaker's" efforts unnecessary. She can expend a minimum of effort and still exist quite comfortably. She often does. But must we let modern life and television win away our home life without a struggle?

I think that the chief enemy of our home life is not, however, modern living so much as modern thinking. There is simply not enough ego satisfaction in making a home. "Occupation, salesgirl" has somehow come to be more respectable than "occupation, house-wife," which now seems to imply that a woman does not have the brains to hold a job. If only the world at large held this view, women might stand up against it, but even a husband is not apt to appreciate the ingenuity and versatility that has gone into making a new blouse, caring for the baby, and cooking his dinner. He, too, has just done a hard day's work, but he gets paid for it. And didn't his mother care for a house too? But every woman must learn this job anew, just as every man must learn his job as CPA or factory worker. The difference is that the woman does her job for love, not money. . . .

I realized that I had not reached a dead end only a few days ago. When I got out of the hospital, practically the first thing I noticed out the kitchen window was that the pregnant cat, too, had recently given birth. It was a neat parallel, a graceful period to a long sentence of time. But just a few days ago, watching the child on Nick's lap staring at the light and the people, refusing to go to bed, I realized suddenly that delivery is not an end but the beginning of something else.

An obvious discovery? Perhaps. But for me, at least, pregnancy was a definite state, to be gotten over, and definitely finished by childbirth. The emotional attachments simply didn't exist. I had conceived of what was happening only in terms of magazine ads and slick fiction: photo of mother-with-baby, cartoon of weary-parent-pacing-floor-with-screaming-baby, what kind of crib to get for baby. It was a static conception. But suddenly I realize that the problems of having a baby will, after all, be brief. The child is a growing organism, not a static magazine photograph. The problems of having a baby will be followed by the even greater problems of having a child, and someday by the astonishing problem of having an adult. Although by that time it will be she who will have the problem—of herself. Having a baby is perhaps an end of a kind; the end of my independent self, which I still rather poignantly regret, but it is also a beginning. I hope I will not be resentful of the fact that when I am an aging forty-five she will be in the most enchanted and difficult period of life, in the full glory and terror of life. May she meet it well. . . .

Barbara Deming
[1917–1984]

Born in New York City, Barbara Deming attended a Quaker school before college at Bennington, Vermont. Her later study of the life and teaching of Ghandi sparked the ardent energy she gave to thinking and writing about nonviolent social change. She also joined in direct action with others for racial justice and civil liberties and against war, as in Vietnam. Evolving with the Women's Movement, she expressed publicly her life-long lesbianism and began to write about and live her philosophy of feminist nonviolence, believing it indispensible to world revolution and peace. Deming also wrote poems, stories, and, most recently, a book about one year of her life, A Humming under My Feet *(London: The Women's Press, 1985). A selection of her work appears in* We Are All Part of One Another: A Barbara Deming Reader, *edited by Jane Meyerding (Philadelphia: New Society Publishers, 1984).*

In 1964, Deming joined the "Quebec—Washington—Guantanamo Walk for Peace." When the group reached Albany, Georgia, city officials prevented them from entering the downtown area and ordered them to march on Ogelthorpe Avenue, a street dividing the black and white communities. On their second attempt to walk through the downtown, the marchers were arrested. Insisting on their rights to freedom of speech and assembly, the marchers were put in jail.

JANUARY 27, 1964

Albany city jail, Georgia. The cop locks the door on us and walks off. Now we're out of mischief. The barred steel door has banged shut; the big key has made a lot of noise; they have "put us away." People still believe there is some magic in the turning of a key.

He walks past some other cages, running his night stick, clattering, along the bars; and then we hear him make a curious little clucking noise to the prisoners—as though human speech were not quite appropriate to cross the distance between us. Magically, now, we are no longer quite of the same species.

As he goes, he glances down at his boots, and he puts his hand—as if to be sure of something—upon his wide leather belt with its creaking tooled-leather holster.

"Sonofabitch cop!" a prisoner rages, and grasps the bars and rattles them. "Oh goddam motherfucking sonofabitch! Wait till I get out of here tomorrow!" . . .

Our cage in Albany is seven by seven by seven. Three bolted steel walls, a steel ceiling, a cement floor. For bunks, four metal shelves slung by chains—two on one wall, double-decker, two on the wall opposite. Thin filthy mattresses. No sheets, no blankets, but, very recently, muslin mattress covers have been added. The chief expects publicity, perhaps. Against the third wall, a tiny washbasin. Cold water. Next to it, a toilet without a lid.

The mattress of the lower bunk rests against the toilet. The upper bunk is so close above the lower that one can only sit up on the lower bunk with a curved spine. The floor space allows one to pace one short step—if there are not too many inhabitants. We are six at the moment, but we'll be more. Other cells are more crowded. It is not by stretching out that the prisoner here will recover himself.

The fourth wall is made of bars and a thick barred door, centered in it. In the corridor outside, guards and plainclothesmen come and go, day or night. If one is sleeping, a sudden knock at the bars: "Hey!" Or a little tug at the hair of the sleeper's head: "What's this one?" No corner of privacy in which to gather oneself together again.

The dirty windows in the corridor look out upon an alley and a brick wall. (They are very dirty. A prisoner long ago has flung a plate of spaghetti against one of them. Shriveled tatters of it still hang there. On the window next to it a shrunken condom hangs.) A little weak sunlight filters through to us at certain hours, but there is no real day.

And no real night. Our only other lighting is a naked bulb hanging in the corridor out of reach, and this burns round the clock.

Not enough space. No real time. . . .

[*Deming's companions have begun a hunger strike, which her health does not permit her to participate in fully.*]

MONDAY, FEBRUARY 10 (15th Day).
. . . Now it is four-thirty. A guard shoves into the cell for me the second of the two meals for the day. I reach under the bunk for a magazine to put the greasy plate on. Then I bend my spine into a curve so that I can sit up without my head knocking the upper bunk. I tuck my feet under my skirt and lean back against the wall, trying to be as little visible as possible while I eat. Yvonne has returned to her bunk across the way and is resting there. As I pick up the small red plastic fork which has been dumped into the middle of the food —and first lick the handle clean and then lick my fingers clean (there is no napkin ever)—I look across at her, and she is watching me, in spite of herself, fascinated. The bologna I leave. It's not hard to resist it. There are also diced turnips today, grits, black-eyed peas. To eat in here always seems to me a gross act—not only because my friends are fasting, but because I feel like a caged animal being fed. The food itself is gross. The grits are easiest to get down. The turnips have a bitter, slightly dirty taste, but I get them down too. I put a forkful of black-eyed peas in my mouth. And then my stomach abruptly revolts. The peas are very thick and pasty and, like the turnips, somehow dirty in taste. They are very nearly daily fare, and I realize with alarm that I just cannot force them down my throat any more. I have pulled myself out of the trouble I was in by beginning to eat a little more now each day—to eat a part of breakfast—and I ask myself: What will happen if my stomach begins to refuse what is put before me? Fear for myself flares up in me for a moment, and then I manage to quiet it. I slide the plate out into the corridor and around the corner a little so my friends won't have to look at it. . . .

[*With the prisoners' fast entering its second week, city officials become concerned about the publicity the hunger strike is generating. They begin to force-feed one prisoner, Yvonne, a struggle that Deming witnesses. As A. J. Muste, Dave Dellinger, and mediators from the American Friends Service Committee negotiate with officials, some prisoners decide to end their fast.*]

MONDAY, FEBRUARY 17 (22ND DAY)
AFTERNOON

There is new reason to hope, and yet I am finding it harder than before to live through the hours. On other days I have suffered from discouragement or fear, and on every day from discomfort, but today for the first time I feel unutterably tired of being in here, and this is harder to bear.

I woke this morning and stared at the ceiling formed by the other bunk, close above me; woke, but felt that some part of me had still to waken; lay there waiting for this to happen, but just as the walls of our cage hold us, so the walls of my own being seemed to hold trapped and inert some formerly active part of me. I climbed out of my bunk, splashed water in my face at the sink, and then tried standing up for a while in the small floor space, but then lay down again—still locked dismally within my own fatigue. For the first time I truly know how it feels to want to rattle the bars. The bars, the steel walls, for the first time impress me as inexorably what they are.

A cockroach is wandering along the wall beside my bunk. A creature able to come and go! I watch him with desperate attention, trying to free my own spirit by following with my eyes his energetic course. His meanderings bring him to the front of the cage, and he begins to walk lightly along one of the horizontal bars. With the window behind him, his delicate hairy legs are outlined with light and his translucent body shines like a piece of amber. I watch him for a long time, finding comfort in it.

I hear Yvonne and Edie talking together. Yvonne is saying, "I begin to feel as though I'm sliding down a toboggan." In the past few days things have of course become harder still for most of my friends. Yvonne has started again to have to be careful each time she stands up—not to black out. Even Erica is beginning to feel the fast now; she has strange sensations in her ears as though she had water in them. And Saturday Michele reported having trouble urinating. Erica wrote a worried note out about this, and a Quaker doctor, Arthur Evans, who is here from Denver to be of what help he can, tried again for permission to get in to see us, but again he was denied—"We can't let every Tom, Dick and Harry in to see them!" Michele is angry at Erica now because of the extra fuss that has been made, and she says she is really all right. When A. J. came at noon yesterday he questioned her carefully, talked with the rest of us for the few minutes allowed him, took Edie's hand and then burst out, "Oh I want to get you all out of here so much!"

He had nothing very new to report. He had told Pritchett, before he left for Nassau, that all bets were off now about terminal dates—as the Albany Movement was planning demonstrations for the twenty-second and we would naturally want to show our solidarity with them. The Chief managed to keep an impassive face. A. J. has sent a wire to the Department of Justice, asking that they investigate the lack of civil liberties here and issue a public report. He and Dave have an appointment to see City Manager Roos and Mayor Davis.

After A. J.'s visit, Edie began to feel very strange. She took her pulse, which is normally between 100 and 108, and it was 55. When C. B. came at the end of the day she was feeling so weak that she didn't even sit up; she just stretched out a limp hand to him, and he stared at her, alarmed. Last night she talked strangely in her sleep. She was awake through most of the night, however; she lies there now, she says, and feels sleep climbing her body, but when it reaches her head, it stops. Today she hasn't moved from her bunk, and so a little while ago I brought her a damp washcloth and washed her face, her hands, her feet for her. She is beginning not to know herself, she told me, and she is going to break her fast, because she doesn't want to reach a state where she would want to bail out.

Yes, one begins to be a stranger to oneself; this is the most difficult feeling of all one has to struggle with in here. Even I, who am merely on a token fast, know it a little. In the middle of the night last night, I was sitting on the toilet and I leaned my elbow on the sink beside me, wearily, and leaned my cheek on my hand—and my face didn't feel to my hand like my own face. A sensation of utter desolation startled me. I felt: Am I sure it is I? How much of me can waste away and my self remain? The day of the meeting I felt a similar shock when Dave and I hugged. When I have hugged people before, there has always been some sort of pillowing of flesh between us, but this day I felt my ribs knock against Dave's ribs. I felt: Is there no more to me than this? . . .

STILL LATER

Clarence, the run-around, with a timid smile, appears at the bars with a large brown paper bag of food for Edie. She has sent a note out to headquarters asking to have a few special things bought for her, because the prison food is harsh fare on which to break a fast. She sits up with a start and holds out her arms for the bag; then, hugging it to her, seating herself crosslegged, opens it and peers in as though afraid to find it empty. She rapidly inspects the contents and her eyes brighten: bananas, apples, a jar of honey, cottage cheese, crackers, some tiny marshmallows. She peels a banana—slowly. She is about to take a bite when she stops, unscrews the top of the honey jar, dips the banana into it, and then puts it into her mouth. We all watch, hypnotized, as she begins to eat it—she is so entirely concentrated upon the act, like someone receiving the sacrament. It is Life itself she eats.

In the distance we hear a strange small cry of joy. Tony has just received *his* bag of special foods.

Yvonne has been reading poetry aloud lately, at my request; a friend has sent in an anthology. Now I hand her the volume and she leafs through it and begins to read one of Donne's sonnets:

> *"At the round earth's imagin'd corners, blow*
> *Your trumpets, Angells, and arise, arise*
> *From death, you numberless infinities*
> *Of soules, and to your scattered bodies goe . . ."*

As she reads, I feel the terrible weariness that has held me cramped within myself crack like a shell; I stare at the walls and they no longer look solid but fragile as shell too, easily burst; the bars look widely spaced; our cells seems airy. A cockroach runs across my foot and out into the corridor and then back into the cell and then out again. Edie spreads some cottage cheese on a cracker. . . .

[*Chief of Police Pritchett has left for his vacation in Nassau and negotiators have reached an agreement with city officials—the march will be permitted on Ogelthorpe Avenue with five marchers allowed to take a route through the downtown shopping area. The jailed protestors accept the agreement. Four days later they are released from prison.*]

SATURDAY, FEBRUARY 22 (27TH DAY) MIDAFTERNOON
. . . There are steps in the corridor and then we hear the key turning in the lock of the cell next door, hear the door grating open. We scramble off our bunks and stand for a moment in the middle of the floor, rigid. Sergeant Hamilton stands at the door of our cell now,

turning the key again; the sound of it echoes and echoes through me, and the sound of the door swinging wide. It takes me a long time to tie my shoe laces; but when I stand up and clutch the bundle I have packed, the door is still wide open.

We file down the corridor and around the corner into the large cell block. Other cops are standing along the way—Assistant Chief Friend, Sergeant Cress, Sergeant Bass—and almost all of them are smiling—smiles that seem half respectful, half puzzled. We shake hands with each of them in turn as we pass. In the large cell block the doors of the men's cells are wide, too, and the men are stepping out of them. We hurry to each other, solemnly kiss each other on the mouth. There is John Papworth, peering into each face. I tell him. "I'm Barbara," and we peer at each other and then we kiss.

Beyond the near cells, then, I notice one cell with its doors still shut. A number of Negro women are crowded against the bars, watching us. For a moment I stare at them. For a long and strange moment I feel an ancient awe. People in a cage! They seem to huddle there at a peculiar distance from me—castoffs. With a start I come to myself, trembling. The thought burns in my head: If, after all these days spent in a cage myself, I can feel this distance, how can I hope that others will learn to cross it? I hurry across the room. Others are walking over to that cell, too. We all clasp hands through the bars, exchange a few quick words—"Good luck . . . Take care . . . Freedom! Freedom!" Edie passes in to them some food she has left.

The wide barnlike door in the back of the room is still closed; apparently it won't be opened until all of us have gathered. My legs are weak and the bundle in my arms heavy, so I sit down on top of a large garbage can that stands by the door.

Now that door has been opened. Tony is standing near, and as he stares outside, into the world beyond this prison, and as he steps forward, I see his eyes change: light wakes in them again, reflecting the light of outdoors; they shine in his withered old man's cheeks. I sit there for a while still, facing into the prison room, and watch the eyes of each of my friends change as they move through the door.

Joan Frances Bennett

[1949–]

Joan Frances Bennett was born in Taylors, South Carolina, the youngest of eleven children. In 1967 she came north to attend Barnard College where she enrolled in an English course taught by Marjorie Housepain Dobkin. The course required daily journals to be kept by the students and Bennett's journal, along with classmate Tobi Gillian Sanders's, was later published in Members of the Class Will Keep Daily Journals . . . *(New York: White House, 1970). After graduating from Barnard in 1971, Bennett attended law school and is currently a practicing attorney in New York City.*

Sometimes when I come across an old photograph of myself, particularly one of those taken when I was ten or twelve or thereabouts, I stare at it for a while trying to locate the person I was then, among all the persons I've been, trying to see stretched out down the years the magnetic chain linking the onlooker and the looked at, the gay expectant child and the sober near adult. If I am successful, and very often I am, the two merge and I recall little snatches of life. Running through the wet grass in the dusk of early evening. My father's vulnerable smile as I walked down the aisle on graduating from kindergarten. A wet kiss on my cheek from a stranger brother on an Atlanta street. Being called *nigger* and straightening my shoulders and lifting my head because I would not let it be known that I was hurt though I didn't fathom the complexities of why I was hurt and why I had to be brave.

From a later journal

From *Members of the Class Will Keep Daily Journals: The Barnard College Journals of Tobi Gillian Sanders and Joan Frances Bennett, Spring 1968* (New York: Winter House, 1970). © 1970 by Tobi Gillian Sanders and Joan Frances Bennett. Reprinted by permission of Joan Frances Bennett.

New York, 12 February 68

The riots at South Carolina State have for the most part left me unmoved. Unmoved in the sense that though I feel that I wouldn't want to die, shot down in my native state—I'm sure there are more congenial areas—I don't in anguish question, "Why there?" Instead, why did it take so long to happen there? The whites in charge are probably outraged. Outraged because their senseless babble about how good race relations in their state were is being seen for exactly that. Why should they be allowed their illusions? Though I wonder if they had illusions or blinders. They hardly seemed the type to nurture illusions, they never seemed to me to have that much imagination.

In my way I hate them. I've always hated them. Thurmond, McNair, Hollings, and the late, thank God, Johnston. Hated them, because that was all permitted me. For eighteen years, I was educated to live under a system invented and sustained by men like them. I'll never be free of the inadequacies and the blows to my spirit, I'll never be able to root out that darker stain, put there because since birth I've been told in words, deeds, and spirit that "you aren't good enough." I'm bitter. It is part of being who I am, my being bitter. Sure, I was one who got away. I beat the system. At a price. A price I pay every day: the burden of looking back and hoping something better is ahead has at times been more than my years could bear. And here I've started to hate too. I've started to root my way into the dirt. I've started to hate faces that have never been looked at and dismissed— faces smug, directed and ignorant, blandly ignorant of the fact of where I've been and how fast I had to run to catch up. . . .

New York, 15 February 68

Black Revolution. White faces. Living in two worlds tends to make you wonder about the validity of one or the other. It tends to make you wonder also about the validity of the people who inhabit these worlds. And contrary to popular notion, the state of wonderment isn't idyllic, not even intellectually stimulating. It's shaking. It makes you a rat in a maze, only there are two ways out, or seemingly so. But they lead to different things, or maybe it's the same thing. Only knowing comes after the fact and facts are finished states.

The whiteness of the environment here tends to strip a Negro of his color, his protective coloration I call it. It protects him because it keeps him black and on the outside of what Baldwin calls the "burning house." Being a Negro is being different, but America is called a melting pot, which I take to mean that everything goes in and one thing comes out. But it hasn't worked that way, somehow thankfully; some elements, the Negro particularly, have not succumbed to the temperature, have not let blow freely the molecules of their makeup. But in places like this there is danger of being blinded, or being bleached. . . .

New York, 14 March 68

I have for the last few days read anything I could get my hands on, and invariably my hands get on something of Baldwin's or some book about writing. They both make me feel so intensely that my head aches and afterwards nothing around me is ever what it could or should be.

The college experience has proved to be unsatisfactory, something is lacking. I'm neither happy, nor stimulated. I'm almost the way I was before the physical transition, before I came here, and I'm afraid I'll be the same when my surroundings become more familiar.

In my sloppy way I am constantly considering career possibilities for it shall be very necessary that I make a living. Newt always suggested quite seriously that I teach English. In fact, according to him, I'm a "born English teacher." But again he's wrong. I'd never make a teacher, good or bad.

Of course I would like to sleep forever and be rid of any necessity for making choices. I anxiously look forward to middle age and being somewhat, but only slightly, settled. By then hopefully things will have come to a head and I'll be on my way somewhere. It would be good to have these painful, indecisive, plodding and thunderous years behind me. . . .

New York, 17 March 68

Big house. Big yard. Big family. Big hopes. Big troubles.

I am the youngest child in a family of eleven children. I am the youngest girl, of four. I grew up surrounded and encouraged by family critics. I have many memories, some I don't want, some I don't need. I was the lone one. Too young to be a companion for the young ones or of interest to the old ones, I was petted and indulged to some extent. I've never had very much to say, which doesn't mean that I'm quiet, but only that I'm not verbal. I think quietness indicates restraint and I've never needed restraint, because there was nothing to restrain. My brothers and sisters are my favorite people, no doubt due to the fact that they are the only people I've ever really come in contact with. My parents are, I think, quite rich in suppressed emotions and unuttered desires. We are kind strangers. I must come to know them.

My friends are few. Truthfully they are nonexistent. I have no impact on anybody's life. I love to sleep, and to be alone. I have headaches frequently and often I hate for no ascertainable cause. I have no past, no present, no future. My great fear is people. I find them the most terrifying objects on this planet. I approach houses of friendship with extreme caution and really my smiles are pleas for mercy. Otherwise I can't give a hoot for anything, and I'm going to hell when I die. . . .

New York, 3 April 68

I went down by the Hudson yesterday. People were lying all around the bank. Some doing nothing, some reading, some sleeping, some couples necking. Children running about. It seemed that everybody was with somebody except me. Some looked at me as if I was waiting for someone. But I wasn't. Not unless I've always been waiting for someone. Which isn't so. I walked up far enough to find a place for myself alone. And I stretched there, watching the cars go by on the freeway. I wondered if I knew any of the people in the cars. I half way expected someone to shout, "Hey, Joan, what are you doing here?!" I probably would have answered "I'll be damned if I know." Everybody was in motion, I was the spectator.

Most of all I wonder what changes these experiences will make in me. I wonder if I'm being broadened, because I need to be broadened. I need to spread myself. Anyway, I probably won't notice any differences in myself, ever. I'll have to be told. I can hear them saying, "Joan! You've changed!" and Newt: "You've done a lot of the living you had to do." I'll say, "Naw, it's just me. I'm coming out at last. I was always like this underneath."

Perhaps people don't grow up or change, just shed skins like snakes do. Or think of a human being as a clothes dummy, and the different ages as layers of clothing. Youth being the underwear, young adulthood the dress or shirt and pants, and old age the coat. Death being total undress—revelation.

New York, 4 April 68

Martin Luther King, the "King," was killed tonight. After the first shock, what did I think? Something perhaps not seemingly sympathetic: such men die in such ways. "To a man of spirit it is more painful to be oppressed like a weakling than in the consciousness of strength and common hopes to meet a death that comes unfelt." Well done, Martin Luther, well done. Let the people say *Amen.*

I can still hear his voice. It was the Negro voice. The deep soulful timbre that only we have. God, how he could move people. "I have a dream that one day on the red clay hills of Alabama, that little black boys and little white boys will walk hand in hand." "We shall overcome."

Some say his philosophy died with him. I would say that the kind of man who could implement that philosophy died with him. The climate of the country will never again produce his like. The conditions are gone. Under him the civil rights movement came of age, and the growth cycle doesn't reverse itself. We have passed that point. There won't be a chance for another little black boy in Atlanta, Georgia, to grow up believing in the innate goodness of man. Would he even be encouraged? God, is there any such thing as innate anything? I mean, doesn't a creed, a hope, a plan, a dream need nourishment, more of its like? And if it doesn't get it, what then? What damn good does it do anybody, man, God, or beast to be born with an innate capacity for goodness, if in his flight through this way the conditions aren't conducive to its development?

New York, 5 April 68

Met that Black Muslim again today. He's disgusting—no, repulsive. Shouldn't brainwashing at best try to be discreet or subtle? Furthermore he's out to seduce me or any woman who would pay heed to his "message," which naturally includes such things as a woman needs a man at certain times. He concedes it his duty to be there when needed. Such rot! Again he assures me that all black men are Gods and all white men devils. That only black men have access to "truth," that the Muslim god, Allah, will outlive God. . . .

I patiently assured him that his incoherence was clear, that I was aware of what he was trying to do, but I had no intention of taking him seriously. He repeatedly asked where I lived and said he hoped

that I would join him for a cup of coffee. He was hard to get rid of
—sickening, the whole incident.

I'm not going to get involved in anything of that kind. I don't
believe any answers are coming from that quarter. Anyway, not the
type of answers consistent with what I believe. Not that I'm unwilling to see anyone's view but my own. But I believe there are certain
basic things any creed, belief or whatever must start with, things like
fairness, decency, dignity, clarity and the like. Any undistorted cause,
any cause that can stand alone and be seen for what it is, shouldn't
have to be rammed down people's throats. It shouldn't have to be
peddled by fast talking men on street corners.

New York, 6 April 68
Walked through Harlem today. Had to. Had to get where I could
feel some currents of compassion. Found them. God, it was sad. The
voice of Martin Luther King, blaring from a small record shop and
people standing around listening. To hear him again, to hear the deep
voice going high and strong in the Baptist church manner, was
enough to carry me back. I believed him then—do I believe him now?
Do I believe in the brotherhood of Man? What else is there to believe
in? What better is there to believe in? They are all so beautiful, the
ideals.

I have not paid my dues to the cause. I haven't been flogged as
heavily and as hard as others like me. There is a gap.

New York, 7 April 68
All the statements I've heard by the great public figures of the
world have not matched the "ungrammatical profundity" of the garbage men of Memphis. What a relief, what a moving relief from the
tons of rhetoric. No care for what they should say, they said what was
in them to say. This is what I'll remember the most about the assassi-
nation of the "King."

Free at last. Thank God almighty. We are free at last.

Lead me on Precious Lord. Lead me on.

The very time I thought I was lost. My dungeon shook and my
chains fell off.

And God gave Noah the rainbow sign, no more water, the fire next
time.

Come by here my Lord, come by here. Oh Lord, come by here.

You've got to walk that lonesome valley. You've got to walk it by yourself.

This time next year, I may be dead and gone, how long Lord, Lord how long.

Shine on, Perishing Republic.

New York, 8 April 68

Tonight Marsha and I walked up and down Broadway after the Memorial for Dr. King. Both of us felt I think, the inadequacy of what we had done in our lives, the way we'd lived. For we hadn't done anything and we hadn't lived. Sure, some would offer us the excuse that we're too young to be expected to have done anything. But I think it wasn't that we weren't activists, but that we weren't believers and we weren't thinkers, we had no visions, no dreams. I told Marsha that we had been sheltered, but I think blinded would be more apt. Blinded because, and I speak only for myself here, I had excused myself with "Not me, but my brother."

I have taken too long to come home.

I acted as if "going home" was what I would do when I finished college, after I had learned certain things, but no. How can you set dates for commitments. That very act would make the idea of a committed life seem a mere choice of career, something one decides after going to the placement office. But it isn't that, it musn't be made that. And I was naive to think of it in those terms. It calls for caring.

New York, 9 April 68

Watched the funeral from 10:00 to about 5:00. Watched the people. Saw the South in bloom. Remembered all the despair there until hope came and watched hope buried today. It was something I shared in. The church atmosphere was very familiar . . . memories of many church mornings, the heat, the flowery hats, the emotionalism. I had forgotten how eloquent an old black woman's face is, I had forgotten the sounds of the "Southern Negro." I had forgotten the feeling that comes from being surrounded by your own people. I think I've tried to flee from all that. I know that in my last years at home, I refused to attend church and sometimes at gatherings I was repulsed by all that I attempted to remember today. I think I felt that they were taking God much too seriously, a borrowed God at that. They put all their hope in the idea of a "heavenly home": "no matter what happens here, everything will be all right up yonder." Well, I ceased to look up "yonder." It was, I felt, a sad trick. I didn't think there was anything "up yonder" but space, and somehow they knew it too. It was a grand illusion, but not compensation enough for hell on earth. . . .

New York, 11 April 68

I've thought about the singing of "We Shall Overcome" at Dr. King's funeral. It was sincere, full-bodied, and emotional. But I know with certainty that that was the last time that song will be sung, that those days of marching and singing are over. And I'm sorry. The movement had beauty to it. There's beauty in going to face unflinchingly those who hate and persecute you. There's beauty in marching to face a man with a gun, a man puzzled because he knows that shooting you is what you dare him to do, and he doesn't want to give you that satisfaction even though he always thought that the worst he could do to you was kill you. But that proves how little he knows about suffering. Your kind of suffering.

But that's over. And I'm nostalgic. Enough of the emotionalism and the Bible are ingrained in me to make me that way. It was peculiar to the South, it could only have flowered there; not because of the number of Negroes, not because of the number of injustices. I think the Southern Negro might be a little more patient, more apt to be caught in a dream, more apt to believe the songs he sings, but even he stops.

New York, 12 April 68

Cecile came by last night. She appears untroubled and as vocal about the "establishment" as ever. She is now a "white revolutionary." And she is quite honest in her reasons for becoming one. She's quite annoyed when people just can't accept other people. Now that she's flown from her comfortable berth in upper middle class white society, she is set on seeing it destroyed because of the prejudices and hate harbored there. According to her the "system" is all wrong and there can be no slight corrections. The entire thing must be changed. She favors violent change because that is the only way. Well, we talked for a long time.

I was again aware that she is the only free person I know. She is free and she has made herself free. She's not like the other girls on the floor—she's deeper and their concerns are not hers. Not many people would have been brave enough to foresake lives of ease and security, but she did. Perhaps, though, she found it suffocating and wanted to get away to breathe. I remember her self-doubts, the time she sat planning to drop out, and the fear on her face. She was afraid because she didn't know what she was going to do, but she knew that she was going to do it. Well, she has conquered all that now and apparently has no regrets about it. The other girls think she's nutty but they are caught up in something that won't let them go, but neither will they let go. I don't envy them but Cecile I admire, because she's free. . . .

New York, 24 April 68
The girl with already sagging chest and popsicle hips. One day I want to grab her by the hair and rub her face into the floor. I get so sick of being around these pseudo-enigmatic white females. Those so soft voices and those prissy ways. The makeup and the dresses. The boys and the fathers. The mothers and the sisters. The way they slide into their established nooks: "I want an undemanding job so that I can raise a family too."
"When I get married . . ."
"Oh, my mother would kill me!"
"So and so doesn't like me with my hair like this."
"Will there be any boys there?" . . .

New York, 25 April 68
So restless. See no sense. So tired. Came here early this morning not knowing that it would be for longer than a few hours. But it looks as if I'll stay overnight and then some. I haven't talked with myself as to why I'm here. It is one of the few times that I have allowed myself to act without formulated reasons. But anyway I feel a little alien even in this black skin. I don't know most of the people here and they don't know me. So maybe my lack of camaraderie is easily explained. But I'm not a traitor, I'm not without identity. I don't think that I'm deluding myself. I hope to God that I'm not.

It doesn't seem strange that we are here, black students, after the seizure of this building that belongs to a white university. As it is, we are guests who have embarrassed our host. I think that black students in white colleges are there (no matter what their personal motives are) to educate the whites, to be their textbooks. Can't you just hear some of the future leaders of the establishment say, "I went to school with Negroes, I KNOW THEM!" which means that he passed them in the hallways on his way to class and was good enough to stop and chat with them some mornings or afternoons. Better still he worked in Harlem under the auspices of the Citizenship Council, thereby discharging his debt to the downtrodden.

New York, 26 April 68

A boy woke me up this morning. He pulled at my hair. Another one asked me loudly, "Hey chick, what's your bag?" I didn't know what he was talking about and I looked the part. He made fun and I only answered with silence.

This looks pretty serious by now. We had a meeting last night. The steering committee guys are really bright, and so are the other kids. I got a feeling of closeness in that room that didn't have anything to do with the fact that it was packed. There is unity here. We have renamed this place Malcolm X University. And we call each other "sister" and "brother." For me it is ironic that as a Southerner I waited until I came North to make my first physical stand against racism. I have been plagued by such thoughts as "Do I mean this as much as the others do? Am I just following a crowd or am I motivated for my own reasons?" I know that I'm not Uncle Tomish, but my fear is that maybe I'm too Joan Bennettish.

New York, 27 April 68

Marcia has not looked well nor happy since we've been here. She's worried about what her parents will think when they find out that she has been in here. I've tried to talk her out of it but I'm not much help.

There are about 90 odd of us in here. We have occupied the first four floors. We have a kitchen, eating rooms, and a supply room and a shower. There is a clean-up detail and a kitchen detail.

Slept on floor again last night. The blanket I have now is not as smelly as the other. I think maybe that I've chucked civilization, Western style, completely. It seems like one long, long day. I wake up, walk around, help, eat, try to study and sleep again. I'm not used to being shut up like this and it's horrible in a way. I keep wondering what it feels like to be outside. I've forgotten what it looks like. I want to leave, just to take a walk, but there are others who got permission to leave before me. People keep asking me if I'm all right. I must look terrible. I don't feel like doing anything. Not even this scrawling. I don't know what I'm writing. Don't really care.

New York, 28 April 68 (early morning)
They played cards and danced for a long time last night. Didn't feel like it. I slept. Talked to some of the kids though, before I slept. No one knew me before. Asked where I've been.

I'm proud of them, of what they are doing. I'm black and I'm here but something like a spectator. But that too will pass. They have not forsaken the other half of themselves because they are here in a white middle class establishment. Maybe some like me feel guilty because they are here and not at Spelman or Morehouse. But things like this remind us of who we are; and if we aren't that we are nobody.

New York, 29 April 68
Cops went in last night. I wasn't there. Feel guilty and cheated. Again I'm left out.

Bonita Wa Wa
Calachaw Nuñez
[1888–1972]

Though Bonita Wa Wa Calachaw Nuñez devoted her life to the study of Indian peoples and the cause of Indian rights, she never knew her own Indian parents. Born in southern California on Christmas day 1888, she was adopted as an infant by a white benefactor, Mary Duggan. Duggan, a member of a very wealthy and prominent New York City family, was a social activist with a commitment to women's rights and the cause of American Indians. Bonita grew up in New York where she lived a sheltered childhood, but where her early interests in her cultural heritage, in science, and particularly in art were nurtured.

Bonita Wa Wa Calachaw married Manuel Carmonia-Nuñez, a Puerto Rican labor organizer in New York City. They had one daughter who died as a young child and the marriage did not last. By 1920, Bonita Nuñez was living in East Harlem supporting herself selling her paintings and healing remedies on the streets. She lived the rest of her adult life as something of a recluse and very poor. When she died at the age of eighty-four, her apartment was filled with her oil paintings and in a trunk were thirty-eight volumes of her writings, including her diaries and memoirs.

[1970]

THE FEMALE HAS THE POWER

A Woman's touch is the same the World over (give our girls a chance to choose their own career). The originality of an Idea as an identity forms in the Mind of a female. Man has sought to control the female (let Me tell you, they do not). The female has the *Power*, and Knowledge of complete Creativeness of the Being she carries.

Some day we are going to have a Woman of Indian Blood as Commissioner of Indian Affairs; regardless whether there is an Interior Department.

Yes, the intellectual Mind of an Indian Woman can become the Dean of our Indian college. Women of Indian Blood, everywhere, will in the future hold the degrees required. We will demand this Right to higher education.

Let Me hear from our youthful females who think as I do. For a brighter tomorrow. At the age of 82 I can think, and have the Creative ability to help and encourage our People to get the opportunity [that] can only be ours so long as we are interested in Knowledge.

If a change is desired the Ideas are the basis for a balance. A Woman can bring this about. Woman has been Humanly neglected. Man has got to change his inferior lack of common sense.

A Nation is recognized by the intelligence of its Citizens. We [Women] are not lost. What we need most is to understand self-motivation.

From *Spirit Woman: The Diaries and Paintings of Bonita Wa Wa Calachaw Nuñez,* ed. Stan Steiner (San Francisco: Harper and Row, 1980). © 1980 by Stan Steiner. Reprinted by permission of Harper and Row and the Harold Matson Company. The introduction by the editor is the source of the biographical information.

Joyce Mary Horner
[1903–1980]

Born in Yorkshire, England, educated at St. Hilda's College, Oxford and at Smith College, Joyce Horner joined the English Department of Mt. Holyoke College in 1944 and remained a member of the college faculty until her retirement in 1969. In 1974, during tests at a hospital, she suffered a fall in which she broke several bones. This accident compounded the effects of her crippling arthritis and forced her to leave the home she had long shared with her friend and colleague, Elizabeth Green, and enter a nursing home. A writer all her life, she kept a journal of life in the nursing home in which she drew witty and kindly portraits of those around her. In the spirit of Alice James, she did not shrink from admitting her increasing infirmity nor from facing death. Yet her avid interest in literature, music, and politics makes the journal an eloquent testimony to the power of the inner life in its struggle with reduced physical circumstances. In her lifetime, Joyce Horner published a number of poems and two novels, The Wind and the Rain *(Garden City, N.Y.: Doubleday, 1943), and* The Greyhound in the Leash *(Garden City, N. Y.: Doubleday, 1949). Forty years before feminist criticism became a recognized field, she published "The English Women Novelists and Their Connection with the Feminist Movement (1688–1797)," in* Smith College Studies in Modern Languages 2, *nos. 1–3 (1930).*

March 11 [1975]

Everyone wants to go home. Perhaps that says too much. Everyone "wants out." Or there may be some who are beyond wanting as much as that. But the woman who calls "Martha" over and over, the woman

From Joyce Horner, *That Time of Year: A Chronicle of Life in a Nursing Home* (Amherst: University of Massachusetts Press, 1982). © 1982 by the University of Massachusetts Press. Reprinted by permission.

who calls "Eileen," want what they used to have and sometimes think they can get it if they call loud enough. (The woman who calls "Eileen" or "Irene" sometimes wants less than that. She wants someone to untie her and asks anyone who passes. Sometimes she'll say "Man, bring a hammer," but it's still to be untied. I wonder if she ever contemplates the next step after being untied; if she can.) As I write I hear a man across the hall say, "I couldn't go anywhere. I don't know where my folks are. I know where they were." That is the situation of many. One of the men in the room opposite owns a house quite near and it is empty, except for a cat whom his sister feeds. His roommate, who is 92 and very ready to be "going on 93," is as nearly reconciled as anyone I have met, the last of his family and with a certain pride in survival, in his able-bodiedness (he can take quite long walks in the right weather) in his appetite. He is deaf and cannot see to read, facts probably overlooked by people like me who think "if I could walk like that, I'd go home." . . .

April 29
In a way both days I wrote nothing down were high days. Sunday, I walked with the walker on the cement walk at the front in a strong, rather cold wind and felt as if I were climbing a mountain. The sun was in and out, the sky blue and grey, the clouds going by fast—an English day. But I wasn't thinking of anything but that I was walking in a wind and managed it.

Yesterday my moment of achievement came when I got out of my chair without help—I haven't been able to repeat it. But oddly another high moment came when I was sitting under the hair dryer with Elizabeth and Millie, and drinking tea and looking out at the still bare trees against another grey-blue sky. It surprises me that it is possible to feel that kind of exhilaration when one is past seventy. Each time I feel it may be the last, but that is partly superstition, partly habit. Partly common sense.

Read the *New Republic* and the world returned. Having read T.R.B. and others on Vietnam, I read Frank Kermode on the perilous state of the arts in London—the taxes, the terrible prices, and the threat of extinction. As he says, no one wants the Old Vic to be turned into a Bingo hall.

Today the hired men are taking people for routine rides in wheelchairs. (It is possible they are volunteers, as any of them might be retirement age. One looks like a church deacon.) I think any way of getting out is good, but do not want that sort of professional jaunt. I walked my three cement blocks in the coolish sun. . . .

June 27
I noted that several of the ninety-year-olds enjoyed their food yesterday more than I did and could eat cucumbers and sauerkraut and onions and peppers better than I could. Not worth being 90 for, though, even if one acquired their appetites. Miss Z. next to me, who *is* 90 and has all her faculties, said she felt 90 was quite enough. One woman at the end of the table who did not eat made plaintive noises all the time, but she does the same thing even when her daughter is wheeling her in a wheelchair. Mrs. Sullivan at another table was still calling out "Martha," and once in a while someone would tell her, "Martha's at work, Kathleen." Miss Z. said, "Does one ever get used to these sounds?" I suppose the answer is yes and no. One cannot hear them for some time and then they sweep over one again, not a *memento mori* but a memento of how it is, not being able to die. . . .

July 3
There was much good in yesterday, including the fact that my knees worked better—better than today. I managed to get outside twice, mostly in the company of the old benchers. One who is 95 told me he'd lost his wife ten years ago after sixty-five years of marriage. "And when you lose your wife. . . ." he said and couldn't go on. I couldn't say much that he could hear. He wears a religious medal and, no doubt, waits upon the good Lord's time for him. I come nearest to conversation with Mr. O., who at least knows a bird when he sees one, and is always gentle and courteous, but he too is going deaf, as no doubt I shall go. Mr. H. went to mass for the first time since he came here. Mr. O. said, "Mister's gone to mass. I can't believe it. He's told the priest he didn't want to see him at all. He said, 'I know where I'm going!' " But he suddenly went. Out of doors, a perfect summer day.

Today another perfect summer day, when I felt for a short time what may be the height of bliss for a septuagenarian with crippled knees. The place was only just round the corner from here, in the shade with a wind blowing, among ferns, and on clover, with long grasses across the road blowing as I have always loved to see grasses blow, whether in a hayfield, cornfield, or on a walk as at the Malvern cottage. And of course in the meadow in Maine. I remember how my first summer in Maine was full of the sense of "days bound each to each," etc. Eating out of doors in the company one loves has been a constant pleasure in my life. Once there was talk on a ship—the old, slow, Baltimore Mail Line—of making the passengers get together and each tell the high moment of his summer vacation. Fortunately it never happened, but I remember telling the young woman I saw most of on that nice slow voyage that I thought mine was biting into a macaroon on Brighton beach—one of those many days of a long sunny summer when G. and S. lived at Brighton and we had sun, sea, tea (bought in a teapot in a little hut) so many times. The macaroon moment must have been an apotheosis. Like an adolescent I must say, "I have had this" and not, "I must pay for this." Or even, "I am paying." . . .

July 30 (*or* 31—*I think I've got a day out in my calendar*)

I keep on being struck by the fact that the people who wait on us are working for very little. They grumble, but also laugh, as they push their mops and cleaners around in the corridor. They have children whose teeth have to be corrected, and things stolen and this or that expense for the car. Often with the women, their husbands are unemployed or part-time. Others, since the governor's threat of laying off state employees, go in fear for their wives or husbands. This is the Middle America Nixon used to talk about and which he (only now it's Ford) is gradually strangling. They are the ones—except for those already unemployed—who take it first. Elizabeth and I will be caught in it a little later, most of our friends later still. After all, I was young when I worked for next to nothing in the Depression and even so I still went home—once I came back with 75 cents in my pocket. It is the middle-aged ones here I feel most sorry for, old enough to be tired, young enough to have children who still depend on them, though I am sorry for the young nurses too whose husbands have been to college and can't get jobs and the humiliation of dependence, not just because they're men.

Visited Miss K., whose birthday it turned out to be and I think it was good for both. We had a subject—Nixon in the *Atlantic* book review—but got ourselves in round the edges. She is almost certain she is losing the sight of the second eye. This was followed by a wonderful surprise visit from Elizabeth and the complete relaxation of being at home with someone who knows all about one, as deep as one goes. . . .

August 31

It can't be possible that August too is gone. Last August I think I'd just got the sling off my arm, but was full of hope.

What a strange spectacle it must have been yesterday to see Miss K. and me at the ends of her telephone hearing aid (a great device for conversation) reciting in concert "To be or not to be." We got most of it but I still forget about "the spurns that patient merit of the unworthy takes." She remembered it better than I did. We then recited "Thou wast not born for death, immortal bird." I don't know what her roommate thinks. She behaves as if we were not there. The gods—the kind in "The Lotus-Eaters"—would laugh. Is it a way of convincing ourselves we are still the same person? Anyhow I found it exhilarating, though rejecting the bare bodkin as beyond my powers, and postponing it even if I could use it—and, of course, if I had one. And rejoicing over "the insolence of office."

Reading further in the *Harvard Advocate*, I realized, what I had not known, that Auden's death was the perfect one—he died in his sleep after a poetry reading that was a success. What more could one ask? Jo once said that Professor Saunders had a perfect death, sitting in his chair reading the *N. Y. Times;* my uncle Ernest, known in the family as a "scamp" (and that's a word I have not heard for decades), had another kind—he was out in the early morning, picking mushrooms. . . .

September 22

I am torn between not wanting the summer to go and wanting Elizabeth to come back. Today very disappointing because warm, and yet cloudy with a shower just when I wanted to go out. From all points of view it is so hard getting out these days and it makes me wonder how I can stand the winter.

We have a new inmate called Dotty, which seems an unhappy name for one who is mental in a fey kind of way, with a high voice and laugh and a way of uttering high birdlike sounds. Last night we think she must have untied herself and when she was being tied up again, took to shouting, "Help, help, police." She kept it up a long time. Since we've lost Martha Danielson with her ring of names, to the West Wing, we haven't had anyone who raised so much noise. There is Mrs. P. who calls, "Nurse," or "Jimmy," or "Rich-ard," persistently, but she knows, I believe, what she's doing. She just wants attention. Well, I want more than I get since Sarah left.

There is a man here (young for here, though he has a grandchild; his daughters look young—girls, and all much alike, including the grandchild) who is dying slowly. His family comes in numbers and there are always some sitting outside his door. I think it is cancer of the throat he has and he is kept under drugs most of the time. One niece, a nun not in the uniform of the order, comes often. I wonder if she prays for his death. I get the impression of a large, religious, and very devoted family. In an old picture they'd be on their knees round his bed. Here they obey rules and sit in the drab, antiseptic corridors while one goes in. I never have spoken to any of them, but two of his sisters who are well-dressed matrons, sociable, hair well-cared for, etc.—they come every day too. But it is the slim dark girls who wring the heart. . . .

September 23

Elizabeth's card about the wildflowers by the beach, somewhere in Maine or New Brunswick, moved me to tears not so much of nostalgia as of *desire.* That is one of my ideal landscapes and no one should live too close to it—one should come upon the beach, with its rocks and wild roses and any sea birds and driftwood. No Daniel Hoffmans to try and tell you it's private.

Cheered up in very low spirits by reading that the Willits-Hallowell Center at Mt. H. promises one "unabated happiness." I thought that was solely within the jurisdiction of heaven.

September 24

A nurse this morning complained that she kept on getting the same patients, one who was always taking her clothes off, one who screamed, "Police!"—and one who fought and bit and scratched. It is hard on these young women. But terrible to think of being reduced to biting and scratching and screaming. And not to be able to say, "There but for the grace of God," as it may happen to oneself, with or without the grace of God.

I suppose the man who is dying so slowly, and I am sure painfully in the hours he can't have the drug, is an example of what one would choose in preference to the hospital method of keeping the body alive. (There's a suit on this in Penna.—or N.J.—at the moment, the parents begging or indeed suing the hospital to let their daughter die, when she is in a coma, and there is no hope of recovery.) I'd still take this way, but it is unbearable for them all that his body clings to life.

September 25

Woke to rain, with the promise of more. There goes my picnic with the Potters. Today Paul has his operation and Connie will be with him. Half the reading group in hospitals, one way or another, the other half on the road in Canada. But we got the G Minor Quintet on *Morning Pro Musica*—I think that would have to be one of my six desert island records, a game they used to play on the BBC. I always marvel that anything can have so much of the sense of tragedy of life in it and rise above it in the last movement. The music was all good this morning—I find I've enjoyed the Chopin series and especially the Preludes.

September 26

The man (Mr. Moriarty) died a few minutes ago. It was strange to realize it by the fact that all of the watchers went away—I'd watched them come in at different times for so long and just now happened to look and see them all going away together, two sisters, two young girls, and an older woman, probably his wife. Someone has been here day and night for what seems a long time—it's been their life and they'll miss it at first. Without knowing them at all, except for an exchange of greetings with the sisters, I have found the whole thing moving, unlike all the other deaths while I've been here. There was something very sad in the little group going away in silence, while up and down the corridor different radios and TVs uttered different sounds, a total din.

September 27

Today a very low point—weather, feelings inside, asthma, minor minimal disappointments, like failing to get my letter to Elizabeth in Nova Scotia and the facts that Bertile did not think my Brighton poem worth commenting on—perhaps it is for the family circle. Having begun to be interested in writing again, I should school myself to the idea, probably the reality, that what I write does not belong to the times.

Listened to a long conversation between Jimmy and Mrs. Hill on the chaos in the kitchen and over the serving of trays that is a result of the new management. And I'd been so much aware of the chaos in the nursing service as compared with, say, the summer. And of course all this coincides with the weather that is not summer, floods of rain, rivers rising, the apple crop spoiling. Summer's over.

Flood warnings out until 2 A.M. Several streets closed.

September 28

At last the rain has stopped and the leaves that have turned yellow behind my back are drifting down in sunlight.

I keep coming back to the man who died, or rather to the mourners. The scene is old, the surroundings new. The privacy of death has been taken away. There were no radios to say I love you and all the other things they are saying one against another, no TVs with the distance of their news from personal loss and their obscene advertising, as they sat there in this long, unlovely corridor—none of this in the old death at home, where I am sure his pain could have been unendurable. I read in the paper that he had two sons—they may have come but I never saw them. It was all women—wife, sisters, daughters. Again the very old scene of "women must weep," though in pant suits. I'd say I'd never forget them going away, turning their backs on the place that had been an everyday occupation—but that I *shall* forget, that and much more.

September 30

Yesterday my nadir so far, chiefly, as I believe, thanks to Dr. LePage's asthma medicine. Today I had a brief sit out of doors, joined by Bea and Jo, followed by a brief visit from Miss K. and managed to pull myself up on the bars, though not brilliantly. I tried to put something down about the mourners, but fear it may be too facile.

VIGIL IN A NURSING HOME

We never saw him, the man who lay dying
In the bare room like the rest of the rooms, rarely
The one, whichever it was, stayed by his bed, only
The watchers outside in the corridor,
All women, wife, sisters, daughters.

I have seen their like often in Italian painting,
Presences at the edge of some holy death, kneeling

Hooded or coifed in the shadows while the sky opened.
But these wore the garments of Middle America
And sat on narrow chairs in a hallway

With an incessant traffic of vacuum cleaners,
Carts with linens, brooms, pills and elixirs,
While from doorways issued conflicting music
Or smooth confident voices; a thoroughfare
Too open and too unquiet for any sorrow.

We hoped that he in his painful wakings
Could warm himself at the flame they tended
All day, then all night too, unremitting,
A way of life. At the distance of the onlooker
It glowed like a brazier in a cloister.

We knew he was dead when we saw them leaving
Not singly or in pairs as they came, but in a huddle,
One already with the mourning women of the ages,
Hurrying to put behind them the bleakness of the corridor.
I could have wished them a few playing angels.

• • •

October 20
   One thing I note since I became more and more preoccupied with
my physical feelings is that I write less about the nursing home, more
about myself, less too of the state of the world, which indeed is harder
for me to reach and less susceptible to letters to one's congressman.
I want to put down my babes-in-the-wood poem, which I'd really like
to be sung.

   WORDS FOR MUSIC

   Come without sound
   Now, while the leaves float brilliant
   Through the air
   Down,
   As the leaves noiseless part from the tree,
   Come to me,

Not with the apple's commotion,
The thud in the grass, or the late shut roses'
Slow inward decay,
Let the last life-thread whatever it be
Give way
With the leaves' lightest severance,
So, on such a day,
Now.

Do not wait for the wind and rain
Thrashing, the boughs' crack and rending,
But on silent final wings, landing
In the garden where we began,
Come
This stillest day of fall—
Leaves in the air, leaves still on the tree
Leaves to cover me.

• • •

March 31 [1976]
   Last night Mrs. R. died. I half expected to hear it this morning,
having heard she'd had the last rites. I expected it before long in any
case. I am surprised to find how much affected I am—it was the visit
of the daughters-in-law and granddaughter that really upset me—the
weeping women again. I have not been able to get Mrs. R. out of my
mind all day. I was so used to her physical presence—her red robe,
her flares of anger, her smile—rare since her illness. I thought, "Well,
Anne, you got the hell out of here as you were always saying you
would." I am afraid to think of what I may get instead.

April 1

IN MEMORIAM
Well, Anne, you got the hell out of here
As you threatened, not quite every day.
No need to walk out of the door in the snow
Or jump in the river. You crossed peacefully.
No more baths from these so-called nurses

(In this place calling itself a hospital)
Who scrubbed you as if you'd been tilling the fields
And shut off the bells when they wanted a smoke.
No more fretting over what you had once, what you had lost,
　　what you had worked for,
The sandwich glass, the Haviland china.
Wherever you are, whether with Jesus, Mary, and Joseph,
Whom—Irish—you invoked in the extremity of
　　exasperation
But believed in simply, firmly, as always;
Or whether you sleep in the *night of nothing*,
You are still in this room
A presence, more than a memory,
In your red robe like a Renaissance pope's,
With your un-Renaissance hair-ribbon, which did not
　　counter
The hint, in some of your moods, of the Cumaean Sybil;
The deepset eyes no one would have known were blind
And the wide beautiful smile when things, meaning people,
Made you, a moment, happy,
Or when music played and you beat time
With your long fingers.

●　　●　　●

June 18

My anniversary. I have lived here two years and survived, though
not without scars and deterioration. (I was deteriorating before the
accident, however.) This morning after hearing Elizabeth was coming out for a picnic and then getting the Academic Overture on the
radio, I felt extraordinarily alive, while yesterday I felt shut in im-
penetrable gloom, changing only to a kind of desperation when I
spilled a glass of milk over everything. I almost cried over the spilt
milk—it was too much. A climax of absurdity and littleness. . . .

July 11

There are many things I've meant to put down, but laziness grows
and I suppose the taking things for granted, as if this were the normal

world. I read less, write less—though more, I suspect, than most people here—enjoy sitting out better than anything, in the shade of warm days with a breeze stirring, sounds of wood thrush and occasional cardinal, very occasionally the smell of pine.

Nevertheless there have been events this week. One was a select dinner for about thirty people, with steak and champagne. It was select, in that all the people there were *compos mentis*. It was an extraordinary mixture as regards clothes, however—some in hospital nightgowns, even in 1776 type—some in lacy, chiffony, old-lady type of things. I wore a cotton dress and my roommate something quite impressive from Angotti's. The food was good, so much above the standard that it's hardly worth comparing them, but the whole thing just missed being festive.

Another event was the arrival yesterday of the wedding party of my roommate's grandniece. The bride and bridesmaids very charming, also the bride's mother in a range of summery colors to match the day. Marian was bowled over by it. It was probably good for everyone to see them—so much youth and freshness, hope and flowers—their floating stuffs, garden party hats, and the perfection of summer weather, the kind every bride must desire.

A sad event was the departure of Jean, the nurse who has been here all the time I have, the one who lends me books and whose high spirits —singing and dancing in the halls—I have partly lived on. Yet she has no easy life.

Background to all this, the sounds from the next room, a Miss T. who calls out incessantly for everything, necessities and trifles, in a faint voice the nurses very rarely hear. "Oh! please come nurse. Louisa. Roger. Boys and girls. Oh! please help me"—then she cries, with the forced tears of a child wanting attention. Then her roommate joins in, "Crybaby," she says. "Get me out of here," says Miss T. over and over, and once a voice very much stronger than Miss T.'s, "Nurse. Come and get this woman off my neck."

July 13

My birthday, the third here and the saddest. The first, though I had to be lifted into the chair, was by far the most festive—champagne under the trees on a hot day and all the Reading Group and Jo sitting there, when I turned round at the bottom of the ramp and saw them. Then I had no doubt I'd get home, though I did not think it would be soon. The second was not strictly speaking here; I had it at home and the same people were there, but I got the cake and the Happy Birthday singing here the next day, to my surprise. Today was a day of cold, gloomy weather, no rain but no sun either—or just gleams now and then. I was still depressed from my visit to the dentist and the knowledge that the tooth that is bothering me can't be saved— and what is that going to lead to? But there was a very good letter from Susan, and one from Bertile with a charming French card of snowdrops—esperance, etc.—and a surprise one from Julia who re-created the prize-giving day at Wells Cathedral School most vividly —as she said, the essence or cliché of all summer prize-givings. Julia renews my youth, but not for long. Several people have told me I don't look 73 and I am glad of it, but Oh! God, today I feel it—73 and falling to pieces, knees, teeth, and insides. I wonder how Lord Clark, whom I still think of as Sir Kenneth, my exact twin at so great a distance, has passed his 73rd birthday?

The hospital gave me another hairbrush. . . .

March 28 [1977]

Yesterday, when someone opened the door, a cat came in, not one of the wild ones who live outside but someone's pet who had strayed. It was a flower of a cat, all the things I like, pansy-tiger markings and a round face and big paws. It stirred all the ailurophile in me as I was allowed to pet it a few moments, to loud purrings and beautiful cat gestures. I thought of the hermit who gave up all but his cat.

My watch is running down, along with my knees. I can buy a new watch and shall have to. At the same time I hanker after a new dress, which seems folly. What is that Hardy poem, "When I behold my face / And view my wrinkled skin" and at the moment my down-trodden-looking hair. Yet I still want a new dress. Renouncing the world is hard.

Poor L.M. distressed this morning because they wouldn't let her telephone her mother in the grave. She knew the number to call too.

Today for the first time I felt my legs were not going to make it back to my room. Today also my watch finally stopped.

Barbara Smith
[1946–]

Born in Cleveland, Ohio, Barbara Smith was raised, along with her twin sister Beverly, in a multigenerational family of black women. A writer, teacher, publisher and political activist, she was a founding member of the black feminist Combahee River Collective in 1974. She was also co-founder of Kitchen Table: Women of Color Press. Among her publications are All the Women Are White, All the Blacks Are Men, But Some of Us Are Brave: Black Women's Studies, *co-edited with Gloria T. Hull and Patricia Bell Scott (Old Westbury, N.Y.: The Feminist Press, 1982);* Home Girls: A Black Feminist Anthology *(New York: Kitchen Table Press, 1983);* Yours in Struggle: Three Feminist Perspectives on Anti-Semitism and Racism, *with Elly Bulkin and Minnie Bruce Pratt (Brooklyn, New York: Long Haul Press, 1984). She is currently completing a collection of her own fiction and lives in Albany, New York.*

Barbara Smith was living in Boston in 1979 when twelve black women were murdered during a four month period. At the time these journal entries were written, she was working with others—black women and men, other women of color, feminists, and lesbians—to bring pressure on law enforcement officials and to educate women about safety and self-defense. Smith writes, "Unlike the murders of Black children (primarily males) in Atlanta two years later, the deaths of the women in Boston received no national media attention and the general public as well as the Black community are, for the most part, still unaware that they occurred." More information about the Boston murders can be found in "Twelve Black Women: Why Did They Die?" by the Combahee River Collective in Fight Back: Feminist Resistance to Male Violence, *edited by Frédérique Delacoste and Felice Newman (Minneapolis: Cleis Press, 1981).*

February 1, 1979

I had two very disturbing dreams last night. The one that woke me up just now concerned Aunt Rosa. We were in Cleveland. There was going to be a big family party (Aunt Bert's family). Susan —— had done a story about all of Aunt Bert's sisters. It was even in the New York *Times* with a color picture. I said something about how it wasn't just in the *Plain Dealer* and also talked about how I had asked Susan —— about being paid a commission for giving her the information she used in the story and she of course brushed it off, as in real life.

Then Aunt Rosa and I and this little girl, all dressed up were waiting for a bus. Aunt Rosa had a cane. While we were standing waiting she did something to her foot/ankle. I asked could she actually ride the bus and she said she could. One bus passed us by. I had to go flag them. One finally came & stopped but as we approached very slowly it began to close its doors. I yelled. Please wait, please wait. Over and over again. And it did. We got on the bus in the back and I went up to pay our fare and also to tell off the bus driver. I was going to say something to him about how Aunt Rosa was so old and would only be here for a few months and that the least he could do was wait. But when I got to the front I saw he was a white man and I didn't want to say anything. I was looking at the fare list and didn't see anything listed for senior citizens or regular fares.

The little girl in the dream was very fair and pretty. When we crossed the street at one point she didn't hold onto my hand. I told her she had to do that. I also said to Aunt Rosa at one point, "Wasn't she the cutest little girl she'd ever seen?" I had to take care of them both.

I woke up furious.

The second dream I remember less clearly, but know that it was about the murders of young Black women they've been discovering this month. (In my dream) a new one had happened on Park Drive near where Ellie lives. It was very upsetting. When I woke I was haunted by these murders and thought about my conversation with Lorraine who wants to "do" something. This morning I want to do something too.

Two dreams about Black women's oppression and powerlessness. Goddamnit I'm sick of this world.

February 7, 1979
... Then there are the murders of four of us right here and the most frustrating meeting I think I've ever attended on Monday at the Blackstone school. Sexual and racial politics with a vengeance. I don't have the strength to write about it. . . . Perhaps I'll tape some thoughts.

March 19, 1979
Random thoughts: Violence against us is overwhelming. A sixth woman was murdered last week. Racism from white women and homophobia from Black people is a vice that will choke the Black feminist movement.

April 28, 1979
I've been awake since 5:54 and didn't go to sleep until around 2:00.
An eighth Black woman was murdered yesterday. There is going to be a demonstration this morning, a march from the common to Pig Mayor White's house. It is an action planned in one night. I think there will be 100s of women there. Practically everyone I called last night already knew, some had gotten four or five calls. But I talked to at least five women who didn't know.

There was a meeting last night in the South End at Harriet Tubman. There were around fifty or sixty women there. Over half of them feminists and Lesbians. Actually more like ¾. The word got out. When I called up Calvin Street Kathy —— answered the phone and before I could say anything she said, "Are you calling about the meeting?" It's happening. This is the third meeting about this violence I've been to this week and at every one we were there giving vital input. The meeting Thursday night at Amaranth was beautiful. So well planned. At least sixty women.

The meeting at Harriet Tubman last night was so intense for this very reason. We were a powerful presence. It just occurred to me that I'm saying we, (meaning feminists & lesbians), but I am a Black woman a part of both we's. Before the issue of race came up Charlotte whispered to me her concern about the action being predominately Black and my forehead furrowed even deeper than it was before. I felt so in the middle. Eventually Charlotte spoke about this and more of that feeling came out. At one point a young Black woman responded to a white woman's suggestion that a group of people take responsibility for security, & that it be someone from the Black organization she belonged to. She said she saw no reason why women in her group should take the weight for this totally and then made some statements indicating her distrust of the white women there, talked about the bad faith that had occurred in other movements.

This is the major issue. Trust and following through. If white feminists ever needed to have their act together it's now. I have faith in a lot of women, because I know their politics, their commitments. But it all has got to be proven.

One idea from that young Black woman and others is that this kind of coalition had happened before and failed. But this is *new*. Black and white, feminist and non-feminists, women have never come together to work on a woman's issue, an issue of racial-sexual politics, at least not in this era. I'm thinking about the anti-lynching movement at the beginning of the century as the nearest parallel—and that of course was different. So this has never been tried before. It could work.

I think about sitting up at Harriet Tubman House three or four years ago in C.E.S.A. [the Committee to End Sterilization Abuse] trying to figure out how to involve Third World Women in our work. And now it's the other way around. White women taking leadership from Black women around one of those "universal" issues we as Black feminists have always said would pull in everyone.

Then there is the emotional level of this, the level so much harder to write about. We are dying. Again the truth I've always talked about that at bottom Black feminism is about keeping Black women from dying, is made frighteningly real.

When Lilly called me yesterday besides being devastated I got scared. I felt cold inside and was afraid. It is an epidemic. When I spoke to Demita about this she said to remember that most of the women who have been killed are very poor and in the streets more. I told her I knew how we lived might be different, but still. We have to tell ourselves something, tell ourselves why we will not be the next victim. And they are arresting Black men. Who knows what it all means, but that's who's getting arrested and we've got to deal with that. Who over time has been the most likely to violate and kill Black women, at least in urban ghettos for the last 20 years? I remember the *Call & Post* in Cleveland. The horrors of sexual politics, particularly that one grisly life-size picture of the dead infant (found in a trash can perhaps?)

I thought about what I was doing yesterday as our sister was dying. Waiting in front of the Harvard Coop for Beth. Eating quiche, but talking to her about the murders too. Lord help . . .

May 7, 1979

Now it's eleven Black women and one white woman. I am numb and aching. They found two on Friday & Saturday, one this morning in Back Bay beaten to death. Naked? Sexual fodder. I'm afraid.

June 26, 1979

I'm sitting by a pond, surrounded by woods listening to birds (and suddenly the inappropriate disturbance of a helicopter.) I cannot believe that I got away, that where I am is real and that I am real in this place. I've had such fantasies already about being here after less than two hours. Fantasies about the kind of writing I could do away from the distractions of oppression. Not just city life which I need and love, but pain. Terror. Knowing from moment to moment that who I am is on all counts hated. Black, woman, Lesbian, my breathing from moment to moment inevitable fear.

I came here on many levels to get away from the murders. To escape death. So they're "over" now. The pressure has "died" down. Not so. Every other phone call that I get concerns them. The poetry reading benefit with Adrienne and Audre, leafletting last week at Dudley station, random conversations . . . For me the deaths of these women has shaped six months of my life. There has never been forgetting. There has been other activity, other moments, definite joy and laughter, but always, always, always, the tragedy. The certain irrefutable and demonstrated knowledge that my Black female life is worth nothing. That my most appropriate fate here in white-boy patriarchy is to be beaten beyond recognition. *Beyond recognition.*

I am furious as I write this. Furious perhaps that the escape will be so temporary. Consciousness does not permit it. But I will rest here and explore.

I wonder how many Black women have *ever* had the chance to do the simple thing that I've just done. To go away by oneself to write.

Bibliography

BIBLIOGRAPHIES

Addis, Patricia K., ed. *Through a Woman's I: An Annotated Bibliography of American Women's Autobiographical Writings, 1946–1976.* Metuchen, New Jersey: Scarecrow Press, 1983.

Arskey, Laura, Nancy Pries, and Marcia Reed, eds. *American Diaries: An Annotated Bibliography of Published American Diaries and Journals.* Detroit: Gale Research Company, 1983.

Begos, Jane Dupree. *Annotated Bibliography of Published Women's Diaries.* Pound Ridge, New York: Privately printed, 1977.

Bitton, Davis. *Guide to Mormon Diaries and Autobiographies.* Provo, Utah: Brigham Young University Press, 1977.

Brignanon, Russell C. *Black Americans in Autobiography: An Annotated Bibliography of Autobiographies and Autobiographical Books Written Since the Civil War.* Durham, North Carolina: Duke University Press, 1974.

Brinton, Howard H. *Quaker Journals: Varieties of Religious Experience among Friends.* Wallingford, Pennsylvania: Pendle Hill Publications, 1983 [1972].

Briscoe, Mary Louise, Barbara Tobias, and Lynn Z. Bloom, eds. *American Autobiography, 1945–1980: A Bibliography.* Madison: University of Wisconsin Press, 1982.

Cox, Edward Godfrey. *A Reference Guide to the Literature of Travel.* 3 vols. Seattle: University of Washington Press, 1935–49.

Fairbanks, Carol, and Sara Brooks Sundberg. *Farm Women on the Prairie Frontier: A Sourcebook for Canada and the United States.* Metuchen, New Jersey: Scarecrow Press, 1982.

Forbes, Harriette Merrifield. *New England Diaries 1602–1800: A Descriptive Catalogue of Diaries, Orderly Books and Sea Journals.* New York: Russell and Russell, 1967 [1923].

Hinding, Andrea, ed. *Women's History Sources: A Guide to Archives and Manuscript Collections in the United States.* New York: R. R. Bowker, 1979.

Jeffrey, Julie Roy. "Bibliography." In *Frontier Women: The Trans-Mississippi West, 1840–1880,* 205–28. New York: Hill and Wang, 1979.

Matthews, William. *American Diaries: An Annotated Bibliography of American Diaries Written Prior to the Year 1861.* Berkeley and Los Angeles: University of California Press, 1945.

———. *American Diaries in Manuscript, 1850–1954: A Descriptive Bibliography.* Athens: University of Georgia Press, 1974.

Morgan, Dale L. "Diaries Kept on the South Pass Route in 1849 by Overland Travelers Bound for California, Oregon, and Utah." In *The Overland Diary of James A. Pritchard from Kentucky to California in 1849,* 177–200. Denver: Old West Publishing, 1959.

Thomas, W.S. *American Revolutionary Diaries: Also Journals, Narratives, Autobiographies, Reminiscences and Personal Memoirs.* 1923.

BOOKS AND ARTICLES ABOUT DIARIES

Literature and History

Begos, Jane Dupree. "Diaries and Journals." *Women's Diaries: A Quarterly Newsletter* 1, no. 1 (Spring 1983): 2–4.

Boerner, Peter. "The Significance of the Diary in Modern Literature." *Yearbook of Comparative and General Literature* 21 (1972): 41–45.

———. *Tagebuch.* Stuttgart: J. B. Metzler, 1969.

Bryant, David. "Reflexions sur le journal intime." *Neuphilologishe Mitteilungen: Bulletin de la Societe Neophilologique* 82, no. 1 (1981): 66–74.

Corbett, William. "Journal Poetics." In *Code of Signals: Recent Writings in Poetics,* edited by Michael Palmer, 158–65. Berkeley: North Atlantic, 1983.

Culley, Margo. "Women's Diary Literature: Resources and Directions in the Field." *Legacy: A Newsletter of Nineteenth-Century American Women Writers* 1, no. 1 (Spring 1984): 4–5.

Cummings, James. "Bookseller's Search for 'The Recorded Life.' " *AB: Bookman's Weekly* (September 6, 1982): 1427–40.

Dedier, Beatrice. *Le Journal Intime.* Paris: Presses Universitaires de France, 1976.

De Pauw, Linda Grant. *Seafaring Women.* Boston: Houghton Mifflin, 1982.

Didion, Joan. "On Keeping a Notebook." In *Sloughing Toward Bethlehem.* New York: Simon and Schuster, 1968.

"Essays, Diaries, Letters." *Book Forum* 4, no. 3 (1979).

Faragher, John Mack. *Women and Men on the Overland Trail.* New Haven: Yale University Press, 1979.

Fothergill, Robert A. *Private Chronicles: A Study of English Diaries.* London: Oxford University Press, 1974.

Godwin, Gail. "A Diarist on Diarists." *Antaeus* 21/22 (Spring/Summer 1976): 50–56.

Gottschalk, Louis, et al. *The Use of Personal Documents in History, Anthropology and Sociology.* New York: Social Science Research Council, 1945.

Hampsten, Elizabeth. *Read This Only to Yourself: The Private Writings of Midwestern Women, 1800–1910.* Bloomington: Indiana University Press, 1982.

Hoffmann, Leonore, and Deborah Rosenfelt, eds. *Teaching Women's Literature from a Regional Perspective.* New York: Modern Language Association, 1982.

Hoffmann, Leonore, and Elizabeth Hampsten, eds. *To Live a Woman: Student Work from the Project "Teaching Women's Literature from a Regional Perspective."* New York: Modern Language Association, 1981.

Hoffmann, Leonore, and Margo Culley, eds. *Women's Personal Narratives.* New York: Modern Language Association, 1985.

Hough, Henry Beetle, and Emma Mayhew Whiting. *Whaling Wives.* Boston: Houghton Mifflin, 1953.

Hyghe, Patrick. "Diary Writing Turns a New Leaf." *The New York Times Magazine,* November 8, 1981, 98–108.

Le Journal intime et ses formes littéraires: actes du colloque de septembre 1975. (Grenoble). Textes réunis par V. Del Litto. Geneve; Paris: Droz, 1978.

Jurgenssen, Manfred. *Das Fiktionale Ich: Untersuchungen zum Tagebuch.* Bern: Francke, 1979.

Kagle, Steven. *American Diary Literature: 1620–1799.* Boston: Twayne, 1979.

Kolodny, Annette. *The Land before Her: Fantasy and Experience of the American Frontiers, 1630–1860.* Chapel Hill: University of North Carolina Press, 1984.

Kuhn-Osius, K. Eckhard. "Making Loose Ends Meet: Private Journals in the Public Realm." *German Quarterly* 54, no. 2 (March 1981): 166–76.

Kurczaba, Alex. *Grombrowicz and Frish: Aspects of the Literary Diary.* Bonn: Bouvier, 1980.

Leleu, Michéle. *Les Journaux Intimes.* Paris: Presses Universitaires de France, 1972 [1952].

Mallon, Thomas. *A Book of One's Own: People and Their Diaries.* New York: Ticknor and Fields, 1984.

Myres, Sandra L. *Westering Women and the Frontier Experience, 1800–1915.* Albuquerque: University of New Mexico Press, 1982.

O'Brien, Kate. *English Diaries and Journals*. London: Collins, 1943.

Ochs, Vanessa L. "Taking Women's Diaries Seriously." *Women's Diaries: A Quarterly Newsletter* 3, no. 1 (Spring 1985): 1, 3–5.

Ponsoby, Arthur. "Introduction on Diary Writing." In *English Diaries: A Review of English Diaries from the Sixteenth Century to the Twentieth Century*, 1–43. New York: George Doran; London: Methuen, [1923].

————. "Introduction on Diary Reading." In *More English Diaries: Further Reviews of Diaries from the Sixteenth Century to the Nineteenth Century*. London: Methuen, 1927.

Ross, Nancy Wilson. "Dear Diary." In *Westward the Women*. San Francisco: North Point Press, 1985 [1944].

Schlissel, Lillian. *Women's Diaries of the Westward Journey*. New York: Schocken, 1982.

Sears, Clara Endicott. *Gleanings from Old Shaker Journals*. Boston and New York: Houghton Mifflin, 1916.

Snow, Edward Rowe. *Women of the Sea*. New York: Dodd, Mead, 1962.

Spacks, Patricia Meyers. *The Female Imagination: A Literary and Psychological Investigation of Writing by Women—Novels, Autobiographies, Letters, Journals that Reveals How the Fact of Womanhood Shapes the Imagination*. New York: Knopf, 1975.

————. "Women's Stories, Women's Selves." *Hudson Review* 30, no. 1 (Spring 1977), 29–36.

Stratton, Joanna L. *Pioneer Women: Voices from the Kansas Frontier*. New York: Simon and Schuster, 1981.

Weinstein, Jeff. "Dear Diaries." *Village Voice*, June 21, 1983, 42–43, 93.

Winter, Metta L. " 'Heart Watching' through Journal Keeping: A Look at Quaker Diaries and Their Uses." *Women's Diaries: A Quarterly Newsletter* 1, no. 2 (Summer 1983): 1–3.

Psychology and Personal Growth

Allport, Gordon W. *The Use of Personal Documents in the Psychological Sciences*. New York: Social Science Research Council, 1942.

Baldwin, Christina. *One to One: Self-Understanding through Journal Writing*. New York: M. Evans, 1977.

Falk, Ruth. *Women Loving: A Journey toward Becoming an Independent Woman*. New York: Random House, 1975.

Harms, Valerie. " 'The Intensive Journal,' One Aspect of the Method Based on Twelve Years of Personal Use." *Women's Diaries: A Quarterly Newsletter* 1, no. 3 (Fall 1983): 1–3, 5.

Moffat, Mary Jane. "On Reading the Diaries of Gifted Women Who Died Young." *Women's Diaries: A Quarterly Newsletter* 2, no. 1 (Spring 1984): 1, 3–5.

Progoff, Ira. *At a Journal Workshop: The Basic Text and Guide for Using the Intensive Journal*. New York: Dialogue House Library, 1975.

Rainer, Tristine. *The New Diary: How to Use a Journal for Self-Guidance and Expanded Creativity*. Los Angeles: J. P. Tarcher, 1978.

Rosenblatt, Paul C. *Bitter, Bitter Tears: Nineteenth Century Diarists and Twentieth Century Grief Theories*. Minneapolis: University of Minnesota Press, 1983.

Simon, George F. *Keeping Your Personal Journal*. New York and Toronto: Paulist Press, 1978.

DIARIES

Collections and Anthologies containing Diaries by American Women

Andrews, Marietta M. *Scraps of Paper*. New York: E. P. Dutton, 1929.

Banks, Mirra. *Anonymous Was a Woman*. New York: St. Martin's Press, 1979.

Berger, Josef, and Dorothy Berger, eds. *Diary of America: The Intimate Story of Our Nation, Told by One-Hundred Diarists*. New York: Simon and Schuster, 1957.

———. *Small Voices*. New York: P. S. Eriksson, 1967.

Cott, Nancy. *Root of Bitterness: Documents of the Social History of American Women*. New York: E. P. Dutton, 1972.

Dow, George Francis, ed. *The Holyoke Diaries, 1709–1856*. Salem, Massachusetts: Essex Institute, 1911.

Drury, Clifford Merrill. *First White Women over the Rockies: Diaries, Letters and Biographical Sketches of the Six Women of the Oregon Mission Who Made the Overland Journey in 1836 and 1838*. 3 vols. Glendale, California: Arthur H. Clark, 1963–66.

Dunaway, Philip, and Mel Evans, eds. *A Treasury of the World's Great Diaries*. Garden City, New York: Doubleday, 1957.

Evans, Elizabeth. *Weathering the Storm: Women of the American Revolution*. New York: Scribners, 1975.

Fischer, Christiane. *Let Them Speak for Themselves: Women in the American West, 1849–1900*. Hamden, Connecticut: Archom Books, 1977.

Hampsten, Elizabeth. *To All Inquiring Friends: Letters, Diaries and Essays in North Dakota*. Grand Forks: Department of English, University of North Dakota, 1979.

Holliday, Laurel. *Heart Songs: The Intimate Diaries of Young Girls*. New York: Methuen, 1980 [1978].

Holmes, Kenneth L. *Covered Wagon Women: Diaries and Letters from the Western Trails 1840–1890*. Glendale, California: Arthur H. Clark, 1983.

Howe, M. A. De Wolfe, ed. *The Articulate Sisters: Passages from the Journals and Letters of the Daughters of President Josiah Quincy of Harvard University*. Cambridge: Harvard University Press, 1946.

Jones, Katharine M. *The Plantation South*. Indianapolis: Bobbs-Merrill, 1957.

Lamp in the Spine, no. 9 (Spring/Fall 1974).

Lifshin, Lyn. *Ariadne's Thread: A Collection of Contemporary Women's Journals*. New York: Harper and Row, 1982.

Luchetti, Cathy, with Carol Olwell. *Women of the West*. St. George, Utah: Antelope Island Press, 1982.

Martinson, Sue Ann, et al. *Sing Heavenly Muse! Women's Poetry and Prose: Journal Issue*. No. 6. Minneapolis, Minnesota, 1982.

Merriam, Eve. *Growing Up Female in America: Ten Lives*. Garden City, New York: Doubleday, 1971.

Millett, Kate, ed. *Caterpillars: Journal Entries by Eleven Women*. Epona Press, 1977.

Moffat, Mary Jane, and Charlotte Painter, eds. *Revelations: Diaries of Women*. New York: Random House, 1974.

Morgan, Dale, ed. *Overland in 1846: Diaries and Letters of the California-Oregon Trail*. 2 vols. Georgetown, California: Talisman Press, 1963.

Myres, Sandra, ed. *Ho for California! Women's Overland Diaries from the Huntington Library*. San Marino, California: Huntington Library, 1980.

So's Your Old Lady 20 (April 1978): 3–26.

Sprigg, June. *Domestick Beings*. New York: Knopf, 1984.

Sterling, Dorothy. *We Are Your Sisters: Black Women in the Nineteenth Century*. New York: W.W. Norton, 1984.

Vanderpoel, Emily Noyes. *Chronicles of a Pioneer School from 1792–1833: Being the History of Miss*

Sarah Pierce and Her Litchfield School. Edited by Elizabeth C. Barney Buel. Cambridge, Massachusetts: University Press, 1903.

————. *More Chronicles of a Pioneer School from 1792–1833.* Cambridge, Massachusetts: University Press, 1920.

Book-length Works

The diarist's name appears in brackets when the title page lists an editor other than the diarist herself and/or when the diary appears in a volume with another diary under whose author the Library of Congress lists the book. Where diaries have been published in multiple editions, the first edition appears here unless otherwise indicated.

Abbott, Elsie (Twining). *Days from a Year in School.* Cornwall, New York: Cornwall, 1930.

[Abzug, Bella S.] *Bella! Ms. Abzug Goes to Washington.* Edited by Mel Ziegler. New York: Saturday Review Press, 1972.

Adair, Cornelia (Wadsworth). *My Diary, August 30th to November 5th, 1874.* Austin: University of Texas Press, 1965.

[Adams, Abigail.] *Journal and Correspondence of Miss Adams, Daughter of John Adams. Written in France and England, in 1785.* Edited by Caroline Amelia (Smith) de Windt. 2 vols. New York: Wiley and Putnam, 1841–42.

Adams, Almeda C. *Seeing Europe through Sightless Eyes.* New York: Grafton, 1929.

Agassiz, Louis, and Elizabeth Agassiz. *A Journey in Brazil by Professor and Mrs. Louis Agassiz.* Boston: Ticknor and Fields, 1868.

[Alcott, Anna Bronson.] In *Bronson Alcott's Fruitlands,* edited by Clara E. Sears. Boston: Houghton Mifflin, 1915.

[Alcott, Louisa May.] *Louisa May Alcott: Her Life, Letters And Journals.* Edited by Ednah D. Cheney. Boston: Little, Brown, 1928.

[Alexander, Eveline M.] *Cavalry Wife: The Diary Of Eveline M. Alexander, 1866–1867. Being a Record of Her Journey from New York to Fort Smith to Join Her Cavalry-Officer Husband, Andrew J. Alexander, and Her Experiences with Him on Active Duty among the Indian Nations in Texas, New Mexico and Colorado.* Edited by Sandra Myres. College Station and London: Texas A & M University Press, 1977.

Alexander, Frances Gordon (Paddock). *Wayfarers in the Libyan Desert.* New York and London: G. P. Putnam's, 1912.

Allen, Harriet Trowbridge. *Travels in Europe and the East: During the Years 1858–59 and 1863–64.* New Haven: Privately printed by Tuttle, Morehouse and Taylor, 1879.

[Allibone, Susan.] *A Life Hid with Christ in God: Being a Memoir of Susan Allibone. Chiefly Compiled from Her Diary and Letters.* By Alfred Lee. Philadelphia: J.B. Lippincott, 1856.

Ames, Mary. *From a New England Woman's Diary in Dixie in 1865.* Springfield, Massachusetts: Plimpton, 1906.

[Amory, Katharine (Greene).] *The Journal of Mrs. John Amory (Katharine Greene) 1775–1777, with Letters from Her Father, Rufus Greene, 1759–1777.* Edited by Martha C. Codman. Boston: Privately printed, 1923.

Anderson, Isabel Weld (Perkins). *Zigzagging.* Boston and New York: Houghton Mifflin, 1918.

Andrews, Eliza Frances. *The War-Time Journal of a Georgia Girl, 1864–65.* New York: D. Appleton, 1908.

[Andrews, Ellen Miriam (Gibson).] *Hudson Diary, 1896–1900.* Edited by Willis Harry Miller. Hudson, Wisconsin: Star-Observer, 1968.

Angle, Helen M. *The Log or Diary of Our Automobile Voyage through Maine and the White Mountains, Written by One of the Survivors.* Stamford, Connecticut: R.H. Cunningham, 1910.

[Anthony, Susanna.] *The Life and Character of Miss Susanna Anthony, Who Died, In Newport (R.I.) June 23, MDCCXCI in the Sixty Fifth Year of Her Age. Consisting Chiefly in Extracts from Her Writings, with Some Brief Observations on Them.* Compiled by Samuel Hopkins. Worcester, Massachusetts: Leonard Worcester, 1796.

Ashe, Elizabeth. *Intimate Letters from France and Extracts from the Diary of Elizabeth Ashe, 1917–1919.* San Francisco: Bruce Brough, 1931.

Atherton, Gertrude Franklin (Horn). *Life in the War Zone.* New York: Systems, 1916.

Atkins, Mary. *The Diary of Mary Atkins: A Sabbatical in the Eighteen Sixties.* Mills College, California: Eucalyptus, 1937.

Avary, Myrta Lockett. *Dixie after the War: An Exposition of Social Conditions in the South, During the Twelve Years Succeeding the Fall of Richmond.* Garden City, New York: Doubleday, Page, 1906.

Ayer, Sarah Newman (Connell). *Diary of Sarah Connell Ayer, 1805–1835. Andover and New-buryport, Massachusetts; Concord and Bow, New Hampshire; Portland and Eastport, Maine.* Portland, Maine: Lefavor-Tower, 1910.

Bacon, Lydia B. (Stetson). *The Biography of Mrs. Lydia B. Bacon.* Boston: Massachusetts Sabbath School Society, 1856.

Bagnold, Enid. *A Diary Without Dates.* New York: William Morrow, 1935.

Baguedor, Eva. *Separation: Journal of a Marriage.* New York: Simon and Schuster, 1972.

[Bailey, Abigail (Abbot).] *Memoirs of Mrs. Abigail Bailey, Who Had Been the Wife of Major Asa Bailey . . . Written by Herself . . . to Which Are Added Sundry Original Biographical Sketches.* Edited by Ethan Smith. Boston: Samuel T. Armstrong, 1815.

Baldwin, Marian. *Canteening Overseas, 1917–1919.* New York: Macmillan, 1920.

[Ballard, Martha Moore.] *The History of Augusta: First Settlements and Early Days As a Town, Including the Diary of Mrs. Martha Moore Ballard, 1785–1812.* By Charles Elventon Nash. Augusta, Maine: Charles E. Nash and Son, 1904.

Banning, Margaret (Culkin). *Salud! A South American Journal.* New York and London: Harper and Brothers, 1941.

[Banyer, Maria Jay.] *A Christian Memorial of Two Sisters.* By John McVickar. New York: Stanford and Delisser, 1858.

[Barbour, Martha Isabella (Hopkins).] *Journals of the Late Brevet Major Philip Norbourne Barbour . . . and His Wife, Martha Isabella Hopkins Barbour, Written During the War with Mexico —1846.* Edited by Rhoda von Bibber Tanner Doubleday. New York and London: G.P. Putnam's, 1936.

Barbour, Mary (Bigelow). *Leaves from My Diary.* Boston: Privately printed, 1932.

Barr, Amelia Edith (Huddleston). *All the Days of My Life: An Autobiography, The Red Leaves of a Human Heart.* New York and London: D. Appleton, 1913.

[Bartlett, Fanny L.] *The Life of Fanny L. Bartlett.* By Rev. A. A. Phelps. Boston: H. V. Degen, 1860.

Barton, Parthena Rood. *Experiences of a Practical Christian Life: In Form of a Journal.* Utica, New York: Curtiss and Childs, 1877.

[Bascom, Ruth Henshaw.] *A New England Woman's Perspective on Norfolk, Virginia, 1801–1802: Excerpts from the Diary of Ruth Henshaw Bascom.* Edited by A.G. Roeber. Worcester, Massachusetts: American Antiquarian Society, 1979.

Bassett, Hannah. *Memoir of Hannah Bassett, with Extracts from Her Diary.* Lynn, Massachusetts: W.W. Kellogg, 1860.

[Bayard, Martha Pintard.] *The Journal of Martha Pintard Bayard, London 1794–1797.* Edited by S. Bayard Dod. New York: Dodd, Mead, 1894.

Beck, Frances. *The Diary of a Widow.* Boston: Beacon Press, 1965.

Beebe, Niles Mary (Blair), and William Charles. *Our Search for Wilderness. An Account of Two Anthropological Expeditions to Venezuela and to British Guiana.* New York: Henry Holt, 1910.

[Belknap, Kitturah Penton.] In *Women of the West*. By Cathy Luchetti. St. George, Utah: Antelope Island Press, 1982.

[Bell, Dwight, Margaret Van Horn Dwight.] *A Journey to Ohio in 1810 as Recorded in the Journal of Margaret Van Horn Dwight*. Edited by Max Farrand. New Haven: Yale University Press, 1912.

Bender, Flora. *Notes by the Way: Memoranda of a Journey across the Plains, From Bull Creek, Washington Co., Nebraska to Virginia City, Nevada Territory, May 7 to August 4, 1863*. Carson City: State, 1958.

Benedict, Clare (Woolson). *The Benedicts Abroad*. London: Ellis, 1930.

[Benedict, Ruth.] *An Anthropologist at Work: Writings of Ruth Benedict*. By Margaret Mead. London: Secker and Warburg, 1959.

Benetar, Judith. *Admissions: Notes from a Woman Psychiatrist*. New York: Charterhouse, 1974.

Bennett, Joan Frances. In *Members of the Class Will Keep Daily Journals: The Barnard College Journals of Tobi Gillian Sanders and Joan Frances Bennett*, by Tobi Gillian Sanders and Joan Frances Bennett. New York: White House, 1970.

Bentley, Toni. *Winter Season: A Dancer's Journal*. New York: Random House, 1982.

[Berenson, Mary.] *Mary Berenson: A Self Portrait from Her Letters and Diaries*. Edited by Barbara Strachey and Jayne Samuels. New York: W.W. Norton, 1983.

[Bethune, Joanna.] *Memoirs of Mrs. Joanna Bethune, by Her Son, the Reverend George Washington Bethune, D.D., with an Appendix, Containing Extracts from the Writings of Mrs. Bethune*. New York: Harper and Brothers, 1863.

Bettle, Jane. *Extracts from the Memorandums of Jane Bettle, with a Short Memoir Respecting Her*. Philadelphia: J. and Kitte, 1843.

Bevington, Helen. *Along Came the Witch: A Journal in the 1960s*. New York: Harcourt Brace Jovanovich, 1976.

———. *The Journey is Everything: A Journal of the Seventies*. Durham: Duke University Press, 1983.

Bird, Isabella. *A Lady's Life in the Rocky Mountains*. New York: G.P. Putnam's, 1900.

Birney, Josephine Churchill (Young). *Journals of Josephine Young*. New York: Privately printed, 1915.

Blake, Mary E. *On the Wing: Rambling Notes of a Trip to the Pacific*. Boston: Lee and Shepard, 1883.

Bloch, Alice. *Lifetime Journey: A Journey through Loss and Survival*. Watertown, Massachusetts: Persephone Press, 1981.

[Bogan, Louise.] *Journey around My Room: The Autobiography of Louise Bogan*. By Ruth Limmer. New York: Viking, 1980.

Bonfield, Lynn A. *Jailed for Survival: The Diary of an Anti-Nuclear Activist*. San Francisco: Mother Courage Affinity Group, 1984.

Borden, Mrs. John (Courtney Louise). *The Cruise of the Northern Light: Explorations and Hunting in the Alaskan and Siberian Arctic*. New York: Macmillan, 1928.

[Bosworth, Joanne Shipman.] *A Trip to Washington*. Edited by Henry M. Dawes. Privately printed, 1914.

[Botta, Anne Charlotte Lynch.] *Memoirs of Anne C. L. Botta, Written by Her Friends. With Selections from her Correspondence and from Her Writings in Prose and Poetry*. New York: J. Selwin Tait, 1894.

[Bowen, Clarissa Walton.] *The Diary of Clarissa Adger Bowen, Ashtabula Plantation, 1865, with Excerpts from Other Family Diaries and Comments by Her Granddaughter, Clarissa Walton Taylor, and Many Other Accounts of the Pendleton Clemson Area, South Carolina, 1776–1889*. Compiled by Mary Stevenson. Pendleton, South Carolina: Research and Publications Committee, Foundation for Historic Restoration in Pendleton Area, 1973.

Bowen, Helen. *Mount Shasta or Bust: A Family Travelogue in the 1890s.* Los Angeles, 1978.

Bowles, Cynthia. *At Home in India.* New York: Harcourt Brace, 1956.

[Bowman, Rachel.] In *The Cormany Diaries: A Northern Family in the Civil War,* edited by James C. Mohr and Richard E. Winslow, III. Pittsburg: University of Pittsburg Press, 1982.

Bradford, Ruth. *"Maskee!" The Journal and Letters of Ruth Bradford, 1861–72.* Hartford, Connecticut: Prospect, 1938.

[Branson, Ann.] *The Journal of Ann Branson, A Minister of the Gospel in the Society of Friends.* Philadelphia: William H. Pile's Sons, 1892.

Braudy, Susan. *Between Marriage and Divorce: A Woman's Diary.* New York: William Morrow, 1975.

Bray, Mary Matthews. *A Sea Trip in Clipper Ship Days.* Boston: Richard G. Badger, 1920.

Bremer, Maura. . . . *And Send the Sun Tomorrow: A Journal of My Father's Last Days.* Minneapolis: Winston, 1979.

➤ Bremser, Bonnie. *Troia: Mexican Memoirs.* Millertown, New York: Croton, 1969.

Brett, Dorothy. *Lawrence and Brett.* Philadelphia: J.B. Lippincott, 1932.

[Bridgman, Laura.] *Life and Education of Laura Dewey Bridgman, the Deaf, Dumb, and Blind Girl.* By Mary Swift Lamson. Boston: New England Publishing, 1878.

Brooke, Mildred. *Mildred Crew Brooke: An Unfinished Manuscript of Reminiscences and Some Extracts from Her Diary.* Casa de Oso, California: Privately printed, 1940.

Brooks, Anne M. *The Grieving Time: A Month by Month Account of Recovery from Loss.* Wilmington, Delaware: Delapeake Publishing, 1982.

Brown, Anna Augusta Fitch. *The Journal of Anna Augusta Fitch Brown.* Privately printed, 1959.

[Brown, Catharine.] *Memoir of Catharine Brown, A Christian Indian of the Cherokee Nation.* By Rufus Anderson. Boston: S.T. Armstrong, and Crocker and Brewster; New York: J. P. Haven, 1825.

Brown, Kathan. *Voyage to the Cities of the Dawn.* Oakland, California: Crown Point, 1976.

Brown, Margaret H. *Mrs. Wang's Diary.* Shanghai: Christian Literature Society, 1936.

[Brown, Sally and Pamela.] *The Diaries of Sally and Pamela Brown 1832–38, and Hyde Leslie, 1887, Plymouth Notch, Vermont.* Edited by Blanche Brown Bryant and Gertrude Elaine Baker. Springfield, Vermont: William L. Bryant Foundation, 1970.

[Bulfinch, Hannah.] *The Life and Letters of Charles Bulfinch, Architect, with Other Family Papers.* Edited by Ellen Susan Bulfinch. Boston and New York: Houghton Mifflin, 1896.

Bullitt, Ernesta Drinker. *An Uncensored Diary from the Central Empires.* Garden City, New York: Doubleday, Page, 1917.

[Bunting, Hannah Syng.] *Memoir, Diary, and Letters, of Miss Hannah Syng Bunting of Philadelphia.* Edited by T. Merritt. New York: Waugh, 1833.

[Burge, Dolly Sumner (Lunt).] *A Woman's War-Time Journal: An Account of the Passage over a Georgia Plantation of Sherman's Army on the March to the Sea, as Recorded in the Diary of Dolly Sumner Lunt.* Edited by Julian Street. New York: Century, 1918.

[Burlingame, Lettie Lavilla.] *Lettie Lavilla Burlingame: Her Life Pages. Stories Poems and Essays. Including a Glimpse of Her Success as the First Lady Lawyer of Will County, Illinois, the Home of Her Girlhood. Also As President, Up to the Time of Her Death, of the First "Equal Suffrage Association," of Joliet, Illinois, to which she Dedicated Her last Work, a Suffrage Song, Words and Music, "Put on the Orange Ribbon," Etc. Etc.* Edited by O. C. Burlingame. Joliet, Illinois: J.E. Williams, 1895.

[Burr, Esther Edwards.] *The Journal of Esther Edwards Burr, 1754–1757.* Edited by Carol F. Karlson and Laurie Crumpacker. New Haven: Yale University Press, 1984.

[Buss, Amelia.] In *Women's Personal Narratives.* Edited by Leonore Hoffmann and Margo Culley. New York: Modern Language Association, 1985.

Butler, Alice. *A.C.B.: A Life in Armor; Extracts from the Notebooks and Letters of Alice Carter Butler.* Chicago: Pascal Covici, 1925.

Butler, Joyce. *Pages from a Journal.* Kennebunkport, Maine: Mercer House, 1976.

Calisher, Hortense. *Herself.* New York: Arbor House, 1972.

[Canary, Martha Jane.] *Calamity Jane, 1852–1903: A History of Her Life and Adventures in the West.* By Nolie Mumey. Denver: Range, 1950.

Cannon, Luella Wareing. *My Cup Runneth O'er.* Salt Lake City: Utah Printing, 1969.

[Carlton, Cynthia Brown.] *Cynthia: Excerpts from the Diaries of Cynthia Brown Carlton, 1841–1900, in the Western Reserve.* Edited by Margaret Patricia Ford. Privately printed, 1976.

Carrington, Margaret Irvin (Sullivant). *Ab-sa-ra-ka, Home of the Crows: Being the Experiences of an Officer's Wife on the Plains, and Marking the Vicissitudes of Peril and Pleasure During the Occupation of the New Route to Virginia City, Montana, 1866–7, and the Indian Hostilities Thereto; With Outlines of the Natural Features and Resources of the Land, Tables of Distances, Maps and Other Aids to the Traveler; Gathered from Observation and Other Reliable Sources.* Philadelphia: J. B. Lippincott, 1860.

Carroll, Gladys Hasty. *To Remember Forever: The Journal of a College Girl, 1922–23.* Boston: Little, Brown, 1963.

[Cary, Anne M., and Margaret Cary.] *The Cary Letters.* Edited by Caroline G. Curtis. Cambridge, Massachusetts: Riverside, 1891.

Cates, Tressa R. *The Drainpipe Diary.* New York: Vantage, 1957.

Cather, Willa (Sibert). *Willa Cather in Europe: Her Own Story of the First Journey.* New York: Knopf, 1956.

Chace, Elizabeth Buffum, and Lucy Buffum Lovell. *Two Quaker Sisters: From the Original Diaries of Elizabeth Buffum Chace and Lucy Buffum Lovell.* New York: Liveright, 1937.

[Chambers, Charlotte.] *Memoir of Charlotte Chambers.* Edited by Lewis Hector Garrad. Philadelphia: Privately printed, 1856.

Champion, Isabelle. *Mother's Memories: A History from Girlhood to the Seventies, 1858–1914.* Eau Claire, Wisconsin: James H. Tifft, 1914.

Channing, Elizabeth Parsons. *Autobiography and Diary of Elizabeth Parsons Channing: Gleanings of a Thoughtful Life.* Boston: American Unitarian Association, 1907.

[Chestnut, Mary.] *The Private Mary Chestnut: The Unpublished Civil War Diaries.* By C. Van Woodward and Elizabeth Muhlenfeld. New York: Oxford University Press, 1984.

[Clairmont, Clara Mary Jane.] *Journals of Claire Clairmont.* By Marion K. Stocking and David M. Stocking. Cambridge: Harvard University Press, 1968.

Clark, Alice Keep. *Letters from Cilicia.* Chicago: A. D. Weinthrop, 1924.

[Clark, Helen E.] *Two Diaries: The Diary and Journal of Calvin Perry Clark Who Journeyed by Wagon Train from Plano, Illinois to Denver and Vicinity over the Santa Fe Trail in the Year 1859, Together with the Diary of His Sister Helen E. Clark Who Made a Similar Journey by the Northern Route in the Year 1860.* Denver: Denver Public Library, 1962.

[Clarke, Aletta.] *Some Records of Sussex County, Delaware.* By Charles Henry Black Turner. Philadelphia: Allen, Lane and Scott, 1909.

Clarke, Caroline Cowles (Richards). *The Diary of Caroline Cowles Richards, 1852–1872.* Canadaigua, New York, 1908.

[Cobb, Eurnic Parsons.] *Mother Cobb or Sixty Years' Walk with God.* By Mary Weems Chapman. Chicago: T. B. Arnold, 1896.

[Cogswell, Alice.] *Father and Daughter: A Collection of the Cogswell Family Letters and Diaries, 1772–1830.* Edited by Grace Cogswell Root. West Hartford, Connecticut: American School for the Deaf, 1924.

Coit, Mehetabel Chandler. *Mehetabel Chandler Coit, Her Book, 1714.* Norwich, Connecticut: Bulletin, 1895.

Colebrook, Joan. *Innocents of the West: Travels through the Sixties.* New York: Basic Books, 1979.

[Coleman, Ann Raney Thomas.] *Victorian Lady on the Texas Frontier: The Journal of Ann Raney Coleman.* Edited by C. Richard King. London and New York: Foulsham, 1972.

Collette, Elizabeth Van Horne. *Journey to the Promised Land: Journal of Elizabeth Van Horne.* Pittsburg: Historical Society of Western Pennsylvania, 1939.

Collins, Septima Maria (Levy). *A Woman's Trip to Alaska: Being an Account of a Voyage through the Inland Seas of the Sitkan Archipelago, in 1890*. New York: Cassell, 1890.

[Colt, Miriam (Davis).] *A Heroine of the Frontier: Miriam Davis Colt in Kansas, 1856. Extracts from Mrs. Colt's Diaries*. Edited by J. Christian Bay. Cedar Rapids, Iowa: Privately printed for the Friends of Torch Press, 1941.

Colt, Miriam (Davis). *Went to Kansas: Being a Thrilling Account of an Ill-fated Expedition to that Fairy Land, and Its Sad Results; Together with a Sketch of the Life of the Author*. Watertown, New York: L. Ingalls, 1862.

Coman, Martha Seymour. *Memories of Martha Seymour Coman*. Boston: Fort Hill, 1913.

[Comly, Rebecca.] *Journal of the Life and Religious Labours of John Comly, late of Byberry, Pennsylvania*. Philadelphia: T.E. Chapman, 1853.

Commons, Marie Andrews. *The Log of Tanager Hill*. Baltimore: Waverly, 1938.

Condict, Jemima. *Jemima Condict, Her Book: Being a Transcript of the Diary of an Essex County Maid During the Revolutionary War*. Newark, New Jersey: Carteret Book Club, 1930.

Congleton, Sarah Robb. *Glimpses of Many Lands*. Chicago: R.R. Donnelly, 1915.

[Cook, Anna Maria Green.] *The Journal of a Milledgeville Girl, 1861–1867*. Edited by James C. Bonner. Athens: University of Georgia Press, 1964.

Cooke, Bella. *Rifted Clouds: or the Life Story of Bella Cooke: A Record of Loving Kindness and Tender Mercies*. New York: Palmer and Hughes, 1885.

Coolidge, Katharine (Parkman). *Selections*. Boston: Privately printed at the Merrymount Press, 1901.

[Cooper, Mary.] *The Diary of Mary Cooper: Life on a Long Island Farm, 1768–1773*. Edited by Field Horne. Oyster Bay, New York: Oyster Bay Historical Society, 1981.

Cooper, Susan Fenimore. *Rural Hours. By a Lady*. New York: G.P. Putnam's, 1850.

Cooper, Viola Irene. *Windjamming To Fiji*. New York: Rae D. Hendkle, 1929.

Coppola, Eleanor. *Notes*. New York: Simon and Schuster, 1979.

Cowell, Christiana B. *The Life and Writings of Mrs. Christiana B. Cowell, Consort of Rev. D. B. Cowell, Who Died in Lebanon, Maine, Oct. 8, 1862, Aged 41 Years*. Biddeford, Maine: John E. Butler, 1872.

Cowles, Helen M. *Grace Victorious: Or, The Memoir of Helen M. Cowles*. Oberlin, Ohio: J. M. Fitch, 1856.

[Cowles, Julia.] *The Diaries Of Julia Cowles, A Connecticut Record, 1797–1803*. Edited by Laura Hadley Moseley. New Haven: Yale University Press, 1931.

Cowman, Lettie (Burd). *The Vision Lives*. Los Angeles: Cowman, 1961.

Craig, Josephine, and Austin Craig. *The Farthest Westing: A Phillipine Footnote. Selections, with Explanations, from a Third of a Century's Correspondence on America's "Farthest Westing" in its Ephemeral Experiment in the Extreme East*. Philadelphia: Dorrance, 1940.

Crane, Florence. *Terrae Incognitae*. Privately printed, 1927.

Crawford, Dorothy (Painter). *Stay with It, Van: From the Diary of Mississippi's First Lady Mayor*. New York: Exposition Press, 1958.

Crawford, Isabel Alice Hartley. *Kiowa: The History of a Blanket Indian Mission*. New York and Chicago: Fleming H. Revell, 1915.

Crile, Grace. *Skyways to a Jungle Laboratory: An African Adventure*. New York: W.W. Norton, 1936.

[Crouter, Natalie.] *Forbidden Diary: A Record of Wartime Internment, 1941–1945*. Edited by Lynn Z. Bloom. New York: Burt Franklin, 1980.

[Crowninshield, Clara.] *Diary: A European Tour with Longfellow, 1835–1836*. Edited by Andrew Hilen. Seattle: University of Washington Press, 1956.

[Culbertson, Manie.] *May I Speak? Diary of a Crossover Teacher*. Edited by Sue Eakin. Gretna, Louisiana: Pelican Publishing, 1972.

Cumming, Kate. *A Journal of Hospital Life in the Confederate Army of Tennessee, from the Battle of Shiloh to the End of the War, with Sketches of Life and Character, and Brief Notices of Current Events During that Period.* Louisville, Kentucky: John P. Morton; New Orleans: William Evelyn, 1866.

Cummins, Margaret. *Leaves from my Port Folio, Original and Selected Together with a Religious Narrative.* St. Louis: William E. Foote, 1860.

Cushman, Mary Ames. *She Wrote It All Down.* New York and London: Charles Scribner's Sons, 1936.

[Daly, Maria Lydig.] *Diary of a Union Lady, 1861–1865.* Edited by Harold Earl Hammond. New York: Funk and Wagnalls, 1962.

Danby, Hope. *In Charming Peking: A Diary of Seven Days Spent in the Old China Capital.* Shanghai: North China Standard, 1930.

Davis, Clara Biddle. *A Winter Journey to the Western Islands, Madeira, Gibraltar, Italy, Egypt, the Holy Land, Turkey, Greece.* Philadelphia: W.B. Wagstaff, 1909.

Davis, Lavinia (Riker). *The Journals of Lavinia Riker Davis.* New York: Privately printed, 1964.

Davis, Mary Elizabeth (Moragne). *The Neglected Thread: A Journal from the Calhoun Community, 1836–1842.* Columbia: University of South Carolina Press, 1951.

Davis, Mary Otis. *The Turning Point: The Dairy of a Debutante.* Privately printed, 1935.

Dawson, Sarah Morgan. *A Confederate Girl's Diary.* Boston and New York: Houghton Mifflin, 1913.

Day, Dorothy. *House of Hospitality.* New York: Sheed and Ward, 1939.

———. *On Pilgrimage: The Sixties.* New York: Curtis Books, 1972.

[Dayton, Maria Annis Tomlison.] *Genealogical Story (Dayton and Tomlinson).* By Laura Dayton Fessenden. Cooperstown, New York: Crist, Scott, and Parshall, 1902.

Dean, Teresa. *White City Chips.* Chicago: Warren Publishing, 1895.

Decker, Mary Bell. *The World We Saw, with Town Hall.* New York: Richard Smith, 1950.

De Laguna, Frederica. *Voyage to Greenland: A Personal Initiation into Anthropology.* New York: W.W. Norton, 1977.

Deming, Barbara. *Prison Notes.* Boston: Beacon Press; New York: Grossman, 1966.

Dewees, Mary (Coburn). *Journal of a Trip from Philadelphia to Lexington in Kentucky, Kept by Mary Coburn Dewees in 1787.* Crawfordsville, Indiana: R.E. Banta, 1936.

Dietz, Nellie Fowler. *A White Woman in a Black Man's Country: Three Thousand Miles up the Nile to Rejaf.* Omaha, Nebraska: Privately printed, 1914.

Dillard, Annie. *Holy the Firm.* New York: Harper and Row, 1977.

———. *Pilgrim at Tinker Creek.* New York: Harpers Magazine Press, 1974.

Djerassi, Norma Lundholm. *Glimpses of China from a Galloping Horse: A Woman's Journal.* New York: Pergamon, 1974.

[Doane, Didama.] *The Cap'n's Wife: The Diary of Didama Kelley Doane of West Harwich, Wife Of Cap'n Uriel Doane, on a Two-Year Voyage with Her Husband aboard the Ship Rival, 1866–1868, and the Log of the Clipper Granger, Uriel Doane, Master . . .* By Albert Joseph George. Syracuse, New York: Syracuse University Press, 1946.

Dodson, Mary L. *Half a Lifetime in Korea.* San Antonio: Naylor, 1952.

[Dow, Peggy.] *The Dealings of God, Man, and the Devil as Exemplified in the Life, Experience and Travels of Lorenzo Dow . . . to Which is Added the Vicissitudes of Life by Peggy Dow.* By Lorenzo Dow. New York: Sheldon, Lamport and Blakeman, 1849.

Downing, Chris, and Gordon Clanton, eds. *Face to Face to Face: An Experiment in Intimacy.* New York: E.P. Dutton, 1975.

Drew, Elizabeth. *Washington Journal: The Events of 1973–74.* New York: Random House, 1975.

[Drinker, Elizabeth.] *Extracts from the Journal of Elizabeth Drinker from 1759–1807 A.D.* Edited by Henry D. Biddle. Philadelphia: J. B. Lippincott, 1889.

[Dunbar-Nelson, Alice.] *Give Us Each Day: The Diary of Alice Dunbar-Nelson.* Edited by Gloria T. Hull. New York: W.W. Norton, 1985.

Dunford, Katherine. *The Journal of an Ordinary Pilgrim.* Philadelphia: Westminster Press, 1954.

Dunham, Katherine. *Katherine Dunham's Journey to Accompong.* New York: Henry Holt, 1946.

[Dunlap, Kate.] *The Mountana Gold Rush Diary of Kate Dunlap.* Edited by J. Lyman Tyler. Denver: F. A. Rosenstock Old West, 1969.

[Dyson, Julia A. (Parker).] *Life and Thought: Or Cherished Memorials of the Late Julia A. Parker Dyson.* Edited by E. Latimer. Boston: Whittemore, Niles and Hall, 1856.

[Eaton, Margaret H., and Vera E. Amey.] *Diary of a Sea Captain's Wife: Tales of Santa Cruz Island.* Edited by Janice Timbrook. Chicago: Rand McNally, 1980.

[Edmondston, Catherine Devereux.] *The Journal of Catherine Devereux Edmondston 1860–66.* Edited by Margaret MacKay Jones. Mebane, North Carolina: Privately printed, 1954.

Elderkin, Kate Denny. *From Tripoli to Marrakesh.* Springfield, Massachusetts: Pond-Ekberg, 1944.

Elliott, L. Louise. *Six Weeks on Horseback through Yellowstone Park.* Rapid City, South Dakota: The Rapid City Journal, 1913.

Elliott, Maud Howe. *Three Generations.* Boston: Little, Brown, 1923.

[Emerson, Ursula Sophia Newell.] *Pioneer Days in Hawaii.* By Oliver P. Emerson. Garden City, New York: Doubleday, Doran, 1928.

Eppes, Susan (Bradford). *Through Some Eventful Years.* Macon, Georgia: J. W. Burke, 1926.

[Erwin, Alice Clementina (Young).] *"Nature Talks": A Book of Days.* Edited by Caroline Harrington. Harbor Springs, Michigan, 1939.

Etnier, Elizabeth. *On Gilbert Head: Maine Days.* Boston: Little, Brown, 1937.

Evans, Mary (Peacock). *The Journal of Mary Peacock: Life, a Century Ago, as Seen in Buffalo and Chautauqua County by a Seventeen Year Old Girl in Boarding School and Elsewhere.* Buffalo, New York: Privately printed, 1938.

Evans, Mary R. *Here and There around the World: Impressions and Notes Taken Day by Day.* La Grange, Illinois, 1930.

[Everett, Anne Gorham.] *Memoir of Anne Gorham Everett; With Extracts from Her Correspondence and Journal.* By Philippa Call Bush. Boston: Privately printed, 1857.

Falk, Ruth. *Women Loving: A Journey toward Becoming an Independent Woman.* New York: Random House, 1975.

[Farmer, Ada.] *Ada Beeson Farmer: A Missionary Heroine in Kuang Si, South China.* By Wilmoth A. Farmer. Atlanta: Foote and Davis, 1912.

[Farnham, Mrs. J.L.] *Log City Days: Two Narratives on the Settlement of Galesburg, Illinois. The Diary of Jerusha Loomis Farnham. Sketch of Log City by Samuel Holyoke.* Galesburg, Illinois: Knox College Centenary Publications, 1937.

Farwell, Ellen (Drummond). *Bird Observations Near Chicago.* Privately printed by John Farwell, 1919.

[Faxon, Mary Josephine.] *Our Own Day.* By Elsie P. Mitchell. Boston: Branden Press, 1976.

Ferland, Carol. *The Long Journey Home.* New York: Knopf, 1980.

Ferris, Mrs. Benjamin G. *The Mormons at Home; With Some Incidents of Travel from Missouri to California, 1852–3.* New York: Dix and Edwards, 1856.

[Fields, Annie.] *Memories of a Hostess: A Chronicle of Eminent Friendships Drawn Chiefly from the Diaries of Mrs. James T. Fields.* By Mark Anthony DeWolfe Howe. Boston: Atlantic Monthly, 1922.

Fisher, Welthy (Honsiger). *Beyond the Moon Gate, Being the Diary of Ten Years in the Interior of the Middle Kingdom.* New York and Cincinnati: Abingdon, 1924.

Fisk, Erma J. *The Peacocks of Baboquivari.* New York: W.W. Norton, 1983.

[Flanner, Janet.] *London Was Yesterday, 1934–1939.* Edited by Irving Drutman. New York: Viking, 1975.

———. *Paris Journal.* Edited by William Shawn. 2 vols. New York: Atheneum, 1965 and 1971.

Fletcher, Ellen Gordon. *A Bride on the Bozeman Trail: The Letters and Diary of Ellen Gordon Fletcher 1866.* Medford, Oregon: Gandee, 1970.

[Fletcher, Sarah Hill.] In *The Diary of Calvin Fletcher,* edited by Gayle Thronbrough. Vol. 1. Indianapolis: Indiana Historical Society, 1972.

Follett, Muriel. *New England Year: A Journal of Vermont Farm Life.* Brattleboro, Vermont: Stephen Daye, 1939.

[Foote, Mary Wilder.] *Caleb and Mary Wilder Foote, Reminiscences and Letters.* By Mary Wilder Foote Tileston. Boston and New York: Houghton Mifflin, 1918.

[Forten, Charlotte L.] *The Journal of Charlotte L. Forten.* Edited by Ray Allen Billington. New York: Dryden, 1953.

[Foster, Emily.] *Journal of Emily Foster.* Edited by Stanley T. Williams and Leonard B. Beach. New York and London: Oxford University Press, 1938.

Francis, Harriet Elizabeth (Tucker). *Across the Meridians, and Fragmentary Letters.* New York: DeVinne, 1887.

Frink, Margaret Ann Alsip. *Journal of the Adventures of a Party of California Gold-Seekers under the Guidance of Mr. Ledyard Frink during a Journey across the Plains from Martinsville, Indiana, to Sacramento, California, from March 30, 1850, to September 7, 1850. From the Original Diary of the Trip Kept by Mrs. Margaret A. Frink.* Oakland, California, 1897.

[Frost, Josephine.] "Loyalists of 1783." In *The Frost Genealogy, Descendants of William Frost of Oyster Bay, New York, Showing Connections Never before Published with the Winthrop, Underhill, Feke, Browne and Wickes Families,* by Josephine C. Frost. New York: F. H. Hitchcock, 1911.

Frost, Lesley. *New Hampshire's Child: The Derry Journals of Lesley Frost.* Albany: State University of New York Press, 1969.

Fry, Elizabeth (Gurney). *Memoir of the Life of Elizabeth Fry with Extracts from Her Journal and Letters.* Philadelphia: H. Longstreth, Moore, 1847–48.

Fuller, Jan. *Space: The Scrapbook of My Divorce.* New York: Arthur Fields, 1973.

Funk, Eleanor, and Wilfred Funk. *A Nostalgic Diary of a Trip We Took These Twenty Five Years Ago.* New York: Privately printed, 1952.

Gag, Wanda. *Growing Pains: Diaries and Drawings for the Years 1908–1917.* New York: Coward McCann, 1940.

Gallagher, Rory. *Lady in Waiting: An Intimate Journal of a Labor of Love.* New York: Stephen Daye, 1943.

[Galloway, Grace (Growden).] *Diary.* Edited by Raymond C. Werner. New York: New York Times, 1971.

Garcia, Virginia May. *Journal of a Young Girl: Being the Impressions of an "Innocent Abroad" and Selected Poems.* Chicago: Privately printed, 1929.

Gardiner, Margaret. *Leaves from a Young Girl's Diary: The Journal of Margaret Gardiner, 1840.* New Haven: Tuttle, Morehouse and Taylor, 1925.

[Gardner, Isabella Stewart.] *Isabella Stewart Gardner and Fenway Court.* By Morris Carter. Boston and New York: Houghton Mifflin, 1925.

Gebhard, Anne Laura (Munro). *Rural Parish! A Year from the Journal of Anna Laura Gebhard.* New York: Abingdon-Cokesbury, 1947.

Gelhorn, Martha. *Travels with Myself and Another.* New York: Dodd, Mead, 1979.

Gibbons, Hannah Pusey. *Memoir of Hannah Gibbons, Late of West Chester, Pennsylvania.* Philadelphia: William H. Pile's Sons, 1873.

Gilman, Marilyn. *Diary of a Woman Doctor.* Zebra, 1981.

Gladding, Mrs. E.N. *Leaves from an Invalid's Journal and Poems.* Providence, Rhode Island: George H. Whitney, 1858.

Glaspell, Kate Eldridge. *A Diary of a Trip Abroad in 1914 When All the World was at Peace and Every Nation Loved the United States of America.* Philadelphia: Dorrance, 1942.

Glynn, Jeanne Davis. *Diary of a New Mother.* St. Meinrad, Indiana: Abby, 1966.

Go Ask Alice: A Real Diary. Englewood Cliffs, New Jersey: Prentice Hall, 1971.

Goldberg, Ruth L. Polhemus. *Ring-around-the-World*. New York: Pageant, 1963.

[Goodnough, Ellen.] In *The Oneidas*, by Julia K. Bloomfield. New York: Alden Brothers, 1907.

Gordon, Julia Weber. *My Country School Diary*. New York: Dell, 1946.

Gorres, Ida Friederike. *Broken Lights: Diaries and Letters 1951–1959. Westminster, Maryland: Newman, 1964*.

[Graham, Bettie Ann.] *Journal of Bettie Ann Graham, October 18, 1860–June 21, 1862. Philadelphia, Pennsylvania, and White County, Virginia.* Edited by Anne Ingles. New York: A. Ingles, 1978.

Graham, C.[ourtney] P. *Journale 1 and 2.* Keswick, Virginia: C.P. Graham Press, 1976.

———. *Journale 5 and 6.* Keswick, Virginia: C.P. Graham Press, 1978.

———. *Poem Stills from Movie Earth with Additions of Poemstills from Journale Notes.* Virginia: Privately printed, 1974.

Graham, Isabella (Marshall). *The Power of Faith: Exemplified in the Life and Writings of Mrs. Isabella Graham, of New York.* New York: Kirk and Mercein, 1819.

Graham, Martha. *The Notebooks of Martha Graham.* New York: Harcourt Brace Jovanovich, 1973.

Gray, Lucy. *Diary of Hope: Reflections of an Alcoholic's Wife.* Grand Rapids, Michigan: Baker Book House, 1970.

Gray, Millie. *The Diary of Millie Gray, 1832–1840 (nee Mildred Richards Stone, wife of Col. Wm. Fairfax Gray) Recording Her Family Life Before, During and after Col. William F. Gray's Journey to Texas in 1835; and the Small Journal Giving Particulars of all that Occurred During the Family's Voyage to Texas in 1838.* Houston: Fletcher Young, 1967.

[Green, Kate.] "Abortion Journal." In *Believing Everything: An Anthology of New Writing,* edited by Margaret Logue and Laurence Sutin. Minneapolis: Holy Cow!, 1980.

Greenleaf, Mary Coombs. *Life and Letters of Miss Mary C. Greenleaf, Missionary to the Chickasaw Indians.* Boston: Massachusetts Sabbath School Society, 1858.

Greenlee, Grace E. *As We Were Journeying: The Hawaiian Islands, Japan, China, Siam, Java and India, as seen from a Girl's Point of View.* Chicago: Blakely, 1900.

Greenwood, Grace [pseud.]. *New Life in New Lands: Notes of Travel.* New York: J.B. Ford, 1873.

Grenfel, Helen. *A Brief Sketch of the Life and Works of Helen Thatcher Loring Grenfel.* Denver: Smith Brooks Printing, 1939.

[Grimké, Angelina.] *The Grimké Sisters: Sarah and Angelina Grimké, the First American Women Advocates of Abolition and Women's Rights.* By Catherine H. Birney. Boston: Lee and Shepard, 1885.

[Gunn, Elizabeth.] *Records of a California Family: Journals and Letters of Lewis C. Gunn and Elizabeth Le Breton Gunn.* Edited by Anna Lee Marston. San Diego: Privately printed, 1928.

[Habersham, Josephine Clay.] *Ebb Tide: As Seen through the Diary of Josephine Clay Habersham, 1863.* Edited by Spencer Bidwell King, Jr. Athens: University of Georgia Press, 1958.

Hadley, Martha E. *The Alaskan Diary of a Pioneer Quaker Missionary.* Mt. Dora, Florida: Loren S. Hadley, 1969.

Hahn, Emily. *Congo Solo: Misadventures Two Degrees North.* Indianapolis: Bobbs-Merrill, 1933.

Haight, Sarah. *The Ralston-Fry Wedding and the Wedding Journey to Yosemite: From the Diary of Miss Sarah Haight.* San Francisco: Grabhorn, 1961.

Halden, Margaret. *First Year Out: The Diary of a Special School Teacher.* London and New York: Thomas Nelson and Sons, 1943.

Hale, Betty May. *My Trip to Europe, 1937.* San Francisco: Wallace Kikbee and Son, 1938.

Hall, Sarah. *Daily Doings of a Voyage around the World.* Privately printed, 1905.

[Hall, Sharlot Mabridth.] *Sharlot Hall on the Arizona Strip: A Diary of a Journey through Northern Arizona in 1911.* Edited by Gregory Crampton. Flagstaff, Arizona: Northland, 1975.

Halsell, Grace. *Bessie Yellowhair.* New York: William Morrow, 1973.

——. *Soul Sister.* New York: World, 1969.

Halsey, Margaret. *This Demi-Paradise: A Westchester Diary.* New York: Simon and Schuster, 1960.

——. *With Malice toward Some.* New York: Simon and Schuster, 1938.

Hamilton-Merritt, Jane. *A Meditator's Diary: A Western Woman's Unique Experience in Thailand Temples.* New York: Harper and Row, 1976.

Hammond, Susan S. *Landfalls Remembered: The Story of Six Summer Cruises in Mediterranean Seas and One Trans Atlantic Voyage.* New York: Barnes, 1963.

[Hansberry, Lorraine.] In *To Be Young, Gifted and Black: Lorraine Hansberry in Her Own Words,* edited by Robert Nemiroff. Englewood Cliffs, New Jersey: Prentice Hall, 1969.

[Hardin, Elizabeth Pendleton.] *The Private World of Lizzie Hardin: A Confederate Girl's Diary of the War in Kentucky, Virginia, Tennessee, Alabama, and Georgia.* Edited by G. Glenn Clift. Frankfort: Kentucky Historical Society, 1963.

Harkness, Ruth. *Pangoan Diary.* New York: Creative Age, 1942.

Harrison, Juanita. *My Great Wide Beautiful World.* New York: Macmillan, 1936.

Harrison, Michelle. *A Woman in Residence: A Physician's Account of Her Training in Obstetrics and Gynecology.* New York: Random House, 1982.

Hart, Marion Rice. *Who Called That Lady a Skipper? The Strange Voyage of a Woman Navigator.* New York: Vanguard, 1938.

Harwood, Michael, and Mary Durant. *A Country Journal.* New York: Dodd, Mead, 1974.

Hathaway, Katharine (Butler). *The Journal and Letters of the Little Locksmith.* New York: Coward McCann, 1946.

Havens, Catherine Elizabeth. *Diary of a Little Girl in Old New York, 1849–50.* New York: Henry Collins Brown, 1919.

[Hawk, Ellen Maria.] *My Mother's Diary and I.* Miami Beach, Florida, 1951.

Hawkins, Frances Pockman. *The Logic of Action: From a Teacher's Notebook.* Boulder: University of Colorado Press, 1969; New York: Pantheon, 1974.

[Hawthorne, Sophie Amelia (Peabody).] *"The Cuba Journal" of Sophia Peabody Hawthorne.* Edited by Claire Badaracco. Ann Arbor, Michigan: University Microfilms, 1978.

——. *Nathaniel Hawthorne and His Wife.* Edited by Julian Hawthorne. 2 vols. New York and Boston: Houghton Mifflin, 1891.

——. *Notes in England and Italy.* New York: G.P. Putnam's, 1869.

Heard, Harriet. *Diary.* Boston: Privately printed at the Merrymount Press, 1942.

[Heath, Betsey.] In *The Crafts Family: A Genealogical and Biographical History of the Descendants of Griffin and Alice Craft, of Roxbury, Mass., 1630–1890,* by James M. and William F. Crafts. Northampton, Massachusetts: Gazette, 1893.

Heckman, Hazel. *Island Year.* Seattle: University of Washington Press, 1972.

Hellman, Lillian. *An Unfinished Woman: A Memoir.* Boston: Little, Brown, 1969.

[Hemenway, Ruth V.] *Ruth V. Hemenway: A Memoir of Revolutionary China, 1924–1941.* Edited by Fred W. Drake. Amherst: University of Massachusetts Press, 1977.

Herdon, Sarah. *Days on the Road: Crossing the Plains 1865.* New York: Burr Printing House, 1902.

Hershaw, Fay McKenne, and Flaurience Sengstacke Collins. *Around the World with Hershaw and Collins.* Boston: Meador Publishing, 1938.

Hewitt, Frances. *Diary of a Refugee.* New York: Moffat, Yard, 1910.

[Heywood, Martha Spence.] *Not by Bread Alone: The Journal of Martha Spence Heywood, 1850–56.* Edited by Juanita Brooks. Salt Lake City: Utah State Historical Society, 1978.

Higbee, Lucy Ann. *The Diary of Lucy Ann Higbee, 1837.* Cleveland, Ohio: Privately printed, 1924.

[Hill, Sarah Jane Full.] *Mrs. Hill's Journal: Civil War Reminiscences.* Edited by Mark M. Krug. Chicago: Lakeside, 1980.

[Hillard, Harriet (Low).] *My Mother's Journal: A Young Lady's Diary of Five Years Spent in Manila, Macao, and the Cape of Good Hope from 1829–1834.* Edited by Katharine Hillard. Boston: George Ellis, 1900.

Hitchcock, Mary E. *Two Women in the Klondike: The Story of a Journey to the Goldfields of Alaska.* New York: G. P. Putnam's, 1899.

[Hobbie, Hannah.] *Memoir of Hobbie Hannah; or, Christian Activity, and Triumph in Suffering.* Edited by Robert G. Armstrong. New York: American Tract Society, 1837.

Hogan, Louise Eleanor. *A Study of a Child.* New York: Harper and Brothers, 1898.

Holley, Mary Austin. *Mary Austin Holley: The Texas Diary, 1835–1838.* Austin: University of Texas Press, 1965.

Holman, Lucia Ruggles. *Journal of Lucia Ruggles Holman.* Berbice Pauli Bishop Special Publications, No. 17. Honolulu: The Museum, 1931.

Holmes, Emma. *The Diary of Miss Emma Holmes, 1861–1866.* Baton Rouge: Louisiana State University Press, 1979.

[Holmes, Sarah Katherine (Stone).] *Brokenburn: The Journal of Kate Stone, 1861–1868.* Edited by John Q. Anderson, Jr. Baton Rouge: Louisiana State University Press, 1955.

Hoover, Helen. *The Gift of the Deer: Pen and Ink Drawings from Life by Adrian Hoover.* New York: Knopf, 1966.

————. *The Years of the Forest: Pen and Ink Drawings from Life by Adrian Hoover.* New York: Knopf, 1976.

Hope, Mary. *Towards Evening.* New York: Sheed and Ward, 1955.

[Hopkins, Louisa.] In *The Life and Letters of Elizabeth Prentiss, Author of Stepping Heavenward,* edited by George L. Prentiss. New York: Randolph, 1882.

Horner, Joyce. *That Time of Year: A Chronicle of Life in a Nursing Home.* Amherst: University of Massachusetts Press, 1982.

Horney, Karen. *The Adolescent Diaries of Karen Horney.* New York: Basic Books, 1980.

Hotchkis, Katharine Bixby. *Trip with Father, 1916.* Balboa, California: California Historical Society, 1963.

Houghton, Adelaide (Louise) Wellington. *The London Years: The Diary of Adelaide Wellington Houghton, 1925–1929.* New York: Privately printed at the Spiral Press, 1963.

Howard, Alice (Sturtevant). *The Yacht "Alice." Planning and Building. A Cruise from New York to Miami through the Inland Water Way.* Boston: Charles E. Lauriat, 1926.

[Howe, Julia Ward.] *Julia Ward Howe, 1819–1910.* By Laura Elizabeth Howe Richards and Maud Howe Elliot. 2 vols. Boston and New York: Houghton Mifflin, 1915.

Hubbs, Rebecca. *A Memoir of Rebecca Hubbs, A Minister of the Gospel in the Society of Friends, Late of Woodstown, N. J.* Philadelphia: Friends Book Store, n.d.

Hughes, Eileen Lanouette. *On the Set of Fellini Satyricon: A Behind-the-Scenes Diary.* New York: William Morrow, 1971.

Hull, Josephine. *Dear Josephine: The Theatrical Career of Josephine Hull.* Norman: University of Oklahoma Press, 1963.

Hunt, Sarah Morey. *Journal of the Life and Religious Labors of Sarah Hunt, Late of West Grove, Chester County, Pennsylvania.* Philadelphia: Friends' Book Association, 1892.

[Huntington, Susan Mansfield.] *Memoirs of the Late Mrs. Susan Huntington, of Boston, Mass., Consisting Principally of Extracts from Her Journal and Letters with the Sermon Occasioned by her Death.* By Benjamin B. Wisner. Boston: Crocker and Brewster, 1826.

Hyde, Nancy Maria. *The Writings of Nancy Maria Hyde, of Norwich, Conn., Connected with a Sketch of Her Life.* Norwich, Connecticut: Russell Hubbard, 1816.

[Ingalls, Grace.] "Diary." In *The Story of the Ingalls,* by William Anderson, Mansfield, Missouri: Laura Ingalls Wilder Home Association, 1967.

Ireland, Tom, and Molly Ireland. *Mostly Mules.* San Cristobel, New Mexico: Laura Foundation, 1974.

[Jackson, Nannie Stillwell.] *Vinegar Pie and Chicken Bread: A Woman's Diary of Life in the Rural South, 1890–1891.* Edited by Margaret Jones Bolsterli. Fayetteville: University of Arkansas Press, 1982.

[Jackson, Rebecca Cox.] *Gifts of Power: The Writings of Rebecca Jackson, Black Visionary and Shaker Eldress.* Edited by Jean Humez. Amherst: University of Massachusetts Press, 1981.

Jacobs, Susan. *On Stage: The Making of a Broadway Play.* New York: Knopf, 1972.

[Jacobs, Victoria.] *Diary of a San Diego Girl, 1856.* Edited by Sylvia Arden. Santa Monica, California: Norton B. Stern, 1974.

[James, Alice.] *Alice James: Her Brothers, Her Journal.* Edited by Anna Robeson Burr. New York: Dodd, Mead, 1934.

[———.] *The Diary of Alice James.* Edited by Leon Edel. New York: Dodd, Mead, 1964.

Janis, Elsie. *The Big Show: My Six Months with the American Expeditionary Forces.* New York: Cosmopolitan, 1919.

Jay, Cornelia. *The Diary of Cornelia Jay, 1861–1873.* Rye, New York: Privately printed, 1924.

Jefferson, Lara [pseud.]. *These Are My Sisters: An "Insandectomy."* Tulsa, Oklahoma: Vickers, 1947.

Jervey, Susan R., and Charlotte St. John Ravenel. *Two Diaries: From Middle St. John's, Berkeley South Carolina, February–May, 1865. Journals Kept by Miss Susan R. Jervey and Miss Charlotte St. John Ravenel, at Northampton and Pooshee Plantations, and Reminiscences of Mrs. [Waring] Henagan with Two Contemporary Reports from Federal Officials.* Pinopolis, South Carolina: St. John's Hunting Club, 1921.

Johnson, Claudia Alta (Tyler). *A White House Diary [by] Lady Bird Johnson.* New York: Holt, Rinehart and Winston, 1970.

Johnson, Edith E. *Leaves from a Doctor's Diary.* Palo Alto, California: Pacific Books, 1954.

Johnson, Mrs. *A New England Pioneer: "The Captivity of Mrs. Johnson." The Story of Her Life with an Account of her Capture and Experiences During Four Years with the French and Indians 1754–1758.* Woodstock, Vermont: Elm Tree Press, 1926. [1841].

Johnston, Adelia [*Antionette Field*]. *Diary.* Cleveland, Ohio: Korner and Wood, 1912.

[Jones, Carolyn.] Greene, Herbert, and Carolyn Jones. *Diary of a Food Addict.* New York: Grosset and Dunlap, 1974.

Jones, Sybil. *Voyage to Liberia.* Philadelphia: Porter and Coates, 1889.

Judd, Laura Fish. *Honolulu: Sketches of the Life, Social, Political and Religious, in the Hawaiian Islands from 1828 to 1861. With a Supplementary Sketch of Events to the Present Time (1860).* Honolulu: Honolulu Star Bulletin, 1928.

[Judson, Emily Chubbuck.] *The Life and Letters of Mrs. Emily C. Judson.* By A.C. Kendrick. New York: Sheldon, 1860.

———. *Memoir of Sarah B. Judson, Member of the American Mission to Burmah.* By Fanny Forester [pseud.]. New York: Colby, 1848.

Judson, Jane C. *A Memoir of Jane C. Judson.* Philadelphia: American Sunday School Union, 1836.

Kane, Elizabeth Dennistoun Wood. *Twelve Mormon Houses Visited in Succession on a Journey through Utah to Arizona.* Philadelphia, 1874.

[Kathie.] *Kathie's Diary: Leaves from an Old, Old Diary, Written by Kathie.* Edited by Margaret Eggleston. New York: George H. Doran, 1926.

[Keays, Elizabeth.] *The Saga of "Auntie" Stone and Her Cabin: Elizabeth Hickok Robbins Stone 1801–1895. A Pioneer Woman Who Built and Owned the First Dwelling, Operated the First Hotel, Built the First Flour Mill and Erected the First Brick Kiln in the City of Fort Collins, Colorado with the Overland Diary of Elizabeth Parke Keays.* Edited by Nolie Mumey. Boulder, Colorado: Johnson, 1964.

Keller, Helen. *Helen Keller's Journal, 1936–1937.* Garden City, New York: Doubleday, Doran, 1938.

Kemble, Frances Anne. *Journal of Residence on a Georgia Plantation in 1838–39.* New York: Harper and Brothers, 1864.

Kennedy, Margaret. *Where Stands a Winged Sentry.* New Haven: Yale University Press, 1941.

Kenny, May. *Well Trodden Paths.* Atlanta: Autocrat 1896.

Kidder, Mary Bigelow. *No Limits but the Sky: The Journal of an Archaeologist's Wife in Peru.* Cambridge: Harvard University Press, 1942.

King, Elizabeth (Taber). *Memoir of Elizabeth T. King; with Extracts from Her Letters and Journal.* Baltimore: Armstrong and Berry, 1859.

King, Josephine. *The King Diaries.* New York: McGraw Hill, 1967.

Kirkpatrick, Katharine. *Mountain Journey.* Birmingham, Alabama, 1948.

Kirkpatrick, Mary. *Around the World on the Laconia.* 1925.

[Klasner, Lily.] *My Girlhood among Outlaws.* Edited by Eve Ball. Tucson: University of Arizona Press, 1972.

[Knapp, Emma (Benedict).] *Hic Habitat Felicita, a Volume of Recollections and Letters, by Mrs. Shepherd Knapp (Emma Benedict).* Boston: W.B. Clarke, 1910.

Knapp, Mrs. M.W. *West Indies, Windward Islands, Demerara, Diary Letters.* Cincinnati: God's Revivalist Office, 1918.

[Knickerbocker, Frances Wentworth Cutler.] *The Minister's Daughter: A Time-Exposure Photograph of the Years 1903–04.* Edited by Charles H. Knickerbocker. Philadelphia: Dorrance, 1974.

Knight, Sarah Kemble. *The Journals of Madame Knight and Rev. Mr. Buckingham.* New York: Wilder and Campbell, 1825.

[Koren, Elisabeth.] *The Diary of Elisabeth Koren, 1853–1855.* Edited and translated by David T. Nelson. Northfield, Minnesota: Norwegian-American Historical Association, 1955.

Kosover, Toni. *The Diary of a New York Career Girl.* New York: Bantam, 1974.

[Laing, Caroline Hyde Butler.] *A Family Heritage: Letters and Journals of Caroline Hyde Butler Laing.* Edited by Edith N. S. Ward. East Orange, New Jersey: Abbey, 1957.

Lamborn, Emma Taylor. *Reminiscences of My First Year in Europe.* Biddle, 1911.

Lamont, Corliss, and Margaret Lamont. *Russia Day by Day: A Travel Diary.* New York: Covici, Friede, 1933.

Lamont, Florence (Corliss). *Far Eastern Diary, 1920.* Edited by Corliss Lamont. New York: Horizon, 1951.

[Lane, Rose Wilder, and Helen Dore Boyleston.] *Travels with Zenobia: Paris to Albania by Model T. Ford. A Journal . . .* Edited by William Holtz. Columbia: University of Missouri Press, 1983.

[Larcom, Lucy.] *Lucy Larcom: Life, Letters, and Diary.* Edited by Daniel Dulany Addison. Boston and New York: Houghton Mifflin, 1894.

Larsen, Gladys. *Lizbeth Jane's Own Diary: The Private Life of a Little Girl.* New York: Exposition Press, 1965.

[Lawrence, Mary Chipman.] *The Captain's Best Mate: The Journal of Mary Chipman Lawrence* on the Whaler Addison, 1856–1860. Edited by Stanton Garner. Providence, Rhode Island: Brown University Press, 1920.

Leadbetter, Annie. *Mother's Diary: An Account of a Trip around the World through Australiasia.* Portland, Oregon: Keystone, 1920.

[Leavitt, Sarah Studevant.] *History of Sarah Studevant Leavitt, from Her Journal, 1865.* Edited by Juanita Leavitt Pulsigher. 1919.

Le Conte, Caroline Eaton. *Yo Semite, 1878: Adventures of N. and C.; Journal and Drawings by Carrie E. Le Conte.* San Francisco: Book Club of California, 1944.

[Le Conte, Emma.] *When the World Ended: The Diary of Emma Le Conte.* Edited by Earl Shenck Miers. New York: Oxford University Press, 1957.

Lee, Andrea. *Russian Journal.* New York: Random House, 1981.

Lee, Eva Ballerini. *Her Recollections.* Boston: Merrymount Press, 1935.

[Lee, Florida (Clemson).] *A Rebel Came Home: The Diary of Florida Clemson Tells of Her Wartime Adventures in Yankeeland, 1863–64, Her Trip Home to South Carolina, and Life in the South during the Last Few Months of the Civil War and the Year Following.* Edited by Charles M. McGee, Jr. and Ernest M. Lander, Jr. Columbia: University of South Carolina Press, 1961.

Lee, Laurel. *Mourning into Dancing.* New York: E.P. Dutton, 1984.

———. *Signs of Spring.* New York: E.P. Dutton, 1980.

———. *Walking through the Fire: A Hospital Journal.* New York: E.P. Dutton, 1977.

[Lee, Margaret Cabot.] *Letters and Diaries of Margaret Cabot Lee.* Edited by Marian C. Putnam, Amy Cabot, and Joseph Lee. Privately printed, 1923.

[Lee, Mary.] *Henry and Mary Lee, Letters and Journals, with Other Family Papers, 1802–1860.* By Frances Rollins Morse. Boston: Privately printed, 1926.

Lee, Nancy Howell. *The Search for an Abortionist.* Chicago: University of Chicago Press, 1969.

[Le Grand, Julia.] *The Journal of Julia Le Grand, New Orleans, 1862–1863.* Edited by Kate Mason Rowl and Mrs. Morris L. Croxall. Richmond, Virginia: Everett Waddey, 1911.

Lemon, Sister Adele Marie. *To You from Hawaii.* Albany, New York: Fort Orange Press, 1950.

Lenski, Lois. *Journey into Childhood: The Autobiography of Lois Lenski.* Philadelphia: J. B. Lippincott, 1972.

Lesley, Susan. *Life and Letters of Peter and Susan Lesley.* New York: G.P. Putnam's, 1909.

Lewis, Abigail. *An Interesting Condition: The Diary of a Pregnant Woman.* Garden City, New York: Doubleday, 1950.

Lewis, Carola Regester. *Ramblings.* Parsons, West Virginia: McClain, 1974.

Lindberg, Anne (Morrow). *Bring Me a Unicorn: Christmas in Mexico, 1927* New York: Harcourt Brace Jovanovich, 1971.

———. *Hour of Gold, Hour of Lead: Diaries and Letters of Anne Morrow Lindberg 1929–1932.* New York: Harcourt Brace Jovanovich, 1973.

———. *Locked Rooms and Open Doors: Diaries and Letters of Anne Morrow Lindberg 1933–1935.* New York: Harcourt Brace Jovanovich, 1974.

———. *The Flower and the Nettle: Diaries and Letters 1936–1939* New York: Harcourt Brace Jovanovich, 1976.

Lindley, Elizabeth. *The Diary of a Book Agent.* New York: Broadway, 1911.

[Lindsay, Elizabeth Dick.] *Diary of Elizabeth Dick Lindsay, Feb. 1, 1837–May 3, 1861.* Edited by Jo White Linn. Guilford County, North Carolina: Salisbury Publishing, 1975.

[Livingston, Anne Home Shippen.] *Nancy Shippen: Her Book; The International Romance of a Young Lady of Fashion of Colonial Philadelphia, with Letters to Her and about Her.* Edited by Ethel Armes. Philadelphia and London: J.B. Lippincott, 1935.

[Lomax, Elizabeth Lindsay.] *Leaves from an Old Washington Diary, 1854–63.* Edited by Lindsay Lomax Wood. New York: E.P. Dutton, 1943.

[Longfellow, Fanny Appleton.] *Mrs. Longfellow: Selected Letters and Journals of Fanny Appleton Longfellow.* Edited by Edward Wagenknecht. New York: Longmans, Green, 1956.

[Longstreth, Mary Anna.] *Memoir of Mary Anna Longstreth by an Old Pupil, with a Sketch of Her Work for Hampton.* By Helen Ludlow. Philadelphia: J.B. Lippincott, 1886.

Longyear, Mary Hawley (Beecher). *The History of a House Built by Squire Bagley, in Amesbury, Massachusetts. Its Founder, Family and Guests.* Brookline, Massachusetts: Zion Research Foundation, [1948].

Loomis, Vivienne. *Vivienne: The Life and Suicide of an Adolescent Girl.* New York: New American Library, 1982.

Lord, Caroline M. *Diary of a Village Library.* Somersworth, New Hampshire: New Hampshire Publishing, 1971.

Lord, Louisa. *Miss Louisa Lord's Diary of a Voyage on the Ship St. Petersburg, 1840.* New York: Ivy, 1975.

Lorde, Audre. *The Cancer Journals.* Argyle, New York: Spinsters Ink, 1980.

Loughborough, Mary Ann Webster. *My Cave Life in Vicksburg. With Letters of Trial and Travel. By a Lady.* New York: D. Appleton, 1864.

Love, Deborah. *Annaghkeen.* New York: Random House, 1970.

Low, Ann Marie. *Dust Bowl Diary.* Lincoln: University of Nebraska Press, 1984.

Lowden, Florence. *A Travel Diary: Egypt, Palestine and Greece, 1929.* Chicago: Lakeside, 1929.

[Lowell, Ellen Bancroft.] In *Arthur Theodore Lyman and Ella Lyman: Letters and Journals with an Account of Those They Loved and were Descended From,* by Ella Lyman Cabot. Menasha, Wisconsin: George Banta, 1932.

[Lowell, Josephine.] *The Philanthropic Work of Josephine Shaw Lowell, Containing a Biographical Sketch of Her Life, together with a Selection of Her Public Papers and Private Letters.* By William Rhinelander Stewart. New York: MacMillan, 1911.

Lowry, Jean. *A Journal of the Captivity of Jean Lowry and Her Children, Giving an Account of her Being Taken by Indians, the 1st of April 1756, from William McCords in Rocky Spring Settlement in Pennsylvania.* Philadelphia: William Bradford, 1760.

Lukens, Matilda Barnes. *The Inland Passage: A Journal of a Trip to Alaska.* 1889.

Lundstrom, Connie. *Connie's Prison Diary.* Sisseton, South Dakota: Message for America Evangelical Association, 1977.

[Lyman, Sarah.] *Sarah Joiner Lyman of Hawaii—Her Own Story.* Edited by Margaret Greer Martin. Hilo, Hawaii: Lyman House Memorial Museum, 1970.

[Lyon, Adelia.] *Reminiscences of the Civil War, from the War Correspondence of Colonel William P. Lyon and from Personal Letters and Diary by Mrs. Adelia C. Lyon.* Edited by William P. Lyon, Jr. San Jose, California: Muirson and Wright, 1907.

MacLane, Mary. *I, Mary MacLane: A Diary of Human Days.* New York: Frederick A. Stokes, 1917.

——. *The Story of Mary MacLane, By Herself.* Chicago: Herbert S. Stone, 1902.

[McCormick, Anne (O'Hare).] *Vatican Journal, 1921–1954.* Edited by Marion Turner Sheehan. New York: Farrar, Straus and Cudahy, 1957.

McDonald, Corenelia (Peake). *A Diary with Reminiscences of the War and Refugee Life in the Shenandoah Valley, 1860–1865.* Nashville, Tennessee: Cullom and Ghertner, 1935.

McGuire, Judith White (Brokenbrough). *Diary of a Southern Refugee, During the War by a Lady of Virginia.* New York: E.J. Hale, 1867.

McKay, Alice. *Diary.* Privately printed by Alice McKay, 1982.

McKenney, Ruth. *Industrial Valley.* New York: Harcourt Brace, 1939.

McLean, Ethel Louise. *A Gentle Jehu in Japan.* New York: Dodd, Mead, 1912.

McNeeley, Sylvia. *Diary of Sylvia McNeeley.* New York and Toronto: Longmans, Green, 1931.

[Magoffin, Susan Shelby.] *Down the Santa Fe Trail and into Mexico: The Diary of Susan Shelby*

Maggofin, 1846–1847. Edited by Stella M. Drumm. New Haven: Yale University Press, 1926.

Mains, Karen Burton. *The Fragile Curtain.* Elgin, Illinois: David C. Cook, 1981.

Malina, Judith. *The Enormous Despair.* New York: Random House, 1972.

[Malone, Blondelle.] *Enigma: The Career of Blondelle Malone in Art and Society, 1879–1951, as Told in her Letters and Diaries.* By Louise Jones DuBose. Columbia: University of South Carolina Press, 1963.

Manalle, Ivor [pseud.]. *Ivor Manalee. Postscript to Life.* Caldwell, Idaho: Caxton, 1938.

Mann, Etta Donnan. *Four Years in the Governor's Mansion of Virginia, 1910–1914.* Richmond, Virginia: Dietz, 1937.

Manning, Nichola. *Historical Document.* Long Beach, California: Applezaba Press, 1982.

Marburg, Winifred Carmer. *"Vagabonding de Luxe": A Journal of Carefree Days around the World.* Berkeley Heights, New Jersey: Oriole, 1937.

Martin, Anna [pseud.]. *Around and about Alaska.* New York: Vantage, 1959.

Martin, Martha. *O Rugged Land of Gold.* New York: Macmillan, 1953.

Martin, Sarah. *Diary Notes and Club Papers.* Boston: George Ellis, 1916.

Mather, Helen. *One Summer in Hawaii.* New York: Cassell, 1891.

Maughan, Mary. *Journal of Mary Ann Weston Maughan.* Daughters of Utah Pioneers, 1959.

Maverick, Mary Ann Adams. *Memoirs of Mary A. Maverick.* San Antonio: Alamo, 1921.

[May, Anna.] *Journal of Anna May, February–July, 1857.* Edited by George Washington Robinson. Cambridge, Massachusetts: Privately printed, 1941.

[(Mayne), Isabella Maud Rittenhouse.] *Maud.* Edited by Richard Lee Strout. New York: Macmillan, 1939.

[Mayo, Abigail DeHart.] *An American Lady in Paris, 1828–1829: The Diary of Mrs. John Mayo.* Edited by Mary May Crenshaw. Boston and New York: Houghton Mifflin, 1927.

Mendenhall, Abby Grant Swift. *Some Extracts from the Personal Diary of Mrs. R.J. Mendenhall; also Press Notices, and Some Early and Later Correspondence to Her, by Her, etc.* Minneapolis, [c. 1900.].

Méras, Phyllis. *First Spring: A Martha's Vineyard Journal.* Riverside, Connecticut: Chatham, 1972.

Merwin, Loretta L. Wood. *Three Years in Chili: By a Lady of Ohio.* Columbus, Ohio: Follett, Foster, 1863.

Meyer, Agnes (Ernst). *Journey through Chaos.* New York: Harcourt Brace, 1944.

[Meyer, Lucy Rider.] *High Adventure: Life of Lucy Rider Meyer.* By Isabelle Horton. New York and Cincinnati: Methodist Book Concern, 1928.

Mickelson, Mary Bikke. *The Northern Light: An American Looks at Finland and Scandinavia.* New York: Exposition Press, 1955.

Milby, Maggie. *Eastward Ho! The Notes of a Globe Trotter.* Houston: Gray Dillaye, 1910.

Miles, Judith. *Journal from an Obscure Place.* Minneapolis: Bethany Fellowship House, 1978.

Miller, Fannie de C. *Snap Notes of an Eastern Trip, from the Diary of Fannie De C. Miller.* San Francisco: S. Carson, 1892.

[Mitchell, Maria.] *Maria Mitchell: Life, Letters and Journals.* Edited by Phebe Mitchell Kendell. Boston: Lee and Shephard, 1896.

Mitchell, Suzanne. *My Own Woman: The Diary of an Analysis.* New York: Horizon, 1973.

Moore, Harriet J. *Memoir and Letters of Harriet J. Moore.* Philadelphia: Merrihew and Thompson's, 1856.

Moore, Jessie T. *Twenty Years in Assam, Or, Leaves from My Journal.* Nowgang, Assam, India: Baptist Mission, 1901.

[Moore, Nancy E.] *The Journal of Eldress Nancy, Kept at the South Union, Kentucky, Shaker Colony. August 15, 1861–September 4, 1864.* Edited by Mary Julia Neal. Nashville, Tennessee: Parthenon, 1963.

Moragne, Mary. *The Neglected Thread: A Journal from the Calhoun Community 1836–42.* Columbia: University of South Carolina Press, 1951.

Morden, Florence. *From the Field Notes of Florence H. Morden.* Privately printed by William J. Morden, 1940.

Morris, Margaret. *Private Journal Kept During a Portion of the Revolutionary War, for the Amusement of a Sister by Margaret Morris of Burlington, New Jersey.* Philadelphia: Privately printed, 1836.

Morrison, Ann. *Diary of Ann Morrison: Those Were the Days.* Boise, Idaho: Em-Kayan, 1951.

Morrison, Helen. *Okanogan to Seattle in 1918.* Fairfield, Washington: Ye Galleon, 1972.

Morrison, Mrs. Terry. *Highcroft, 1895–1952.* 1952.

Morrow, Elizabeth (Cutter). *The Mexican Years: Leaves from the Diary of Elizabeth Cutter Morrow.* New York: Spiral Press, 1953.

Morton, Margaret Gray. *Around the World.* Privately printed, 1931.

[Mott, Lucretia Coffin.] *James and Lucretia Mott: Life and Letters, by their Granddaughter.* By Anna Davis Hallowell. Boston and New York: Houghton Mifflin, 1884.

————. *Slavery and 'The Woman Question'; Lucretia Mott's Diary of Her Visit to Great Britain to Attend the World's Anti-Slavery Convention of 1840.* Edited by Frederick B. Tolles. Haverford, Pennsylvania: Friends Historical Association, 1952.

[Mugford, Sarah S.] *Triumph in Trial: A Memorial of Sarah S. Mugford, of Salem, Mass.* By S. M. Worcester. Boston: Crocker and Brewster, 1862.

Napear, Peggy. *Brain Child: A Mother's Diary.* New York: Harper and Row, 1974.

Nef, Elinor (Castle). *In Search of the American Tradition.* New York: University Publishers, 1959.

[————.] *Letters and Notes.* Edited by John U. Nef. Los Angeles: The W. Ritchie Press, 1953.

Neilson, Eliza Lucy Irion. *Lucy's Journal.* Greenwood, Mississippi: Baff, 1967.

Nesbitt, Victoria Henrietta (Kugler). *White House Diary, by F.D.R.'s Housekeeper.* Garden City, New York: Doubleday, 1948.

Newberry, Julia Rosa. *Julia Newberry's Diary.* New York: W.W. Norton, 1933.

Newell, Fanny. *Memoirs of Fanny Newell, Written by Herself.* Springfield, Massachusetts: Merriam, Little, 1832.

Newlin, Dika. *Schoenberg Remembered: Diaries and Recollections 1938–1976.* New York: Pendragon, 1980.

[Newport, Elizabeth.] *Memoir of Elizabeth Newport.* By Ann Townsend. Philadelphia: J. Comly, 1874.

Newton, Esther, and Shirley Walton. *Womenfriends: A Soap Opera.* New York: Friends Press, 1976.

Nice, Margaret (Morse). *The Watcher at the Nest.* New York: Macmillan, 1939.

Nicholson, Asenath Hatch. *Ireland's Welcome to a Stranger; or an Excursion through Ireland, in 1844 and 1845, for the Purpose of Personally Investigating the Condition of the Poor.* New York: Baker and Scribner, 1847.

O'Brien, Margaret. *My Diary.* Philadelphia: J.B. Lippincott, 1948.

[Olnhausen, Mary (Phinney) von.] *Adventures of an Army Nurse in Two Wars; from the Diary and Correspondence of Mary Phinney, Baroness von Olnhausen.* By James Phinney Monroe. Boston: Little, Brown, 1903.

[Orr, Lucinda (Lee).] *Journal of a Young Lady of Virginia, 1782.* Edited by Emily V. Mason. Baltimore: John Murphy, 1871.

[Orvis, Marianne Dwight.] *Letters from Brook Farm, 1844–1847.* Edited by Amy L. Reed. Poughkeepsie, New York: Vassar College, 1928.

[Osborn, Sarah.] *Memoirs of the Life of Mrs. Sarah Osborn, who Died at Newport, Rhode Island, on the Second Day of August, 1796. In the Eighty Third Year of Her Age.* By Samuel Hopkins. Worcester, Massachusetts: Leonard Worcester, 1799.

O'Shaughnessy, Edith. *My Lorraine Journal.* New York: Harper and Brothers, 1918.

[Otis, Harriet.] In *Cary Letters,* edited by Caroline Cardiner Curtis. Cambridge, Massachusetts: Riverside, 1891.

Otto, Madeline. *Madeline Bird Otto: A Memorial.* Milwaukee: Privately printed, 1964.

Owen, Belle. *A Prairie Winter, by an Illinois Girl.* New York: The Outlook Company, 1903.

Owen, Ruth (Bryan). *Leaves from a Greenland Diary.* New York: Dodd, Mead, 1935.

Page, Charlotte Augusta Johnson. *Under Sail and in Port in the Glorious 1850s: Being the Journal from 1 May to 3 October 1852. Kept by Charlotte A. Page.* Salem: Peabody Museum, 1950.

[Page, Mary Ann Reynolds.] *Memoir of Mrs. Mary P. Reynolds.* Edited by A.G. Pease. Cambridge, Massachusetts: Riverside, 1873.

Paige, Harriette Story White. *Daniel Webster in England: Journal of Harriette Story Page, 1839.* Boston and New York: Houghton Mifflin, 1917.

[Paine, Abiel.] *The Discovery of a Grandmother: Glimpses into the Homes and Lives of Eight Generations of an Ipswich-Paine Family Gathered Together by one of the Ninth for the Tenth, Eleventh, and Twelfth Generations.* Edited by Lydia A. Carter. Newtonville, Massachusetts: H. H. Carter, 1920.

Parker, Cornelia Stratton. *More Ports, More Happy Places: Further Adventures of an American Mother and Her Children in Europe.* New York: Boni and Liveright, 1926.

———. *Ports and Happy Places: An American Mother and Her Sons See Europe.* New York: Boni and Liveright, 1924.

———. *Wanderer's Circle.* Boston and New York: Houghton Mifflin, 1934.

[Parkman, Anna Sophia.] In *The Hundreth Town: Glimpses of Life in Westborough, 1717–1817,* by Harriette Merrifield Forbes. Boston: Rockwell and Churchill, 1889.

Parton, Margaret. *The Leaf and the Flame.* New York: Knopf, 1959.

Patterson, Cissy. *Diary of a Voyage down the Salmon River in Pioneer Days in Idaho.* Caldwell, Idaho: Caxton, 1951.

Paxson, Mary Scarborough. *Mary Paxson, Her Book.* Garden City, New York: Doubleday, Doran, 1931.

Paz, Juana Maria. *The La Luz Journal: Autobiographical Account of Lesbian of Colour Land.* Fayetteville, Arkansas: Paz Press, 1982.

Peabody, Elizabeth Palmer. *Record of a School: Exemplifying the General Principles of Spiritual Culture.* Boston: J. Monroe, 1835.

[Peabody, Josephine Preston.] *Diaries and Letters of Josephine Preston Peabody.* Edited by Christina Hopkinson Baker. Boston and New York: Houghton Mifflin, 1925.

Peabody, Marian Lawrence. *To be Young Was Very Heaven.* Boston: Houghton Mifflin, 1967.

Peake, Elizabeth. *Pen Pictures of Europe.* Philadelphia: J.B. Lippincott, 1874.

Peary, Josephine (Diebitsch). *My Arctic Journal: A Year among Ice-Fields and Eskimos; with an Account of the Great White Journey Cross Greenland by Robert E. Peary.* New York and Philadelphia: Contemporary, 1893.

Peattie, Donald Culross, and Loyise Redfield Peattie. *Bounty of Earth.* New York and London: D. Appleton, 1926.

Pepin, Yvonne. *Cabin Journal.* Berkeley, California: Shameless Hussy Press, 1984.

[Perkins, Arozina.] In *Women Teachers on the Frontier,* by Polly Welts Kaufman. New Haven: Yale University Press, 1984.

[Perkins, Edith (Forbes).] *Letters and Journal of Edith Forbes Perkins, 1908–1925, Edited by Her Daughter.* Edited by Edith Perkins Cunningham. Cambridge, Massachusetts: Riverside, 1931.

[Perkins, Eleanor Ellis.] *Eve among the Puritans: Biography of Lucy Fitch Perkins*. Boston: Houghton Mifflin, 1956.

Pflager, Alyce (Barber). *Glimpses of Africa and England*. St. Louis: Clark-Sprague, 1937.

———. *Prancing around the World*. St. Louis: Clark-Sprague, 1931.

[Phelps, Elizabeth Porter.] In *Under a Colonial Roof-Tree: Fireside Chronicles of Early New England*. Boston and New York: Houghton Mifflin, 1891.

[Phinney, Rose.] In *An American Family in the Nineteenth Century*. Touret, 1973.

[Pickard, Hannah Maynard (Thompson).] *Memoir and Writings of Mrs. Hannah Maynard Pickard; Late Wife of Rev. Humphrey Pickard*. By Edward Otheman. Boston: David H. Ela, 1845.

Pinckney, Eliza (Lucas). *Journal and Letters of Eliza Lucas*. Wormsloe, Georgia, 1850.

[Piozzi, Hester Lynch.] *Observations and Reflections Made in the Course of a Journey through France, Italy and Germany*. Edited by Herbert Barrows. Ann Arbor: University of Michigan Press, 1967.

Pitcairn, Dora. *The Oswin Prosser Memorial Booklet*. Kilvert Society, n.d.

Plath, Sylvia. *Johnny Panic and the Bible of Dreams: Short Stories, Prose and Diary Excerpts*. New York: Harper and Row, 1979.

[Plath, Sylvia.] *The Diaries of Sylvia Plath*. Edited by Frances McCullough. New York: Dial, 1982.

Porter, Anna. *A Moscow Diary*. Chicago: Charles H. Kerr, 1926.

[Porter, Deborah H. Cushing.] *Memoir of Mrs. Deborah H. Porter, Wife of Rev. C. G. Porter of Bangor*. By Anne T. Drinkwater. Portland, Maine: Sanborn and Carter, 1848.

[Porter, Eliza Chappell.] *Eliza Chappell: A Memoir*. By Mary Porter Harris. New York: Fleming H. Revell, 1892.

Porter, Lillian Russell. *Choice Seeds in the Wilderness, from the Diary of Ann Eliza Bacon Porter, Cooksville, Wisconsin, 1845–1890*. Rockland, Maine: Seth Low, 1964.

[Post, Lydia (Minturn).] *Personal Recollections of the American Revolution: A Private Journal*. Edited by Sidney Barclay [pseud.]. New York: Rudd and Carleton, 1859.

Potter, Blanche. *Recollections of a Little Life*. New York: Privately printed by William Edwin Rudge, 1927.

Potwin, Julia Hedges. *Fourteen Months Abroad: A Simple Record of a Foreign Trip from July 18, 1897, to September 19, 1898*. Cleveland, Ohio: Privately printed, 1911.

Powers, Elvira. *Hospital Pencillings: Being a Diary while in Jefferson General Hospital, Jefferson Indiana and Others at Nashville, Tennessee*. Boston, 1866.

[Preble, Harriet.] *Memoir of the Life of Harriet Preble; Containing Portions of Her Correspondence, Journal and Other Writings, Literary and Religious*. By R. H. Lee. New York: G. P. Putnam's, 1856.

Prentice, Eliza. *Diary of Eliza Ann Prentice of Lockport, New York 1849–1893*. Privately printed, 1946.

Prentiss, Elizabeth Payson. *The Life and Letters of Elizabeth Payson Prentiss: Author of Stepping Heavenward*. New York: Randolph, 1882.

[Preston, Margaret Junkin.] *The Life and Letters of Margaret Junkin Preston*. By Elizabeth Preston Allan. Boston and New York: Houghton Mifflin, 1903.

[Preus, Caroline Dorothea Margrethe (Keyser).] *Linka's Diary: On Land and Sea, 1845–1864*. Edited by Johan Carl Keyser Preus and Diderikke Margrethe Brandt. Minneapolis: Augsburg, 1952.

[Prince, "Grandma."] *Grandma's Album Quilt*. By Helen Prince. Portland, Maine: Falmouth Book House, 1936.

[Pringle, Elizabeth Waties Allston.] *A Woman Rice Planter by Patience Pennington*. New York: Macmillan, 1913.

[Pugh, Sarah.] *The Memorial of Sarah Pugh: A Tribute of Respect from Her Cousins*. Philadelphia: J. B. Lippincott, 1888.

Putnam, Sallie A. (Brock). *Richmond during the War: Four Years of Personal Observation. By a Richmond Lady*. New York: G.V. Carleton, 1867.

Raitt, Helen. *Exploring the Deep Pacific*. New York: W.W. Norton, 1956.

[Ramsey, Martha Laurens.] *Memoirs of the Life of Martha Laurens Ramsey: Who Died in Charleston, S.C., on the Tenth of June, 1811, in the Fifty-Second Year of Her Age. With an Appendix, Containing Excerpts from Her Diary, Letters, and Other Private Papers, and Also Letters Written to Her by Her Father, Henry Laurens, 1771–1776*. By David Ramsey. Philadelphia: James Maxwell, 1811.

Randall, Margaret. *Part of the Solution: Portrait of a Revolutionary*. New York: New Directions, 1973.

Rankin, Hattie Love. *I Saw It Happen to China, 1913–1949*. Baton Rouge: Claitor's Book Store, 1960.

Ranous, Dora Knowlton Thompson. *Diary of a Daly Debutante: Being Passages from the Journal of a Member of Augustin Daly's Famous Company of Players*. New York: Duffield, 1910.

Ratcliff, Mildred Morris. *Memoranda and Correspondence of Mildred Ratcliff*. Philadelphia: William H. Pile's Sons, 1890.

[Raymond, Sarah.] *Overland Days to Montana in 1865: The Diary of Sarah Raymond and Journal of Dr. Waid Howard*. Edited by Raymond W. and Mary Lund Settle. Glendale, California: Arthur H. Clark, 1971.

Read, Jennie. *In Pursuit of Art and Life: The Journals and Letters of a Young Sculptor, San Francisco, 1970–1976*. Burnsville, North Carolina: Antioch University, with Celo Press, 1982.

[Reed, Anna Morrison.] *Anna Morrison Reed, 1849–1921*. Edited by John E. Keller. Layfayette, California: John E. Keller, 1979.

Richards, Caroline Cowles. *The Diary of Caroline Cowles Richards, 1852–1872*. Canadaigua, New York, 1908.

Richards, Ellen H. *Life of Ellen H. Richards*. Boston: Whitcomb and Barrows, 1912.

Richards, Eva Louise Alvey. *Arctic Mood: A Narrative of Arctic Adventures*. Caldwell, Idaho: Caxton, 1949.

Rickover, Ruth Masters. *Pepper, Rice, and Elephants: A Southeast Asian Journey from Celebes to Saim*. Annapolis, Maryland: Naval Institute, 1975.

Rizzi, Marcia Salo. *Some Pictures from My Life: A Diary*. Washington, New Jersey: Times Change, 1972.

[Roberts, Deborah.] In *Memoir of Catharine Seeley, late of Darien, Connecticut*. New York: Collins Bros., 1843.

Roberts, Louisa. *Biographical Sketches of Louise J. Roberts, with Extracts from Her Journal and Selections from Her Writings*. Philadelphia: Alfred J. Ferris, 1895.

Robeson, Eslanda. *African Journey*. New York: John Day, 1945.

Robinson, Dorothy Atkinson. *The Diary of a Suburban Housewife by Dorothy Blake*. New York: William Morrow, 1936.

———. *It's All in the Family: A Diary of an American Housewife, December 7, 1941–December 1, 1942 by Dorothy Blake*. New York: William Morrow, 1943.

Robinson, Ione. *A Wall to Paint on*. New York: E.P. Dutton, 1946.

Roderick, Mary Louise Rochester. *A Nightingale in the Trenches*. New York: Vantage, 1966.

[Rogers, Clara Kathleen (Barnett).] *Journal-letters from the Orient*. Edited by Henry Munroe Rogers. Norwood, Massachusetts: Plimpton, 1934.

Rogers, Dale Evans. *My Spiritual Diary*. Westwood, New Jersey: F.H. Revell, 1955.

Rogers, Emma Winner. *Journal of a Country Woman*. New York: Eaton and Mains, 1912.

[Ropes, Hannah Anderson.] *Civil War Nurse: The Diary and Letters of Hannah Ropes.* Edited by John R. Brumgardt. Knoxville: University of Tennessee Press, 1980.

Rose, Hilda. *The Stump Farm: A Chronicle of Pioneering.* Boston: Little, Brown, 1928.

Rose, Rev. Mother Mary. *A Mission Tour in the Southwest Pacific.* Boston: Society for the Propogation of the Faith, 1942.

[Royce, Sarah (Bayliss).] *A Frontier Lady: Recollections of the Gold Rush and Early California.* Edited by Ralph Henry Gabriel. New Haven: Yale University Press, 1932.

Russell, Amelia Eloise. *Home Life of the Brook Farm Association. With a Short Biographical Sketch.* Boston: Little, Brown, 1900.

Russell, Linda. *Diary.* New York: Vantage, 1982.

Salisbury, Charlotte Y. *Asian Diary: A Personal Record of a Trip to the Far East.* New York: Scribners, 1967.

————. *China Diary.* New York: Walker, 1973.

————. *China Diary, after Mao.* New York: Walker, 1979.

————. *Russian Diary.* New York: Walker, 1974.

————. *Tibetan Diary and Travels along the Old Silk Route.* New York: Walker, 1981.

Sanders, Tobi Gillian, and Joan Frances Bennett. *Members of the Class Will Keep Daily Journals: The Barnard College Journals of Tobi Gillian Sanders and Joan Frances Bennett.* New York: Winter House, 1970.

Sanford, Mollie Dorsey. *Mollie: Journal of Mollie Dorsey Sanford in Nebraska and Colorado Territories, 1857–1866.* Lincoln: University of Nebraska Press, 1959.

Santa Maria, Frances Karlen. *Joshua: Firstborn.* New York: Dial, 1970.

Sargeant, Alice Applegate. *Following the Flag: Diary of a Soldier's Wife.* Kansas City: E.B. Barnett, 1919.

Sarton, May. *At Seventy: A Journal.* New York: W.W. Norton, 1984.

————. *The House by the Sea: A Journal.* New York: W.W. Norton, 1977.

————. *Journal of a Solitude.* New York: W.W. Norton, 1973.

Sauro, Joan. *Inner Marathon: The Diary of a Jogging Nun.* New York: Paulist Press, 1982.

Schuyler, Philippa Duke. *Adventures in Black and White.* New York: Robert Speller, 1960.

Schwarcz, Vera. *Long Road Home: A China Journal.* New Haven: Yale University Press, 1984.

Schwerin, Doris Halpern. *Diary of a Pigeon Watcher.* New York: William Morrow, 1976.

Scott, Fanny. *Our Trip to California to Attend the Twenty-Sixth Convention of the Order of Railway Conductors at Los Angeles, Cal.* 1897.

Scott-Maxwell, Florida Pier. *The Measure of My Days.* New York: Knopf, 1968.

Scrivener, Jane [pseud.]. *Inside Rome with the Germans.* New York: Macmillan, 1945.

[Sedgwick, Catharine Maria.] *Life and Letters of Catharine M. Sedgwick.* Edited by Mary E. Dewey. New York: Harper and Brothers, 1871.

Seeley, Catharine. *Memoir of Catharine Seeley, Late of Darien, Connecticut.* New York: Collins Bros., 1843.

Segale, Sister Blandina. *At the End of the Santa Fe Trail.* Columbus, Ohio: Columbian, 1932.

[Sellers, Martha.] *M.S.: The Story of a Life.* Edited by Frances Sellers Garrett. Philadelphia: Alfred J. Ferris, 1901.

Sergeant, Elizabeth Shepley. *Shadow Shapes: The Journal of a Wounded Woman, October 1918– May 1919.* Boston and New York: Houghton Mifflin, 1920.

[Seton, Elizabeth Ann Bayley.] *Memoir, Letters and Journal of Elizabeth Seton, Convert to the Catholic Faith, and Sister of Charity.* By Robert Seton. 2 vols. New York: P. O'Shea, 1870.

Sewell, Elizabeth Missing. *A Journal Kept During a Summer Tour for the Children of a Village School.* New York: D. Appleton, 1859.

Seymour, Helen Wells. *A Japanese Diary.* New Haven, 1956.

Shannon, Elizabeth. *Up in the Park: The Diary of the Wife of the American Ambassador to Ireland, 1977–1981.* New York: Atheneum, 1983.

Shapiro-Bertolini, Ethel. *"I Never Died," Said He.* Los Angeles: Agency Lithograph, 1970.

Sheilds, Mary Lou. *Sea Run: Surviving My Mother's Madness.* New York: Seaview Books, 1981.

Sheldon, Carrie (Brooks). *A Summer across the Sea.* Red Wing, Minnesota: Red Wing, 1905.

Sherman, Jane. *Soaring: The Diary and Letters of a Denishawn Dancer in the Far East, 1925–1926.* Middletown, Connecticut: Wesleyan University, 1976.

[Sherman, Martha.] *The Pastor's Wife: A Memoir of Mrs. Martha Sherman.* By James Sherman. Philadelphia: Robert Peterson, 1850.

[Sherwood, Laura.] *Letters and Journals of Samuel and Laura Sherwood, 1813–1823.* Edited by J.D. Crocker. Delhi, New York, 1967.

Shunk, Caroline Saxe (Merrill). *An Army Woman in the Phillipines: Extracts from Letters of an Army Officer's Wife, Describing Her Personal Experiences in the Philippine Islands.* Kansas City: Franklin Hudson, 1914.

Simon-Smolinski, Carole. *Journal Eighteen Sixty Two: An Historical Account of Early Riverboat Travel on the Columbia and Snake Rivers.* Northwest Historical Consultants, n.d.

Slayden, Ellen (Maury). *Washington Wife: Journal of Ellen Maury Slayden from 1897–1919.* New York: Harper and Row, 1963.

Sloane, Florence Adele. *Maverick in Mauve: The Diary of a Romantic Age.* Garden City, New York: Doubleday, 1983.

Smedley, Agnes. *China Fights Back: An American Woman with the Eighth Route Army.* New York: Vanguard, 1938.

[Smith, Abigail Willis (Tenny).] *Lowell and Abigail: A Realistic Idyll.* By Mary Dillingham Frear. New Haven: Privately printed, 1934.

Smith, Alice. *Alice Weston Smith, 1868–1908: Letters to Her Friends and Selections from Her Note-Books.* Boston: A.C. Getchell, 1909.

Smith, Elizabeth A. *A Wanderer's Journal.* New York: Privately printed, 1889.

[Smith, Elizabeth Murray.] *Letters of James Murray, Loyalist.* Edited by Nina Moore Tiffany. Boston: W. B. Clarke, 1901.

Smith, Jane (Baldwin). *Diary of Jane Baldwin Smith, 1867, with Letters of Eva Smith [and] Genealogy.* Yonkers, New York: Privately printed, 1930.

Smith, Jennie. *Valley of Baca: A Record of Suffering and Triumph.* Cincinnati: Hitchcock and Walden, 1876.

[Smith, Sarah.] *First White Women over the Rockies: Diaries, Letters and Biographical Sketches of Six Women of the Oregon Mission Who Made the Overland Journey in 1836 and 1838.* Edited by Clifford Merrill Drury. Glendale, California: Arthur H. Clarke, 1963–66.

[Smith, Sophia.] *Sophia Smith and the Beginnings of Smith College.* By Elizabeth Deering Hanscom and Helen French Greene. Northampton, Massachusetts: Smith College, 1925.

Snodgrass, Martha. *Extracts from the Writings of Martha Snodgrass.* St. Paul, Minnesota: Webb, 1900.

Snow, Alice (Rowe). *Log of a Sea Captain's Daughter: With Adventures on Robinson Crusoe's Island by Alice Rowe Smith who Sailed with Her Father, Captain Joshua N. Rowe, on the Bark Russell during a Voyage of Four Years and a Half.* Boston: Meador, 1944.

Snow, Maria Cobb. *Jane Grabhorn's Grandmother's Diary: Being the Faithful Accounting of Her Life in the Year 1919 . . . and the Final, Fragmentary Book of Her Grand Daughter, now Printed Posthumously in 1974.* San Francisco: Jumbo, 1974.

[Spencer, Cornelia.] *Old Days in Chapel Hill: Being the Life and Letters of Cornelia Phillips Spencer.* By Hope Summerell Chamberlain. Chapel Hill: University of North Carolina Press, 1926.

[Spring, Augusta Murray.] *Gideon Lee Knapp and Augusta Murray Spring, His Wife: Extracts from Letters and Journal.* New York, 1909.

[Springer, Helen.] *I Love the Trail: A Sketch of the Life of Helen Emily Springer.* By John McKendree Springer. Nashville, Tennessee: Parthenon, 1952.

Standley, Emma (Bartlett). *What I Saw in Foreign Lands of Interest and Beauty.* Galesburg, Illinois: Wagoner, 1913.

[Stanton, Elizabeth Cady.] *Elizabeth Cady Stanton As Remembered in Her Letters, Diary and Reminiscences.* Edited by Theodore Stanton and Harriot Stanton Blatch. New York and London: Harper and Brothers, 1922.

Starkey, May Chapman. *Westward to Europe.* Los Angeles: Suttonhouse, 1937.

Starr, Eliza Allen. *The Life and Letters of Eliza Allen Starr.* Chicago: Lakeside, 1905.

Steele, Eliza R. *A Summer Journey in the West.* New York: J.S. Taylor, 1841.

Steger, Jane. *Leaves from a Secret Journal: A Record of Intimate Experiences.* Boston: Little, Brown, 1926.

Stein, Gertrude. "A Diary." In *Alphabets and Birthdays.* New Haven, Yale University Press, 1957.

———. *Notebooks.* New York: Liveright, 1975.

———. *Wars I Have Seen.* New York: Random House, 1945.

Stephens, Louisa. *Golden Adventure: A Diary of Long Ago.* Pasadena, California: San Pasqual Books, 1941.

Stern, Susan Harris. *With the Weathermen: The Personal Journal of a Revolutionary Woman.* Garden City, New York: Doubleday, 1975.

Stevenson, DeLoris. *Land of Morning.* St. Louis: Bethany Press, 1956.

[Stickney, Elizabeth.] *Records of a California Family: Journals and Letters of Lewis C. Gunn and Elizabeth Le Breton Gunn.* Edited by Anna Lee Marston. San Diego: Johnck and Seeger, 1928.

Street, Margaret Frink. *Dakota Diary: The Westerners 1948 Brand Book.* Denver, 1949.

[Sulzberger, Marina.] *Marina: Letters and Diaries of Marina Sulzberger.* Edited by C.L. Sulzberger. New York: Crown, 1978.

Susan. *Diary by Susan.* Santa Fe, 1970.

[Swift, Mary.] *The First State Normal School in America: The Journals of Cyprus Peirce and Mary Swift.* Cambridge: Harvard University Press, 1926.

Szold, Henrietta. *Henrietta Szold: Life and Letters.* New York: Viking, 1942.

[Taber, Gladys Bagg.] *Still Cove Journal.* Edited by Constance Taber Colby, New York: Harper and Row, 1981.

———. *Stillmeadow Calendar: A Countrywoman's Journal.* Philadelphia: J.B. Lippincott, 1967.

Talbott, Katharine Houk. *Talbott Family.* Mount Vernon, New York: Peter Beilenson, 1949.

Tanner, Annie Clark. *A Mormon Mother: An Autobiography.* Salt Lake City: University of Utah Library, 1969.

Taylor, Elizabeth Rosemond. *Nibbles and Me.* New York: Duell, and Sloane and Pearce, 1946.

Taylor, Kathrine Kressman. *Diary of Florence in Flood.* New York: Simon and Schuster, 1967.

Thaxter, Celia. *An Island Garden.* Boston and New York: Houghton Mifflin, 1894.

Thomas, Emma. *Three Months in Europe: A Journal of Travel in England, France, Switzerland, Germany, Italy and Belgium.* Boston: DeWolf and Fiske, 1892.

Thomas, Margaret. *Around the World in 1912 and 1914: Diary of Margaret Thomas.* Boston: Privately printed, 1961.

[Thomas, Martha Carey.] *The Making of a Feminist: Early Journals and Letters of M. Carey Thomas.* By Marjorie Housepain Dobkin. Kent, Ohio: Kent State University Press, 1979.

[Thompson, Dorothy.] *Dorothy and Red.* By Vincent Sheean. Boston: Houghton Mifflin, 1963.

Thompson, Jean [pseud.]. *The House of Tomorrow.* New York: Harper and Row, 1967.

[Thompson, Josephine.] *The Scenes of My Childhood.* By James Allen Thompson. Garden City, New York: Doubleday, 1948.

Thompson, Juliet. *Diary of Juliet Thompson.* Los Angeles: Kalimat, 1983.

Thompson, Mary (Breckinridge). *Breckie: His Four Years, 1914–1918.* New York: Privately printed, 1918.

[Thorne, Ethel.] *Joy is the Banner: The Life of Ethel M. Cheney Thorne.* By Olive Floyd and Samuel Thorne. Rye, New York: Privately printed, 1950.

[Thwing, Carrie F. Butler.] *Carrie F. Butler Thwing: An Appreciation by Friends, together with Extracts from Her "Journal of a Tour of Europe."* Cleveland, Ohio: Herman Taylor, 1899.

[Timbres, Rebecca (Janney).] *We Didn't Ask Utopia: A Quaker Family in Soviet Russia.* By Harry and Rebecca Timbres. Englewood Cliffs, New Jersey: Prentice Hall, 1939.

[Todd, Mabel Loomis.] In *Austin and Mabel: The Amherst Affair and Love Letters of Austin Dickinson and Mabel Loomis Todd,* by Polly Longsworth. New York: Farrar, Straus, Giroux, 1984.

[Todd, Martha Nancy (Gaddis).] *Life and Letters of Martha Gaddis Todd.* Edited by Arthur James Todd. Chicago: School of the Art Institute, 1940.

[Towne, Laura Matilda.] *Letters and Diary of Laura M. Towne. Written from the Sea Islands of South Carolina, 1862–1884.* Edited by Rupert Sargent Holland. Cambridge, Massachusetts: Riverside, 1912.

Tree, Viola. *Castles in the Air: A Story of My Singing Days.* New York: George H. Doran, 1926.

Truitt, Anne. *Daybook: The Journal of an Artist.* New York: Pantheon, 1983.

Turnbull, Grace Hill. *Chips from My Chisel: An Autobiography.* Rindge, New Hampshire: Richard B. Smith, 1953.

[Tyler, Mary Hunt (Palmer).] *Grandmother Tyler's Book: The Recollections of Mary Palmer Tyler (Mrs. Royall Tyler, 1775–1866).* Edited by Frederick Tupper and Helen Tyler Brown. New York: G.P. Putnam's, 1925.

Ueland, Brenda. *Me.* New York: G.P. Putnam's, 1939.

Underwood, Enda (Worthley). *The Taste of Honey: The Note Book of a Linguist.* Portland, Maine: Mosher, 1930.

Van Denburg, Elizabeth Douglas (Turrill). *My Voyage in the United States Frigate "Congress."* New York: Desmond-Fitzgerald, 1913.

[Van Lennep, Mary E.] *Memoir of Mrs. Mary E. Van Lennep: Only Daughter of the Rev. Joel Hawes and Wife of the Rev. Henry J. Van Lennep, Missionary in Turkey.* By Louisa Fisher Hawes. Hartford, Connecticut: Wm. Jas. Hamersley, 1847.

Van Patten, Barbara. *Diary of the Honeymoon of Charles and Barbara Van Patten, 1932–1933.* Charles Van Patten, 1977.

Vining, Elizabeth. *Windows for the Crown Prince.* Philadelphia: J.B. Lippincott, 1952.

Volk, Katherine Magdalene. *Buddies in Budapest: An American War Nurse's Narrative.* Los Angeles: Kellaway-Ide, 1936.

Wadelton, Maggie Jeanne (Melody) Owen. *The Book of Maggie Owen.* Indianapolis and New York: Bobbs-Merrill, 1941.

———. *Maggie No Doubt.* Indianapolis and New York: Bobbs-Merrill, 1943.

[Walker, Georgina Freeman (Gholson).] *The Private Journal of Georgina Gholson Walker, 1862–1865. With Selections from the Post-War Years 1865–1876.* Edited by Dwight Franklin Henderson. Tuscaloosa, Alabama: Confederate Publishing, 1963.

[Walker, Mary.] *Elkanah and Mary Walker: Pioneers among the Spokanes.* By Clifford Merrill Drury. Caldwell, Idaho: Caxton, 1940.

———. *Mary Walker: Her Book.* Edited by Ruth McKee. Caldwell, Idaho: Caxton, 1945.

[Wallace, Elizabeth Curtis.] *Glencoe Diary: The War-Time Journal of Elizabeth Curtis Wallace.* Edited by Eleanor P. and Charles B. Cross, Jr. Chesapeake, Virginia: Norfolk County Historical Society, 1968.

Wallis, Mary Davis (Cook). *Life in Feejee; Or, Five Years Among the Cannibals by a Lady.* Ridgewood, New Jersey: Gregg, 1967.

[Ward, Frances Elizabeth.] *Frankie's Journal by Frances Elizabeth Ward, Daughter of the Prairie Schooner Lady.* Edited by Florence Stark DeWitt. Los Angeles: Western Lore, 1960.

[Ward, Harriett (Sherrill).] *Prairie Schooner Lady: the Journal of Harriett Sherrill Ward.* Edited by Ward G. DeWitt and Florence DeWitt. Los Angeles: Western Lore, 1959.

Warde, Beatrice. *"Bombed But Unbeaten": Excerpts from the War Commentary of Beatrice L. Warde.* New York: Printed for the Friends of Freedom by the Typophiles, 1949.

Ware, Mary Smith (Dakney). *From Mexico to Russia.* Sewanee, Tennessee, 1929.

[Warner, Edith.] *The House at Otowi Bridge: The Story of Edith Warner and Los Alamos.* By Peggy Pond Church. Albuquerque: University of New Mexico Press, 1960.

[Warner, Susan.] *Susan Warner.* By Anna B. Warner. New York: G. P. Putnam's, 1909.

Watson, Jeanette Grace. *"Our Sentry Go."* Chicago: Ralph Fletcher Seymour, 1924.

Weber, Julia. *My Country School Diary: An Adventure in Creative Teaching.* New York and London: Harper and Brothers, 1946.

Webster, Barbara. *The Green Year.* New York: W.W. Norton, 1956.

Webster, Caroline Le Roy. *"Mr. W. and I": Being the Authentic Diary of Caroline Le Roy Webster, during a Famous Journey with the Honble. Daniel Webster to Great Britain and the Continent in the Year 1839.* New York: Washburn, 1942.

Weingarten, Violet. *Intimations of Mortality.* New York: Knopf, 1978.

Wells, Suszanna Louisa Aikman. *The Journal of a Voyage from Charlestown, S.C., to London, Undertaken During the American Revolution by a Daughter of an Eminent American Loyalist in the Year 1778, and Written from Memory Only in 1779.* New York: New York Historical Society, 1906.

Wernher, Hilda. *My Indian Family.* New York: John Day, 1945.

————. *My Indian Son-in-Law.* Garden City, New York: Doubleday, 1949.

West, Jessamyn. *Double Discovery: A Journey.* New York: Harcourt Brace Jovanovich, 1980.

————. *Hide and Seek: A Continuing Journey.* New York: Harcourt Brace Jovanovich, 1973.

————. *To See the Dream.* New York: Harcourt Brace, 1957.

What! No Igloos? Fairbanks, Alaska: Sitka Printing Co., 1955.

[Wheaton, Eliza Baylies (Chapin).] In *The Life of Eliza Baylies Wheaton: a Chapter in the History of Higher Education of Women,* by Harriet Eliza Paine. Cambridge, Massachusetts: Riverside, 1907.

Wheaton, Ellen Douglas Birdseye. *The Diary of Ellen Douglas Birdseye Wheaton.* Boston: Privately printed by D.B. Updike, 1923.

[Whitall, Ann and Hannah.] In *John M. Whitall: The Story of His Life. Written for His Grandchildren by His Daughter,* by Hannah Whitall Smith. Philadelphia: Privately printed, 1879.

White, E. *Ten Years in Oregon: Travels and Adventures.* Ithaca, New York: Mack, Andrus, 1848.

[White, Mary Wilder.] *Memorials of Mary Wilder White: A Century Ago in New England.* By Elizabeth Amelia (White) Dwight. Edited Mary Wilder Tileston. Boston: Everett Press, 1903.

[White, Tryphena Ely.] *Tryphena Ely White's Journal: Being a Record, Written One Hundred Years Ago, of the Daily Life of a Young Lady of Puritan Heritage, 1805–1905.* By Fanny Kellogg. New York: Grafton, 1904.

White, Viola Chittenden. *Not Faster Than a Walk: A Vermont Notebook.* Middlebury, Vermont: Middlebury College, 1939.

[————.] *Partridge in a Swamp: The Journals of Viola C. White, 1918–1941.* Edited by W. Storrs Lee. Taftsville, Vermont: The Countryman Press, 1979.

————. *Vermont Diary.* Boston: Charles Branford, 1956.

Whiteley, Opal Stanley. *The Story of Opal: The Journal of an Understanding Heart.* Boston: Atlantic Monthly Press, 1920.

[Whitford, Maria.] *And a White Vest for Sam'l: An Account of Rural Life in Western New York.* Edited by Helene C. Phelan. Almond, New York: 1976.

[Whiting, Martha.] *The Teacher's Last Lesson: A Memoir of Martha Whiting, Late of Charleston*

Female Seminary. Consisting Chiefly of Extracts from Her Journals, Interspersed with Reminiscences and Suggestive Reflections. By Catharine N. Badger. Boston: Gould and Lincoln, 1855.

Wilder, Laura Elizabeth (Ingalls). *On the Way Home: The Diary of a Trip from South Dakota to Mansfield, Missouri, in 1894.* New York: Harper and Row, 1962.

[Wilkins, Mesannie.] *Last of the Saddle Tramps.* With Mina Titus Sawyer. Englewood Cliffs, New Jersey: Prentice Hall, 1967.

Willard, Emma (Hart). *Journal and Letters, from France and Great Britain.* Troy, New York: N. Tuttle, 1833.

Willard, Frances Elizabeth. *Glimpses of Fifty Years: The Autobiography of an American Woman.* Chicago: Women's Temperance Publication Association, 1889.

[————.] *Nineteen Beautiful Years: Or, Sketches of a Girl's Life.* By Mary S. Willard. New York: Harper and Brothers, 1864.

Williams, Celia Ann. *The Diary of a Teacher along the Journey to Siberia.* New York: Exposition Press, 1972.

[Williams, Eliza Azelia.] *One Whaling Family.* Edited by Harold Williams. Boston: Houghton Mifflin, 1964.

Williams, Frances (Coleman). *Aloha Comes of Age.* New York: J.J. Little and Ives, 1932.

Williams, Rebecca (Yancey). *Carry Me Back.* New York: E.P. Dutton, 1942.

[Willson, Elizabeth (Lundy).] *A Journey in 1836 from New Jersey to Ohio: Being the Diary of Elizabeth Lundy Willson.* Edited by William C. Armstrong. Morrison, Illinois: Shawver, 1929.

Wilson, Helen Calista, and Elsie Reed Mitchell. *Vagabonding at Fifty: From Siberia to Turkestan.* New York: Coward McCann, 1929.

[Winslow, Anna Green.] *Diary of Anna Green Winslow, A Boston School Girl of 1771.* Edited by Alice Morse Earle. Boston and New York: Houghton Mifflin, 1894.

[Winslow, Harriet Wadsworth (Lathrop).] *Memoir of Mrs. Harriet L. Winslow, Thirteen Years a Member of the American Mission in Ceylon.* By Miron Winslow. New York: American Tract Society, [1840].

[Wister, Sarah.] *Sally Wister's Journal, a True Narrative: Being a Quaker Maid's Account of Her Experiences with Officers of the Continental Army, 1777–1778.* Edited by Albert Cook Myers. Philadelphia: Ferris and Leach, 1902.

Woodman, Abby (Johnson). *Picturesque Alaska: A Journal of a Tour among the Mountains, Seas and Islands of the Northwest, from San Francisco to Sitka.* Boston and New York: Houghton Mifflin, 1889.

[Woodward, Mary Dodge.] *The Checkered Years.* Edited by Mary Boynton Cowdrey. Caldwell, Idaho: Caxton, 1937.

[Woolson, Constance Fenimore, and Hanna Cooper Pomeroy Woolson.] *Five Generations 1785–1923: Being Scattered Chapters from the History of the Cooper, Pomeroy, Woolson and Benedict Families, With Extracts from Their Letters and Journals.* Edited by Clare Benedict. London: George Ellis, 1930.

Wright, Billie. *Four Seasons North: A Journal of Life in the Alaska Wilderness.* New York: Harper and Row, 1973.

[Yarnall, Hannah Haines.] In *Thomas Richardson of South Sheilds, Durham County, England, and His Descendants in the United States of America.* New York: T.A. Wright, 1929.

Young, Josephine. *Journals of Josephine Young.* New York: Privately printed, 1915.

Note: Many hundreds of American women's diaries have been published in whole or part in journals and magazines. Space does not permit listing them here.

The Feminist Press at the City University of New York offers alternatives in education and in literature. Founded in 1970, this non-profit, tax-exempt educational and publishing organization works to eliminate sexual stereotypes in books and schools and to provide literature with a broad vision of human potential. The publishing program includes reprints of important works by women, feminist biographies of women, and nonsexist children's books. Curricular materials, bibliographies, directories, and a quarterly journal provide information and support for students and teachers of women's studies. In-service projects help to transform teaching methods and curricula. Through publications and projects, The Feminist Press contributes to the rediscovery of the history of women and the emergence of a more humane society.

FEMINIST CLASSICS FROM THE FEMINIST PRESS

Antoinette Brown Blackwell: A Biography, by Elizabeth Cazden. $19.95 cloth, $9.95 paper.

Between Mothers and Daughters: Stories Across a Generation. Edited by Susan Koppelman. $8.95 paper.

Brown Girl, Brownstones, a novel by Paule Marshall. Afterword by Mary Helen Washington. $8.95 paper.

Call Home the Heart, a novel of the thirties, by Fielding Burke. Introduction by Alice Kessler-Harris and Paul Lauter and afterwords by Sylvia J. Cook and Anna W. Shannon. $8.95 paper.

Cassandra, by Florence Nightingale. Introduction by Myra Stark. Epilogue by Cynthia Macdonald. $3.50 paper.

The Changelings, a novel by Jo Sinclair. Afterwords by Nellie McKay; and by Johnnetta B. Cole and Elizabeth H. Oakes; Biographical Note by Elisabeth Sandberg. $8.95 paper.

The Convert, a novel by Elizabeth Robins. Introduction by Jane Marcus. $6.95 paper.

Daughter of Earth, a novel by Agnes Smedley. Afterword by Paul Lauter. $7.95 paper.

A Day at a Time: The Diary Literature of American Women from 1764 to the Present, edited and with an introduction by Margo Culley. $29.95 cloth, $12.95 paper.

The Defiant Muse: French Feminist Poems from the Middle Ages to the Present, a bilingual anthology edited and with an introduction by Domna C. Stanton. $24.95 cloth, $9.95 paper.

The Defiant Muse: German Feminist Poems from the Middle Ages to the Present, a bilingual anthology edited and with an introduction by Susan L. Cocalis. $24.95 cloth, $9.95 paper.

The Defiant Muse: Hispanic Feminist Poems from the Middle Ages to the Present, a bilingual anthology edited and with an introduction by Angel Flores and Kate Flores. $24.95 cloth, $9.95 paper.

The Defiant Muse: Italian Feminist Poems from the Middle Ages to the Present, a bilingual anthology edited by Beverly Allen, Muriel Kittel, and Keala Jane Jewell, and with an introduction by Beverly Allen. $24.95 cloth, $9.95 paper.

The Female Spectator, edited by Mary R. Mahl and Helene Koon. $8.95 paper.

Guardian Angel and Other Stories, by Margery Latimer. Afterwords by Nancy Loughridge, Meridel Le Sueur, and Louis Kampf. $8.95 paper.

I Love Myself When I Am Laughing . . . And Then Again When I Am Looking Mean and Impressive, by Zora Neale Hurston. Edited by Alice Walker with an introduction by Mary Helen Washington. $9.95 paper.

Käthe Kollwitz: Woman and Artist, by Martha Kearns. $7.95 paper.

Life in the Iron Mills and Other Stories, by Rebecca Harding Davis. Biographical interpretation by Tillie Olsen. $7.95 paper.

The Living Is Easy, a novel by Dorothy West. Afterword by Adelaide M. Cromwell. $8.95 paper.

The Other Woman: Stories of Two Women and a Man. Edited by Susan Koppelman. $8.95 paper.

Mother to Daughter, Daughter to Mother: A Daybook and Reader, selected and shaped by Tillie Olsen. $9.95 paper.

Portraits of Chinese Women in Revolution, by Agnes Smedley. Edited with an introduction by Jan MacKinnon and Steve MacKinnon and an afterword by Florence Howe. $5.95 paper.

Reena and Other Stories, selected short stories by Paule Marshall. $8.95 paper.

Ripening: Selected Work, 1927–1980, by Meridel Le Sueur. Edited with an introduction by Elaine Hedges. $8.95 paper.

Rope of Gold, a novel of the thirties, by Josephine Herbst. Introduction by Alice Kessler-Harris and Paul Lauter and afterword by Elinor Langer. $8.95 paper.

The Silent Partner, a novel by Elizabeth Stuart Phelps. Afterword by Mari Jo Buhle and Florence Howe. $8.95 paper.

Swastika Night, a novel by Katharine Burdekin. Introduction by Daphne Patai. $8.95 paper.

These Modern Women: Autobiographical Essays from the Twenties. Edited with an introduction by Elaine Showalter. $4.95 paper.

The Unpossessed, a novel of the thirties, by Tess Slesinger. Introduction by Alice Kessler-Harris and Paul Lauter and afterword by Janet Sharistanian. $8.95 paper.

Weeds, a novel by Edith Summers Kelley. Afterword by Charlotte Goodman. $7.95 paper.

A Woman of Genius, a novel by Mary Austin. Afterword by Nancy Porter. $8.95 paper.

The Woman and the Myth: Margaret Fuller's Life and Writings, by Bell Gale Chevigny. $8.95 paper.

Women and Appletrees, a novel by Moa Martinson. Translated from the Swedish and with an afterword by Margaret S. Lacy. $8.95 paper.

The Yellow Wallpaper, by Charlotte Perkins Gilman. Afterword by Elaine Hedges. $3.95 paper.

OTHER TITLES FROM THE FEMINIST PRESS

Black Foremothers: Three Lives, by Dorothy Sterling. $8.95 paper.

But Some of Us Are Brave: Black Women's Studies. Edited by Gloria T. Hull, Patricia Bell Scott, and Barbara Smith. $12.95.

Complaints and Disorders: The Sexual Politics of Sickness, by Barbara Ehrenreich and Deirdre English. $3.95 paper.

The Cross-Cultural Study of Women. Edited by Margot Duley-Morrow and Mary I. Edwards. $29.95 cloth, $12.95 paper.

Feminist Resources for Schools and Colleges: A Guide to Curricular Materials., 3rd edition. Compiled and edited by Anne Chapman. $12.95 paper.

Household and Kin: Families in Flux, by Amy Swerdlow et al. $8.95 paper.

How to Get Money for Research, by Mary Rubin and the Business and Professional Women's Foundation. Foreword by Mariam Chamberlain. $6.95 paper.

In Her Own Image: Women Working in the Arts. Edited with an introduction by Elaine Hedges and Ingrid Wendt. $9.95 paper.

Integrating Women's Studies into the Curriculum: A Guide and Bibliography, by Betty Schmitz. $9.95 paper.

Las Mujeres: Conversations from a Hispanic Community, by Nan Elsasser, Kyle MacKenzie, and Yvonne Tixier y Vigil. $8.95 paper.

Lesbian Studies: Present and Future. Edited by Margaret Cruikshank. $9.95 paper.

Moving the Mountain: Women Working for Social Change, by Ellen Cantarow with Susan Gushee O'Malley and Sharon Hartman Strom. $8.95 paper.

Out of the Bleachers: Writings on Women and Sport. Edited with an introduction by Stephanie L. Twin. $9.95 paper.

Reconstructing American Literature: Courses, Syllabi, Issues. Edited by Paul Lauter. $10.95 paper.

Salt of the Earth, screenplay by Michael Wilson with historical commentary by Deborah Silverton Rosenfelt. $5.95 paper.

Witches, Midwives, and Nurses: A History of Women Healers, by Barbara Ehrenreich and Deirdre English. $3.95 paper.

With These Hands: Women Working on the Land. Edited with an introduction by Joan M. Jensen. $9.95 paper.

Woman's "True" Profession: Voices from the History of Teaching. Edited with an introduction by Nancy Hoffman. $9.95 paper.

Women Have Always Worked: A Historical Overview, by Alice Kessler-Harris. $8.95 paper.

Women Working: An Anthology of Stories and Poems. Edited and with an introduction by Nancy Hoffman and Florence Howe. $8.95 paper.

For free catalog, write to The Feminist Press at the City University of New York, 311 East 94 Street, New York, N.Y. 10128. Send individual book orders to The Feminist Press, P. O. Box 1654, Hagerstown, MD 21741. Include $1.75 postage and handling for one book and 75¢ for each additional book. To order using MasterCard or Visa, call: (800) 638-3030.